RETOOL
YOUR SCHOOL
THE EDUCATOR'S ESSENTIAL GUIDE
TO GOOGLE'S FREE POWER APPS

**JAMES LERMAN
& RONIQUE HICKS**

International Society for Technology in Education
EUGENE, OREGON · WASHINGTON, DC

RETOOL YOUR SCHOOL

THE EDUCATOR'S ESSENTIAL GUIDE TO GOOGLE'S FREE POWER APPS

JAMES LERMAN & RONIQUE HICKS

© 2010 International Society for Technology in Education

World rights reserved. No part of this book may be reproduced or transmitted in any form or by any means—electronic, mechanical, photocopying, recording, or by any information storage or retrieval system—without prior written permission from the publisher. Contact Permissions Editor: www.iste.org/permissions/; permissions@iste.org; fax: 1.541.302.3780.

Director of Book Publishing: *Courtney Burkholder*
Acquisitions Editor: *Jeff V. Bolkan*
Production Editors: *Lynda Gansel, Tina Wells*
Production Coordinator: *Rachel Williams*
Graphic Designer: *Signe Landin*
Copy Editor: *Kärstin Painter*
Proofreader: *Barbara J. Hewick*
Cover Design: *Emily Lewellen*
Book Design and Production: *Kim McGovern*

Library of Congress Cataloging-in-Publication Data

Lerman, James, 1946-
  Retool your school : the educator's essential guide to Google's free
 power apps / James Lerman and Ronique Hicks.
    p. cm.
  ISBN 978-1-56484-267-1 (pbk.)
  1. Internet in education—United States. 2. Google Apps. 3. School
improvement programs—United States.   I. Hicks, Ronique. II. Title.
 LB1044.87.L46 2010
 371.33'44678—dc22

                                                    2010021983

First Edition
ISBN: 978-1-56484-267-1

Printed in the United States of America

ISTE® is a registered trademark of the International Society for Technology in Education.

ABOUT ISTE

The International Society for Technology in Education (ISTE) is the trusted source for professional development, knowledge generation, advocacy, and leadership for innovation. ISTE is the premier membership association for educators and education leaders engaged in improving teaching and learning by advancing the effective use of technology in PK–12 and teacher education.

Home of the National Educational Technology Standards (NETS) and ISTE's annual conference and exposition (formerly known as NECC), ISTE represents more than 100,000 professionals worldwide. We support our members with information, networking opportunities, and guidance as they face the challenge of transforming education. To find out more about these and other ISTE initiatives, visit our website at www.iste.org.

As part of our mission, ISTE Book Publishing works with experienced educators to develop and produce practical resources for classroom teachers, teacher educators, and technology leaders. Every manuscript we select for publication is carefully peer-reviewed and professionally edited. We value your feedback on this book and other ISTE products. E-mail us at books@iste.org.

Contact Us

Washington, DC, Office:
   1710 Rhode Island Ave. NW, Suite 900, Washington, DC 20036-3132
Eugene, Oregon, Office:
   180 West 8th Ave., Suite 300, Eugene, OR 97401-2916
Order Desk: 1.800.336.5191
Order Fax: 1.541.302.3778
Customer Service: orders@iste.org
Book Publishing: books@iste.org
Book Sales and Marketing: booksmarketing@iste.org
Web: www.iste.org

ABOUT THE AUTHORS

James Lerman creates educational environments and experiences for learners of all ages. Design, in its many forms, is a particular passion of his, as are educational technology, politics, and the arts. He has been a classroom teacher, principal, staff development director, director of technology, assistant superintendent of schools, college professor, nonprofit organization executive, national conference presenter, consultant, founder of four public schools, and author. He currently serves as Director of the Progressive Science Initiative at Kean University, a highly innovative program for experienced high school teachers that educates them to become teachers of physics, chemistry, and biology. Jim's other affiliations include being a Google Certified Teacher and an adjunct faculty member in the Departments of Educational Leadership at both Kean and William Paterson Universities. Between 2009 and 2010, he was instrumental in writing federal grant proposals that raised over $15 million.

Ronique Hicks is an educational consultant specializing in instructional design, including differentiated instruction and technology integration, to meet the needs of 21st-century learners. She engages in professional development activities including workshops, seminars, conference presentations, and mentoring for educators in varied programs. Additionally, she shares her ed tech expertise as an independent consultant for industry-leading companies such as Discovery Education, eInstruction, and PLATO Learning. Her professional memberships and affiliations include ASCD, ISTE, Google Certified Teacher, and STAR Discovery Educator.

Contributors

Jerome Burg taught high school English for 38 years. Now retired, he spends his time doing professional development, training educators across the country for Apple. He is also a member of the Board of Directors for Computer Using Educators, Inc. (www.cue.org), the founder of the award-winning GoogleLitTrips.com project, and a brand-new grandfather.

Cheryl Davis is the Acalanes Union High School District curriculum and instruction technology specialist. She works with teachers to create and develop 21st-century lessons for the classroom. A former high school history and digital arts teacher, she has created and published Web 2.0 lessons as a Google Certified Teacher and as an Apple Distinguished Educator.

Pamela Friedman is an instructional technology specialist and computer technology teacher for the Westfield (New Jersey) School District, as well as a Google Certified Teacher. In addition to professional development for her district, she has presented and facilitated at the NJECC Annual Conference, the Montclair State University Classroom 2.0 Learning Institute, the

New Jersey School Boards Association Conference, the NJ Elite Conference, and the NJSBA Annual Technology Conference on subjects ranging from technology integration to Web 2.0 communication tools.

John Hrevnack is an assistant professor and coordinator of the Middle School Program at Kean University of New Jersey. He has presented at the New Jersey Middle School Association Conference, the New Jersey School Boards Association Conference, the Annual NJSBA Technology Conference, and the New Jersey Principals and Supervisors Association Conference on integration of technology into the curriculum and related topics. He previously served as superintendent of schools, principal, basic skills supervisor, and taught Grades 3–8.

Carol LaRow taught language arts for 33 years in the Niskayuna School District (New York). She is an Apple Distinguished Educator, a Smithsonian Laureate, and a Google Certified Teacher. LaRow received WNYT's Educator of Excellence Award and was nominated for Disney's American Teacher Award. She has written curriculum for Apple and Adobe, taught at the Apple Teacher Institutes, and is one of the authors of Google Lit Trips and Apple's 21st Century Learning Collection. She is a technology consultant and provides staff development and keynote addresses for faculties and administrators throughout the Northeast United States.

Harold Olejarz is a Google Certified Teacher. He teaches digital media at Eisenhower Middle School in Wyckoff, New Jersey. On the forefront of infusing technology in arts education, Olejarz has presented at numerous state and national conferences. His essay, "Digital Video in the Art Room," is included in *Video Art for the Classroom*, a National Art Education Association publication. Visit his website at www.digitalharold.com.

Sarah Rolle is the director of technology at The Elisabeth Morrow School in Englewood, New Jersey, and a Google Certified Teacher. She holds a Master of Education in Educational Media and Computers from Arizona State University. When not involved in technology, Sarah enjoys crafts including knitting, weaving, and pottery.

Eleanor Funk Schuster is a library media specialist at Suffern Middle School in Rockland County, New York. She holds a Master of Science in Library and Information Science from Long Island University and a Master of Science in Technology with Distinction from the New York Institute of Technology. Eleanor coordinates Suffern Middle School's videoconferencing program, connecting her students to content and conversation around the globe.

Andrea Tejedor is a consultant for e-learning and instructional technology. As the coordinator for e-Learning for the Orange-Ulster BOCES in New York, she currently assists the educators in 17 school districts in the design, planning, and integration of instructional technology across the curriculum. Tejedor is currently a candidate for an EdD in Education Leadership, Management, and Policy at Seton Hall University.

CONTENTS

SECTION IV
DO SCHOOL DIFFERENTLY

SECTION V
LESSON PLANS

INTRODUCTION

DICTIONARIES
DON'T "GET" GOOGLE

google *(verb)*: to search for information on the Internet,
esp. using the Google search engine

—WEBSTER'S NEW MILLENNIUM DICTIONARY OF ENGLISH

The word google first appeared in the *Merriam Webster Collegiate Dictionary* and the *Oxford English Dictionary* in 2006. In its lower-case form, these dictionaries say *google* is a verb. Obviously in its upper-case form, we all know that Google is a company in California that developed a popular Internet search engine.

Is that all?

To think of Google as merely a company or a search engine, or *to google* as only *to search*, is to overlook its dozens of incredibly powerful and useful online applications and to deprive oneself and one's students of the best collection of free online learning tools that exists today.

This book attempts to forge a new understanding of what Google is, and how to google. In it, we describe many of Google's most widely used online applications for education, lead you through step-by-step instructions for how to operate them, and provide lesson plans for how to integrate them into classroom practice.

That alone would constitute a really practical book ... we thought. Then we found CIS 339, a large school in the Bronx, New York, with a visionary and driven principal, Jason Levy, that went from one of the lowest performing to one of the best performing schools in New York City. The centerpiece of its improvement strategy was Google Applications.

The first chapter of this book tells CIS 339's story in detail, giving numerous specific examples of how Google Applications moved the entire school community to extraordinary levels of communication, collaboration, and creativity, and to compelling levels of performance.

We believe CIS 339's story is important for numerous reasons: First, for demonstrating how truly significant Google Applications can be in transforming a school's culture; second, for showing beyond question that the resources and the know-how exist today to move inner-city schools (and indeed all schools) to levels of accomplishment that conventional thinking says are reserved only for the privileged elite; and third, for exhibiting once again the transformative power of technology to make a meaningful difference in the lives of learners.

We also realized that the Google Apps Education Edition constitutes a virtually cost-free way to completely retool the communication infrastructure of a school, so Section IV includes step-by-step directions for how to do that.

With this lineup of content, we feel strongly that *Retool Your School* is a book in which both new and experienced users of Google Applications will find many ideas for how to improve the levels of communication, collaboration, and creativity in their schools and classrooms.

In fact, we hope our efforts contribute to a much-needed transformation of schooling for the benefit of learners around the world.

HOW THIS BOOK IS ORGANIZED

We've divided *Retool Your School* into five sections, with 17 chapters and 43 lesson plans.

Section I contains a chapter devoted to how Google helped a visionary principal transform a highly challenged school, CIS 339, in the Bronx, New York. We start with the story of how Google transformed a school because we think it brings to life the inherent possibilities in all the material that follows.

Section II includes detailed guidance on how to employ the Google Applications most widely used in schools: Documents, Presentations, Spreadsheets, Forms, Blogger, Maps, and Earth.

Section III moves on to provide detailed descriptions of how to use seven more great Google applications: Advanced Search, Calendar, Groups, iGoogle, News, Picasa, and Sites. Each chapter in this section contains helpful Teacher Tips, with ideas for using the application and where to go for more information.

Section IV provides step-by-step explanations for how to bring the Google Apps Education Edition suite of applications to your school or district. Google Apps Education Edition enables a school or district to substantially increase collaboration, communication, and creativity, while cutting costs, by moving much of its computing functionality to the web, instead of maintaining its own local infrastructure. The chapter is written by Harold Olejarz, a Google Certified teacher who personally managed the process of bringing Google Apps Education Edition to his school.

The lesson plans in Section V contain well-defined ideas developed by a number of experienced educators. The plans focus on the applications in Section II, since they are the most widely used. Lesson plans address the major subject areas and are organized into elementary, middle, and high school groupings.

SECTION I

THE TRANSFORMATIVE EDUCATIONAL POWER OF GOOGLE APPLICATIONS

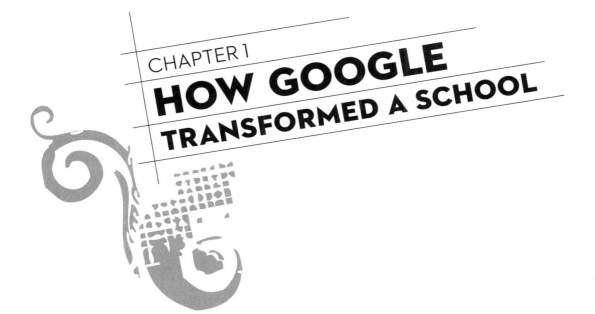

CHAPTER 1
HOW GOOGLE
TRANSFORMED A SCHOOL

Community Intermediate School 339 (CIS 339) occupies a large swath of real estate on Webster Avenue in the South Bronx. The school is a big brick building hunkered down on an expansive asphalt-covered playground that surrounds most of the school. The school is two blocks from a major interstate highway: blocks filled with ten tire and auto repair shops, two lumberyards, a Taco Bell, and a McDonalds. The school doesn't have a parking lot, and everyone must pass through a metal detector to enter the building. CIS 339 is a no-nonsense kind of place in a no-nonsense kind of neighborhood.

CIS 339 educates approximately 900 students in Grades 6, 7, and 8. Roughly two-thirds of the students are of Hispanic background, and just under one-third are African American or African; approximately 80% of students are eligible for free lunch.

As one of over 1400 schools administered by the NYC Department of Education, in the spring of 2007, CIS 339 failed its NYC Quality Review assessment and was placed on the New York State Schools Under Registration Review (SURR) list for low test scores, meaning it was on a path to possibly being closed. Less than a year later, the school had made such startling progress that a team of its teachers and administrators were invited to the national conference of High Schools That Work in Nashville, Tennessee, where they presented the transformation of CIS 339 from SURR to showcase.

This is the story of how Google transformed a school.

THE PRINCIPAL

Any consideration of CIS 339 has to start with Jason Levy, its principal since 2003. As befits his school, Levy is a big man: he stands approximately 6′2″, presents a handsome appearance and a sporty physique. In his youth the left-hander was a pretty good football, basketball, and baseball player. Behind his affable smile and ready laugh there is a razor-sharp mind and a must-do (not can-do) attitude. Levy has high expectations for both himself and everyone in his school.

Patrick Wagner, a consultant who has worked closely with Levy for two years, says, "As an only child [of two New York City high-school teachers], he has all the attributes of the oldest and youngest child wrapped into one—confidence, ambition, being cute, and needing someone to talk to about what he's doing. He can think logically and laterally. With both parents being educators, he's well schooled in schooling." You can see a video of Levy doing the "chicken noodle soup" dance at a school assembly on YouTube (www.youtube.com/watch?v=kpfsPTQPV_g). That he can do this, allow it to be online, and be a respected and effective school leader tells you a lot about the man.

> **THERE IS VIDEO** on CIS 339's transformation, produced by PBS *Frontline*, available at www.pbs.org/wgbh/pages/frontline/digitalnation/learning/schools/how-google-saved-a-school.html.

In college he didn't plan to be a teacher. He considered a career in law, but instead joined Teach for America, taught elementary school in Houston from 1993 to 1996, and then came back to New York. After five more years in the classroom, he became an Assistant Principal at Middle School 390 in the Bronx, earned a Master's degree at Teachers College, Columbia University, and became Principal of CIS 339 in 2004.

When Levy came to CIS 339, he had a big job on his hands. In 2001, the state took the former Junior High School 147 and broke it into two schools. (339 shares its building with another middle school consisting of approximately 450 students.) Levy says, "JHS 147 had a reputation as being a tough place with lots of problems and issues and challenges. It was big, with lots of teacher turnover, behavior problems, and issues in the community. This school is not a neighborhood school; nearly everyone has to travel to it from all across the Bronx. There's no cohesive community immediately surrounding the school." The previous principal had been there for approximately four years and had a reputation as a strong disciplinarian, but little learning had been taking place.

In his first two years as principal, Levy worked hard to implement the human and programmatic infrastructures necessary for progress. Despite some improvement, the hammer fell in 2007 when CIS 339 failed its Quality Review (largely due to poor math scores) and was placed on the dreaded SURR list.

New York State reports student test performance in four levels (level one is the lowest performance, while level four is the highest). In 2003, approximately 70% of CIS 339's students scored at level one in math; in 2008 that dropped to 14% scoring at level one. In 2003, only 9% of students tested at grade level in math; in 2008 the number jumped to 47%. In 2008, the school passed its Quality Review and was ready to be removed from the SURR list. Nestled within these numbers lies a fascinating story, and much of it revolves around Google Applications.

WHAT WERE THE KEYS TO CHANGE?

This chapter focuses mainly on the events of the 2007–08 school year. During this time, both staff and students became involved in using several Google Applications for purposes of administration, teaching, learning, and communication. The Applications used were Gmail, Google Documents (Docs, Spreadsheets, and Presentations), Blogger, Calendar, and Chat. Implementation of Google Applications became the magnetic force that brought people together within the school community as well as the lubricant that made communication faster, easier, and more effective. This combination of factors produced a real-time, real-life organizational transformation.

Patrick Wagner notes that incorporating Google Applications was more than simply incorporating technology: "What's been different this year especially is that we don't just do this stuff, we live it. We have immersed ourselves in this stuff so heavily ... put such investment into it. It's been incredibly rewarding; and the rewards only started to show around the end of the school year. It's also been the platform for a lot of very interesting and exciting things that will be happening next year and beyond."

Levy adds, "We're looking to get faster, smarter, better, and more connected and looking for everything to be seamless. We want it to be in real time; we want everything to make sense, to be connected, and be efficient. Not for the purposes of saving time, but so we can do the things that are most important most often."

Going into the 2007–08 year, CIS 339's organizing slogan was "Communication, Collaboration, and Consistency." All new strategies and procedures were intended to align with, or be derived from, those three overarching concepts.

TIMELINE

WHAT WAS THE SEQUENCE OF EVENTS?

The critical events in the transformation of CIS 339 during 2006–2008 can be quite confusing in their complexity. This chronology of the events may be useful.

2006–2007

School adds more technology

Beginning in the previous school year, and continuing through 2006–07, CIS 339 adds technology with a few laptop carts and has one technology teacher.

iTeachiLearn grant

CIS 339 is chosen as one of 22 middle schools throughout the city for iTeachiLearn, a major public/private grant to upgrade equipment, tech use, and professional development. The school receives 300 iBooks for sixth graders and their teachers as part of the grant.

Teaming begins

CIS 339 implements teacher and student teaming throughout the building.

APRIL 2007: Principal's inspiration

Levy attends a workshop featuring Will Richardson, and the meaning of Web 2.0 becomes a clear inspiration to action.

MAY 2007: Wiki implemented

Levy implements a wiki to replace the paper daily announcements and professional resources for teachers. This becomes the first significant schoolwide technology initiative and continues to the present day.

▶ ▶

TIMELINE (*CONTINUED*)

MAY 2007: CIS 339 fails Quality Review and is placed on SURR list

At the end of the 2006–07 year, the school learns that it has not passed its city-administered Quality Review assessment. Primarily because of low mathematics scores on the state test, the state places the school on the SURR list.

2007–2008

SUMMER 2007: Informal administrative reorganization

Prinstein's position as Literacy Coach is dissolved and a new Dean of Instruction position is created, to which he is duly appointed. Wagner is hired full-time as a technology consultant to the school. Levy, Wagner, and Prinstein become the inner circle for school reform through technology innovation.

JULY 2007: Summer meeting of Principal, Consultant, and Dean of Instruction

On July 18, Levy, Wagner, and Prinstein meet in a restaurant and sketch out the improvement agenda for the year on a paper napkin. The motto for the coming year, "Communication, Collaboration, and Consistency," begins to take shape.

SEPTEMBER 2007: Fall implementation of Google Applications

Program rollout of Google Applications begins with the school's opening. By now, nearly all teachers at CIS 339 have laptops. Gmail is instituted for all staff.

➤➤

In his first two years as principal, Levy worked hard to implement the human and programmatic infrastructures necessary for progress. Despite some improvement, the hammer fell in 2007 when CIS 339 failed its Quality Review (largely due to poor math scores) and was placed on the dreaded SURR list.

Leadership

As mentioned previously, this story really begins with the arrival of Jason Levy as principal for the 2003–04 school year. Levy had been an assistant principal under Robert Mercedes for three years at MS 390, another middle school in the Bronx. Mercedes was a technology supporter, and had introduced a modified 1-to-1 laptop program in the early 2000s. In this setting, Levy began to see the power of technology and started articulating his vision.

Upon arriving at CIS 339, Levy knew he faced a challenging situation. He recalls, "We didn't necessarily have all the resources we needed, nor all the people we needed to have on staff who were excited. I told the teachers, 'You're going to see a lot more tech in this building. I promise you I will get the resources you need to prepare students for the future.'"

Veteran teachers could be forgiven their skepticism as there were no laptops in the school at the time, the only desktops were five years old, and there weren't many of them. But Levy persisted, and the next year CIS 339 received a grant for several laptop carts and added a technology teacher. The following year, the school received another grant through the city's iTeachiLearn program for 300 iBooks for the sixth grade. Things were starting to happen.

Jumping forward to the present day, Levy says, "We don't see the separation of technology and what goes on in an excellent educational organization. I can't imagine the improvement we've done without the Google Apps, but I can imagine the Google Apps working without the approach we've taken. It's an interwoven ethos."

He continues, "At some point in early 2008, I looked up at a staff training, and everyone had their laptops out, and I hadn't said to anyone that they should bring them. That's when I realized they were doing much more work with their laptops than without them. It was very exciting to see that people had fully evolved to be connected in those ways. The Google Apps helped us create a common language in the building around collaboration, connection, and creativity."

The *aha* moment for Levy about the power of technology came in the spring of 2007. "I went to a training where Will Richardson spoke. I had never heard of RSS, Google Reader, or seen the power of blogging. The second I realized what Web 2.0 really meant, the meaning of education shifted for me at the same moment. My entire framework for teaching and learning in schools was completely different.

"It's like this ... once you know there are airplanes, why would you want to drive across the country? Once you know there's laparoscopic surgery, why would you want the kind of operation that will lay you up for six or eight months?

"There's no choice anymore. Unfortunately in education, many see technology as an option. I see it as oxygen. When people say that kids don't need laptops or that tech is a waste of time, I say, 'Would you cut off the oxygen supply to a school?'"

Reflecting on the 2007–08 school year and its many notable accomplishments, Levy says about Google Apps, "They allow for rapid improvement, reflection, response, and communication that wouldn't be possible any other way. What we're doing isn't stuff that hasn't been done before, but *the way* we're doing it makes the work much more enriching and meaningful. You're able to focus on what's important quicker; you're able to spread best practices much more readily.

"Communication here is extremely tight and our organization is extremely focused. A lot of

TIMELINE (CONTINUED)

JANUARY 2008: Staff presentations at Google and state conference

After the holiday break, several activist staff members make public presentations about their work; first to a group of Google executives in New York City and then to a state-level education conference involving the five largest districts in the state of New York.

FEBRUARY 2008: School holds mock Quality Review

In preparation for CIS 339's upcoming city Quality Review assessment, city officials hold a mock Quality Review in the winter. During this time, the motto of Communication, Collaboration, and Consistency is modified to more accurately characterize the threads (centers of activity) that would drive school improvement efforts in the future.

These threads are identified as follows: Data and Differentiation, Environment and Engagement, Curriculum and Collaboration, Responsibility and Rigor, and Communication and Celebration.

APRIL 2008: School holds parent open house

CIS 339 holds a parent open house about technology on April 30. Several hundred parents attend. It is the largest instance of parent turnout anyone at the school can remember.

JUNE 2008: THE WEEK

The first week of June is filled with significant events and becomes a pivotal moment in solidifying and celebrating CIS 339's remarkable story of improvement.

- On Monday, a half-day professional development session is held in the school library. CIS 339 staff

>>

collaboratively develop the five key goals to drive the organization for 2008–09.

■ On Thursday, an all-day PD is held. Teachers engage in round-robin sessions devoted to differentiation, school environment, and innovative teaching. Teachers are given digital cameras and asked to document their perception of the school environment at that moment.

■ On Friday morning, CIS 339 hosts a technology open house for over 150 visitors from across the NY metro area. Dozens of staff members make presentations to the visiting dignitaries.

■ On Friday evening and Saturday morning, CIS 339 holds a staff retreat at a local, off-site location. During this weeklong period of reflection and planning, everyone becomes much more fluent in articulating a common language dealing with the most vital elements and concerns that truly drive the school.

JUNE 2008: School passes Quality Review

Just a few days later, CIS 339 learns that it has passed its latest Quality Review and that student scores on the state tests qualify it to be removed from the SURR list.

JULY 2008: School presents at High Schools That Work conference

A team from CIS 339 travels to the national High Schools That Work conference in Nashville, Tennessee, sponsored by the Southern Regional Education Board. Over 300 people attend the team's presentation, titled "How Google Changed My School."

it is because we are streamlining our processes and systems through these tools. They are a filter that allows you to do your best work more frequently. I can't imagine school leadership without the Google tools. Now that I've seen how it works this way, I would never want to go back."

Jesse Spevack, a four-year language arts teacher at CIS 339 says, "Levy has a definite vision of the school, but he's happy to let everyone in and come up with things on their own. He's the kind of boss where if you have an idea, he'll say, 'Run with it.' His strategy is not a top-down strategy, it's much more consensus. He's more of a carrot guy [than a stick guy]."

Wagner has formed definite opinions about Levy and his leadership. "A lot of principals get sucked into thinking that they have to be authoritarian, and if they're not, they're not doing their job properly. Levy is someone who is prepared to share his leadership, and he does this incredibly well. He has the confidence, and the naïveté in some regards, to say, 'OK, what do you think we should do?'

"He's really got it together. He's very positive and very positive publicly. When people start to panic about different things, he always says, 'Right. Let's start with what's going well.' Then he says, 'OK, what's the issue?' He can take the personal out of the professional. He can get people to say what the issue is. He does that very, very well."

Leadership, however, does not reside only in Levy. Many people contribute their ideas and energy to moving CIS 339 forward. Clearly, he encourages and welcomes such input, and without it the school's progress would not be possible. Among the many activists, three people have formed the "kitchen cabinet" that constitutes CIS 339's inner circle. They are Levy, Wagner, and Dean of Instruction, David Prinstein. Together, they are the core that ignites the flame of instructional technology progress at CIS 339.

The Faculty

Two important developments greatly affected the instructional staff from 2003 to 2008. First, the culture of the school changed. Second, there was considerable turnover of personnel.

Wagner describes the culture when Google Apps were implemented in fall 2007: "Right from the first week in September, there was a lot of resistance. I think a lot of it was due to a sheer lack of understanding. The teachers were still going, 'Yeah, this is kind of interesting, but it's still just another fad.' There was a history within 339 of innovations that didn't go anywhere."

Jesse Spevack illustrates how the school culture changed from a teacher's perspective.

> During my first year (2004–05), this was a terrible place to work. People took a lot of mental health days. I had coverages two or three times a week because people weren't coming in. Classroom management was the only thing we could think about. We did not have control over the kids. That doesn't happen any more. I hated coming into work every day then. Now, I enjoy coming to work. And I think that's a sentiment held throughout the building.
>
> People are proud to be a part of what's going on here. Not just new teachers, not just the tech wizard teachers; everyone sees that what we're doing is new and having real positive effects on our kids. I mean not just academically, though test scores have gone up. Instruction is definitely our focus now.
>
> The culture of the building is so much more positive. There's a spirit of collaboration that all the teachers have. Everyone wants to share and everyone wants to get better by watching one another. We feel we've got the expertise in the building to keep this movement of school change going.
>
> People have the feeling we can, as a school and as individuals, change behaviors of kids. We were more resigned in my first year. There was the feeling, 'This is how it's going to be.' Now more and more people are saying, 'That is not how it's going to be. We can change it. Things can improve.'

Usually when a troubled school gets a new principal, particularly one who expresses a definite (and different) vision of the future, a certain number of teachers feel they will be better suited teaching somewhere else. CIS 339 was no exception. At the end of Levy's first year, approximately 15 of the school's 75 teachers chose to go elsewhere. Since that time, the number of teachers who choose to leave each year has dwindled substantially. Nevertheless, the regular course of retirements and other customary reasons for teachers to leave contributed to approximately a 60% personnel turnover during Levy's first four years. This has enabled a new and fairly consistent way of thinking to be built across the faculty, including numerous veteran faculty members who have transformed their teaching practices to incorporate technology.

Levy says, "The approach was not from the position of 'This is mandatory' or 'This is by tomorrow.' The approach was 'Eventually' and 'Why not do it?' We looked for early adapters and people we could encourage. My theory is that people who are not interested in connecting in the 2.0 ways aren't interested in connecting in the 1.0 ways either. The same people who are resistant to setting up a Gmail account aren't checking their other e-mail account either.

"At no point have I written a letter of discipline or a warning letter to anyone for not engaging with the Google tools. I don't want this to be anything but useful and exciting. If we're not giving people enough of a reason, or there isn't enough incentive for people to use the tools, then they shouldn't have to use the tools.

"We have the right mindset, vision, and approach. In the wrong hands, or with the wrong or ineffective approach, tech tools could be sources of frustration or divisiveness or gotcha. Or without the right training and support they could be tools for working on incompetence. The tools seamlessly merge with our approach to help us catapult the school."

Wagner sees an additional dimension to the impact on staff members: "Even though Levy says we didn't make this compulsory for staff, that staff just picked up on it, that's not quite accurate. Not that he made it compulsory—what he did was open it up to the entire staff. And that's what I think was a crucial thing.

"A lot of technology conferences you go to, they talk about 'trialing' it, about using a small pool of people. I think that's the first mistake they make. What happens with that is you have this culture where some people are the shining lights and the others have no part of it. They have no motivation to be part of it because the other ones are the ones who go off and get the kudos.

"Whereas what Levy did was: Everyone had a laptop, and everyone was involved with the technology. There was the potential there for different people to grow. It all snowballed. The second half of the 2007–08 school year, it just took off. Suddenly people who were only halfway there were saying, 'Oh, how do I do that?' or 'Can you show me, too?' Interest was coming from all different places slowly, and each of those new bits of interest added to the momentum of what we were doing."

Spevack adds, "It's so clearly in everyone's best interest to teach using the Google Apps that everyone's getting on board. People who had never used e-mail before in their lives are now asking to be shared on documents. Teachers who were afraid of the tech or didn't want it in their classrooms now see that there's some benefit there."

Another key individual in the school's efforts has been David Prinstein, Dean of Instruction, who serves as CIS 339's educational leader. Prinstein was a literacy coach for two years before being named to his current position in 2007–08. He is part of the principal's administrative team, but he doesn't perform formal teacher evaluations. In this way, teachers view him as a peer, not someone with the power to hire and fire. His suggestions and leadership are taken as from a colleague, not a boss. This provides Prinstein with greater access to teachers and they can be more open with him. On the other hand, this challenges Prinstein to rely on the power of his ideas and the effectiveness of his communication, rather than the power that comes with a position that affects teacher evaluation.

Prinstein's view of faculty participation is that "People move at their own pace. Just because someone's moving at a different pace, doesn't mean they're not moving. Teachers who we thought were being totally resistant would seem to wake up one morning and get it. It wasn't that they were being resistant; it was that they were coming to it at their own pace. We were never punitive. There was never any kind of discipline if people weren't using tech or the Google Apps. People came to the movement when they were ready and when they felt it was necessary."

Teaming and Teacher Leadership

What grade-level groups are to elementary schools and departments to high schools, teams are to middle schools—the fundamental unit of administrative organization. Yet, many middle schools do not organize their faculties into teams, and until the 2006–07 school year, neither did CIS 339.

The importance of moving the CIS 339 faculty into teams cannot be overemphasized. Levy explains, "Movement into teaming was critical. There was a lot of isolation previously. Teaming built structures where people could connect and collaborate. Later, when we added the technology, that really helped keep people aligned within their teams." The existence of teams gave teachers a reason to collaborate, communicate, and create with one another.

In a faculty of 75 teachers, CIS 339 has seven teams. Each team consists of an interdisciplinary group of teachers on a grade level responsible for a common group of approximately 120 students. They plan instruction, assessment, team activities, motivation, and behavioral interventions for their team. At CIS 339 there are two teams on each grade level and one additional team, for a total of seven.

Each team has a designated team leader. The leaders organize the work of their teams, have modified schedules, and also receive a stipend. There are also approximately a dozen content area leaders, who work with the teams as curriculum specialists. Until the spring of 2008, these were volunteer classroom teachers. In the fall of 2008, the content area leaders started receiving a stipend. The money to support these teacher leadership positions came from a reorganization of staff using the existing building budget.

The creation of teacher teams changed the work atmosphere for faculty. Spevack says, "The institution of teams was a huge change in the school. Instead of not having anywhere to turn, there was a lot of team spirit and pride in our group. Teams wanted to be the one to come up with the next big thing in the school. Now we have structured meetings and really help ourselves get a tremendous amount of constructive work done."

Commenting on this initiative, Levy states, "Leadership is distributed in our school. We involve staff in hiring and interviewing and the selection process for new faculty. We have promoted people from within to leadership positions, too: assistant principals, deans, coaches, facilitators, and team leaders."

As examples of teachers who really stepped up, Wagner mentions Christina Jenkins, CIS 339's Tech Coordinator, and Abby Lovett, a Special Education teacher. "Christina is a very hard worker, a detail person who takes care of things, and is very intelligent. Abby gave people confidence that technology wasn't getting in the way of education, that it was actually making things better and helping education."

In addition, as excitement at CIS 339 began to build, teachers became involved in providing professional development programs to one another and represented the school at local, regional, and national conferences.

Administration

Communication

Administrative operations changed in a number of startling and profound ways, some expected and some completely unanticipated. Prinstein gives an example: "For my job, the Google Apps enable me to be meeting with one team and have windows up on my computer seeing the meetings of other teams happening simultaneously. I can chime in whenever I want. I can be there and not there at the same time. I can be out of the building entirely and still be present." He continues, "We couldn't anticipate how valuable Chat was going to be. Just to be able to find people makes the phone system and walkie-talkies obsolete."

Examples of other forms of administrative operations improved by Google Applications include:

- Contact lists for easy distribution of e-mail in Gmail;

- Chat with colleagues. The Chat client indicates whether a person is online (available). Full text of the Chat is archived for permanent future reference in a separate section of Gmail;

- Newsletter creation in Docs and distribution to targeted audiences using Gmail;

- Public and private calendars for schoolwide, group, and personal use in Calendar;

- Meeting schedules with automatically e-mailed RSVP requests in Calendar. Confirmations appear on one's own personal calendar;

- Single school start page created in Google Apps for Education;

- Managed Gmail accounts for all students established in Google Apps for Education. (Parent permissions are necessary for students under the age of 13); and

- Color-coded schedule matrices for personnel created in Spreadsheets for distribution online or posting in Docs or elsewhere.

To view a Google Presentations slide show detailing the use of Google Applications at CIS 339, go to http://docs.google.com/present/view?id=dd2xg6bf_294zqzf47xg.

Instructional Improvement

Prinstein summarizes CIS 339's approach to teacher supervision: "Our idea is: We'll evaluate when there's a problem. Aside from that, we're supporting, pushing, and giving ideas." A key to accomplishing this task is the online Class Visit Feedback Document, a Google Doc hosted online. To view a video of Prinstein describing use of the Class Visit Feedback Document, go to www.youtube.com/watch?v=jwMvL8-C9zA.

A team of nine people at CIS 339 is charged with the responsibility of visiting teachers' class-rooms and providing feedback on teachers' performances. This team includes the school's administrators as well as a few senior level instructional leaders who do not possess administrative certification. The faculty has agreed to this arrangement.

Teachers receive many visits from team members, often several at different times over a single day. Comments from visitors, along with responses from the teacher, are compiled in an online document seen only by the teacher and the visitors (see Fig. 1.1). The document serves as a volu-minous running record of visits, comments, and responses compiled over the full length of the year—becoming a rich repository of information for teacher reflection, professional growth, and instructional improvement. The document serves as a virtual, personal, professional learning community for each teacher in the building.

This is a new Class Visit Feedback Document we have developed at CIS 339. It will be shared only between the Curriculum Team and you. You are encouraged to respond in the far right-hand column, and we look at feedback as a two-way street.

Thank you for being receptive to professional feedback. We hope that consistent communication can develop a common understanding of quality, and we stand ready to support you in any way possible. If you have questions, kindly e-mail to: Jason, Georgina, Ivory, Daniel, Florence, David, Jose, Abby, Maggie.

I SAW AND HEARD	ELEMENTS OF QUALITY	QUESTIONS AND SUGGESTIONS	FEEDBACK FROM TEACHER

FIGURE 1.1. Sample Class Visit Feedback Document used in Google Docs

Planning

The school developed a form to be used in Docs to record, summarize, and track the work of CIS 339's many committees and teams. All members of a group and the administration are able to access the form in Google Docs to make contributions and keep up to date on current developments. The forms serve as running records of groups' work over time, keeping people on track and on time. They are available online anytime, anywhere, to designated individuals. All administrative and instructional groups use the form (see Fig. 1.2).

DATE TIME, LOCATION	ATTENDEES	AGENCIES	MINUTES	QUESTIONS AND NEXT STEPS
Date: 9/4/07 Time: 12:15–1:00 Location: Levy's Office	Facilitator: All In Attendance: PW DP JL	1. September PD Calendar 2. Staff Gmail accounts 3. Creating spreadsheets 4. Content facilitator selection 5. Designed template for meeting notes	1. September PD Calendar 2. Staff Gmail accounts 3. Creating spreadsheets 4. Content facilitator selection 5. Designed template for meeting notes	■ How do we generate and share this template with all teams? ■ Plan meeting for Weds @ 1:00 ■ Get 5 key people to sign up for Gmail ■ Plan PD for Weds after school ■ Plan PD for Thurs. for Team Leaders

FIGURE 1.2. Sample form to archive agendas, minutes, and next steps for teams in Google Docs

Discipline

CIS 339 experiences its fair share of student behavior issues and, until the early part of the 2007–08 school year, had two Deans of Students to handle this work. However, one of the Deans had to leave the position in mid-September, which resulted in the remaining Dean, Noelle Burns, having to take on a seemingly Herculean mountain of paperwork to process and incidents to address. Burns and the leadership team huddled and—you guessed it—developed a few procedures through Google Applications, and the seemingly insurmountable became fully manageable.

Burns describes the situation: "I became inundated with referrals, dealing with such big things that I wasn't able to support the teachers when they needed help with little things. Little things like insubordination, or throwing paper, or just dancing in class. Teachers were coming to me and they would say, 'You're not supporting me. You're only coming to me when we have a major physical altercation.' I was so busy helping other people's children that I was starting to neglect my own child at home."

A method was created to recognize students for positive behavior, including participation, effort, helpfulness, organization, creativity, improvement, and quality of work. Using the Forms feature of Google Spreadsheets, an online form was developed for teachers to send instant reports of commendable student behavior to the administration so students and their families could receive appropriate recognition and reinforcement. As part of the daily announcements over the loudspeaker, Levy regularly commended these Tech Tiger All-Stars, as they are called.

Like many schools, CIS 339 had a system of daily behavior sheets for misbehaving students that teachers had to fill out at the end of each period. With the potential for several such students in every class, managing all this paperwork was frequently a nightmare. Enter Google Spreadsheets. A spreadsheet was created for each section (class) of students. Every Monday, teachers received a new set of section spreadsheets in their e-mail, listing every student by class. Teachers were able to record both attendance and behavior information with just a keystroke or two.

Anytime during a period, if a teacher needed to note a student's misbehavior, they could enter the information in the appropriate spreadsheet and it would appear instantly on the Dean's computer. As she strolled down the hall with her laptop in hand, she could check the behavior status of an entire class as she passed the door. If particular students required attention, they could be addressed immediately. Word soon got out among the students that, as they say in Star Trek, "Resistance is futile."

Burns now says, "Student behavior changed. I started to have a lot less low-level infractions and was really able to focus on correcting behavior instead of fixing it." To view a video of Burns describing the use of behavior management forms in Google Spreadsheets, visit www.youtube.com/watch?v=iJpixeZWDFg.

This behavior tracking form (see Fig. 1.3) shows one team for two days. The form is maintained on a Google Spreadsheet and always accessible in real time to all team teachers, the Dean of Students, and administration. The periods of the day appear across the top of the spreadsheet: M1 for Monday, first period; M2 for Monday, second period; T3 for Tuesday, third period, and so on. Teachers enter a behavior assessment for every student for every period. (This is not quite as onerous as it might sound. CIS 339 has a block schedule, consisting of many double-length periods.)

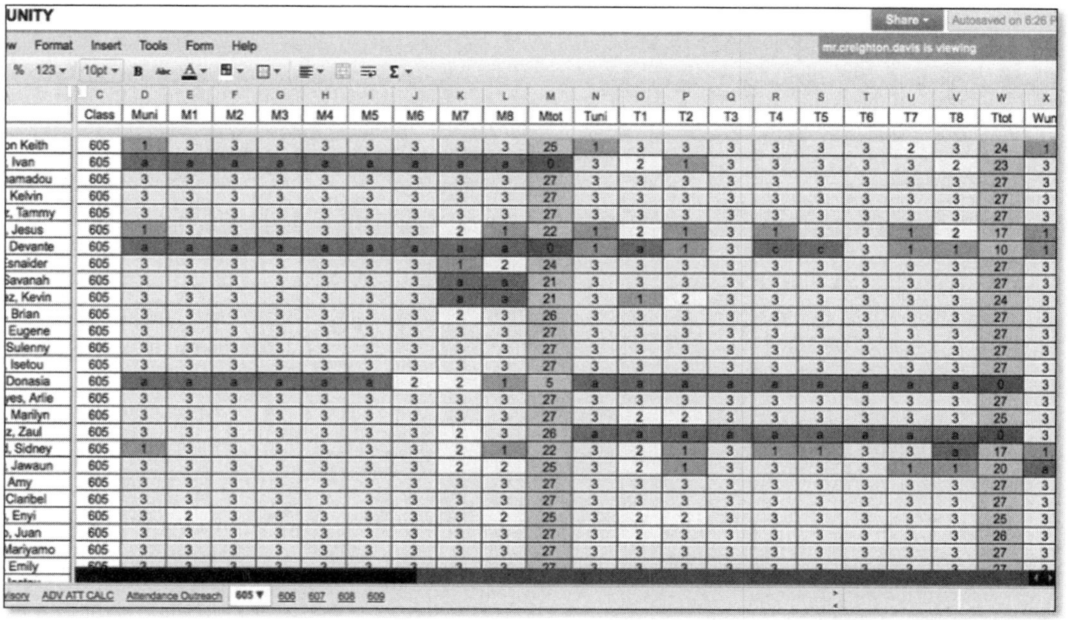

FIGURE 1.3. Sample behavior management form in Google Speadsheets

A 3 signifies good behavior, 2 signifies minor infractions such as talking out of turn or littering the room, and 1 stands for a significant problem needing rapid attention. The cells in the form are color-coded. The same form is used to record student absences, indicated by the letter A.

Burns frequently walks the halls with her laptop and can move quickly from one end of a long corridor to another, stopping at classrooms where needed to conference with students whose behavior requires attention. In this manner, she can attend to the behavioral concerns of an entire hallway of students in just a brief period of time. She mentions that students often remark to her, "How did you get here so fast? That just happened 30 seconds ago!"

The behavior tracking system serves as a just-in-time, short-term monitoring system, but it is also organized for long-term reinforcement of positive behavior. Formulas have been developed in the spreadsheet to total each student's behavior assessments on both daily and weekly bases. If a student's daily score falls below a certain threshold, that student may be called in for a conference or receive detention. At the end of the week, each student receives a "paycheck" based on behavior score. More points yield a bigger paycheck. The paychecks are redeemable at the school store for supplies and school gear such as pens, notebooks, hats, and T-shirts.

Planning

The institution of teams provided CIS 339 with an organizational structure on which to build with Google Applications. The planning form (see Fig. 1.4) was a key element to move this process forward. In addition, teams were urged to collaborate in the development of common unit plans, with all members contributing to their development, implementation, and revision. This was done through Google Docs, and the resulting plans were saved in team as well as personal archives. This planning process was reinforced in regular team meetings that occurred several times per week, which led to greater consistency in lesson design and implementation.

CIS 339 UNIT PLANNER

Teacher _____ Class(es) _____

DATES OF UNIT	TOPIC/TITLE OF UNIT
From: To:	

TEACHERS COMMITTED TO COLLABORATING ON THIS UNIT

ESSENTIAL QUESTIONS (What BIG IDEAS or OVERARCHING THEMES will my students take away from this unit?)

GUIDING QUESTIONS (What THEMES will tie together or drive groups of lessons?)

KEY CONCEPTS/VOCABULARY (What important ideas, concepts, words, or terms will need to be pre-taught?)

PERFORMANCE INDICATORS (Which NYS performance indicators will this unit align to? Click the hyperlinks below to browse.)	
READING	WRITING
6th Grade Reading	6th Grade Writing
7th Grade Reading	7th Grade Writing
8th Grade Reading	8th Grade Writing

(Continued)

DATES	Mini-Lessons What will I teach to support these skills? RIGOR	Activities/Assessments How will I know if each student has mastered the mini-lesson? ENGAGEMENT	Opportunities for Differentiation How can the activity or assessment be modified to meet the needs of all learners? DIFFERENTIATION

TECHNOLOGY INTEGRATION OPPORTUNITIES (How will you infuse 21st-Century instructional technology in the unit?) ENGAGEMENT

CULMINATING ACTIVITY/FORMAL ASSESSMENT (What will my students be able to show at the end of the unit that displays their learning? Click here for a link to the RUBRIC)

RESOURCES AND MENTOR TEXTS (What texts, exemplary samples, or finished products will I show my students to guide their work?)

FIGURE 1.4. CIS 339's Unit Planning Form, used in Google Docs

Assessment

Teams were encouraged to develop common assessments for their units. These assessments separated overall grades into subcategories that lent themselves to the development of scoring rubrics. In this manner, each student received a grade for a unit assignment that was composed of several parts, each of which could be related to a specific rubric element that yielded practical information to the student and the teacher for feedback and conferencing purposes (see Fig. 1.5).

ELA Writing Common Assessment Data Tr... View only

File ▾   View   Create a Map, Chart or Table

This spreadsheet is receiving entries via a form.   🔲 Go to live form

Last, First	GR LVL	OFF CLS	ELA Teacher	FOCUS	ELABORATION	STRUCTURE	VOICE & VOCAB	TOTAL
Average for each column:				3.03	3.17	3.10	3.08	12.38
na	6	605	Spevack	2	4	4	3	13
	6	605	Spevack	3	4	5	4	16
ey	6	605	Spevack	2	2	3	3	10
	6	605	Spevack	5	3	4	4	16
el	6	605	Spevack	3	3	3	3	12
	6	605	Spevack	3	4	4	4	15
	6	605	Spevack	3	2	2	2	9
	6	605	Spevack	2	3	3	3	11
n	6	605	Spevack	4	3	4	4	15
	6	605	Spevack	4	4	4	4	16
	6	605	Spevack	3	4	4	4	15
	6	605	Spevack	2	2	1	1	6
	6	605	Spevack	2	3	3	2	10
	6	605	Spevack	2	1	1	1	5
	6	605	Spevack	3	2	2	2	9
	6	605	Spevack	3	4	5	4	16

FIGURE 1.5. Sample of a common assessment spreadsheet for one teacher

Perhaps the most powerful element in this process, however, was that teachers also entered the grades for each student in a teamwide spreadsheet. This was a factor that made the common unit plans such powerful forces for student learning. The grades included the score for each subpart of the student's overall grade. All teachers did this within roughly the same time period, so that in short order a spreadsheet became available for the unit that incorporated the subscore and total score for every student on the team. By color-coding, grouping, and sorting the scores, teachers were able to analyze performance patterns, strong and weak points of the unit, and groups of students who could benefit from either re-teaching or enriched experiences (see Fig. 1.6). This made reflection on the design, delivery, and effectiveness of the unit much easier and faster, as well as a collaborative rather than individual endeavor on the part of the teachers. More minds were able to work together quickly and effectively—a win-win situation for teachers and students alike. Keep in mind that, once the spreadsheets are set up, these types of data displays are almost automatic, and accessible online 24 hours a day, 7 days a week.

Using the Forms feature in Google Spreadsheets, some teachers were able to build tests and quizzes that fed student responses immediately into a self-scoring spreadsheet that could return results to students and provide the teacher with full data for the whole class ... instantly. This was done for pre-assessments as well.

Using Docs for student writing, teachers provided feedback directly in the writing assignment. Students could peer review one another's work as well. Hosting student writing online enabled the school day to extend to anytime the student could access the Internet. The built in date- and time-stamp for Docs enabled teachers to see every instance of when a student worked on an assignment. Having unhindered access to Gmail enabled students to e-mail their teachers anytime they had a question. All of these features contributed to an expansion of the school day. Students were willing and able to engage in education beyond the confines of the school walls and hours.

common assessment

Format | Insert | Tools | Form | Help

First Name	Total	Autho purpo 15	Cause and effect 14	16	Chara motiv 17	Figura Langu 18	Inferences 7	8	9	10	13	Main idea 1	4	Predic 3	Summ 6	Text conne 2	Text Featu 5	Vocabulary 11	12
	48.6	58.3		41.7	25	12.5					54.2		83.3	83.3	45.8	12.5	58.3		29.2
Ivan	22.2	0	0	0	0	0	0	100	100	0	0	100	0	100	0	0	0	0	0
Mahamadou	55.6	100	100	100	0	0	100	0	100	100	0	100	0	100	100	0	100	0	0
Kelvin	66.7	100	100	100	0	0	100	0	0	0	100	100	100	100	100	100	100	0	100
Tammy	50	0	100	0	0	0	100	100	100	100	0	100	0	100	100	0	0	0	100
Jesus	83.3	100	100	100	100	0	100	100	100	100	100	100	100	100	100	0	100	0	100
Esnaider	66.7	100	100	100	0	0	100	100	100	0	100	100	100	100	100	0	100	0	0
Savanah	38.9	100	0	0	0	0	100	0	100	0	0	100	100	100	0	0	0	0	100
Kevin	50	0	0	0	100	0	100	100	0	100	0	100	100	100	0	0	100	0	100
Brian	44.4	100	100	0	0	0	100	0	0	100	0	100	100	100	0	0	100	0	100
Eugene	61.1	100	0	100	0	100	100	0	100	0	100	100	100	0	100	0	100	0	100
Sulenny	38.9	0	100	100	0	0	0	0	0	0	0	100	100	0	100	0	100	0	100
Isetou	38.9	0	0	0	0	0	100	100	100	0	0	100	100	100	0	0	0	0	100
Donasia																			
Arlie	77.8	100	100	0	100	0	100	100	100	100	100	100	100	100	100	0	100	0	100
Marilyn	55.6	0	0	0	0	0	100	100	100	100	100	100	100	100	0	0	100	0	100
Zaul	16.7	0	0	0	0	0	0	0	100	0	0	100	100	0	0	0	0	0	0
Sidney	38.9	100	0	100	0	0	100	100	0	0	0	0	0	0	0	100	100	0	100
Jawuan	22.2	0	0	0	100	0	0	100	0	0	100	0	0	0	0	0	100	0	0
Amy	55.6	100	100	0	0	100	100	100	0	0	0	100	100	100	100	0	100	0	0

FIGURE 1.6. Sample of a common assessment spreadsheet for a unit test for part of a team.

Classroom Instructional Organization and Delivery

Sixth grade language arts teacher and team leader, Dena Wolk, describes the way Docs changed her teaching experience.

> Google Docs saved my life. I truly mean that: *saved my life*. I e-mailed my lessons to students each day. They understood the routine. They would come into class, take out their laptops, open their e-mail, see my reading and writing workshops, and the first thing on there would be a "Do Now." I would walk around as the students were completing their Do Nows and make sure they were on task. These lessons would also set up a paper trail for me for students who were absent, and for collaborating with other teachers. I became more organized, and so did the students.
>
> Short little story: We were having a lesson about *The Giver*. All of a sudden, one of my students said, 'Shakir is online.' Shakir was not in school. I had received a phone call earlier that he couldn't come to school. All of sudden, here he was, opening up his e-mail and doing his Do Now and actually completing the work. I was floored.
>
> All of this added up to my wow moment when I realized that Google had transformed my classroom. I looked over at my desk and I could actually see it. The papers that were to be graded had disappeared.
>
> In the beginning of the year, I was receiving only 14% of my students' home-work. By March it was over 70%.
>
> *To view Wolk's description of how Google Docs changed her classroom, visit:* www.youtube.com/watch?v=_ZBF8tg-ht0 *and* www.youtube.com/watch?v=VhIp1dFsslM.

Spevack began using Docs for lesson planning out of necessity. He had always kept his lesson plans on his laptop's hard drive, but during the holiday break in 2007, he left his laptop at school. He had no choice but to create his plans online, in Docs. He never went back.

Spevack uses Docs regularly with his language arts students. "Let's say a group of students is reading a book in common. They do a response to it in a Doc, just like a notebook. What's great is, they can't lose it. For the first time as a literacy teacher, I can document the kids using specific reading strategies that I'm teaching. On a blank page, students write their names and 'Reading Journal' and send me a running list of the pre-reading strategy and explain how they used it. It's set up like a blog; the newest one goes on top.

"We use a similar strategy for writing: one writing Doc for a unit. [A student's] name and 'Short Story' go on top ... shared with me, maybe shared with their writing group. Start at the top, whatever the activity is to get started, maybe a brainstorming list or a freewrite. Open up one another's documents and comment. They love that because I tell them they can do it in a different color. The next day, maybe the next assignment is outlining, so that goes in at the top of the page. The next day it might be the draft and that goes at the top; and so on and so forth. I find that the real trick is to keep it as simple as possible ... one document. Just keep it all in one place and you have a good record of all that's been done."

Prinstein says that from a schoolwide perspective, as opposed to an individual classroom, "Collaborative writing was surprising, the long routes it took. A lot of teachers I wouldn't have expected to get on the bandwagon quickly set up writing groups for their kids. It makes management a lot easier because kids can just sit where they are and work together online. We have a schoolwide writing rubric. We do writing in math and science, all the content areas."

Spevack's comments shed light on the transformative power inherent in Google Docs. First, communication is public. Students no long write only for themselves and their teacher; they have a wider audience. In this case, Spevack restricts the audience to fellow classmates, but in other instances in CIS 339, such as student blogs, their work is open to the world.

Engaging in more public communication produces two immediate effects: students pay more attention to conventions of expression (spelling, grammar, and voice) and the learning becomes more social (as in social constructivism). Students' written communication about their work among themselves develops learning networks that contribute to knowledge creation by and among students, enabling student roles that formerly were reserved exclusively for the teacher. Also, engaging in visible online peer discussions also teaches important 21st century skills in giving and receiving feedback.

Finally, having all the communication exist online, in an easily manageable format, produces tremendous efficiencies in paper management. Papers are no longer lost or misplaced. Students no longer need to carry bulky notebooks, bursting with loose teacher handouts and mixed-up collections of class notes, homework, and other assignments. Everything lives on the web, always ready for easy access for all intended readers and collaborators. Less time is spent on management tasks; more time can be devoted to learning.

All eighth graders have blogs. The school newspaper is a blog. "We have a blogging mentor program. We paired eighth graders with people in the community to give them feedback on their writing. We paired up Frederick [not his real name] and his blog, Fred on Food, with a chef, who showed him how to write about food. Frederick was a kid with behavior problems, a kid who was uninterested in school but passionate about food. Through his blog, and through the mentoring he received, Frederick became engaged with school. He even became a student instructional leader. His teachers, to a one, recognized that he had an absolutely great year. He won a couple of awards at the end of the year. His sixth grade teacher, who had him two years ago, said that back then he was a real pain in the rear. Now he's looking at this mature kid who's a writer and he said, 'This is great. What happened?'"

CIS 339 even has a rubric for blogging (see Fig. 1.7). Big posters of the rubric, two feet by three feet, adorn the walls of every eighth grade classroom. What's especially important about this rubric is not that some external body has dubbed it the best, but that the school's own staff developed it in-house. It belongs to them, and they think it's good. Not only that, but they're more than happy to have anyone use it or suggest improvements. This demonstrates the power of collaboration in an exemplary fashion.

Research Blog Rubric				
CONVENTIONS	FOCUS	ORGANIZATION	VOICE/ VOCABULARY	ELABORATION
4 All online sources are properly hyperlinked. Very few errors in punctuation, spelling, grammar, and usage.	Focus is maintained throughout. Choice of material supports purpose of the post. Author's opinion is clear, and woven right through each post. Theme of the blog is well developed.	Subject ideas are synthesized smoothly with ideas of the writer. Logical progression of ideas. Writing is fluent and cohesive.	Directly engages the reader through a conversational tone. Has a strong imprint of the writer.	Provides an insightful and original explanation/ opinion that relates to or extends aspects of the text.
3 Most online sources are properly hyperlinked. Some errors in punctuation, spelling, grammar, and usage.	May lose focus at times. Choice of material supports purpose of the post. Theme of the blog is generally developed.	Subject ideas are presented but not smoothly incorporated. Logical progression, but may not be fluent and/or cohesively presented.	May engage the reader in the conversation. Writing is sometimes too academic or too informal in tone.	Provides an original explanation/ opinion using situations or ideas from the text as support.
2 Hyperlinks don't work or are nonexistent. Consistent errors in punctuation, spelling, grammar, and usage.	Frequently loses focus. Material chosen is questionable in terms of accuracy or doesn't clearly relate to topic.	Subject ideas are poorly presented and a relationship with ideas of the writer is lacking. Lack of cohesion.	Little imprint of the writer who, at times, seems to care little for the topic and/or audience.	Provides an opinion or explanation that seems uninformed and/or unrelated to text.
1 Hyperlinks don't work or are nonexistent. Contains errors that interfere with meaning.	Unfocused. Material chosen is questionable in terms of accuracy and doesn't clearly relate to topic.	Subject ideas are poorly presented or not presented at all. Writer's ideas are difficult to follow. Post is incoherent and poorly organized.	Writing that is "going through the motions." No acknowledgment of audience.	Opinion or explanation is flawed, inconsistent, and/or makes no attempt to relate to ideas in the text.

FIGURE 1.7. CIS 339's rubric for blogging for eighth graders

Levy says the enhanced communication due to all students and teachers having Gmail, and all eighth graders maintaining blogs, is particularly significant because "Kids become known. When they get their Gmail and Blogger accounts, their personalities come out. They feel connected with teachers on a daily basis. The Google platforms really create a sense of harmony and equity among the staff and students. Everyone becomes an equal when they're editing a document collaboratively. It becomes really powerful in that way. The kids' work becomes known. As an administrator, I can drop by a class and say to a kid, 'Hey, I read your story. It was great.' The kid would look at me and realize he's not alone. Kids read one another's blogs. That allows these social tools to become more intellectual and educational."

There have been many unanticipated instructional benefits as well. Prinstein reflects on the changes he hadn't predicted: "I didn't expect to be presenting at the New York Google office to Google staff. I didn't expect our school to be presenting at national educational conferences about the things we dreamed up on a napkin in a restaurant. I didn't expect in my wildest dreams for the Docs and Apps to have this galvanizing effect on the entire school community. Students are proud of this stuff and that they're the only ones doing it. That they're doing stuff that's different and better than how their friends, or their brothers, or their parents did when they were in school. We're meeting kids where they live. We're equating being smart with being cool."

SEVEN FACTORS CONTRIBUTING TO SUCCESS

Seven factors converged to motivate, drive, and support CIS 339: necessity, leadership, efficacy, expertise, support, reliability, and critical mass. Many of the school's successes can be attributed to the vigorous intentions of the people involved on-site, but some must be viewed as having occurred due to larger forces in the world outside the school.

One of the most important factors driving the school's improvement was *necessity*. In the spring of 2007, it failed its Quality Review and was placed on the SURR list. Those events were strong motivators for change; to ignore the situation would have inevitably led to the school's closure.

On the other hand, without the collection of capable and dynamic leaders at CIS 339, it would have been impossible for the school to improve so dramatically. *Leadership*, then, was also a key determinant of CIS 339's transformation: Not only the leadership of Levy but also Wagner, Prinstein, and all the teachers who stepped up and assumed more responsibilities and agreed to perform roles different from those of a traditional classroom teacher. Leadership at CIS 339 was active, focused, and purposeful; it was also distributed among the faculty. It was not merely a case of one heroic leader, but rather the success of a large group of people demonstrating the effectiveness of concerted cooperation.

A third key factor was the *efficacy* of the strategies and technologies used to implement the school's new agenda. In other words, the plans were capable of producing the desired results. Using Google Apps to promote communication, collaboration, and creativity was about selecting the right tool for the job. If your car has a flat tire, but you decide to fix the heater, the tool makes no difference because it doesn't address the problem. By focusing on communication, collaboration, and creativity, the people at CIS 339 addressed the real problems and were smart enough to select the best tools for the job.

A fourth key factor was appropriate recognition of *expertise* in achieving the desired results. Levy had a vision for what he wanted to accomplish but knew he would need to rely on the various knowledge and experiences of others to implement that vision.

He saw Patrick Wagner as a catalyst for change in the way CIS 339 used technology, so Levy figured a way to harness Wagner's expertise and put it to work for the school. Wagner was a model for the effective use of the technology and also a valuable resource for the staff when Google Apps were implemented. Wagner says, "The way Levy put me in the [consultant's] role, not only was I there to discuss ideas and be a sounding board, I was also there to monitor, too. Not monitor in a bad way, like Big Brother. I actually interviewed and made videos of the staff right from the start. I said to them, 'This is just about concerns you have at the moment. This is so we can address your concerns, not to bulldoze you.'"

When Wagner returned to Australia after two years in New York, the two created a way for him to remain as a full-time consultant for CIS 339 and to be present virtually. Wagner spent hundreds of hours videoconferencing via Skype conversations, chats, and virtual meetings using shared Docs, supplemented with a few in-person visits to the school. By interacting with teachers remotely, and using the technology in ways that were personally relevant to the faculty (their own learning) they were better able to see how easy it was to use and how they could apply it with their students. There was also an important "coolness" factor. During his time of intense involvement with CIS 339 (2006–2008), engaging in the skillful use of the type of distance learning that he promoted was a rare occurrence in an NYC school. Many in the CIS 339 community (students, faculty, and parents) could sense they were on the leading edge of something very exciting.

David Prinstein's role change was a similar story. Moving him from Literacy Coach to Dean of Instruction utilized his particular skills and knowledge and moved him from the periphery to the center of the school network. Recognizing, and building upon, Prinstein's expertise in curriculum and instruction strengthened CIS 339 in important ways.

Both symbolic and practical results occurred because of the Prinstein move. Symbolically, creating a Dean of Instruction sent a powerful message. In NYC, a Dean's position usually focuses on student discipline. To create a Dean of Insruction in a school that had both student academic and behavior challenges told everyone that in this school, learning was very important. Further, including Prinstein in the principal's inner circle, or cabinet, even though he did not have administrator's position, gave the faculty a sense that Levy valued their input and expertise. Rather than feeling that their educational role was marginalized in favor of an emphasis on discipline, teachers came to see learning as the number one priority of the school.

From a practical standpoint, Prinstein could operate as the inside expert on technology and learning while Wagner served as the outside expert. Everyone knew that Wagner's role would eventually diminish or fade away. This was not the case with Prinstein, who would remain present to remind everyone everyday about the importance of teaching and learning in this school.

And finally, Prinstein was a skillful practitioner of educational technology in his own right. He was constantly present to ask the right questions, provide encouragement, model best practice, and provide exemplary collegial leadership. To use a baseball analogy, in many ways he was like the captain of a team—the first among equals. Wagner was like the hitting coach who is brought in during spring training, and made available when players (teachers) needed a bit of private, extra help.

The expertise of faculty was recognized and utilized in other meaningful ways by empowering the staff through quality professional development, coaching, and support. The emphasis was always on contributing to the collective expertise in the building. This emphasis on *support* represents the fifth key factor. As Prinstein says, "We had paid professional development every Monday afternoon. Every day we had team meetings where development happened. We had regular surveys to ask people what they needed. We had in-class support and technical help. We were trying to get ahead of any problems that we could anticipate."

AN ARTICLE on CIS 339 appeared in the October 2008 issue of the *Village Voice*. To view the article, visit www.villagevoice.com/2008-10-22/news/learning-2-0-brings-schools-into-the-digital-age. *(Please be advised that the* Voice—*though not this particular article—contains material that may be offensive to some readers.)*

Professional development changed from the typical drive-by variety, in which teachers endure one-shot workshops planned for them by administration. It became much more focused on what the teachers indicated they needed, when they needed it. Specialists were made available to work with teachers at times that were convenient for them. The educational technology innovations were not treated as thing added on to an already overcrowded agenda, the innovations *were* the agenda. The business of the school—teaching, learning, communicating, creating—was to be accomplished through the use of technology. In Levy's words, it became like oxygen and was everywhere. Teachers were not evaluated separately on whether they incorporated technology into their lessons, it was just assumed that everyone would use technology for everything they did; from taking attendance, to conducting meetings, to writing lesson plans, and to teaching and learning in the classroom.

On why the development of expertise through Google Apps is essential, Levy adds, "You're able to focus on what's important quicker, you're able to spread best practices much more readily. The level of satisfaction and engagement, and the type of motivation that comes from knowing your work can be known, knowing that you have partners helping with your work, knowing that you can challenge yourself to be innovative—that creates a different type of school, different type of classroom, and a different type of student."

Further forms of support were also present to develop expertise. Collaborative classroom visits by the instructional leaders of CIS 339 were enhanced by use of the online form, and enabled a rich coaching to occur continuously. The team structure, along with the use of Google Apps, fostered collegiality among staff. The spirit of collaboration was infectious—it created a sense of community for both teachers and students. CIS 339 even formed a student tech squad to support teachers in need of technical support at a moment's notice.

Levy praises the excellent support provided to CIS 339 by Lisa Nielsen, Professional Development Manager from the Office of Instructional Technology at the NYC Department of Education. As the school's designated liaison for the iTeachiLearn grant, Nielsen has been instrumental almost from the beginning in providing resources, on-site and off-site professional development, encouragement, motivation, and ideas.

Of course, the reliability of Google Applications cannot be underestimated as a source of support. On-again, off-again school technology was a thing of the past. Everyone in CIS 339 knew that if they wanted to use technology, it would be there for them. This *reliability* served as an all-important sixth success factor.

Finally, an implementation strategy that focused on awareness of *critical mass* served as the seventh factor. The term is derived from the study of nuclear reactions. Critical mass is the smallest amount of fissionable material needed for a self-sustained nuclear chain reaction. Applied to CIS 339, the notion is that both the number of people using an innovation, and the sustained frequency with which they use it, will significantly affect the effectiveness of consistent, successful implementation. If only some people use an innovation only some of the time, its effects are not likely to be particularly widespread or viewed as an important priority in the school culture. On the other hand, if many people use an innovation most of the time, and if it's a good idea, its effects are much more likely to be widespread and important. The trick is to get the innovation up to critical mass so that both the number of people and frequency of their use cause the innovation to become as self-sustaining as possible.

Wagner referred to this when quoted earlier about the wisdom of Levy's providing laptops to every staff member. Other strategies to achieve critical mass included involving all staff in professional development, requiring all staff to read and sign off on the daily notices in the school's wiki every day, using Docs to conduct the work of all teams, requiring staff to use Gmail, moving main school discipline systems to Google Docs, and implementing online class visitation forms. Sooner or later, every teacher discovered for herself some way in which the technology made her life easier and better. After that, the gradual movement toward incorporation of the Google Apps and other technological innovations would follow more or less naturally. Looking back, we can see that CIS 339's implementation of Google Apps positively influenced every aspect of teaching and learning at the school. As long as Google Apps worked reliably, they could be counted on to make a real difference—and they did. Google Apps were successfully woven into the essential everyday fabric of CIS 339, and that's how they helped transform the school.

WHAT DOES THIS ALL MEAN?

For Other Schools

Expanding this snapshot of one year at CIS 339 into a global portrait of many schools over many years calls for some deep reading of the tea leaves. Yet, some tentative forecasting may be possible. Besides, making predictions is fun.

Based on what we've seen at CIS 339, there is little doubt that many more schools will start to use Google Apps. In fact, Google announced in May 2010 that 8 million students in the U.S. were now served by Google Apps, up from 7 million only 60 days earlier. As pioneers like CIS 339 jump into the deep end of the pool, more cautious educators will be encouraged to at least stick their toes in the water. Perhaps encouraged by CIS 339, in spring 2008 the NYC Department of Education launched an initiative to encourage use of Google Apps by what it terms its Empowerment Schools. There are more than 500 of these schools in the city. Once New York schools get behind an idea, many schools across the country follow. Interested readers may follow developments regarding this emerging program at www.nycempowerment.org/handsontrainingdays/.

Google is publicizing use of Apps in schools with greater energy and reach, both online and in face-to-face settings—in the fall of 2008, Google sponsored a national bus tour of college campuses to promote use of its Apps, which signals a shift in marketing for a company that has tended to primarily focus on the business applications of its products.

Google continues to invest in the development of its Apps. The company seems to unveil a new feature or a major new tool every few weeks. We will likely witness an active changing lineup of apps and features as well as improved interoperability among apps. It is logical to assume that the ability of the apps to interact and support one another eventually will yield even greater variety and usefulness. They will likely morph into a more seamless, multipurpose, user-friendly, and highly capable suite of tools.

And Google represents only one company on the web. As the notion of Web 2.0 prolongs its explosive growth, new applications appear daily from multitudes of sources. The idea of cloud computing, with applications hosted on the Internet rather than residing on one's local hard drive, continues to grow as well. These trends suggest that the tremendous expansion of online applications that enable increasingly intelligent ways of communicating, as well as accessing and manipulating data and media, will continue for some time.

As indicated by the experience of CIS 339, these trends also suggest that teaching and learning conducted in schools may become more tightly coupled and focused ... that learning experiences for students may become more individually tailored and personally meaningful. At the same time, the confines of classroom walls and school schedules may become increasingly less of a consideration. More teaching and learning will certainly occur outside of school walls and schedules than occurs now. When considered in light of the predicted exponential growth of online classes, where most or all teaching/instruction is delivered online, a picture begins to emerge of a potential transformation of the entire school experience for most students over the age of 12 or 13. It is likely that at least secondary level students in the future will experience school as a much more customized, personal experience, and one that takes place with a decreasing amount of time spent within the schoolhouse walls.

The lock-step processing of students in batches, like so many cookies on a baking sheet, with periodic testing to weed out those who differ from externally imposed norms, may begin to become another relic of the industrial age. More students who differ from the norms may begin to learn in ways and to levels of accomplishment that may surprise many. In fact, the idea of the norms themselves may begin to change.

A new educational model may emerge for educating older students as what was formerly the physical schoolhouse becomes a virtual meeting place: to meet with teachers and negotiate learning contracts and engage in two-way exhibitions of learning with feedback ... and to meet with classmates for socialization, athletics, and creative experiences in the fine- and performing arts. By spending less time in school as we currently know it, students may actually learn better and learn more. This is one possible scenario strongly suggested by current trends in educational technology.

For This School

Levy is the first to acknowledge that what is written in these pages is but a single chapter in a much larger story. "The amount of rapid improvement that I've seen in a big, unwieldy, urban middle school that came from, in part, adopting some new and simple tech tools ... not simplistic, but simple ... I think the sky's the limit. We have to embrace things we don't yet fully understand. This is the next frontier. Everyone has to get their boots on and wade in.

"But we're just on first base, we haven't fully used the tools that are out there, and there are tons more coming. What's transferable for us is our approach and philosophy.

"The Google tools allow us to do our best work more often. They create a lot of opportunities for great things to happen. We integrate the tools into all aspects of school ... not just one classroom or one grade. That's been rewarding. We have been able to model the tools at an administrative level and also see the same kinds of benefits and excitement from the deans, to the attendance teachers, to the secretaries, to all the classrooms. That's been fulfilling.

"Next year we will focus on the parents. This year it was the leadership team, the teachers, and the kids. Until the adults are comfortable with the tools, they're not going to help the kids be comfortable with the tools. Until the kids are excited about the tools, the parents aren't going to be motivated about the tools. We're ready to move on to the parents now."

Wagner adds: "Next year, we want to get faculty writing articles, presenting at conferences, doing action research. We want to organize an international educational conference at CIS 339, in person and online. We want at least some of the kids to see themselves as world leaders.

"We want to make a total change about the way the kids and teachers in the Bronx are viewed. This year it was, 'Wow, that's really good for a school in the Bronx.' Next year we want it to be, 'That school, wherever it is in the world, is phenomenal.'" Not look at what they've overcome, but look at what they're doing. It might be located geographically in the Bronx, but it should live in cyberspace with people all over the world."

A FINAL WORD

Is there a way to succinctly sum up how Google transformed a school, to encapsulate the experience of over 1,000 people in just a few words? Perhaps the best person to do this is Jason Levy. He says, "You need the skills, the tools, and you also need the approach. Just the tools alone without the approach aren't going to work. And the tools without the skills aren't going to work. And the skills and the approach aren't going to work without the tools. Those three things are totally interconnected."

In Section II of this book we take you through step-by-step instructions on how to set up a Google account and how to benefit from each of the seven most commonly used Google Applications: Documents, Presentations, Spreadsheets, Forms, Blogger, Maps, and Earth. Let's go!

THE MOST
WIDELY USED
GOOGLE APPLICATIONS
IN SCHOOLS

CHAPTER 2
FIRST THINGS FIRST
SET UP A GOOGLE ACCOUNT

Setting up a Google account is easy and free! This chapter walks you through the process.

Go to the Google search page (www.google.com). Select Sign In, located at the top right corner (see Fig. 2.1).

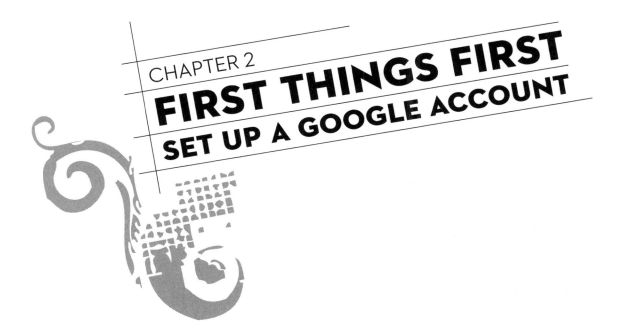

FIGURE 2.1. Google's home page for searching

This Google Accounts screen will open (see Fig. 2.2). Click on Create An Account Now.

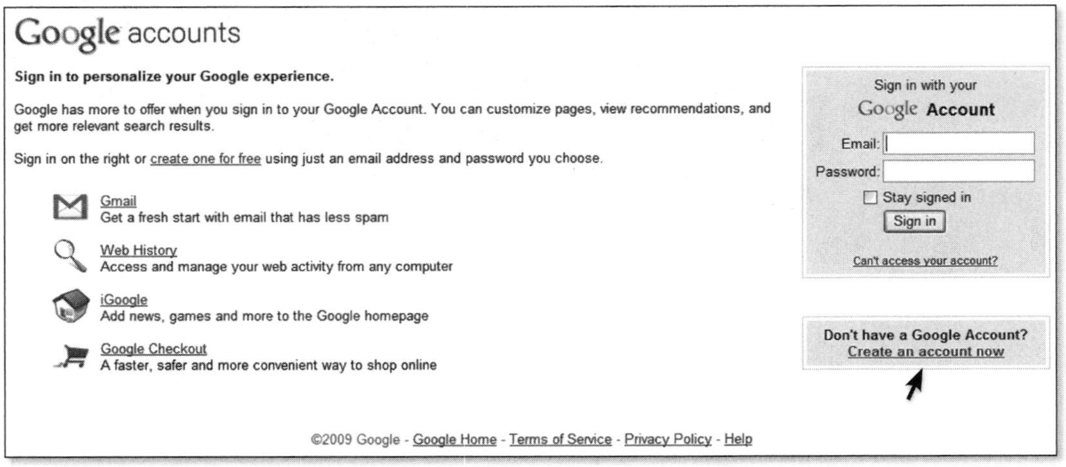

FIGURE 2.2. Sign-in page for Google Accounts. Create An Account Now appears at bottom right.

Fill out the form that appears (see Fig. 2.3). Do not check the box labeled Stay Signed In. It's OK to check the box labeled Enable Web History.

Google will send an e-mail to the address you entered in the top box in this form. Go to your e-mail, open the e-mail from Google, and click on the blue hyperlink. This will confirm that you did, in fact, register for an account, and it will open your account. If you don't see an e-mail from Google, be sure to check your e-mail junk folder.

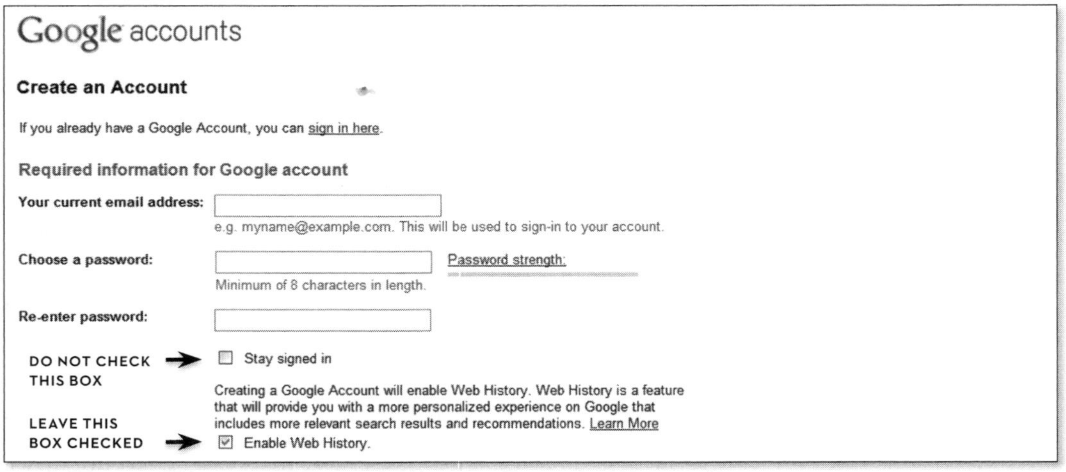

FIGURE 2.3A. The form to create a Google account (part 1)

Default Homepage
☑ Set Google as my default homepage.
Your default homepage in your browser is the first page that appears when you open your browser.

Location: United States

Word Verification: Type the characters you see in the picture below.

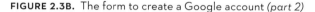

ENTER THESE LETTERS ...

IN THIS BOX

Letters are not case-sensitive

Terms of Service: Please check the Google Account information you've entered above (feel free to change anything you like), and review the Terms of Service below.

Printable Version

Google Terms of Service

Welcome to Google!

1. Your relationship with Google

By clicking on 'I accept' below you are agreeing to the Terms of Service above and the Privacy Policy.

I accept. Create my account.

FIGURE 2.3B. The form to create a Google account *(part 2)*

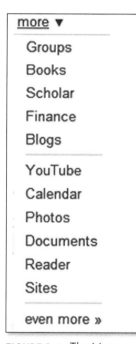

FIGURE 2.4. The More drop-down menu and the Even More command

Google strives to make its products as user-friendly as possible, and accessing Google Applications (Apps) is no exception. Just go to the famous Google search page (www.google.com), and click More at the top of the page. Figure 2.4 shows the drop-down menu that will appear. Select Even More.

The More Google Products window will open (see Fig. 2.5). Click on any icon or its name to use the application.

Google changes its products often. Most of the time, these changes involve improvements to existing applications or roll-outs of entirely new ones. Occasionally, applications that have not met a great deal of public acceptance are dropped from the active roster and become unavailable.

Gpanion (www.gpanion.com) is a nifty and user-friendly third party application that makes it easier to navigate through the numerous Google Apps. This application can be added to your browser's bookmarks toolbar.

Google has also launched Google Dashboard (www.google. com/dashboard/) to provide easy access to all the Google Apps to which you are subscribed. Dashboard also gives you a summary of your activity for each app and direct access to your profile in each app.

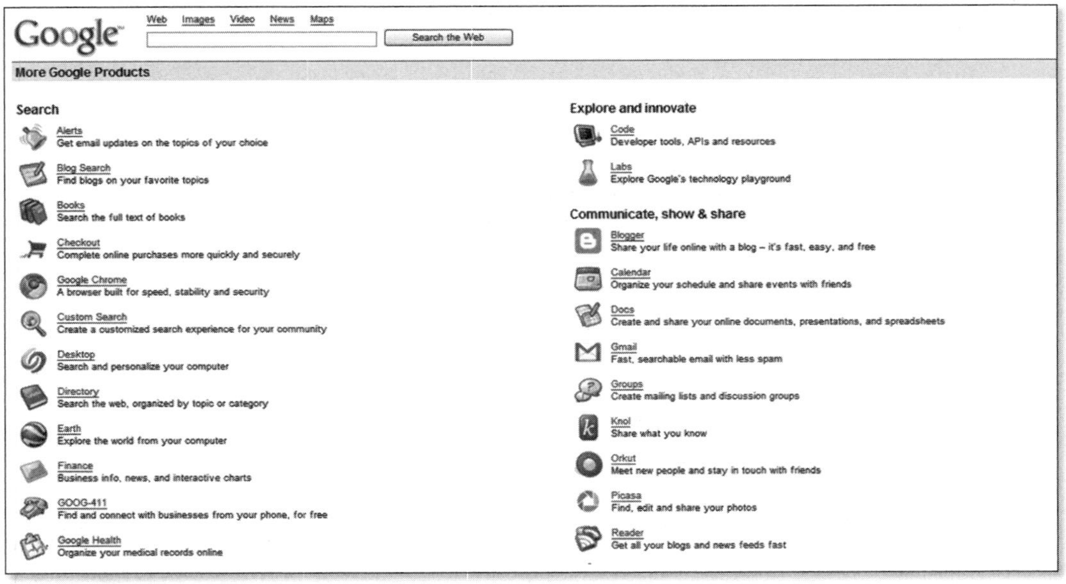

FIGURE 2.5. The Even More window displaying some of Google's more than four dozen applications. The window into Google's world!

One way to keep up with what's happening at Google is to subscribe to its free, monthly Google Friends Newsletter (http://groups-beta.google.com/group/google-friends?pli=1) or visit the company's official blog (http://googleblog.blogspot.com).

CHAPTER 3
DOCUMENTS

CHAPTER AT A GLANCE

- A Brief Word about Google Docs
- Snapshot Description
- How It Works
  - Creating a New Document
  - Working with a Document
  - Comments
  - Sharing
  - Templates
  - Managing the Google Docs Home Page
  - Changing Ownership of a Document
- Teacher Tips

A BRIEF WORD ABOUT GOOGLE DOCS

An explanation of terminology may be helpful for first-time users of Google Docs.

The term *Google Docs* refers to a collection of applications, just as a *Whitman's Sampler* refers to an assortment of various candies, such as caramels, almond nougats, cherry cordials, and toffee chips. In computer terms, Google Docs is composed of a collection of applications much like Microsoft Office is composed of a number of programs, including Word, Excel, and PowerPoint.

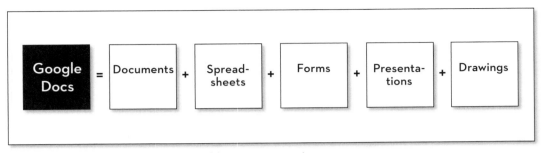

FIGURE 3.1. Google Docs is composed of five separate applications

In the case of Google Docs, the collection consists of five online computer applications: Documents, Spreadsheets, Forms, Presentations, and Drawings.

Documents is roughly equivalent to Microsoft Word, Spreadsheets to Microsoft Excel, and Presentations to Microsoft PowerPoint. In our opinion, Forms does not closely resemble any Microsoft product. Drawings enables users to create graphics and visuals roughly equivalent to what can be done in PowerPoint and Microsoft Paint.

We use the term "roughly equivalent" because Google Apps operate similarly to Microsoft applications, but they do not do exactly the same things. You will make your own discoveries as you become proficient in using Google Docs.

The point here is simply regarding terminology. We hope Figure 3.1 clarifies this.

SNAPSHOT DESCRIPTION

Now we turn to the first application in the Google Docs suite: Documents. Users of Documents can create, store, share, and collaborate on documents. Word processing software is unnecessary; everything is done on the web.

This means up to 50 people can work on the same document simultaneously, or at different times, from any location with Internet access. No one needs a separate copy of the word processing software; it's already there in Documents. Students or teachers can save their work, from single assignments to extensive online portfolios. Users publish their work so that it may be shared privately (with only invited viewers), publicly (visible to all via the web), or not at all (visible only to the author). Students may work together, and teachers may collaborate with students (or other adults), either individually or in groups. Comments, as well as images and charts, may be added to documents.

Documents may be revised, and all versions of a document are saved and dated. Versions may be compared side by side. When collaborators update a document, each individual's work is color-coded for easy identification of who is working on what. Updates occur in real time and may be seen letter-by-letter as they are typed. Documents may also be published to blogs. With a little creative pre-planning, a teacher may even have students submit assignments via Documents so that they arrive in their folder neatly sorted by class and in alphabetical order by student name. All work in Documents is automatically saved on Google's servers every 20 seconds, so no one has to worry about losing work.

Perhaps the best feature of Documents is that it totally eliminates the clutter and confusion of multiple e-mails sent among groups of people making multiple edits to a document. When a pair of people, or a group, works on something in Documents, everyone looks at the same item concurrently, in real time. They may be in the same classroom, separated by just a few feet, or halfway around the world from one another—what enables them to collaborate is their connection through the web.

> **IT WILL BE USEFUL** to review chapters that deal with Google Docs: Chapter 3: Documents; Chapter 4: Presentations; and Chapter 5: Spreadsheets. Some information provided in these chapters applies to these three Google Apps but, for the sake of brevity, is provided only once.

HOW IT WORKS

Creating a New Document

To create a Google document, visit the Google Docs home page (http://docs.google.com), and click on the Create New command tab. There are many choices, but for now, select Document. (We will return to the other choices and this home page later.)

Working with a Document

Once a new document is open, simply begin typing, as in any word processing document. The icons in the formatting toolbar at the top of the page closely resemble those found in Microsoft Word. To read a description of an icon button's function, mouse over an icon and a dialog box will appear. Experiment with these icons and the tools their drop-down menus contain.

The top toolbar (referred to as the Menu Toolbar in Microsoft Word) contains commands with additional drop-down menus. These menus provide much of the functionality of the Documents application. Click on each menu and experiment with its functions.

Some notable commands

FILE

See Revision History: see all previous versions of a document

Rename Document: use the File menu or just click on the name of the document at the top of the page to rename it

Download As: offers a variety of formats in which to save the file, including PDF

INSERT

Image: insert a picture from your computer or online (click on More Image Options to manage image size and alignment)

Drawing: insert line drawings and shapes

Table: create tables

Link: make hotlinks to websites, other documents, bookmarks, or e-mail messages

Comment: insert comments

Footnote: for research papers

Page Break: tell the printer how to paginate documents for proper printing

Table of Contents: automatically create a TOC

TOOLS

Check Spelling

Word Count: find out how many words a document contains

Look Up Word: find definitions, synonyms, encyclopedia entries, and translations for words

HELP

Get Help: from the Google Docs Help Center or from other Google users

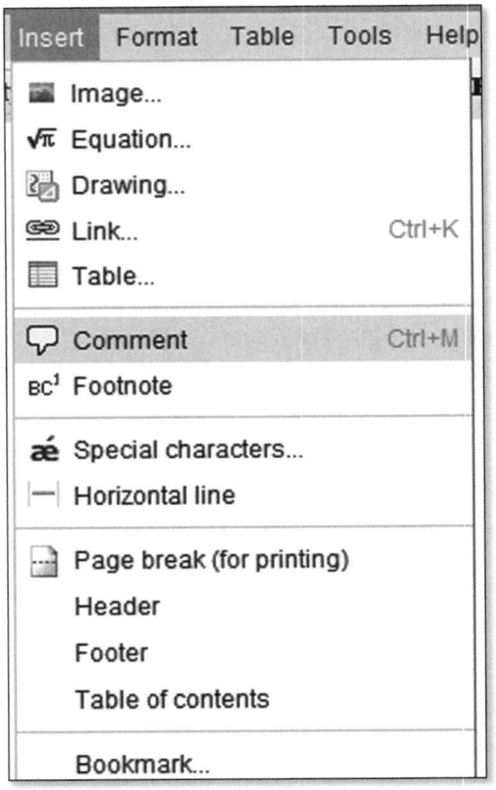

Comments

Let's take a little time to examine the comment function in greater detail, since it is so valuable in an educational setting. Comment is found under the Insert menu when a document is open on the screen. Alternatively, users may employ the key combination Control+M to insert a comment (see Fig. 3.2).

To insert a comment, place your cursor where the comment is to appear. Select Comment from the Insert menu or enter the Control+M key combination. A small dialog box appears that reads "type here" and gives the user's name and the date and time of the entry. Right-clicking (or simply clicking for Mac users) enables the user to select a color for the comment. A comment of any length may then be entered. Comments may appear anywhere in a document, and there is no limit to their number.

FIGURE 3.2. Inserting a comment in Documents

These following suggestions about student editing are offered by Google Certified Teacher Erica Hartman in a Google Presentation posted online (http://docs.google.com/present/view?id=dfkhjt2n_3fm4k5kf5).

> Establish guidelines for peer reviewers early on. Have students skip a few lines or insert a horizontal line and list their feedback at the end of their partner's work. Another way to give feedback without interrupting the flow of student work is to insert a Footnote. Click Insert and then Footnote for noninvasive commenting.

Sharing

An important function in Documents is Share. The Share button is located on the upper right of the page when a document is open (see Fig. 3.3). Share enables the author to invite others to view a document and to give them editing privileges. Simply click Invite People, which opens a window that allows the user to do this, as well as to send an e-mail message to invitees. Using the Advanced Permissions command (at the top right of the Invite People window) also enables the user to designate editors who may then invite additional people to view or edit the document. As many as 50 people may edit a document simultaneously, and the document may be shared with as many as 200 people (although only the first 50 will be able to edit).

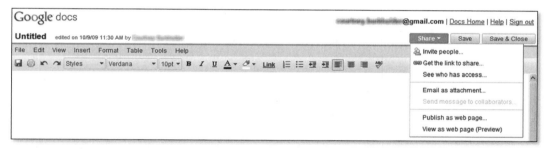

FIGURE 3.3. Share options in Documents

The Get The Link To Share command enables a user to obtain a unique URL for the document so others may be directed to it. The See Who Has Access command opens a list of everyone who has access to the document and the privileges each person has been granted.

Other commands in the Share drop-down menu are also important. They enable a user to e-mail the document as an attachment and publish the document as a web page.

Documents published as web pages receive their own URLs and may be accessed by anyone who knows the web address. This can be a great aid for publishing work. Bear in mind that because of the unique nature of this process, such documents cannot be indexed by search engines. People must know or be told how to find these documents; they cannot be located otherwise. Documents may also be posted to a user's blog using this command.

Templates

Many times educators find themselves performing repetitive tasks that require the same formats. They make lesson plans, meeting agendas, and outlines—they take notes, create resumes, and use fax cover sheets. To avoid recreating these documents from scratch each time they are needed, many educators have created templates that have been uploaded to Google Docs for use by anyone. There are thousands of templates available, in several languages, and more are added daily. Templates can be great time savers.

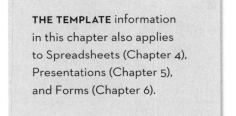

FIGURE 3.4. Search for templates in Google Docs

To search for templates, return to the Google Docs home page (http://docs.google.com). You may enter a search term and click on Search Templates, (see Fig. 3.4) or, to see a wide selection, leave the search box empty and click on Search Templates to be taken to the templates gallery, where templates are organized by type and category. Alternatively, click on Browse Template Gallery. It is also possible to navigate to the templates gallery by using the New command in the File drop-down menu and selecting From Template: File > New > From Template.

> **THE TEMPLATE** information in this chapter also applies to Spreadsheets (Chapter 4), Presentations (Chapter 5), and Forms (Chapter 6).

The templates gallery has tabs for a user to keep track of Templates I've Used and My Templates (those created by the user). The default setting gives access to all templates that are available for public view. It is simple to submit a template to be housed in the gallery: click on Submit A Template and fill out the form.

Erica Hartman reported this creative example of template use in a Google Presentation posted online (http://docs.google.com/present/view?id=dfkhjt2n_3fm4k5kf5):

> A science teacher creates a lab report template for her students to use for every lab they complete in a year. She shares the template with all of her students. After they click on the document to open it, they must choose File and then Save As New Copy to ensure that they do not make changes to the original template. What if they forget to save as a new copy? Simply go to File > Revision History and revert to the original template.

To view an informative video on using templates, go to: www.screencast.com/users/ EricaHartman/folders/Jing/media/a6619411-30dc-4bdf-8b27-f3a7ebbf269a.

Google Certified Teacher Chris Clementi has posted a very helpful handout (in PDF format) on using templates. It can be viewed or downloaded online: http://sites.google.com/site/ onlinetoolssite/google-templates.

Managing the Google Docs Home Page

Once a document has been created or shared, it appears in the master Docs list on the Docs home page. In Figure 3.5, the user has created two documents, "Jim's great American novel" and "Jim's book report on 'The Giver.'" In addition, the spreadsheet "Enriching Learning with Visual Processes" has been shared with the user.

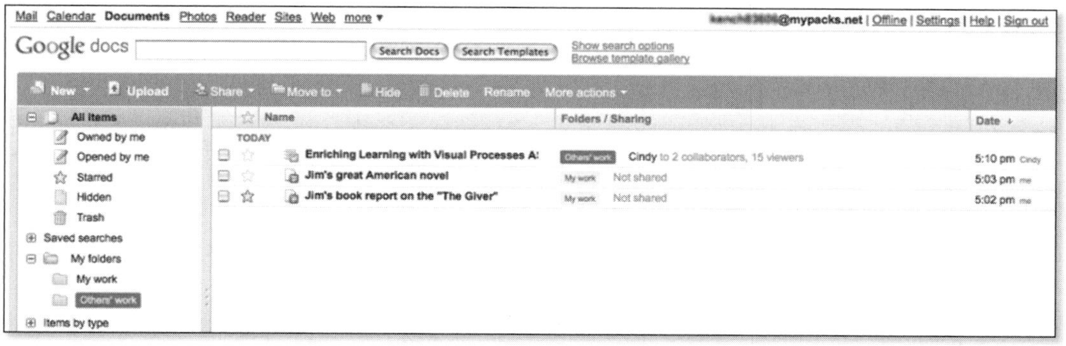

FIGURE 3.5. A Google Docs homepage with 3 documents and 2 folders shown

Figure 3.5 shows that the user has created two folders in the navigation bar on the left of the page, under My Folders. The folders are labeled My Work and Others' Work. It is possible to color code folders; note that the Others' Work folder is colored. This makes it possible to drag and drop each document in the central, main area of a user's page (called the Docs list) into the appropriate folder for easy filing. In the Docs list, one can also see how each document has been filed and with whom it has been shared. Color-coding folders can be an effective way to manage submission of student work.

To create a new folder, go to the Create New button (in the upper-left corner) and select Folder. (Make sure you are on the Google Docs home page when looking for this button.) Folders may contain other folders or only documents.

Documents may be moved into folders by dragging and dropping, or by using the Move To command in the toolbar. To use this function, check the box on the far left of the document name in the central Docs list. Click Move To and designate the desired folder. This is particularly helpful when moving a number of files to the same folder all at once.

Using the Upload command tab (on the upper-left corner of the Docs home page), users may upload files to their Documents account from their own computer or the web. You may upload existing documents, spreadsheets, or PowerPoint presentations. Some size limitations and formatting restrictions apply.

The Share command tab functions similarly to the Share command discussed earlier. First, the user selects as many documents as she wishes using the check boxes to the far left of each document in the Docs list. The user then selects Share > Invite People and enters the e-mail addresses of the invitees, indicating them as either collaborators (by clicking the To Edit button) or viewers (by clicking the To View button). The user may customize the e-mail invitation sent to invitees. If the invitees have Gmail accounts, the user's contact list may be used instead of entering e-mail addresses individually.

It is possible to search the Documents application by entering keywords in the search box or by using other search criteria. Click on Show Search Options to view the criteria. They resemble the search criteria used in Advanced Search in Google's regular online search engine (see Chapter 10). Once a search has been conducted, it can be saved and easily retrieved for future use. Searching becomes very helpful once a list of files starts to grow.

Users may also wish to take advantage of the star feature to identify frequently used documents. Click on the faint outline of the star next to the document you wish to identify in the Docs list. This highlights the star. Then, to view a list of all starred documents, click on Starred in the navigation menu on the left of the page.

The other command tabs—Hide, Delete, Rename, and More Actions—are self-explanatory.

Changing Ownership of a Document

Once a user has shared documents, a time may come when the user no longer wishes to be the owner of a document, or wants to delete it from the Docs list but still wants to allow viewers or collaborators to see it. This poses a problem: If an owner of a document deletes it, the document becomes inaccessible for all users. The solution is to transfer ownership to someone else.

To do this, check the document's name in your Docs list. Click More Actions > Change Owner. Enter the e-mail address of the new document owner. Then click Change Owner. Bear in mind that Google requires the new owner to be in the same domain as the original owner. In layman's terms, this means that the part of the e-mail address after the @sign has to be the same for both owners (e.g., both @gmail.com, or @yahoo.com, etc.). This is another good reason for everyone at school to have a Gmail address!

TEACHER TIPS

■ Make sure your students add you as a collaborator on every document they submit. This ensures you will be able to edit and comment on everything.

■ Just like most teachers have a convention for heading hard-copy papers, you will want to follow a convention for how students name their electronic documents. A tried-and-true method is to have students put down their class period (usually for secondary) or subject (usually for elementary), followed by last name, first name, and name of the assignment.

   ■ An elementary document might be titled:
   Science—Zimmerman, Robert—Photosynthesis Worksheet

   ■ A secondary document might be titled:
   3—Quinones, Sarah—Macbeth Paper

In this manner, when items appear in your inbox they will be sorted by period or subject, and students will be listed in alphabetical order. This will make it easy for you to place student work in the proper folders and to check submissions against your class roster to make sure all work has been submitted properly. To keep your inbox tidy, hide documents after they have been filed.

- Practice procedures with students at the beginning of the term. This will enable you to focus on content rather than method later on, and will enable both you and your students to realize the maximum benefits of the application.

- Promote honesty among students by having them compose their work within Documents. Encourage students to work online with Documents, not offline with a software application on a local computer. In this way, every entry is time-and date-stamped with the identity of the author and all versions are archived.

- Helen Barrett has written a great article titled "How to Create an Electronic Portfolio with Google Docs—Documents" (http://sites.google.com/site/eportfolios/How-To-Create-ePortfolios-with-GoogleApps). She has also written an informative piece on "Marking work in Google Docs" (http://tbarrett.edublogs.org/2008/06/29/marking-work-in-google-docs).

- Google has joined with *Weekly Reader* to publish the comprehensive *Teaching Reading with Google Docs* (www.google.com/educators/weeklyreader.html). It contains extensive materials for students as well as a teacher's guide.

- Google Certified Teacher Mary Fran Lynch wrote about why she loved Docs in her blog (http://sites.google.com/site/techtipstuesday):

  > My favorite characteristic of Docs is its collaborative feature. It has helped Colette and me coordinate our schedule, my third grade team and I work together on the Educational Action Plan while I spent two weeks in Buffalo in September, my grade level team share grades for our rotation students, and my students to put together two presentations while working on it at the same time in the Media Center (thank you, Kelli Glass for putting up with the noise and confusion). And because it is all stored in "the Cloud," I have access to my Docs wherever and whenever I have a device that can access the Internet. This came in super handy when I went to give a presentation with my laptop and forgot to bring along the connector to hook my Mac up to the projector … . I was able to turn on their Dell and access my slides!

- A third-party application, Textify (www.textify.com), has been created to simplify the inclusion of mathematical expressions in Google Documents. This application provides a simple means to write the expressions (in LaTeX format), which are turned into code to drop into Google Docs, e-mail, web pages, and forums. The expressions display as images.

- Google has recently made it possible to upload any type of file to Google Docs (not just files created in Google Apps, as was previously the case). Any file up to 25 MB in size is acceptable. Up to 1 GB of storage is free. Additional storage is available at a cost of 25 cents per GB, per year. This makes it easy for collaborators to share, download, or print any file they are working on together.

CHAPTER 4
PRESENTATIONS

CHAPTER AT A GLANCE

- Snapshot Description
- How It Works
  - Naming
  - Menu Toolbar
  - Customizing Slide Backgrounds
  - Sample Slide Show
  - Revision History
  - Copy and Paste Slides
  - Saving
  - Printing a Slide Show or Saving as a PDF
  - Chat in Presentation View
  - Uploading PowerPoint Presentations
  - Publishing and Embedding a Presentation
- Teacher Tips

SNAPSHOT DESCRIPTION

Presentations enables users to create, upload, save, and print functional equivalents of Microsoft PowerPoint slide shows. This Google App comes with much of the functionality users are familiar with and has the added capabilities of real-time chat and collaborative, simultaneous editing. Existing PowerPoint slide shows from your computer or the web may be uploaded to Presentations. Another neat feature is the ability to perform a live Google search from any point in any slide.

HOW IT WORKS

To use Presentations, go to the Docs home page, click on Create > Presentation. Figure 4.1 shows what the home page looks like when a new presentation is opened for the first time.

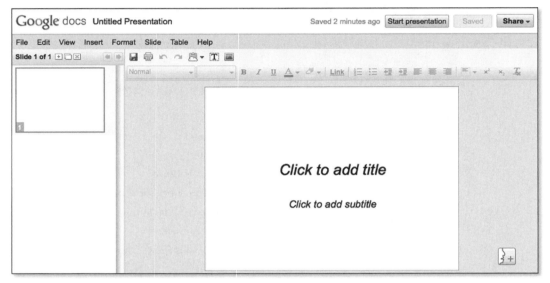

FIGURE 4.1. A new, blank presentation

Notice the light blue Menu toolbar. It has eight menu choices listed from left to right (currently File, Edit, View, Insert, Format, Slide, Table, and Help). Click on each menu to see the commands listed under it. The grey Formatting toolbar is just below the Menu toolbar. There are two main windows on the Presentations page: the slide sorter window on the left and the current slide window on the right. In the bottom right corner, notice the rectangular icon with a head silhouette and a plus sign. This icon opens a panel on the page for speaker's notes.

Naming

Once a new presentation is created, it should be immediately named and saved. This will cause it to show up in the Docs list and will also enable the autosave feature so presentations in progress will not be lost. Once autosave is activated, the presentation is saved approximately every 20 seconds.

To name the presentation, click on Untitled Presentation in the upper-left corner. A small dialog box will open with a space to name the presentation. After entering the name, click OK. Then click File > Save. This saves any new work and allows the user to remain on the current page. Clicking Save & Close will save new work and close the slide show. If a user inadvertently clicks this command, the presentation can be re-selected from the Docs list.

Menu Toolbar

View Menu

Speaker Notes may be activated using the View menu.

Slide transition effects are currently unavailable in Presentations, and the application is not equipped to insert audio files. If it's essential to include audio, one could insert a video and hide the image by shrinking or partially covering it.

Insert Menu

The Insert menu enables a user to add text, images, drawings, videos, tables, and shapes into the slide. It also permits importing of slides.

Insert > **Text.** This command opens a centered textbox in the current slide window.

Insert > **Image.** This command enables placement of images into the slide from a computer or the web. It is also possible to drag and drop images from an open web page directly into an open slide. Presentations allows only proportional resizing of images by selecting the image and dragging the corners. If cropping is necessary, it must be done before inserting the image into the slide show. No image enhancement tools are provided; most manipulations of images must be done offline.

Insert > **Shape.** This command opens a menu of shapes that may be inserted in the slide. Once a shape has been inserted into the slide, it can be manipulated by selecting the shape and right-clicking. A menu will open that enables vertical and horizontal flipping of the shape, as well as layering. Notice that when a shape is inserted into the slide, the slide toolbar changes to allow filling of the shapes and varying the thickness of their outlines.

Insert > **Video.** This command enables insertion of YouTube videos. At the time of this writing, YouTube is the only source available for compatible videos. If a user wishes to include a video, it must first be uploaded to YouTube, at least for now.

Format menu

Themes for the slide show may be changed by using the Format menu. This is also the menu to use for changing the background of an individual slide or the entire slide show (see the following section). It is possible to customize slide backgrounds with images or background colors. This will override the theme selection. Be sure to try all the commands in the Format menu to see what functions each can perform.

Slide Menu

To begin working on the first slide, click Slide > New Slide. A window will open, displaying the slide layouts available for selection. One is not restricted to these layouts; they are merely starting points. As in Microsoft PowerPoint, elements in a slide may be moved freely, and the appearance of any slide may be customized.

In the Slide menu, clicking on Duplicate Slide will create a copy of the slide displayed in the current slide window. The duplicate will appear in the slide sorter window and may be dragged and dropped to place it in the proper sequence. Delete Slide does just what it says.

Customizing Slide Backgrounds

Make sure the slide to be changed is displayed in the current slide window. Right-click (Ctrl+click on a Mac) anywhere on the slide and a small window will open. Select Change Background (see Fig. 4.2), and a new dialog box will open.

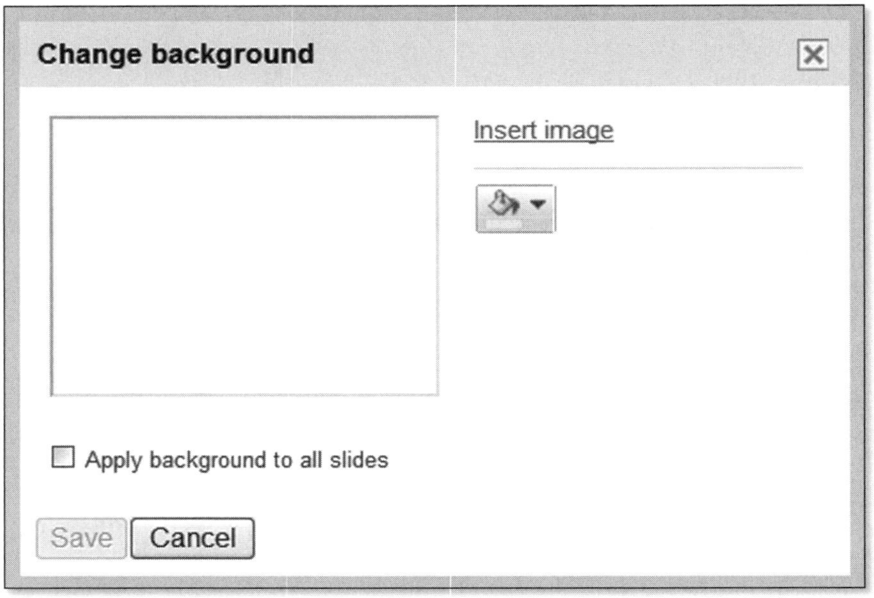

FIGURE 4.2. The Change Background work window

Insert an image from a local computer by clicking Insert Image then browsing to the file's location. The image must be on the computer; if it is not, it must be downloaded first. Modification of a background image is impossible; if changes are needed, they must be made before insertion. When the image has successfully uploaded to the slide, it will appear as a thumbnail in the Change rectangle on the upper left of the dialog box. You may also create a color background by selecting the paint bucket icon in the dialog box. By checking the box Apply Background To All Slides the background image or selected color becomes a template for all slides in the presentation.

Sample Slide Show

Figure 4.3 shows a sample slide show consisting of three slides. No templates were used; the background for slide 1 is just a color. For slides 2 and 3, the backgrounds are images downloaded from Flickr that have attribution licenses from Creative Commons. (Owners have granted permission to use the images as long as attribution is given.) The image used in slide 2 is from www.flickr.com/photos/16961193@N06/2267862256/, and the image in slide 3 is from www.flickr.com/photos/brendaannerl/2352248802/sizes/m/.

FIGURE 4.3. Sample presentation with three slides. The Speaker Notes window is open.

Please note a few things about Figure 4.3. There are three slides in the show. The second slide is highlighted in the slide sorter window on the left, and it is also displayed in the current slide window. To change the sequence of the slides, one would simply click on a slide and drag it to the desired location in the slide sorter window.

View > Show Speaker Notes was selected, so the Speaker Notes window is open. A fictitious sentence about enjoyment of graphic organizers was inserted. Notes placed in this window will be visible to all collaborators and viewers. To control the font size of Speaker Notes, type everything in the default size. Then, highlight the text and change the size using the commands on the Formatting toolbar.

To view the presentation as a regular slide show (nearly full-screen) click on the Start Presentation button indicated by the arrow at the top right of the page in Figure 4.3. To revert to the editing page, during or at the end of the slide show, close the slide show.

To insert a live link to a website, highlight the text in the slide to which the link should apply. Click the blue Link command in the Formatting toolbar and the Edit Link dialog box will open. Enter the URL of the website. The dialog box also offers the option of testing the link before it is inserted.

Revision History

To open the complete revision history of a slide in the current window, click on File > See Revision History. A new page will open to display every revision made to the slide, including the time, date, and name of every reviser.

Copy and Paste Slides

It is possible to move a single slide, as described previously, or a series of sequential slides, or a scattered number of slides all at one time. This is done in the slide sorter window. To move a sequence of slides, click and hold the Shift key while selecting each slide. Right-click (Ctrl+click on a Mac) and select Copy Slide. Move the cursor to the desired location in the slide sorter window, right-click again, and select Paste Slide. To move a scattered number of slides, click and hold the Ctrl key (Command key on a Mac) instead of the Shift key while selecting each slide and repeat the rest of the procedure.

Saving

It is possible to save slide shows to a local computer as PDF, PowerPoint, or text files. Select File > Download As and choose the desired option.

Printing a Slide Show or Saving as a PDF

To print a slide show, select File > Print, or press Ctrl+P (Command+P on a Mac). The Print Preview dialog box will open, displaying the first slide in the presentation. You can customize the print job in a number of ways (see Fig. 4.4). It is possible to select how many slides to print on a page (from 1 to 12 slides), whether to print the slide with or without the background, and whether to include the Speaker Notes on the printed page.

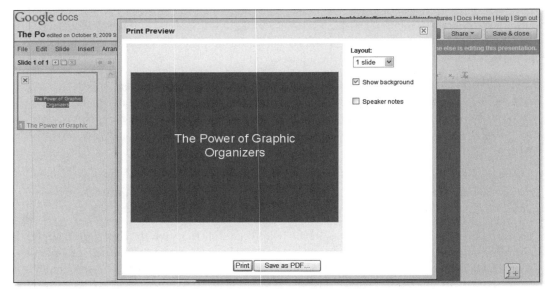

FIGURE 4.4. The Print work window

To save the slide show as a PDF, rather than print, click the Save As PDF button at the bottom of the dialog box.

It is also possible to print, or save as a PDF file, a slide show from the full presentation view. The commands are located on the toolbar at the bottom of the page. Select Actions > Print Slides or Actions > Save as PDF as appropriate. The same dialog box opens as shown in Figure 4.4.

Chat in Presentation View

Chat is a powerful feature of Presentations. It allows viewers to comment on a slide presentation while it is being given. Questions can be posted, links to relevant websites can be added, videos and images can be incorporated, and conversations can be conducted.

As many as 50 people may edit a presentation simultaneously, and it may be shared with as many as 200 people at the same time (including collaborators).

To participate in Chat with collaborators, a user must be in Presentation view. To open the slide show in Presentation view, click the Start Presentation button in the top right corner of the page. A new window will open. A list of all collaborators will appear under the word *Audience* in the Chat window. Enter text directly in the rectangle at the bottom of the Chat window (with the smiley face). The Print command from this view is to the left of the box where one enters chat text (in white letters).

In the center of the border between the Chat window and the slide show itself, there is a very small right-pointing triangle. Clicking this triangle will close the Chat window so that only the slide show is visible.

Uploading PowerPoint Presentations

It is quite easy to upload preexisting PowerPoint presentations from a local computer or the web. Go to the Docs home page and click on the Upload button in the top left area of the page. Presentations will accept both .ppt and .pps files as large as 10 MB from a local computer and 2 MB from the web. Individual slides may also be uploaded. Once uploaded, the items appear in the Docs list and may be edited.

Don't be one of the brokenhearted people who can't figure out why her pictures didn't upload with their PowerPoint file! Don't copy and paste images into PowerPoint because the images don't transfer. Images must be dragged onto the slides; then they'll "stick."

Publishing and Embedding a Presentation

Publishing a Presentation has numerous advantages. Obviously, it makes it easy for anyone to view the Presentation online. Also, the published version of the Presentation cannot be edited, so students will not be tempted nor will their attention wander as much. Every student can be directed to access the Presentation at the same time, and a teacher can control the timing of the slides, creating the possibility of a synchronized slide presentation on each student's individual computer. No need to darken the room to be able to see a projected image!

A Google presentation can be embedded in any blog or website that accepts HTML code (this includes Google Blogger and Google Sites, as well as many others). This can be a great way for students to embellish group reports or to provide updates or background to developing events on a blog.

Whether publishing or embedding, the first step is to publish the presentation to the web. To do so, click the Share button near the top right corner of the window. Then select Publish/Embed from the drop-down menu. A new window will open. Click Publish Document and the presentation will be published. The Publish This Presentation window will open. If the user only wants to publish the presentation, he can exit. The unique URL for the presentation appears near the top of this window (see Fig. 4.5). The Stop Publishing command will remove your presentation from the web.

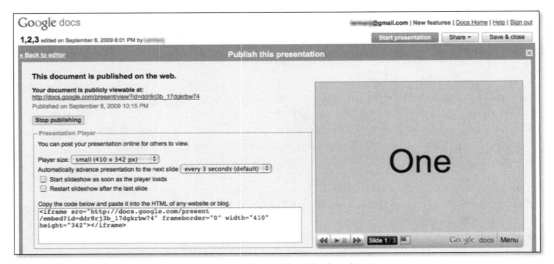

FIGURE 4.5. The Publish This Presentation window, with embed code

To embed the presentation in a website or blog, set the Presentation Player options then copy and paste the HTML code into the desired web location. The Player size option controls the display size of the presentation. Small and medium sizes are good for blogs or embedding in websites, and large is good for larger group displays, projecting, or extensive reading. The HTML code for embedding the presentation in any website or blog is displayed in the text box on the lower-left corner of the window.

TEACHER TIPS

- Google's help for Presentations is located at http://documents.google.com/support/presentations/.

- For pointers on how to make great presentations, see David Jakes's presentation at the 2008 NECC conference (with related material), "One Hour PowerPoint: 10 Strategies for Improving Presentations" (http://jakes.editme.com/onehourppt/).

- Another terrific resource for improving presentations is Garr Reynolds' blog titled "Presentation Zen" (www.presentationzen.com/presentationzen). Reynolds has also written an excellent book with the same title.

- When using the Chat feature in Presentations, it is possible to show actual videos and images in the chat, not just their URLs. Videos must be from Google Video or YouTube. Images must be from Picasa or Flickr (for Flickr use the Grab The Link URL).

- In an e-mail message, Google Certified Teacher John Sowash shared this creative idea for using Presentations:

  > This year I am going to publish my PowerPoint slides as Google Presentations and have my students review them as homework before class. They will be asked to write down 2–3 questions prompted from the slides. Then, instead of lecturing during class, I'm going to answer the questions.

- Google Certified Teacher Erica Hartman offers another great idea for Presentations in a Google Presentation posted online at: https://sites.google.com/site/cuegli/events/2009-06-19/docs/:

  > When students are using the side chat in Google Presentations, assign students roles to keep them interested and on task. The "Word Wizard" looks up words that students are not familiar with. The "Moderator" picks essential questions from the side chat to ask the presenter. The "Link Looker" shares links to topics mentioned in the presentation.

CHAPTER 5
SPREADSHEETS

CHAPTER AT A GLANCE

- Snapshot Description
- How It Works
  - Naming
  - Modifying Row Height and Column Width
  - Other Formatting
  - Sorting
  - Formulas
  - Auto-Filling and Copying
  - Managing Rows and Columns
  - Managing Cells
  - Gadgets
  - Search
  - Images
  - Motion Charts
  - Chat
  - Collaboration
  - Importing and Exporting
  - Publishing and Embedding
  - Making a Form from a Spreadsheet
- Teacher Tips

SNAPSHOT DESCRIPTION

If you have spent any time working with spreadsheets, chances are you have come to appreciate how very powerful they are. Google Spreadsheets offers an incredible range of functionality, often surpassing Microsoft Excel's capabilities. At the present time, Spreadsheets is definitely the most robust among the Google Docs suite of Documents, Presentations, and Spreadsheets. Spreadsheets is not a lightweight application, but a compelling and potent tool.

Spreadsheets performs all of the basic spreadsheet operations easily: adding, deleting, and moving rows and columns; inserting color, pictures, and charts; creating and using formulas; sorting and formatting; auto-filling and copying; and adding comments.

While there are some things that Spreadsheets doesn't (yet) do as well as Excel, here are some dazzling options Spreadsheets offers that Excel doesn't:

- Engage in real-time editing of spreadsheets online with multiple collaborators simultaneously

- Chat with collaborators while working on a spreadsheet, in the same window

- Create animated Motion Charts, capable of depicting up to six variables at the same time

- Create surveys and questionnaires online that feed live data from respondents directly into spreadsheets (see Chapter 6, Forms)

- Add dozens of Gadgets that create unique functions, such as the ability to display data as gauges, easily create organization charts, or translate written information from English into several languages

- Quickly and easily publish your spreadsheet to the web, with a unique URL

- Search Google from any cell in a spreadsheet

It will be useful for readers to look at the four chapters that deal with Google Docs: Documents, Presentations, Spreadsheets, and Forms (Chapters 3–6). Some information provided in these chapters applies to all four applications, but for the sake of brevity, has been given only once.

HOW IT WORKS

To use Spreadsheets, open Docs. From the home page, click on Create New > Spreadsheet. Navigation of Google Spreadsheets will be quite familiar to Excel users. Many functions and operations are similar. To enter data in an empty cell, click on it and begin typing. To edit a cell after leaving it, double click the cell (or press Ctrl+Enter).

Figure 5.1 shows a simple spreadsheet and chart (graph), listing 11 students in Class 204 and data collected from them.

Naming

New spreadsheets should be named immediately. An easy way to do this is to click on Unsaved Spreadsheet in the upper-left corner. A dialog box will open asking for the name of the new spreadsheet. Name the file and click OK.

The file name will appear on the spreadsheet, and from this point forward the spreadsheet will save automatically (approximately every 20 seconds, and each time a change is made). The file name will also appear in the Docs list on the Google Docs home page. No more saving will be needed.

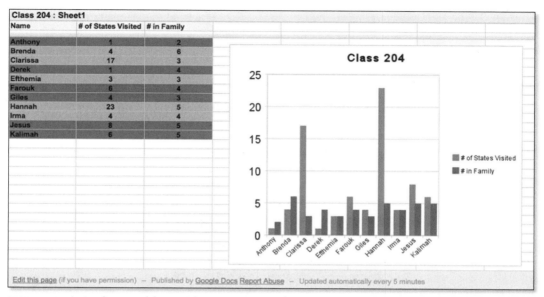

FIGURE 5.1. A simple spreadsheet with accompanying chart

To change the name of a spreadsheet, click on its file name and a dialog box will appear again, allowing the file to be renamed.

Modifying Row Height and Column Width

To modify the row height or the column width, work with the row number cells on the left or the column letter cells at the top of the spreadsheet (multiple rows or columns can be selected and modified at the same time). To modify the height of a row, place your cursor over the bottom border of the cell containing the number of the row you wish to modify (far left of spreadsheet); the cursor will change into a horizontal line with an upward-pointing arrow. Drag the border down to create the desired row height. Drag the border up, and the row will become smaller until it is hidden.

To modify the width of a column, place your cursor over the right border of the cell containing the letter of the column you wish to modify (top of the spreadsheet); the cursor will turn into a vertical line with a right-pointing arrow. To make the column wider, drag the line to the right. To make it narrower, drag it to the left.

Other Formatting

There are numerous types of formatting that can be applied to cells, rows, columns, or selected areas of the spreadsheet. Mouse over the icons in the Formatting toolbar, and the name of the function will be displayed.

To format numbers, use the 123 icon's drop-down menu. Formatting of rows and columns works exactly like formatting in Microsoft Excel. Click on the row number cell or the column letter cell to apply formatting to all the cells in a row or column. To apply formatting to multiple rows or columns, hold down the Shift key while selecting the row numbers or column letters.

Horizontal and vertical alignment of data within cells is managed using the Align icon's drop-down menu. To freeze rows or columns, click on the Tools menu and make the appropriate selection.

Sorting

Sorting may be accomplished in two basic ways: by using the Tools > Sort command or by using the Sortbar (the default location of the Sortbar is just below the header row).

To use the Tools > Sort command, click on the cell where sorting should begin. Then click on the Tools menu, where Sort options are found. It is possible to sort by descending (A–Z) or ascending (Z–A) order, and to freeze selected rows or columns so they are not included in the sort. To select more than one column, hold down the Shift key.

The Sortbar allows users to sort data in a single column. It's light grey in color and is located between the header row and row 1. To use the Sortbar, mouse over the grey letter cell at the top of the desired column and the Sortbar will turn orange. Click on the small arrow at the right end of the Sortbar to select descending or ascending order.

The Sortbar may be moved up and down so that rows at the top of the spreadsheet will not be affected by the sort. To move the Sortbar, click and drag in the shaded cell at the far left of the bar (in the column of row numbers). At the time of this writing, this action only applies to the top 11 rows of the spreadsheet.

Formulas

One of the great features of spreadsheets is the formula function, which automatically computes values related to other parts of the sheet. For two useful tutorials on how to use formulas in spreadsheets, go to Utah State University's website (http://cil.usu.edu/files/uploads/tutorials/ss/index.cfm?p=formula) or the Microsoft Office website (http://office.microsoft.com/training/training.aspx?AssetID=RC011870911033). Both tutorials specifically address Microsoft Excel, but the same principles apply to Google Spreadsheets.

Auto-Filling and Copying

Auto-fill is a useful function that automatically completes any series or pattern that the program is able to identify.

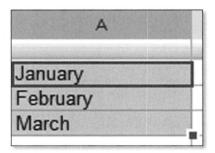

FIGURE 5.2. Preparing to use Auto-fill

In Figure 5.2, three cells show the beginning of a series (months of the year). Type this series into a spreadsheet and click on the January cell. Now, hold down the Shift key and use the Down Arrow key to highlight February and March. Notice the small blue square that appears in the bottom right corner of the last cell. Click and drag this blue square down as many rows as desired to complete the series. The program will complete the series automatically, if it is able to understand it. Auto-fill only works on cells immediately below or to either side of the selected cell(s). You cannot jump over cells and use Auto-fill.

If Auto-fill does not recognize the series you have entered, it will simply copy the last cell in the series. This is actually a good way to copy single cells, if that is desired. To copy a single cell, highlight it and drag the blue square as many cells down or to the side as desired. The data in the selected cell will automatically copy into all the newly selected cells.

To copy an entire spreadsheet, open it then click File > Copy Spreadsheet. A dialog box appears, allowing the user to rename the copied spreadsheet. The copy will appear in the Docs list.

To copy a portion of a spreadsheet, highlight the cells you desire to copy, then click Edit > Copy. Paste into a new sheet within the current spreadsheet, or paste into a new spreadsheet.

To copy one sheet within a multisheet spreadsheet, click on the tab of the desired sheet in the bottom left corner of the spreadsheet. A pop-up menu will appear. Select Duplicate. An exact copy of the sheet will be made, and its name will appear in a new tab next to the one you selected. (Note: for ease of navigating multiple sheets, it is possible to name individual sheets using this same pop-up menu.)

Notice that the position of the sheets can be modified by selecting the Move Right command. When a spreadsheet contains multiple sheets, a Move Left command will also appear.

It's not possible to use an entire, multi-page spreadsheet as a template. However, you can use an individual sheet as a template. To do this, enter the horizontal and vertical headings desired and save the sheet without entering data. Make as many duplicates of this sheet as desired (see previous discussion of duplicates) and enter data.

Managing Rows and Columns

A number of operations may be applied to an entire row or column at once. To apply a desired operation, right-click on the row number or column letter (Ctrl+click on a Mac) and a pop-up menu will appear. Operations include Cut, Copy, Paste, Insert, Delete, Clear, Hide, and Change Format.

Rows and columns may also be inserted or deleted using the Insert menu. Select the desired row number or column letter and click Insert.

Managing Cells

A number of operations may also be applied to a single cell. To apply a desired operation, after entering data in the cell, right-click on it (Ctrl+click, on a Mac) and a pop-up menu will appear with the following options: Cut, Copy, Paste, Insert Comment, Clear Comment, Clear Selection, Change Colors With Rules, Validate Data, Search The Web, Insert Gadget, and Find And Replace. In addition to right-clicking for a pop-up menu, comments can be added by using the Insert menu: click Insert > Comment.

Comments may be inserted into any cell. Comment length is not restricted. Once Insert Comment is selected, the user's name is added along with a time- and date-stamp.

Once a comment has been entered, click anywhere outside the cell and the comment will be hidden. Notice that a cell containing a comment has a small orange-colored shape in the upper-right corner. To view the comment, click the orange shape. To delete the comment, select the cell, right-click (Ctrl+click on a Mac), and choose the Clear Comment command.

Gadgets

In addition to functionality similar to the Microsoft Excel graphs, Google now features a large and growing collection of additional functionalities called Gadgets. Gadgets represent an expansion on the idea of charts (or graphs) and display data in a wide variety of ways.

Examples of current Gadgets include Flash Cards, Gauges, Interactive Time Series Chart, Word Search, Motion Chart, Organization Chart, Timeline, Gannt Chart, Pile Chart (actually a pictograph), and English Translation.

Gadgets may be added to a spreadsheet by right-clicking (Ctrl+click on a Mac) within a cell, or by selecting a cell and using the Insert menu.

Search

Searching the web while using a spreadsheet couldn't be easier. To search from any cell, type a term or phrase, or highlight previously entered words. Right-click (Ctrl+click on a Mac) on the cell, select Search The Web, and search results will appear in a new window. When finished with the search, close the window to return to the spreadsheet.

Images

Images from a web source such as Google Images can easily be inserted into a spreadsheet. However, you cannot use images from your own computer or photo sites such as Picasa or Flickr without some hefty manipulation first—at least for now. Surely, this functionality will come soon.

To insert images, place your cursor anywhere in the spreadsheet. Click on Insert > Image. Make sure you have the URL for the image because you will need to insert it into the Insert Image URL dialog box.

We experimented with an image from Google Images. Once we found an image on the search results page, we clicked on it to open the Web page containing only the image. Then we clicked on See Full-Sized Image near the top of the page, which opened a new page containing only our chosen image. The URL of this page is what should be copied and pasted into the Insert Image URL dialog box in the spreadsheet. Images larger than 500 pixels (length or width) will not be accepted.

After a few seconds, the image will appear several cells below and to the right of your cursor placement. It's easy to drag and drop the image into any position. The image may be resized by placing the cursor on the image's borders or bottom corners. When in the proper position, the cursor turns into a small black bar. Placing the cursor on the borders enables either horizontal or vertical resizing; placing the cursor in the bottom corners enables proportional resizing. To delete the image, click on it, click on the small blue word Image then select Delete Image.

Motion Charts

A Motion Chart is an animated graph of multiple variables. Without a doubt, it serves as a very powerful and compelling tool for understanding. Trying to describe a Motion Chart is like trying to describe ice cream to E.T. Words are inadequate ... but we'll give it a try! A Motion

Chart is an animated graph, meaning that the elements move. It can depict up to six variables simultaneously, using colored shapes that change in size as they move within the axes of the graph. For example, Figure 5.3 shows the price of housing relative to the amount of unemployment in each of the 50 states from 2000 to 2005.

Motion Charts are based on the Trendalyzer software made famous by Hans Rosling. Google purchased Trendalyzer and used it as a basis for Motion Charts. To see examples of Motion Charts in action, go to the Gapminder website (www.gapminder.org). The video that's Mr. Roslings' top ten hit is "The seemingly impossible is possible." You can manipulate a sample Motion Chart at Google's website (http://spreadsheets.google.com/pub?key=pCQbetd-CptE1ZQeQk8LoNw). This same Motion Chart appears in Figure 5.3.

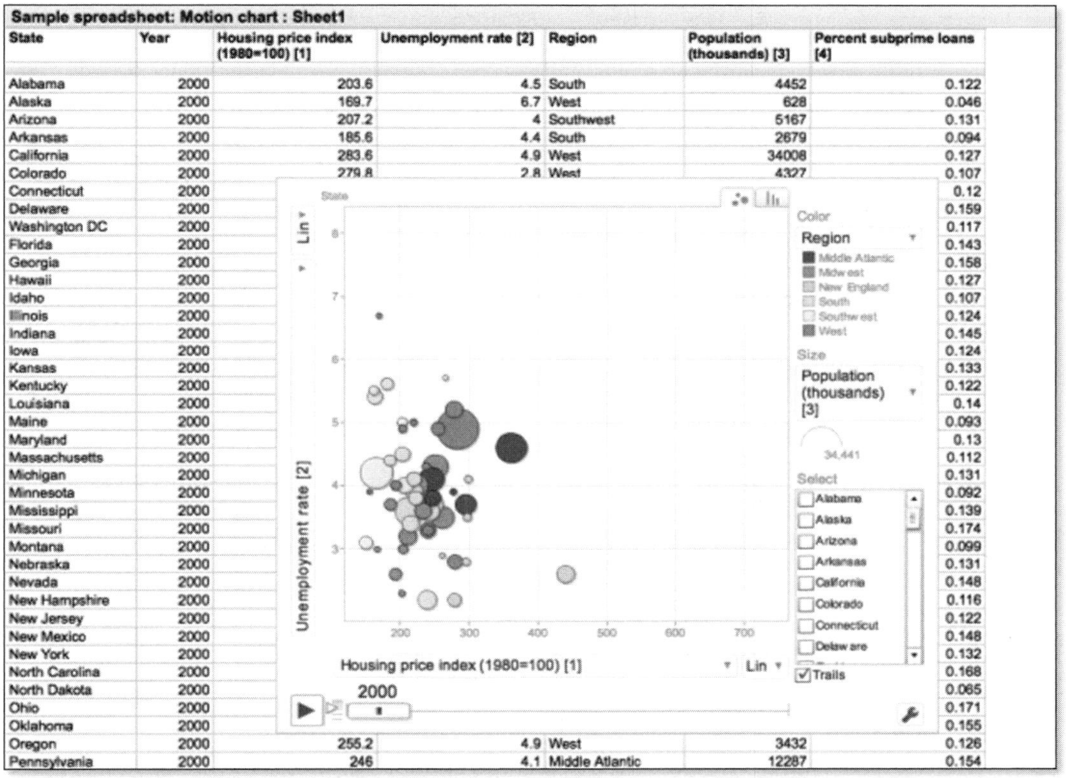

FIGURE 5.3. A sample spreadsheet with Motion Chart displayed

The maximum number of factors for a Motion Chart (number of columns on the spreadsheet = number of factors) is six. One may have as few as three with no problem, but the application can display only a maximum of six factors at one time. Additional factors may be used, but they must be moved into the display function and a factor already in the display function must be removed (see "changing the data display settings" following).

To set up a Motion Chart after data has been entered into the spreadsheet, go to Insert > Gadget. A menu will appear; find Motion Chart and click on Add To Spreadsheet. The following dialog box will appear (see Fig. 5.4).

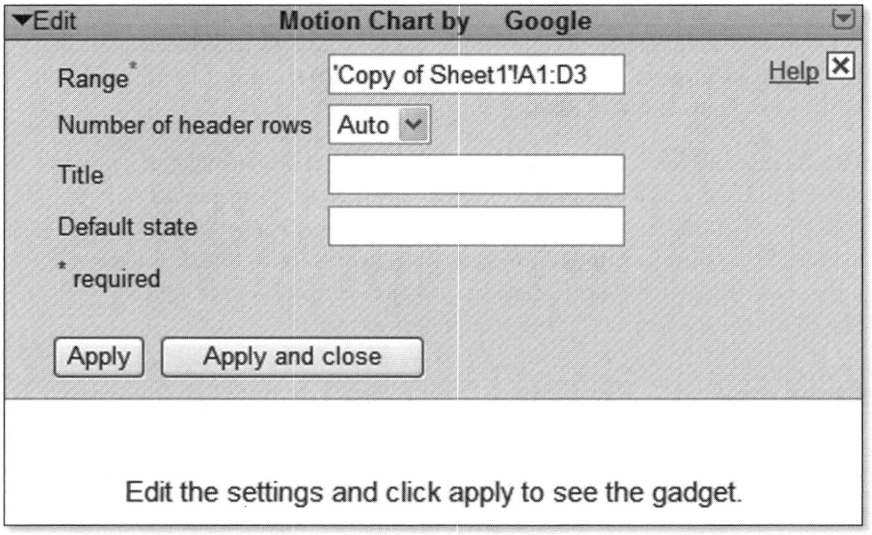

FIGURE 5.4. The initial Motion Chart setup dialog box

It is essential to enter the range of cells you want the Motion Chart to include, in the box marked Range. It is also essential to leave the characters "Sheet1!" in the box. For example, if you want to include data from cells A1 through F26, the Range box should read: "Sheet1!A1:F26". The beginning cell is separated from the ending cell by a colon. There are no spaces between characters. Indicating the range of cells is a required action. You may also give your Motion Chart a title. We advise doing this; it makes it easier to locate the chart later.

You may either Apply the Motion Chart or Apply & Close. Clicking on Apply creates a copy within the dialog box. This is useful if you want to experiment with the chart by altering the settings. Apply & Close will save the chart in its current format and close the dialog box. To edit the chart, it will be necessary to reopen it by clicking on the visible chart and selecting the Edit command in the upper-left corner of the box.

To activate motion on the chart, click the Start button in the lower left (it looks like a Play button). The slider, right of the start button, manually adjusts the time and location of the motion (see Fig. 5.5).

Changing the data display settings on the chart is a powerful feature. As you may have noticed by now, the first column of the spreadsheet names the subject under study. By default, this data will be displayed on the Motion Chart by mousing over the circles. In Figure 5.3, the second column of data, Year, is displayed on the bottom left of the chart by default. This covers two of our six data sets.

In Figure 5.5 you will see there are drop-down menus available to change the x-axis category, y-axis category, color for a category, and size of a category. By clicking on the small arrow next to the menu name, a selection box will open permitting you to select which data category (column of data in the spreadsheet) will be depicted using the particular display feature. For example, in Figure 5.3, "Unemployment rate" is shown on the y-axis, "Housing price index" is shown on the x-axis, "Region" is shown by the color of each circle, and "Population" is shown by the size of each circle. Each of these named categories may be switched to display them

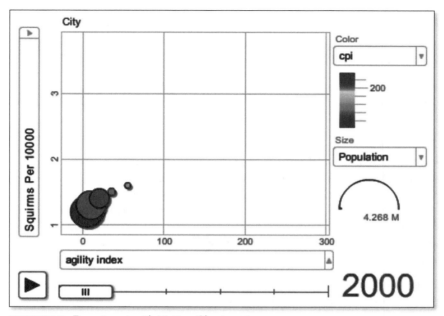

FIGURE 5.5. Experiment with Motion Chart settings

differently. This feature of Motion Charts allows a user to swap categories and create multiple charts using the same spreadsheet if there are more than six data categories.

To delete a Motion Chart, select it, click on the downward-pointing arrow in the upper-right corner, and select Delete Gadget. To publish a Motion Chart to the web, for public viewing, click on the same arrow and select Publish Gadget. To move a Motion Chart within a spreadsheet, click and drag it. To resize a Motion Chart, place the cursor over the vertical borders, the bottom border, or the bottom corners. When it reaches the proper position, the cursor will turn to a bar icon. Moving the vertical borders horizontally will widen the Motion Chart. Moving the bottom border up and down will lengthen or shorten the chart's height. Dragging the corners will resize the chart proportionally

Using Motion Charts is not as complicated as it sounds. Try it a few times; you will get it … and you will be glad. Motion Charts enable viewers to easily identify patterns and trends from mountains of data that seem impossible to analyze because of the sheer volume. Try plotting a dozen zip codes from cities and suburbs versus percent of population under 15, infant mortality, incidence of diabetes, population density, and standardized test scores, and see what your students conclude.

Chat

You may chat with anyone you have named as a collaborator, and chats may be initiated by you or your collaborators. This is a great way to work on a spreadsheet together and talk about it at the same time. Names of people working on a spreadsheet are listed near the top of the screen. An arrow appears next to the names, on the right. Click the arrow to open the chat window. Note that a collaborator must be actively logged into the spreadsheet for his name to appear and thus enable the chat function.

Collaboration

There are two classes of service regarding collaboration: those who may edit, and those who may view. Editors are also sometimes referred to as collaborators.

In order for all users to see the changes in a document or presentation, the page must be refreshed or autosaved. In order to see the changes in a spreadsheet, the data in a cell must be changed, and the cell must be exited by pressing enter, using an Arrow key, or clicking on another cell.

If collaborators are working on a spreadsheet at the same time, the Discuss window will open automatically and the collaborators' names will be displayed. As many as 50 people may collaborate simultaneously. (As many as 200 people can view a spreadsheet simultaneously.) To avoid collaborators working on the same cell at the same time, each time a collaborator begins working in a new cell, it will display in a different color. In other words, if three collaborators are working on a spreadsheet at the same time, each of the three cells they are working in will be highlighted in a different color.

It is not necessary to have a Google account to view a document; this can be accomplished through an invitation. However, to edit a document, a Google account is required. Keep in mind that it is possible to obtain a Google account without having a Gmail address—any e-mail address will suffice. This is important if you do not want to require students to have Gmail addresses.

To invite collaborators or viewers, click on the Share button near the upper-right corner of the spreadsheet. The window depicted in Figure 5.6 will open.

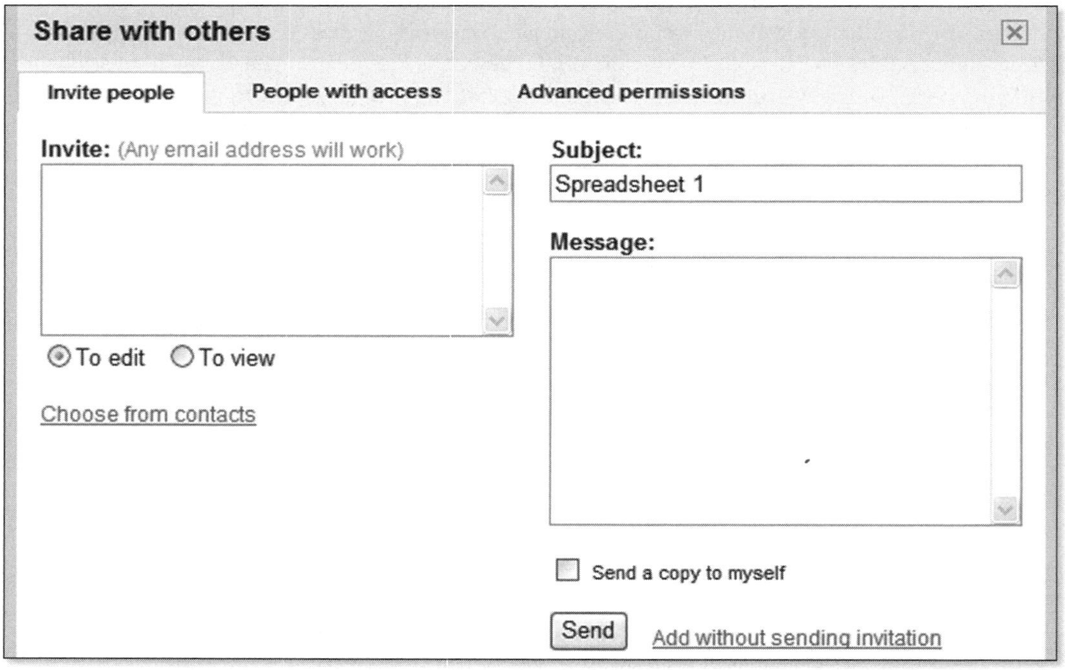

FIGURE 5.6. The Share Invitation window, where users may invite others to become viewers or collaborators

Select the radio button for either collaborators (To Edit) or viewers (To View) and enter the e-mail addresses of the people you want to invite. Notice the Choose From Contacts command just under the box for entering addresses. If you maintain contacts in your Gmail account, simply select invitees from the contacts list and their e-mail addresses will be entered automatically.

To include a message with an invitation, type it in the Message box. To send yourself a copy of the invitation (ensuring that it went out, or as a record for yourself) check Send A Copy To Myself. The Add Without Sending Invitation command adds the e-mail addresses with rights to either edit or view, but does not send an invitation.

Don't click the Send command yet!

Click on the Advanced Permissions command near the top of the window to control what people can do with your invitation. These decisions are important to make before sending out invitations. You can change them later, but it's a big waste of time to go back and do it over when you can take care of it now.

Figure 5.7 shows the Google default selections. "Allow editors to invite others to edit or view" enables people you invite as editors to act like owners of the spreadsheet (they can invite others to edit or view it). If this is OK, leave it checked. If you want to be the only one who controls invitations, make sure this box is unchecked. "Allow invitations to be forwarded" enables people you have invited to resend your invitation to anyone. The people they send your invitation to will have the same rights to edit or view that you gave in your original invitation. If you don't want people to forward your invitation, make sure this box is unchecked.

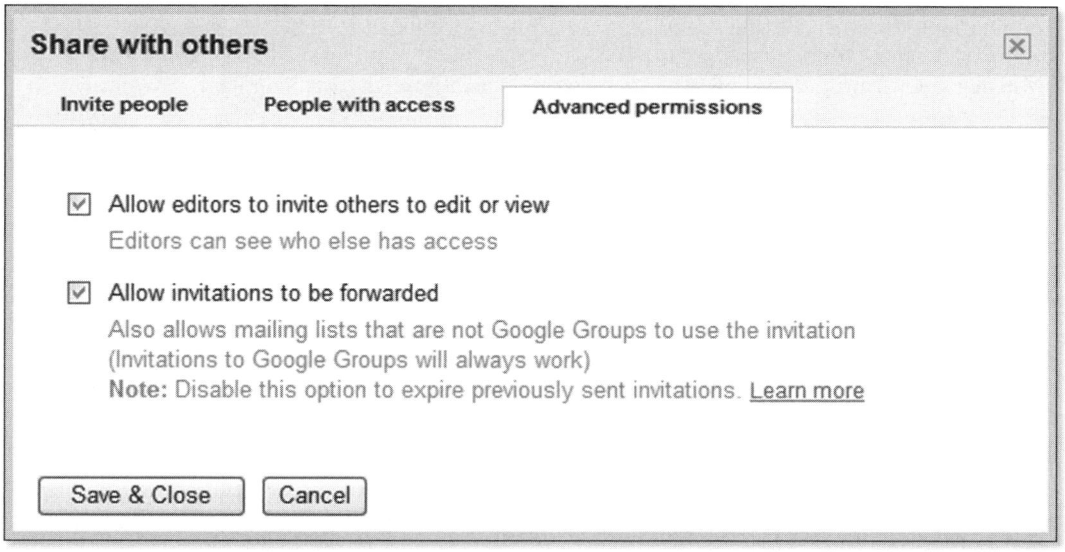

FIGURE 5.7. The Advanced Permissions window

Please note that it's also possible to send invitations to groups of people, using groups that were set up in Google Groups. Each group has its own contact information.

After you have made these selections, click Save & Close to return to the Share With Others window.

Importing and Exporting

Importing (or "uploading") spreadsheets (as well as documents and presentations) involves only a few steps. Go to the Docs home page, select the Upload button (above the sidebar, on the left). Browse to the location of the file to upload, or to the URL on the web, and click Start Upload. The file will now appear in the Docs list.

If the spreadsheet you are uploading contains a chart along with the spreadsheet, the chart will not upload. It is possible to copy and insert the chart in a separate process. Instructions for this are online: http://docs.google.com/support/bin/answer.py?hl=en&topic=11319&answer=63834. There are limits to the size and types of file formats that may be used; however, as is typical of Google, the options are rather generous.

To export a spreadsheet, click on File > Export and select the desired format. Spreadsheets may be exported in the following formats: CSV, HTML, text, Excel, OpenOffice, or PDF. If you wish to work on your spreadsheet offline, exporting as an Excel spreadsheet is probably best. To publish to the web, use HTML. To send as an e-mail attachment or to print, use PDF, to preserve the formatting.

Publishing and Embedding

Publishing is great because it allows a user to turn a spreadsheet into a website. You can publish one sheet or a collection of sheets. Spreadsheets can be automatically updated on the web whenever changes are made, or they can remain in a static format, so changes are not reflected in web copy. Entire spreadsheets (or specific parts) can be embedded in blogs or other web pages. To publish a spreadsheet, open the file and click on Share > Publish As A Web Page. A window will appear asking what parts of the spreadsheet you want published. Then select Start Publishing.

Before a spreadsheet can be embedded in a website or blog, it must be published. The URL from the published spreadsheet is used to embed it. In Google Sites, go to Edit Page > Insert > Spreadsheet and enter the spreadsheet's URL when asked to do so. (When using Google Sites for the first time you will have to create a site. See Chapter 16 for details on creating a site.) For an excellent article on how to embed spreadsheets in a website or blog, go to the Vertex42 website (www.vertex42.com/News/embedding-google-spreadsheets.html).

Making a Form from a Spreadsheet

To create a form that will function as a questionnaire based on a spreadsheet, click on the Form menu at the top of the spreadsheet. A drop-down menu will open, and the only choice will be Create A Form. Click this command and a web-based questionnaire will be created using the column headings in your spreadsheet. This questionnaire carries the same title as the spreadsheet. If you send this form to people, or send them its URL, their answers will feed into your spreadsheet.

This can be a convenient way to collect data for both you and your students. In addition, because the form is online and can be e-mailed, anyone with an Internet connection can fill it out. This makes the form-spreadsheet combination just as useful for professional and community work as it does for use in the classroom.

For more information on how to use Forms, please see Chapter 6.

TEACHER TIPS

- We don't want to go into a big explanation of what spreadsheets can do or how they can be used, but to spur readers' imaginations, here is a list of ideas. Spreadsheets:

    - Let users experiment with numbers without having to redo calculations

    - Permit the exploration of "what-if" scenarios

    - Enable easy and attractive graphic layouts

    - By the use of charts (graphs), make possible the identification of patterns and trends that otherwise might be difficult or impossible to discern

    - Make the use of real-time data easy and practical

    - Greatly simplify the sorting and filtering of data

    - Make the recording of survey data or experimental data very straightforward

    - Operate effectively as simple databases

    - Enable mail merging

    - Can be made into a gradebook

    - Greatly simplify the making of all kinds of lists and charts

    - Are very useful for purposes of comparing and contrasting, classifying, and making timelines

    - Make it easy to organize interviews of multiple people using the same questions or to record survey responses

    - Allow the creation of digital worksheets that give students immediate feedback without need to consult with the teacher

    - Can plan a trip, keep track of expenses, develop and maintain a budget, keep track of passwords

- In our experience, spreadsheets are best taught incrementally, as an integrated part of a content lesson. Students can better appreciate the usefulness of spreadsheets when they are used to address meaningful situations, rather than taught as an isolated exercise ... relevance is a more powerful motivator than abstraction.

We suggest giving students problems in which the use of spreadsheets makes it much easier to get to an answer. Basically, spreadsheets should enable students to see relationships and patterns faster, easier, and perhaps in ways that they could not otherwise recognize. We also believe that the levels of complexity in using spreadsheets are best introduced in a sequential, or incremental, manner rather than all at once.

■ For resources on using spreadsheets across disciplines and grade levels go to:

Dr. Christie's Using Spreadsheets in K–12 Classrooms:
http://alicechristie.org/edtech/ss/
(elementary)

Buddy Project: ResourceCentral Computer Capers:
http://buddyproject.org/capers/
(search for spreadsheets/graphs)

Education World Technology Center EXCEL-lent Middle School Math Lessons:
www.educationworld.com/a_tech/tech/tech079.shtml
(middle school)

Center for Technology and Teacher Education: Microsoft Excel Activities:
http://teacherlink.org/content/math/activities/excel.html
(middle and high school)

LT Technologies: Spreadsheet Resources:
www.lttechno.com/links/spreadsheets.html
(K–12, across the disciplines)

■ Google's excellent online instructions for using Spreadsheets are located at http://docs.google.com/support/spreadsheets.

■ Google has recently made it easy to copy a single sheet (known as a worksheet in Excel) from one spreadsheet to another. Click on the Sheet Name tab at the bottom of the page (e.g., Sheet 1, Sheet 2) and then select Copy To. A dialog box appears that lists all the spreadsheets you own or for which you have editing rights. Select the spreadsheet you want and the single sheet will be added to it.

CHAPTER 6
FORMS

CHAPTER AT A GLANCE

- Snapshot Description
- How It Works
  - Getting Started
  - Creating Questions
  - Managing Forms
  - Understanding Data with *See Responses*
- Teacher Tips

SNAPSHOT DESCRIPTION

Forms allows a user to create a questionnaire and send it to a list of people or make it public via the web. Responses to the questionnaire are fed automatically to a spreadsheet in the Docs list, and you can even receive e-mail updates when you get new responses. This makes quick work of administering and taking a survey, registering people for a conference or meeting, submitting data from fieldwork, or even giving students a self-scoring homework assignment, quiz, or test.

Forms started off in Google Docs as a service within Spreadsheets; however, users rapidly realized the terrific things they could do with Forms, so Google devoted a significant amount of resources to making it more robust. Now it's a grown-up, stand-alone App.

HOW IT WORKS

Getting Started

To begin using Google Forms, open Docs. From the home page, click on New > Form. Figure 6.1 shows the window that will open.

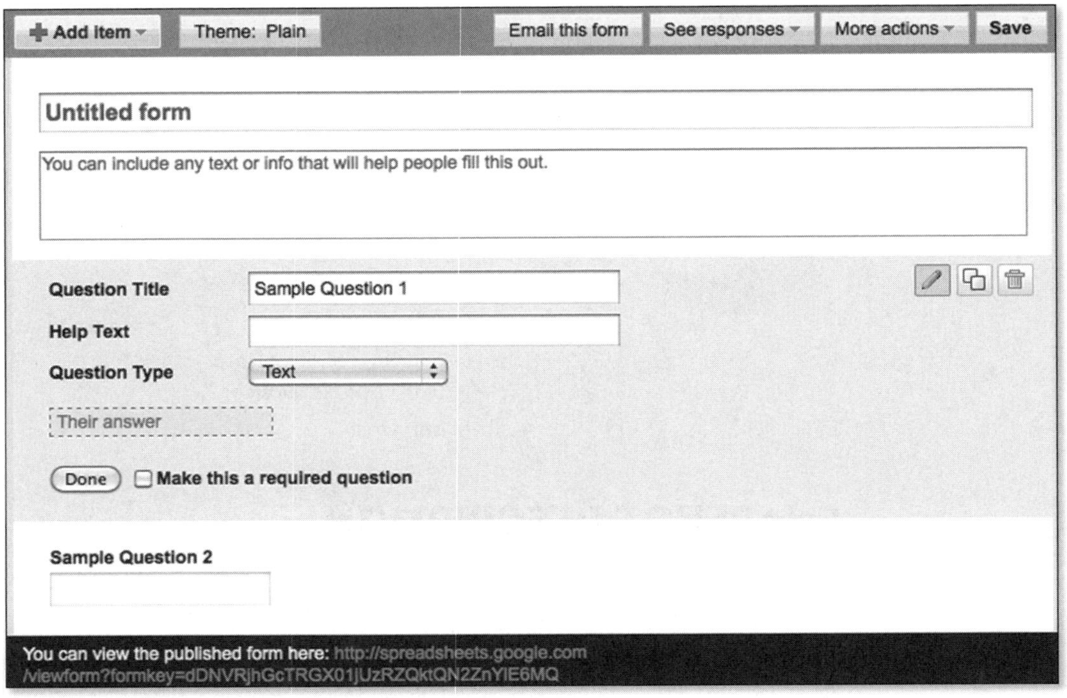

FIGURE 6.1. The first window you'll see when developing a Form

Give your form a name in the box that reads Untitled Form. You can easily change this later. Don't worry about the file name; it is only necessary to find the form again.

After you name your form, click Save (top right of the window). When saved, the form will appear by name in the Spreadsheets section of the Docs list. If you save at this point, you will need to mouse over Sample Question 1 and click on the pencil icon that appears to edit the question.

Notice the dark horizontal bar at the bottom of the window. This contains the URL for your form. You can send the URL to people so they can access the form themselves.

There is a box below the Untitled Form area that reads, "You can include any text or info that will help people fill this out." This is an area to place general information about your form and is also a place to provide instructions on how to fill it out.

Creating Questions

The Question Title field is for the name of the question, for reference. It is not the text of the question. Many forms use a simple sequential number or letter system (i.e., 1, 2, 3 or A. B. C.). That's a fine system to use. You can use just about any naming system that uses letters and numbers.

The Help Text field is for the text of the question. For example, if the form reads "7. At what time of day is the sun at the lowest point in the sky?" The Question Title in this case is "7," and the Help Text is "At what time of day is the sun at the lowest point in the sky?"

The Question Type drop-down menu allows you to select the type of question. At this time, Google offers seven different choices for type of questions: Text (short answer), Paragraph text (long answer), Multiple choice, Checkboxes, Choose from a list, Scale (e.g., rate from 1 to 5), or Grid (see Fig. 6.2).

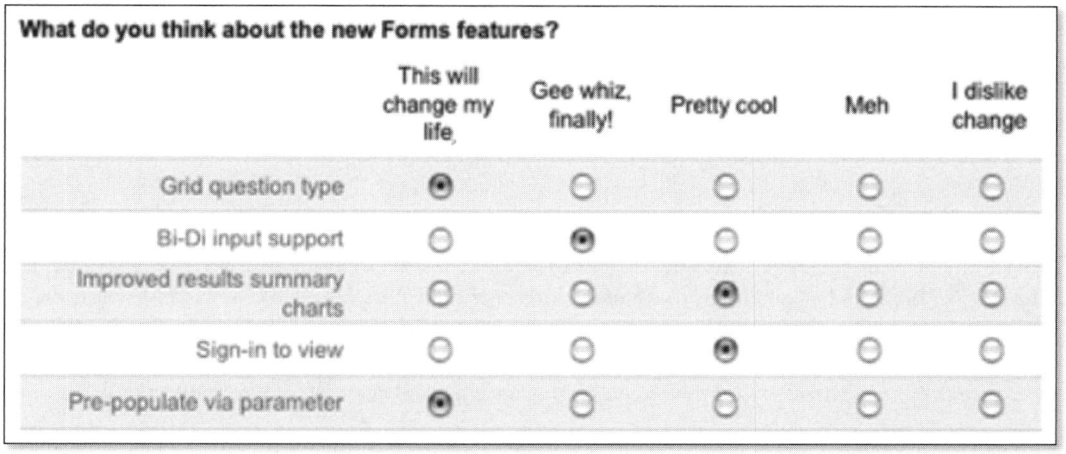

What do you think about the new Forms features?

	This will change my life	Gee whiz, finally!	Pretty cool	Meh	I dislike change
Grid question type	●	○	○	○	○
Bi-Di input support	○	●	○	○	○
Improved results summary charts	○	○	●	○	○
Sign-in to view	○	○	●	○	○
Pre-populate via parameter	●	○	○	○	○

FIGURE 6.2. Example of a grid-type question. The results of each row appear in a separate column in the associated spreadsheet.

Once you select the question type, depending on the type chosen, an additional window may open prompting you to enter text for the particular items (such as multiple choice items or items in a list). The faint box that reads "Their answer" is actually showing the response type expected of the person filling out the form. As different question types are selected, the response type also changes.

When you are finished with the question, you may click on Done. If you wish to make the question required for those filling out the form, check the box next to Make This A Required Question. If you leave this box empty, viewers of the form will not be required to answer the question if they don't want to.

After you click Done, your question will display in a preview of how it will appear to your viewers. The actual form will look slightly different.

Next, proceed to Sample Question 2 and repeat the process. When you finish this question and click Done, additional editable questions will not automatically appear. You will have to create them. To do this, go to the Add Item drop-down menu at the top left of the window (see Fig. 6.3). The familiar list of question types appears in the top portion of the list. Select one and it will appear below question 2. You may continue for as many questions as necessary.

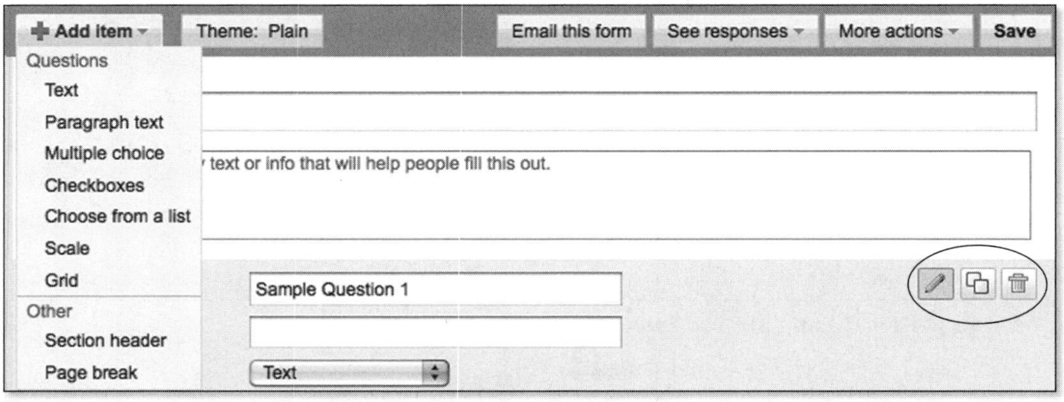

FIGURE 6.3. The Add Item drop-down menu allows you to create additional questions

Managing Forms

Notice the Section Header command at the bottom of the Add Item drop-down list. You may add section headers to your form to divide it into sections. This may make it easier for respondents to read, follow, and understand the questionnaire. Section headers can have a title, which appears in a larger font, and also a description. To change the order of questions simply click and drag them. Remember, you may need to change the question title if you move a question.

In Figure 6.3, note the three icons in the oval to the right of Sample Question 1. They appear next to every question. Use them to edit a question (pencil icon), duplicate a question (2 squares icon), or delete a question (trash can icon).

Please also note the other tabs in the toolbar at the top of the window shown in Figure 6.3:

> **Theme: Plain.** Select a theme for the form's appearance when published to its own website. There are over a dozen themes from which to choose.

> **E-mail this form.** Send the form directly to anyone's e-mail address.

> **See responses.** See the spreadsheet containing responses to the form, or see a complete graphic summary of the responses (see Fig. 6.4).

> **More actions.** Obtain the code to embed the form into a website or a blog, or edit the confirmation message that is sent to respondents after they complete and send a form.

Understanding Data with *See Responses*

See Responses is one of the two greatest features for educators in Forms. With See Responses, viewers are able to easily retrieve visual summaries of responses to the form.

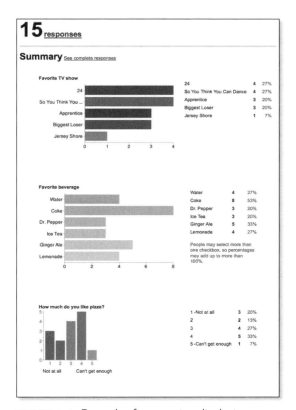

FIGURE 6.4. Example of summaries, displaying graphic representations of data

This feature is important because gathering data is one thing, but interpreting the meaning of the data is another thing altogether. The See Responses feature greatly simplifies the process of engaging students in seeing patterns and trends—one of the most important 21st-century skills.

The other very important feature of Forms is that *students* can create forms and the questions that make them up. This is an essential activity in design: identifying what you want to discover (or accomplish) and figuring out the necessary steps (or the building blocks you need) to get there. Creating environments for students to figure out *what they need to know* and *how to know it* is another of the most important 21st-century skills.

The spreadsheets that display the data in raw form are additional playgrounds for mental growth. The data may be sorted, manipulated through computations and formulas, and many types of graphs can be displayed. Spreadsheets can even be exported to Excel for use of its greater graphic display capabilities.

TEACHER TIPS

■ One of the absolutely greatest things to do with Forms is to create self-scoring worksheets, quizzes, and tests. This takes quite a bit of preparation, but the results are simply wonderful. Students can receive instant feedback on their work and you are saved the drudgery of grading, while enjoying the luxury of seeing results and being able to analyze them in a spreadsheet—perfect for item analysis and grouping for reteaching, enrichment, or acceleration.

A great way to implement Google Forms in your classroom is with common tests developed with members of your team. Chapter 1 describes how CIS 339 in the Bronx, New York, uses Forms to create end-of-unit tests that instantly provide the results to all the students and teachers in an entire grade or team.

CIS 339 teacher and Google Certified Teacher Jesse Spevack has created a video to show how to do this: "How to Create Self-Grading Quizzes Using Google Forms" (www. screencast-o-matic.com/watch/cjXeqwnDe). For those who prefer a print tutorial, see

"Self-grading Multiple Choice Tests with Google Docs" (http://rpollack.net/2008/09/ self-grading-multiple-choice-tests-with-google-docs). This lengthy and informative blog post is by R. Pollack, a teacher who has worked in Mississippi and the Southwest. Also, do not miss "How to Make a Self-Calculating Survey" by Colette Cassinelli (http://drop.io/cassinelli/asset/how-to-make-a-self-calculating-survey-pdf). All three tutorials are very valuable.

■ Tom Barrett, an elementary teacher from Great Britain, offers a goldmine of ideas for using Forms in his blog (http://tbarrett.edublogs.org/2008/02/10/ using-google-forms-in-the-classroom) and (http://tbarrett.edublogs.org/2008/ 08/23/10-google-forms-for-the-classroom). Among Barrett's ideas are:

  ■ Beginning and end of term surveys

  ■ Beginning of the year student profiles (likes, dislikes, multiple intelligence questions, other views)

  ■ Student-ranked factors of what they think makes a good piece of work, creating a rubric for teaching, assessment, and learning

  ■ Technology survey among students or teachers

  ■ Staff poll on professional development preferences

  ■ Graph of the emotional ups and downs in a story

  ■ Spelling tests (phenomenal time saver)

  ■ Weekly reading record of time spent reading by each student

  ■ Data collection from classes for later instructional use (head size, shoe size, height, weight, number of siblings, number of pets)

  ■ Prior learning assessment (see what students know about a topic before teaching it)

  ■ Student assessment of learning success (students rate their confidence in the skills at the conclusion of a unit; great instant feedback for teacher to determine whether to move ahead or reteach)

  ■ Book reviews, website reviews

  ■ Parent questionnaires

■ Google's Help for Forms is at http://docs.google.com/support/bin/topic. py?hl=en&topic=15166. It includes a nice video for beginners.

CHAPTER 7
BLOGGER

CHAPTER AT A GLANCE

- Snapshot Description
- How It Works
  - Getting Started
  - Making Your First Blog Post
  - Blogger Dashboard
  - Managing Your Blog
- Teacher Tips

SNAPSHOT DESCRIPTION

A blog (from "web log") is best described as a diary or journal maintained on the web. Blogs are not meant to be static. They are meant to be dynamic, with authors posting entries regularly, perhaps weekly, daily, or more frequently, depending on the blog's purpose.

Blogs can be used as an education tool to communicate beyond the classroom's four walls. Whether for day-to-day lessons and projects, or for dissemination of class information, blogs give students the opportunity to connect with their peers and experts through writing. Blogs can instantly provide a worldwide audience for critical thought, opinion, observation, or accolade. Discussions are threaded (meaning all thoughts on a given topic are grouped together sequentially), giving individuals the chance to reflect on comments being made and learn from new information presented.

Both teachers and students may maintain blogs, as they can serve many purposes. For example, blogs may be used as the following:

Bulletin board. Post important information for a class, for parents, or students in a collaborative learning group. Study notes for important tests may be posted, or students may take turns summarizing what occurred in class each day.

Discussion center. Questions may be posed for discussion, and responses may be opened to anyone or limited to certain individuals. Readers may comment on responses to questions, or readers may start their own discussions.

Personal expression journal. This is probably the most common purpose for which blogs are used. Students may be encouraged, or required, to maintain an individual blog that contains personal reflections, assigned work, poetry, videos, images, and comments on the work of their peers. Many teachers maintain anonymous personal blogs of thoughts and reflections on their own work.

Notebook. If you are just beginning and wish to start in a simple way, you may choose to use a blog as a simple online notebook, serving as a collection point for all assignments, thoughts, and communications.

HOW IT WORKS

Getting Started

Blogger, powered by Google, is a free blog application accessible from any computer with Internet access. Blogger features include publishing, posting comments, and uploading photos and videos from your computer or even your cell phone.

It's easy to create a blog with Blogger. The onscreen directions help to simplify the process (see Fig. 7.1). Blogger works best with either the Explorer or Firefox browsers; Google recommends Firefox.

1. Go to the Blogger website (www.blogger.com) to get started.

2. Sign in to your Google account (see Chapter 2).

3. Name your blog. The name can be whatever you like: perhaps your class name or the project you are working on (e.g., Biology Class 101).

4. Choose your design from the many templates available. We recommend using the default selection just to speed things along. You can change or customize your design at any time.

That's it! You're ready to start blogging.

FIGURE 7.1. The Blogger home page

Making Your First Blog Post

Placing material on a blog is called posting. "Hi, Tanya," you might say to a friend, "Check out what I posted on my blog yesterday!"

Figure 7.2 shows an example of what a blog post looks like. Yours will look different if you chose a different template for your blog's appearance. Here, we "prettied up" the blog with a photo.

FIGURE 7.2. A sample blog post

When you start blogging, this screen will greet you (see Fig. 7.3).

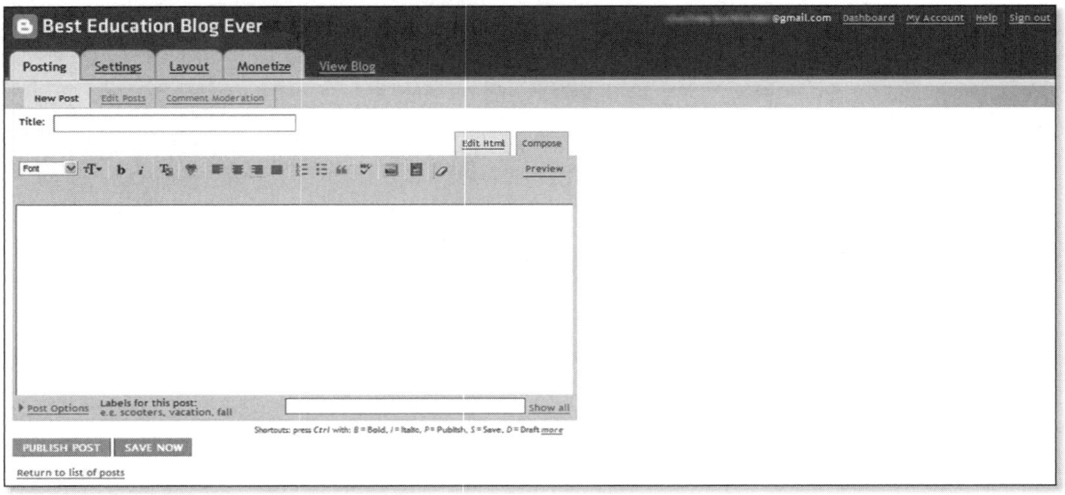

FIGURE 7.3. Creating a new blog post

Name your post using the Title box. A post title is similar to a headline in a newspaper article. Every blog post should have a title, even if it's only something like the date or Number 34.

Note the following choices: Compose, Edit HTML, and Preview. You will probably find yourself working mostly in Compose, as this is the default and is easiest to use. Compose is a What You See Is What You Get (WYSIWYG—pronounced "wiziwig") editor. Here you can type and format your text, including fonts, colors, adding links, images, and videos. When typing in Compose, what you see on the screen is what appears in the blog, thus the term WYSIWYG. Figure 7.3 shows the Compose mode.

If you know HTML (hypertext markup language), then the Edit HTML mode will be useful. If you do not know how to use HTML, it's probably best to leave this alone.

The Preview mode (just below Compose) allows you to see exactly how your blog post will look before you publish it to the web.

The formatting toolbar for Blogger contains a number of icons. If you mouse over each icon for 2 seconds, a tiny window will open that names the icon's function. These include font style, size, bold, italic, and color; creating hyperlinks; text and image alignment; list bulleting and numbering; block quotes; spell check; inserting images and videos; and remove formatting (an advanced feature).

Type and post your images and videos in the large text box. An individual post can be as lengthy as you wish.

On the lower left, find the Post Options command. This enables you to choose whether readers may add comments to your post after it is published.

Now find the text box that reads: Labels For This Post. This is a very helpful feature; it is similar to the tagging done on many social networking and bookmarking sites. Labeling your posts enables you to provide certain keywords that describe the topic or topics addressed in your post. These tags automatically index your blog posts, which makes specific posts easy to find when you have a long list.

For example, say you've posted a few paragraphs about going to the beach with your dog and having a great conversation about surfing with someone you met there. You could add the labels beach, dog, and surfing in this box. Now, if you have written other posts about the beach, they will be indexed together in your blog.

The Show All command displays all of the labels you have previously used in your blog. This is very helpful if you can't remember whether you used the label *dog* or *Rex* when writing about your dog Rex. You don't want to use more labels than you have to, or things can get pretty confusing.

Clicking Publish Post will publish the post you've been writing to your actual blog on the web. If you make a mistake and publish before the post is completed, don't worry—you can always edit or delete a post you've made.

Clicking Save Now will save what you are working on as a draft so you can return to it later for more editing. It will not be published.

Clicking Return To List Of Posts will take you to a new page that lists all of your blog posts, by title. You may choose posts to edit, view, or delete. The Edit Posts command, above the Title box, does the same thing as Return To List Of Posts.

When the Publish Post command is clicked, a screen will open announcing "Your blog post published successfully!"

From this page, you may select either of the two View Blog links, and your blog will open in the same browser window. Select In A New Window and your blog will open in a new browser window.

From this same page, Edit Post takes you back to edit your original post, and Create a New Post opens a new Create window to make a new post to your blog.

Commenting is one of the most powerful features of blogging because it allows two-way communication between the blogger and an audience. Commenting is one of the features that makes a blog such a powerful advance from a website that may only be read.

The moderation of comments controls how comments are handled on your blog. Google offers many options to you as the administrator of your blog. For example, you control whether comments are shown or hidden, and whether they may be made by anyone, or only by individuals or categories of individuals that you specify. You also control where comments appear in your blog, and you can show or hide links back to other pages on the web that connect to your blog post (this is a good way to know who thinks your blog is important enough to link to). You may also choose to moderate comments (approve them before they appear publicly) or not. Click Comment Moderation to control how comments are displayed, who may comment, and whether your approval is required for comments to display. This command appears on numerous pages.

Blogger Dashboard

The Dashboard is the main screen you will see whenever you sign in to Blogger. From the Dashboard you may begin a new post, edit an existing post by clicking View Blog, create a new blog, and update your account profile.

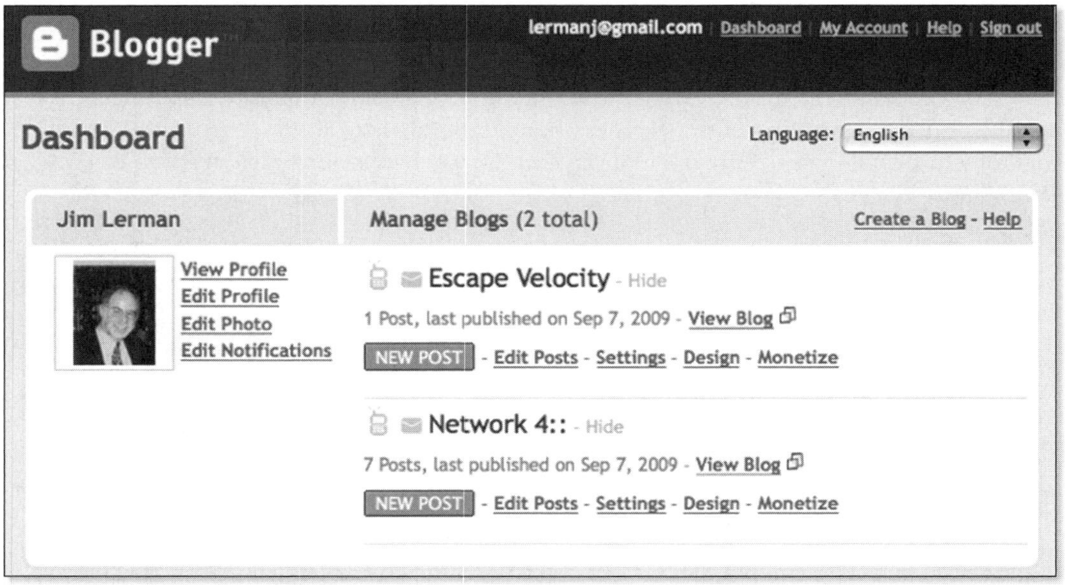

FIGURE 7.4. The Google Dashboard

In Figure 7.4, two blogs are displayed. Their names are *Escape Velocity* and *Network 4::*. Click on the View Blog command to the right of each title to go to that blog. Each blog has a unique URL.

To create multiple blogs for different classes or projects, use the same Google account so you can access all of your blogs within Dashboard. If you are in another area of Blogger and need to get back to Dashboard, look for the Dashboard command, or click the orange Blogger icon in the top left corner of the page.

Managing Your Blog

Unless you change your blog settings, it will be available to the public. So, depending on the grade level you work with or the purpose of your blog, you may consider controlling who reads and comments on your blog. If this is not a concern for you, simply leave the default settings as they are.

Note the tabs just below the name of your blog on the Create A Post page (see Fig. 7.5).

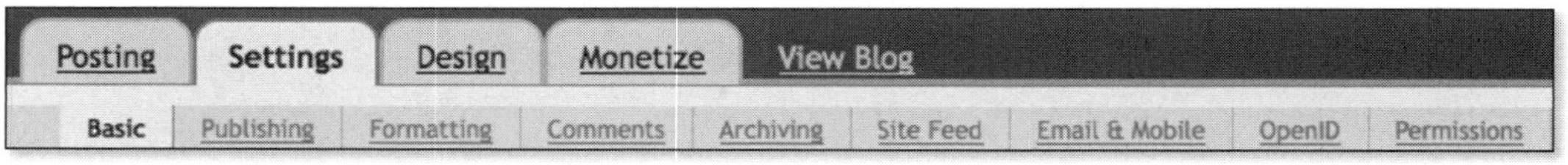

FIGURE 7.5. Tabs and related blog management toolbar

Just below the tabs you will see a management toolbar containing commands for the selected tab. In Figure 7.5, the Settings tab is selected and its toolbar is displayed, with the Basic command selected. Take the time to view each of these commands and see the wide variety of choices provided to manage your blog's settings.

You may also navigate to these tabs from the Dashboard page. Below the name of your blog, click on the commands Posting, Settings, Design, or Monetize (allow advertising to be displayed on your blog for a fee).

Take a moment to explore the Permissions command on the far right of the management toolbar under the Settings tab (see Fig. 7.5). Click on Permissions to add authors or readers. Add additional authors to give others permission to post on your blog. Complete the form by entering each person's e-mail address and clicking Add Authors. In the Blog Readers section, the default selection is Anybody. Other choices are Only People I Choose and Only Blog Authors.

If you select Only People I Choose, you must grant access to readers by entering their e-mail addresses. Separate multiple addresses with commas.

Keep in mind that these settings will send an invitation requiring invited readers to either create a new Google account, sign-in to an existing Google account, or view your blog as a guest without an account. While readers are not required to have a Google account, they will be able to view your blog for only two weeks until they decide to create a Google account, or you will need to send them another invitation.

To remove a reader from your list, click the remove link next to the individual's name in the Blog Readers list. Make your blog public anytime by switching back to the Anybody option.

Finally, let's take a look at the management toolbar under the Design tab.

Page Elements. Manages the position of various sections of your blog on the screen

Edit HTML. Displays your blog page in full HTML code, which can be edited

Template Designer. Offers a selection of attractive, ready-made template designs or allows you to create your own templates

TEACHER TIPS

- People have written at great length about their meaningful experiences with blogging in the classroom. Clarence Fisher, a middle school teacher in northern Canada, speaks eloquently about the topic (www.evenfromhere.org/?p=665):

  I've been a subscriber to the main feed from [the blog] Global Voices for only a few weeks and I find my Bloglines account constantly filled with new perspectives from around the globe.

  Miguel originally picked up this post and I want to echo most of it: "For many, blogs have become the door to the rest of the world. In writing a blog, you are inviting other people to know your life, and it is inevitable that this sentiment will be reciprocated. You ultimately read others' blogs and discover their lives in other places."

This is exactly one reason why I want my kids to blog; and just as importantly, to read the blogs of others. Blogs are doors to the rest of the world. This is a powerful explanation of what we try to do. We "invite other people to know our lives," you "read others' blogs and discover their lives in other places." This is why I am adamant that my kids link to, read, and comment on the blogs of people who live in other parts of the globe. I want them to hear from Australian kids, from Brazilian kids. From kids who live in major urban centres, and from those who live in small towns just like they do. They need to learn about their differences, see their similarities, and understand about how, on this ever-shrinking globe, they are a generation of people who will have many problems to solve when they inherit what we are leaving behind.

Blogging may bring us into a new community of learners, but it also drives us from a "regular" place of comfort where the rules are steady, change is slow, and things are predictable. Instead, we leave this behind, and are driven towards trying to understand concepts of change in all of its facets and its impact on our lives, the lives of our students, and what we are trying to accomplish in our classrooms. This process is not easy or steady, and it provides us with little comfort outside of the constancy of change.

But it is only through this exile from "regular" teaching, a place I feel driven more and more towards, that we can open the peek through the doors into the lives of others in ways that are honest, respectful, and open to dialogue and understanding.

- Blogger provides numerous resources for help (http://help.blogger.com).

- Steve Hargadon maintains a website, Support Blogging (http://supportblogging.com), that contains a host of information and resources about blogging. It includes links to numerous articles, websites, videos, and podcasts about how to blog in schools and its benefits. Don't miss Steve's great list of teacher, student, administrator, and parent blogs.

- The Classroom 2.0 Ning website (www.classroom20.com/forum/topic/listForTag?tag=blogging) contains a rich collection of resources and posts about blogging in schools.

- Science blog idea: Create a blog for the science lab. Students can post their experiment findings with their class or group and discuss or compare observations.

- Social Studies blog ideas: Have students present research or discuss issues as they relate to themes and events around the world. Maintain a blog to talk with experts or e-pals from various countries or neighboring towns to compare lifestyles and the issues that matter most.

■ Art blog ideas: With the ability to import pictures, classes can analyze classic and modern works, including their own. Inspire creativity by sharing designs, resources, and reviews.

■ Math blog ideas: Students can create and solve problems posted by the teacher or classmates. This is an excellent method for students to learn collaboratively and show their work!

■ Language Arts blog ideas: Students can publish creative writing, essays, and literary analysis for peer editing and sharing.

■ More ideas for using blogs in the classroom can be found at:

Assorted Stuff—Ideas: Using Blogs in the Classroom:
www.assortedstuff.com/stuff/?p=71
This site presents numerous ideas for teachers and students to use blogs in the classroom.

International Edubloggers Directory: http://edubloggerdir.blogspot.com
This directory includes nearly 500 edubloggers from around the world.

K12 Online Conference 2009—*Sustained Blogging in the Classroom* video:
http://k12onlineconference.org/?p=170

Edutopia—Digital Discussion: Take Your Class to the Internet:
www.edutopia.org/digital-discussion-take-your-class-to-Internet
This article presents a variety of approaches to using blogs.

The Edublog Awards: http://edublogawards.com
Lists of the best education blogs of the year in 16 categories, chosen by the public, starting in 2004.

Blogger Buzz: http://buzz.blogger.com
Google's blog about what's happening at Blogger.

CHAPTER 8
MAPS

CHAPTER AT A GLANCE

- Snapshot Description
- How It Works
    - Learning Your Way Around
    - Searching
    - Getting Directions
    - My Maps—Creating a Map and Adding Your Own Content
    - Adding Content Created by Others to Your Map
    - Collaborating and Sharing
- Teacher Tips

SNAPSHOT DESCRIPTION

Google Maps provides searchable and customizable maps your class can use to find places in many parts of the world and display geographic data. Without boarding a plane, see details through high-resolution satellite images or aerial photographic views that bring viewers to only a few feet above ground level. Search the globe by address, click and drag, zoom then pan, or navigate to street view to see area surroundings. As you begin to use Google Maps in the classroom, you will learn ways to go beyond searching, to personalize and annotate maps, making them come alive in your daily lessons and projects.

HOW IT WORKS

Learning Your Way Around

While you do not need a Google account to use Google Maps, you will need a Google account to create and customize maps. See Chapter 2 for help on creating a Google account. The Google Maps opening page (http://maps.google.com) looks like Figure 8.1.

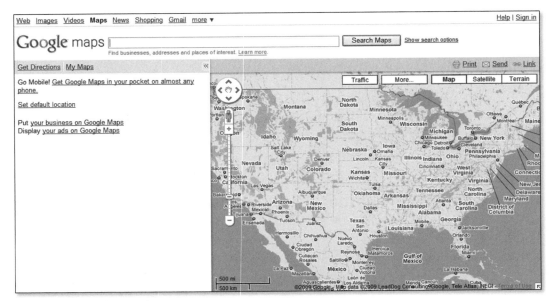

FIGURE 8.1. Google Maps home page

Near the top of the page, you will find the familiar Google search box. In Google Maps, search terms entered into the box will return a map with information about a particular area. You may enter an address, a city, a place of interest, a business, or latitude and longitude coordinates. For example, entering "pizza Houston" will give a map of pizzerias in the city of Houston. You can also search for a topic and a geographic location, for example, "jazz New Orleans."

To the right of the search box is a small, downward-pointing arrow. Click on this to access your saved locations. This is very convenient for returning to places for repeat visits. Google's default setting saves all searches. This is easy to turn off using the same downward arrow control.

Note the Get Directions and My Maps commands. Get Directions enables you to get precise directions from one place to another by car, on foot, or by public transportation (in major metro areas). My Maps shows views of custom maps you make yourself, or maps made by others. Instructions for creating your own maps and using others' maps appear later in this chapter.

The navigation controls (a white circle with arrow icons in the upper-left corner of the map) enable users to manipulate the map. Find the circle with arrows. Use these arrows to move the map view up, down, or sideways. To drag the map, move the cursor over it. When the cursor changes to a hand, click and drag the map in the desired direction.

The Icon bar that looks similar to a thermometer, with a little Person icon at the top, is used for zooming in and out on the map. Use the Person icon to obtain a street view if you are using a map of a metro area. Simply click on the Person icon and drag it to a particular location on a street. The icon will display yellow if a street view is available. The display will change to offer a photo of that specific location. If Google doesn't have this information, no picture will show.

Turn on the Overview map by clicking on the small white box with the arrow in the lower-right corner of the page. This thumbnail shows a slightly wider view of the area displayed in the main map on the page. It helps viewers better understand their general location.

Searching

Next, take a look at what a page looks like with search results (see Fig. 8.2).

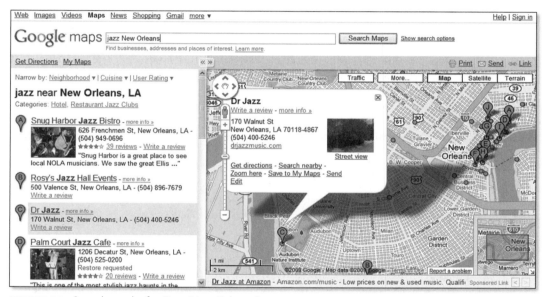

FIGURE 8.2. Search results for "jazz New Orleans"

The main map area shows downtown and uptown New Orleans in Map view. The pushpin markers with letters in them represent search results described in the search results panel to the left. Circles without letters represent other locations that Google has identified, but which are not returned in the Search results panel. If somebody asked where the jazz action was in New Orleans, it wouldn't be hard to figure out from this map.

In the search results panel, you'll find a short description of each pushpin marker. Click on More Info to open a window with extensive information and links about the location. Click on the pushpin title line (e.g., "Snug Harbor Jazz Bistro"), and the search results and the map will move that location to the center of the main map and open an Info window (in Fig. 8.2, the Info window shows Dr. Jazz). There is a More Info command inside the Info window as well. This may provide reviews, photos and videos, web pages, and other user-contributed content. (Teachers, take note: Google does not usually edit user-contributed material unless there is a complaint regarding its inappropriateness or inaccuracy.)

The Print, Send, and Link commands are located in the upper-right corner of the map. After you are satisfied with your map, either as it is or after modification, you can print it, send it, or publish it on the web, including any modifications. Print prepares a copy of your map for sending to your printer, including the search results panel information. Send enables transmission of your map by e-mail to a phone, a car's navigation system, or another GPS device. Link provides a URL for pasting into an e-mail or instant message, and HTML code for embedding the map in a website or blog by copying and pasting.

The viewing controls are located along the top of the main map area (directly below the Print, Send, and Link commands). The viewing control buttons are titled Traffic, More, Map, Satellite, and Terrain. Traffic shows live traffic conditions on main arteries and highways in metro areas. More offers views of photos, videos, and webcams located in the area shown on the map. Icons appear on the map in specific locations. In addition, Wikipedia entries for specific locations may be shown.

Map is the default view and shows the street grid, public transit stops, and places of note. Satellite shows satellite imagery of the location. Viewing a map in Satellite view, followed by Street view, provides a remarkable amount of detail. Most satellite images are one to three years old, according to Google. Terrain gives a topographic view of the area.

Street view is not accessible using the viewing controls. Remember, you'll need to click and drag the Person icon in the navigation controls to access the street view of a specific location. The Person icon must be yellow to see a street view of the map. Streets outlined in blue indicate that an active street view is possible. A second way to access street view is to type a specific address into the search box. A new map will open with a pushpin marker denoting the address location, and an Info window will point to it. A Street view command will be located within the Info window. A third way to access street view is to zoom in to the greatest magnification in map view. At the highest magnification, Map view turns into Street view.

Traffic view is good to check before going on a field trip or taking a team to an out-of-town game. Traffic flow on major roads is shown by colors, according to the legend in the upper-right corner. Icons display things such as road closures, construction, medical emergencies, and caution zones. Click on the icon to view a date- and time-stamped description of the specific problem. Google says the traffic information is "real time," but bear in mind that all traffic data has some time lag. Google says it has full data for 30 American cities, partial data for many more, and that it is working to add cities all the time.

Getting Directions

To get directions, click on Get Directions on any page in Maps. A box will open. Enter the address of your starting point in text box A and your ending point in text box B. If you have a trip with several stopping points, use the Add Destinations command. This opens additional text boxes for entering addresses. To delete an address, click the faint X on the right of the text box.

The Show Options command allows you to specify a route that avoids tolls or highways. It also permits distances to be shown in miles or kilometers. The drop-down menu below these two commands permits users to choose among directions for traveling by car, public transit (where available), or walking.

After entering your desired information and options, click Get Directions, and Google will customize a map and provide step-by-step travel instructions. Once you have generated directions, it's easy to reverse everything and get new directions for the trip back. Click the curved, two-headed arrow icon to the right of text boxes A and B and your directions will be reversed.

When you have finalized a map, you may print it, send it, or create a link to it. By clicking on Save To My Maps, at the bottom of the directions in the left panel, you can save your map for future reference.

My Maps—Creating a Map and Adding Your Own Content

You must sign in to your Google account to use this feature. Login to Maps, then click on My Maps. A new window opens. Click on the Get Started button.

FIGURE 8.3. Start page for Create A New Map, with placemark info window open

Provide a file name for your map in the Title box. You can always change it later; just give it a working name so you can find it again. Write a brief description of the map in the Description box. Next, use the radio button options to choose whether to make the map public or unlisted. Selecting Public allows anyone to view the map, and it will possibly be published in search results and user profiles. Selecting Unlisted makes the map private; it can be viewed only by people who have its URL. These settings may be changed later. Click Save, and your map will be saved to your My Maps page so you can find it whenever you want.

When a user selects Create A New Map or edits an existing map, three tool icons appear at the top left of the map: the hand tool, pushpin marker, and drawing tool. The hand tool enables dragging of the whole map in any direction. Click on the pushpin marker in order to place a placemark at any location on the map. Place your cursor where you want the placemark to appear, and click. The pushpin will appear on the map, and an Info window will open (see Fig. 8.3).

This Info window gives My Maps its greatest capability—to add custom information, pictures, links, and even videos. To start, give the placemark a name in the Title box.

Below the Title box, notice the Plain Text, Rich Text, and Edit HTML commands. The default choice is Plain Text—it shows in bold type. To place plain text in the Info window, simply type in the Description box.

Choose Rich Text if you wish to customize the appearance of the message, create a hyperlink, or insert a photo from the web. Photos may not be inserted in the Info window from your computer; they must come from the web. If you have a photo on your computer you wish to use, upload it to a service such as Picasa or Flickr.

To add a video from YouTube or Google Video (these are the only sources allowed), click on Edit HTML. Then copy the embed code from the website where the video appears into the box in the Info window.

Notice the (blue) pushpin marker icon in the upper-right corner of the Info window (see Fig. 8.3). Click on it to choose a different, custom icon from the list that appears, or you can upload an icon from the web. Using custom icons is a good way to help the viewers of your map to find exactly the information they need. Match the icon to the type of location you are highlighting—for example, a school, a park, a restaurant, a campground, or a movie theater.

To close the Info window, click the Close icon (a blue X surrounded by a circle) in the upper-right corner. To delete the Info window, click the Delete command in the lower-left corner.

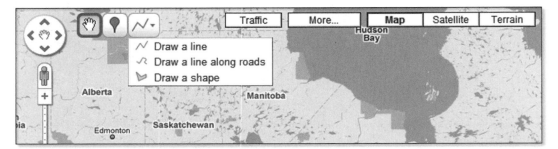

FIGURE 8.4. The drawing tool, showing options

The drawing tool enables users to draw a line, draw a line along a road, or draw a shape (see Fig. 8.4). Click on the Drawing icon (a jagged line) and then select the operation you wish to perform from the drop-down menu. Once any of these three operations is completed, an Info window opens for you to include descriptive information, upload pictures or videos, or make hyperlinks similar to the pushpin markers described previously.

Draw A Line makes a straight line from point to point on the map; it also measures distance from the line's beginning to its end. This tool is particularly good for areas where roads do not exist, or for tracing routes that do not follow roads. To draw the line, click the Drawing icon and select the Draw A Line command. Place your cursor on the map where you want the line to begin. Click once, but do not hold the cursor down. After clicking, move the cursor to the destination spot. If that is the end of the line, click twice. The dotted line will change into a solid line and an Info window will open. If it is not the end of the line, click once. A small white box will appear on the map and you will be able to continue dragging the line to another destination. Basically, it's one click to continue drawing the line and two clicks to end it.

Draw A Line Along Roads does exactly what it says. Click the command and start your cursor anywhere on the map. Control the line as you did with Draw A Line. No matter where you start on the map, as soon as you move the cursor, Google will jump your line to the nearest road and continue to draw the line along roads until you reach your destination. It will measure the distance travelled along the way as well. The same single- and double-click operations are used when drawing a line along a road or simply drawing a line. The controls work the same way. This is great for marking walking routes or designing tours. Placemarks can be dropped along the way to provide descriptive information.

Draw A Shape enables you to designate an area that is too large for a single placemark by enclosing an area on a map in a semi-transparent shape. Once an area is enclosed and the Info window appears, you may customize the shape's appearance by clicking on the colored square at the top right of the Info window.

VERY IMPORTANT: When you have finished working on your map, click on the Done command in the left panel. You have previously saved your map to the My Maps page. Done retains any new work. Failure to click Done will cause work to be lost. Don't let this happen to you or your students!

Adding Content Created by Others to Your Map

You can add content created by others to your map by browsing the Directory. After you have created a map, it is easy to create overlays that show things such as the weather, U.S. census demographics, local gas prices, places of interest, the effects of rises in sea level due to global warming, world oil consumption, the effect of drilling a hole directly through the earth from any spot, and over 1500 other options.

Begin this process from the Google Maps home page. Click My Maps. In the left panel, you will find three categories of maps: Created By Me, Created By Others, and Featured Content. Created By Me shows maps you have created, named, and saved previously. Created By Others shows maps you have saved from the Directory or maps created by others to which you have subscribed or become a collaborator (this option will not show if you have not saved maps created by others). Featured Content shows maps that Google thinks you might be interested in. You cannot control this list.

Click the Browse The Directory command. A new window will open, giving you over 1500 map overlays from which to choose. Some maps were created by Google; most were created by users.

Let's say you know you want to add a population density overlay to a map you have created and saved. On the Browse The Directory home page, type *population density* into the search box. A new page will open, showing the overlays that meet your search criteria. To read a brief description of the item, click on either the overlay title (in blue) or on its image. Once you decide you'd like to use an item, click Add It To Maps. The name of the overlay will now appear on your My Maps home page, in the Created By Others list.

To return to the My Maps page once you have selected an overlay, click Back To Google Maps in the upper-left corner. To delete an overlay or map on the My Maps page, click the Close icon (X in a box), to the far right of its name.

To display more than one map at the same time, return to the My Maps page. Select each map or overlay you wish to display by clicking on its name. The list of chosen maps or overlays will display at the bottom of the left panel. Click in the checkbox next to the name of each map or overlay to show or hide the particular map. (You may need to zoom in or out.) Not all overlays will display properly when used with another map.

Collaborating and Sharing

The Collaborate option within Maps gives you the opportunity to have students work on map projects together. When you display a previously made map (or once you've clicked Done on a map you're editing), the Collaborate command becomes visible under the Directions and My Maps commands. Invite collaborators by entering their e-mail addresses in the dialog box that appears once you click the Collaborate command. Additional options for collaborators include: Collaborators May Invite Others and Allow Anyone To Edit This Map.

If Google Earth is installed on your computer, the map you created and saved in Maps may be viewed in Google Earth by clicking the link in the toolbar above the Views menu (see Fig. 8.5). When you click the link, a .kml file will be created and you may choose to open it or save it to your computer. For more on opening a .kml file in Google Earth, see page 101.

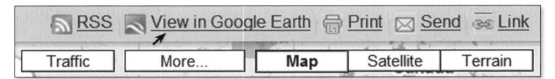

FIGURE 8.5. This link allows you to view your saved map in Google Earth

TEACHER TIPS

Ideas from Thomas Cooper

Thomas Cooper offers these wonderful ideas about goals for students using Google's geographic apps (Maps and Earth) at www.slideshare.net/tcooper66/learning-expeditions-1092504/:

- Discover (conduct research and identify problems)

- Engage in discourse (participate in civil discussions on current events)

- Become aware and analyze their surroundings (use spatial tools and math skills to solve problems)

- Negotiate (to understand and appreciate others' points of view)

- Be aware (look at global issues that affect us all)

- Engage themselves (to become part of civil and social engagement efforts to solve problems in our community and abroad)

Google Education Geo Education

The following ideas are from the Google Education Geo Education website (www.google.com/educators/geo_class.html).

Art History

- Search for photos and user-created maps showing famous museums like the Louvre in Paris.

Biology & Ecology

- Track routes of chimpanzees in Tanzania's Gombe Forest. See the Jane Goodall Institute Chimpanzee blog (www.janegoodall.org/gombe-chimp-blog).

Environmental Science & Climatology

- See how Google and the United Nations Environment Programme teamed up to use collaborative MyMaps for the International Cleanup Weekend Initiative (http://maps.google.com/help/maps/cleanup).

- Use the Google Maps Mashup, Earthquakes in the Last Week, to locate and learn about recent earthquakes around the world (http://earthquakes.tafoni.net).

- Celebrate the 2007–2008 International Polar Year and add your classroom's plans to their global map (www.ipy.org/index.php?/ipy/launchmap).

Geology

- Find images, links, and descriptions, with information about thousands of volcanoes around the globe, thanks to organizations like the Smithsonian Institution's Global Volcanism Program (www.volcano.si.edu/world/globallists.cfm?listpage=googleearth).

History

- Take a virtual tour of the 21 California Missions (http://maps.google.com/maps?q=http://bbs.keyhole.com/ubb/download.php?Number=558454&t=k&om=1).

Literature & Humanities

- Bring class or contemporary tales to life with Google LitTrips (www.googlelittrips.org).

Physics

- Use Google Maps to teach speed, velocity, and displacement (http://google-latlong.blogspot.com/2007/11/map-of-day-my-maps-for-teaching-physics.html).

For Further Exploration

- Google Maps Mania—a blog about Google Maps (http://googlemapsmania. blogspot.com).

- Ten Ideas for Using Google Maps and Earth in the Classroom—a blog post (http://olliebray.typepad.com/olliebraycom/2007/11/ten-ideas-for-u.html).

CHAPTER 9
EARTH

CHAPTER AT A GLANCE

- Snapshot Description
- How It Works
  - Getting Started
  - Navigating the Home Page
  - The 3D Viewer and Controls
  - Adding Content
  - Searching for Content
  - Adding Your Own Content
  - Image Overlay and Photos
  - Viewing and Creating Virtual Tours
- Teacher Tips

SNAPSHOT DESCRIPTION

Google Earth: *"The globe that sits on your PC."*

Google Earth is a free application that must be downloaded to your computer. It allows you to "travel" around the world by viewing satellite images and information about the Earth's terrain, its oceans, and now the Moon and Mars as well. Search by entering locations, then explore using tools to zoom, pan, spin, and tilt. Organize your searches to create virtual tours that include content provided by partners or yourself. Version 5 has a unique history twist: you can turn back the clock with Historical Imagery. There are endless possibilities for use in the classroom and across the curriculum.

It would be severely limiting to consider Google Earth as suitable for teaching only geography. It represents a highly compelling way to connect users with multiple types of information associated with locations on Earth, the Moon, and Mars.

There are so many features available in Google Earth, we could write an entire book on it. This chapter will help you get a good start by becoming familiar with the basics. You can test the waters with a simple project of your own.

Speaking of waters, you can now see the ocean and explore material from National Geographic, the Cousteau Society, BBC, the National Oceanic and Atmospheric Administration (NOAA), and more. There are locations of shipwrecks, tracks for ocean expeditions, GPS tracks of sea animals, and lots of information about the ocean environment.

HOW IT WORKS

Getting Started

Since this is an application that must be installed, you do not need a Google account to use Google Earth. To download or upgrade to the latest version, go to the Google Earth website (http://earth.google.com) and click on the Download Google Earth icon on the right side of the web page.

Read and agree to the terms appearing on the next page, confirm by clicking, and the installation will begin. For system requirements or additional information, visit the Google support page (http://earth.google.com/support). Please note that all material in this chapter relates to version 5.0 of Google Earth.

Google Earth Pro and Google Earth Plus have associated costs. For regular use in the classroom, the free version has all the capabilities you need to build content-rich activities.

Navigating the Home Page

Before you begin, get to know the tools available to you. Figure 9.1 points out various features with definitions of Google Earth 5 tools. Both text and the figure are from the Google Earth User Guide at http://earth.google.com/userguide/v5/ (*Used with permission*).

1. **Search panel.** Use this to find places and directions and manage search results.

2. **3D Viewer window.** View the globe and its terrain in this window.

3. **Icon Toolbar buttons.** See Figure 9.2 for details on the function of each icon.

4. **Navigation controls.** Use these to zoom, look and move around (see The 3D Viewer and Controls section for details).

5. **Layers panel.** Use this to display points of interest.

6. **Places panel.** Use this to locate, save, organize, and revisit placemarks.

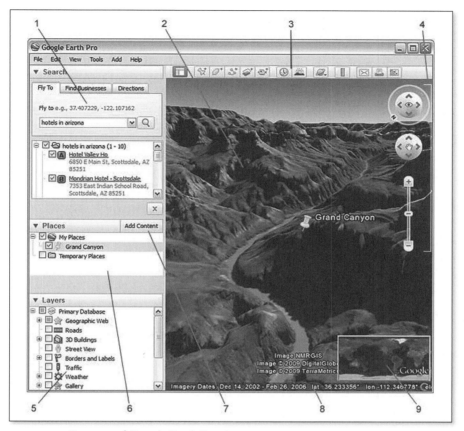

FIGURE 9.1. Features of Google Earth 5 tools

7. **Add Content button.** Click this to import exciting content from the KML Gallery.

8. **Status bar.** View coordinates, elevation, imagery date, and streaming status here.

9. **Overview map.** Use this for an additional perspective of the Earth.

Figure 9.2 details the icon functions in the toolbar at the top of the 3D Viewer window.

Use the Search panel to find a desired location. Click the Fly To tab to enter details about your search in the box. You can search for a place as specific as latitude/longitude coordinates, an address, landmark, or city; or as general as a state, country, or zip code. Enter information in the search box, click the magnifying class, and the 3D Viewer takes you there.

Next to the Fly To tab, you will see the Find Businesses tab. Click on it to find a particular type of business in a particular location.

When you search in Fly To or Find Businesses, you will usually receive numerous search results. Exactly like a regular Google search, not all of the results will be useful or meaningful. You may wish to save the results that seem worthwhile for future use. To save a search result to My

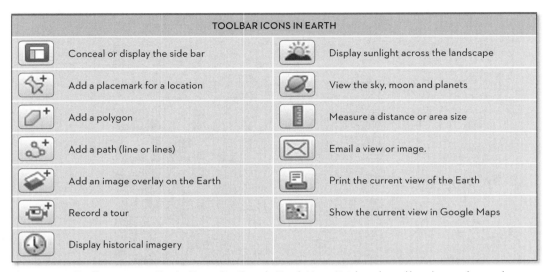

FIGURE 9.2. Toolbar icons in Earth. From the Google Earth User Guide at http://earth.google.com/userguide/v5/. *Used with permission.*

Places, select File > Save > Save to My Places. To save the search result to your computer, select File > Save > Save Place As. To save all the items in your My Places file, so they will be there the next time you open Google Earth, select File > Save > Save My Places.

To move items up and down in your My Places folder, simply select the item by clicking on it and drag it to the desired position. This applies to moving items within My Places and Temporary Places as well as moving items back and forth between them.

Next to the Find Businesses tab you will see the Directions tab. Click on it to obtain driving directions from one location to another. A difference between Maps and Earth in getting directions is that in Earth you can virtually "drive" the route by moving along images following the route.

Search results compiled by Google are marked by red pushpin placemarks. User submitted content shows up with blue pushpin placemarks. For many historical or natural landmarks, user submitted content is more interesting. Pushpin placemarks are denoted by red or blue letters in the search results panel and by corresponding letters on the display map.

Delete the entire contents of a search by right-clicking (Ctrl+click on a Mac) in the search panel and selecting Delete. Alternatively, click on the Close icon (small x in the box) below the search panel, on its bottom right.

The 3D Viewer and Controls

The window that displays search results, the 3D Viewer, allows you to see different perspectives—from aerial to ground level—with navigation tools to rotate, tilt, zoom, move up and down, and grab.

With the mouse you can grab the globe (the cursor turns into a hand) and move it to your desired view in any direction. Right-click (Ctrl+click on a Mac) and hold to zoom in or out. To zoom in, move the cursor downwards, to zoom out, move the cursor upwards.

In addition to the mouse, Google Earth navigation controls let you move and manipulate the globe in your view. Move your mouse over the upper-right corner of the 3D Viewer for them to appear (see Fig. 9.3).

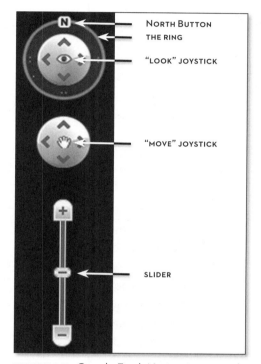

1. Click the North button to reset the view so that north is at the top of the screen.

2. Click and drag the Ring to rotate the view.

3. Use the Look joystick to look around from a single vantage point, as if you were turning your head. Click an arrow to look in that direction or continue to press down on the mouse button to change your view. After clicking an arrow, move the mouse around on the joystick to change the direction of motion.

4. Use the Move joystick to move your position from one place to another. Click an arrow to look in that direction or continue to press down on the mouse button to change your view. After clicking an arrow, move the mouse around on the joystick to change the direction of motion.

FIGURE 9.3. Google Earth Navigation controls

5. Use the zoom slider to zoom in or out (+ to zoom in; - to zoom out) or click the icons at the end of the slider. As you move closer to the ground, Google Earth swoops (tilts) to keep your viewing angle parallel to the Earth's surface. You can turn off the automatic tilt by selecting Tools > Options > Navigation > Navigation Controls (on a Mac: Google Earth > Preferences > Navigation > Navigation Controls).

Adding Content

In Google Earth, you can populate your view with content accessible within the application or with your own content, or you can open files created by others.

The Layers feature of Google Earth (see Fig. 9.4) provides overlays to see more detail and get more information about an area.

In Layers, you are provided with a list of options for Roads, 3D Buildings, Borders and Labels, Weather, Places of Interest, and more. If you click the gray triangle to the left of any feature, the drop-down menu displays additional options.

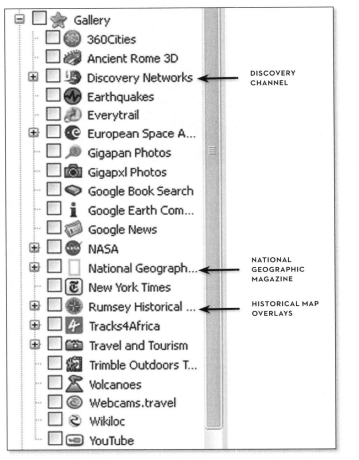

FIGURE 9.4. The Layers panel

When you check an option box, the information it contains will appear in the 3D Viewer, usually in the form of icons. Content can include pictures, videos, maps, markers, and articles. You simply must experiment with this feature to discover its many capabilities.

Don't overlook The Gallery just because it is a single entry on the list. When you open it, you will see the names of many, many agencies and organizations that have contributed content (see Fig. 9.5). Navigate the Gallery within Layers just as you do the menu for Layers, using the gray triangles and checkboxes.

FIGURE 9.5. The Gallery option within Layers, with some useful sources highlighted

Searching for Content

Files created in Google Earth are made in Keyhole Markup Language (KML). Google files will have a suffix code of .kml. Occasionally Google Earth files also appear as KMZ files. KMZ is a compressed version of KML. Both KML and KMZ files will open in Google Earth, and most will open in Google Maps.

Search for content available in the Google KML Gallery by clicking the Add Content button found next to Places (see #7 in Fig. 9.1). Alternatively, access the Google Gallery (www.google.com/gadgets/directory?synd=earth&preview=on&cat=featured).

Much like a search using the Google search engine, you can type in keywords related to what you hope to find. Alternatively, use the category links to browse. There are approximately 1700 tours in the Gallery. Many are in languages other than English. The "Popular" and "New" categories list all the files in the Gallery.

When you are ready to select a file, click Open In Google Earth. The selected file will automatically download into the Places folder on your Google Earth home page. When you get ready to close Google Earth, a pop-up window will ask if you wish to save the content (the file that you opened inside Google Earth). Click Save, and that KMZ tour file will be saved in your Google Earth.

For guidance in how to play tours, see the upcoming section "Viewing and Creating Virtual Tours."

Adding Your Own Content

Use the pushpin icon in the top toolbar to add a placemark. Alternatively, choose Add > Placemark from the Earth menu at the top of the page. The pushpin will appear in the 3D Viewer, and you may drag it to the desired location. A dialog box will also open (see Fig. 9.6). Earth will automatically display the exact latitude and longitude of the pushpin in the dialog box.

Title your pushpin placemark in the Name box.

Notice the Description; Style, Color; View; and Altitude tabs below the latitude and longitude boxes.

Figure 9.6 shows the Description tab selected. In the box, type a description of the location you are placemarking. Earth will recognize URLs that you place in the description and will automatically turn them into hyperlinks. It is possible to insert images in the description box, but this must be done using HTML code (the code is simple to use; examples are given at http://earth.google.com/userguide/v4/ug_editing.html#writing—scroll down to "Writing Descriptions").

The Style, Color tab allows you to choose the color, opacity, and size of your pushpin icon. The View tab offers a more exact way of positioning your placemark. The Altitude tab allows you to determine the placemark's distance from the ground in your viewer.

If you would like to change the pushpin icon to a different image, click the pushpin icon in the upper-right corner of the dialog box, and select from the menu or provide your own graphic from your computer. If you want to use something from the web, you have to capture it and save it to your computer first.

When you are finished, click OK to save your selections.

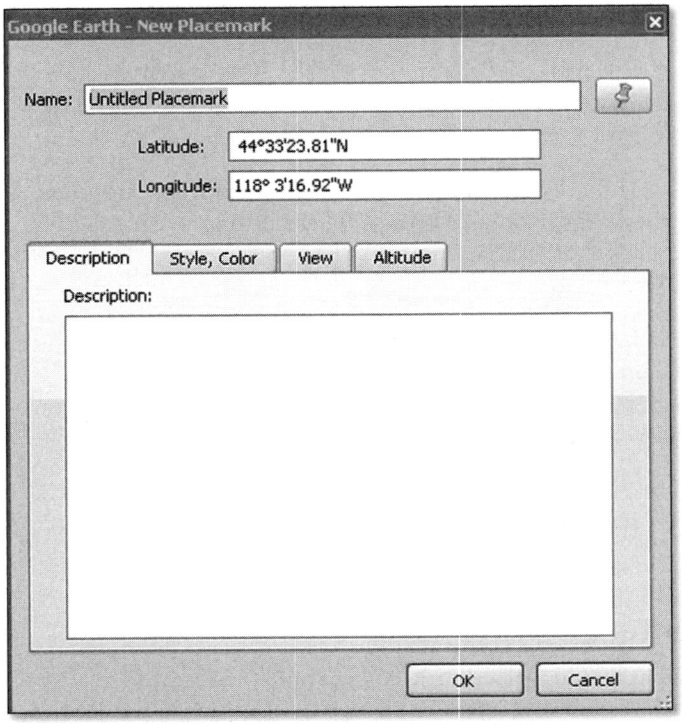

FIGURE 9.6. New Placemark dialog box

Image Overlay and Photos

Adding your own images will enhance your Google Earth project or file. Perhaps you have a picture of a main literary character, place, or object. Or perhaps you have a more detailed map you would like to include. These two options give you this opportunity.

Let's explore the difference between Image Overlay and Photos. Image Overlay conforms images to the shape of the Earth. In Photos, images exist in two-dimensional space between the globe and the screen. In viewing the Pacific Ocean, for example, you could place an Image Overlay of your face on the globe, and if you made it a little transparent, your face would resemble the man in the moon. The picture would conform to the curvature of the Earth. Use the same image and place it as a Photo and it shows as a rectangle covering the Pacific.

Locate the Image Overlay icon in the toolbar at the top of the page (see Fig. 9.2). Alternatively, select Add > Image Overlay. To add a photo select Add > Photo. The Add Photo dialog box looks like, and operates almost identically to, the Image Overlay dialog box illustrated and described immediately following this paragraph.

Here's an example of one way to use an image overlay: Locate an image of an old map of the 1904 World's Fair and lay it directly on top of the same area now (Forest Park in St. Louis, Missouri). Then you can make the image appear and disappear by toggling on the switch located just below the Places tab.

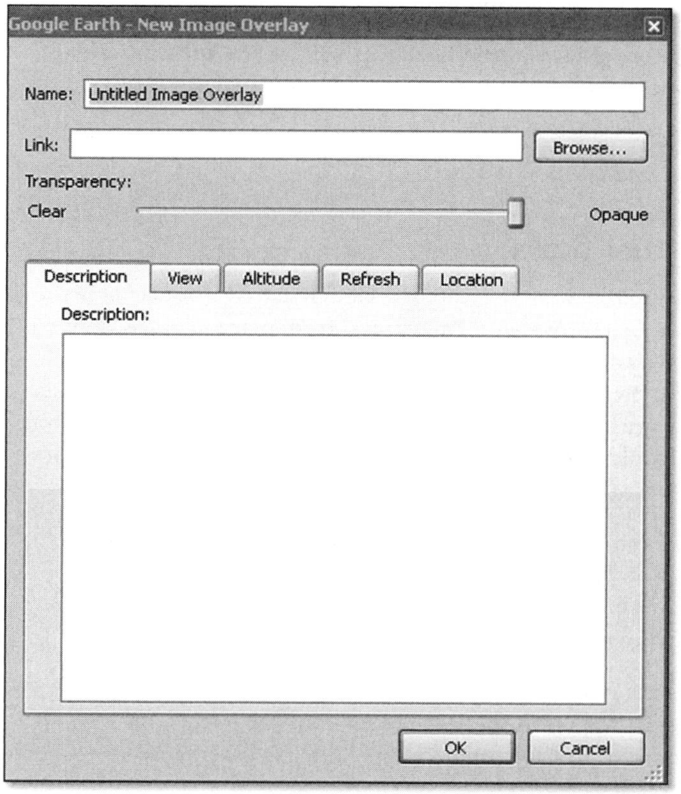

FIGURE 9.7. New Image Overlay dialog box

1. Adjust the positioning of your desired location in the 3D viewer by clicking the globe and moving it. Zoom in or out, depending on where you want to place the image and how large of an area you are going to cover. Select the Image Overlay icon from the toolbar in the top center of your screen. A dialog box will open (see Fig. 9.7).

2. Type a descriptive name for your image in the Name field.

3. Use the Browse button to locate your image file on your computer. Common image file types include JPEG, GIF, BMP, or TIFF.

4. If your image is on the web, type the web address (URL) of the image file in the Link field. This is different from using the web address of the web page the picture is located on. Typically, you can obtain the URL of the image by right-clicking on the image and selecting Copy Image Location from the sub menu (Firefox), or Copy Image Address (Safari). Of course, be sure to get permission if an image is copyrighted.

5. Use the transparency slider to select the opacity.

6. Using the Description tab, enter information for your overlay, such as text or links to additional websites.

7. Click OK to save your image and information.

The additional tabs in this area, Altitude, Refresh, and Location, will let you add additional specifications related to where your image is placed and refreshing intervals for viewing.

For more information about Image Overlays, go to Google's Help (http://earth.google.com/intl/en/userguide/v5/ug_imageoverlays.html).

Viewing and Creating Virtual Tours

Virtual tours, or simply tours, are animated movies created in Google Earth. Tours enable the telling of a story in a compelling way. In a tour, viewers may travel from place to place along custom-made routes, observe content, and listen to audio narration or music. You may watch an already-created tour or make your own. A great feature of tours is that a viewer may pause a tour at any time to "walk around" and explore the current view at their leisure, and then rejoin the tour with a single mouse click. In addition to an audio track, a tour may fly viewers around the globe and contain pop-up content balloons.

We already learned how to search for tours. Another way to acquire a tour is for someone to e-mail one to you or share it on a CD or flash drive, or you may create you own. You may play tours directly from your hard drive (if they have been saved to your computer), or you may play them within Google Earth. Those in Google Earth will be located in your My Places folder.

To play a tour, double click its file name in My Places, or its icon if playing from your hard drive. After a few moments, the tour will start to play in the 3D Viewer (tours are fairly large files, so they can take a little time to get started). The tour controls appear in the lower left corner of the 3D Viewer (see Fig. 9.8).

If you click the Go Back and Fast Forward buttons repeatedly, the tour will rewind or go forward more quickly. If the tour controls disappear from the screen, just mouse over the area where they were, and they will reappear.

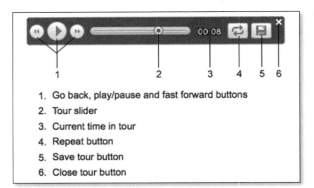

FIGURE 9.8. Tour controls for playing a tour

When a tour is playing, click and drag the view in the 3D Viewer to look up and down or side to side. The tour will continue to play. For more thorough exploration, pause the tour and you may navigate freely. When you resume the tour, the view will return to where you left off.

To record a tour, there are two ways to start. You may either click the small icon that looks like a camcorder in the icon toolbar at the top of the 3D Viewer, or you may select View > Tour. The controls for recording the tour will appear in the bottom left of the 3D Viewer (see Fig. 9.9).

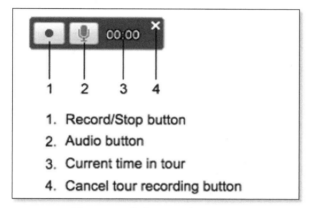

FIGURE 9.9. Tour controls for recording a tour

Record the tour by clicking the Record button. It will turn red to indicate that recording is taking place, and the time will start to count in seconds. The tour actually records what occurs on your 3D Viewer screen, so pan, tilt, zoom, rotate the globe, and fly just as if you were giving a live presentation. Fly from place to place by double clicking on placemarks in your Places panel.

Google has created an excellent tutorial on creating a virtual tour (http://earth.google.com/outreach/tutorial_kmltours.html#tourtips). It is detailed, clearly written, easy to follow, and contains a sample data set to download for practicing.

When you have finished creating your tour, click the Stop button. Your recorded tour will immediately start playing and the tour controls for recording will be replaced by those for playing. To save your tour, click File > Save. To save the tour to My Places, choose Save to My Places. To save to your hard drive, choose Save Place As.

TEACHER TIPS

- One of the first challenges that newcomers to Google Earth and Maps often encounter is how to decide which application to use and when to use it. Table 9.1 summarizes the main features of each App (from a slide presentation by Thomas Cooper at http://docs.google.com/present/view?id=dgdwkz9w_33d224pgft).

GOOGLE MAPS	GOOGLE EARTH
Viewed in a web browser; you must be connected to the Internet	A free software package that has to be downloaded
Custom maps may be created	Highly realistic depictions with tilt, rotate, and zoom functions as well as 3D terrain and buildings
Collaboration with others is easy	
Provides map, satellite, and street-level views	Virtual flights may be done within much of the depicted content
Sharing is easy using web links	
May be embedded easily in a website or other Google Application	Use of overlays (layers) creates great opportunities for customization and learning

TABLE 9.1. Google Maps versus Google Earth. *Used with permission.*

It's best to start working with Google Maps before moving on to Google Earth. First, Maps is a bit simpler to learn and manipulate. Second, many of the features in Maps are also present in Earth, so when Maps users encounter these features in Earth, they will have a better understanding of their functions. A useful metaphor might be to consider Maps as the on-ramp to the Earth superhighway.

■ Google Earth is not only about geography; it represents a powerful way to connect many types of information to location. For example, with a view of the United States, placemarks may be placed for each of the locations in Steinbeck's *The Grapes of Wrath*. Content may be added to each placemark, including photos of the location, page numbers where the place is featured in the book, or recordings of students reading Steinbeck's descriptions of the area. Google Certified Teacher (and contributor to this book) Jerome Burg pioneered this approach, and calls it Google Lit Trips. His website (www.GoogleLitTrips.com) now contains dozens of Lit Trips for Grades K–16.

■ In a Google Earth file on the Lewis and Clark expedition (www.gearthblog.com/blog/archives/2005/11/lewis_and_clark.html), the historical, geographical, and literary aspects of the trip were merged by noting the routes taken and key stops made. These were combined with selected contemporary diary entries from members of the expedition team. Viewers may tilt the view of key sites to see the tremendous variations between flat and mountainous terrain, explore additional folders to learn about the Louisiana Purchase (which prompted the trip), and even activate the Roads layer to compare what exists today to what existed then.

It is important to understand that these large-scale projects do not necessarily need to be constructed by one student or one teacher working alone. Creation of interdisciplinary, collaborative efforts such as these make learning come alive for students, cause it to be ingrained deep in their memories, and contribute to development of lifelong learning skills.

■ Google has produced an interactive game to help beginners quickly learn how to use Earth. It's the most painless way we know of to become familiar with Earth. Access it at http://earth.google.com/support/bin/static.py?hl=en&page=guide.cs&ctx=go&guide=22550.

- For beginning users of Google Earth (as well as those who are more advanced) Google Earth Lessons (http://gelessons.com) is an outstanding resource. Designed by another Google Certified Teacher who touts it as "GE lessons for teachers, by teachers," it includes lessons, a community of discussion forums, pictures for use in GE lessons, and a blog from the site's author. Readers will find the lessons area particularly helpful. It contains how-tos for the basics, and examples of student-controlled lessons, teacher-controlled lessons, and mini-sized lesson starters.

- Thomas Cooper has also posted an uncommonly rich collection of ideas for beginning and intermediate Google Earth–based lessons for preschool to advanced placement educators at these sites:

    Pre-School Classroom:
      http://docs.google.com/Doc?id=dgdwkz9w_65dzbp67gs

    Lower School Classroom (Grades 1–5):
      http://docs.google.com/Doc?id=dgdwkz9w_66dvcqqbrh

    Middle School Classroom (Grades 6–8):
      http://docs.google.com/Doc?id=dgdwkz9w_68dp4wdxcc

    Upper School Classroom (Grades 9–12):
      http://docs.google.com/Doc?id=dgdwkz9w_69chpv96f8

- These websites will give you the opportunity to explore, learn, and share additional fertile resources.

    Archive of *The Sightseer* monthly newsletter about Google Earth (*dating back to 2004*):
      http://bbs.keyhole.com/ubb/ubbthreads.php?ubb=postlist&Board=13&page=1

    Atomic Learning Tutorials (*fee applies*):
      http://movies.atomiclearning.com/k12/google_earth

    GoogleEarthGoods: a terrific collection of resources for Google Earth and Maps, put together by Google Certified Teacher, Cindy Lane:
      GoogleEarthGoods.pbworks.com

    Geo Education: www.google.com/educators/geo.html

    Geo Education Classroom Ideas: www.google.com/educators/geo_class.html

    Google Earth Blog: www.gearthblog.com

    Google Earth Community: http://bbs.keyhole.com/ubb/ubbthreads.php/Cat/0

    Google Earth Education Community:
      http://edweb.tusd.k12.az.us/dherring/ge/googleearth.htm

    Google Earth User's Guide Project: http://googlearthusersguide.blogspot.com

    Google KML Gallery of tours (*several dozen*):
      http://earth.google.com/gallery/index.html

Google LatLong Blog: http://google-latlong.blogspot.com

Tech-Ease: Classroom Tech Help—podcasts by Luis F Perez to help you get started in Google Earth *(Requires iTunes):* http://deimos3.apple.com/WebObjects/Core. woa/Browse/usf.edu.1255574854.01282530001

- Don't forget that Google Earth is not confined solely to the land surface of our planet. It also contains bountiful resources for the moon, Mars, and the sky. Access these from the View menu at the top of the page. Click on Explore, and choose what you would like to view. It also contains a nifty Flight Simulator, located in the Tools menu at the top of the page.

- Google says it will give a free Google Earth Pro license to educators who plan to use it for purposes of teaching and research. To request the Pro license, send an e-mail to geec@google.com, identifying yourself as an educator. Google Earth Pro works much more rapidly than the free version, prints images with almost five times the resolution (4800 pixels vs. 1000 pixels), provides access to e-mail technical support, enables geographic identification of hundreds (even thousands) of addresses simultaneously, and computes area and radius of identified geolocations.

MORE GREAT
GOOGLE APPLICATIONS
FOR SCHOOLS

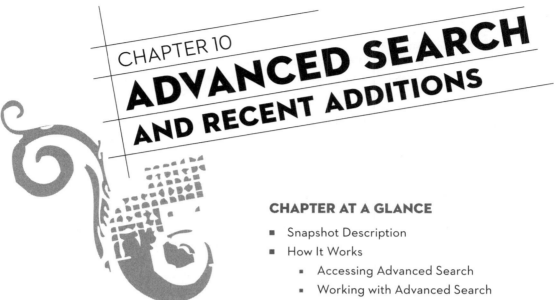

CHAPTER 10

ADVANCED SEARCH
AND RECENT ADDITIONS

CHAPTER AT A GLANCE

- Snapshot Description
- How It Works
    - Accessing Advanced Search
    - Working with Advanced Search
    - More Advanced Search Parameters
    - Recent Additions to Search
- Teacher Tips

SNAPSHOT DESCRIPTION

At some point, nearly everyone who performs Google searches wonders if there might be an easier or better way to improve results. Scrolling through a seemingly endless list of hits to find only bits and pieces of useful information can be frustrating and very time consuming.

That's when it's time to start using Advanced Search. This tool enables users to tailor searches with considerable precision, yielding a much higher percentage of quality results. This leads to happier researchers who produce higher quality work. Most users can master the basics of Advanced Search in an hour or two. From then on, they will be better able to clearly articulate what they are seeking, find it, and use it to achieve their goals.

HOW IT WORKS

Note that Google "simplified," or changed, its Advanced Search page in March 2008. This chapter addresses the March 2008 version. By most accounts, just about all the functions of the old version have been retained; the differences are in style and the words on the page.

Google has also added a search bar at the top of the page to show the syntax of the search query as you build it in the page below. This can work to your advantage, if you're interested, because it can teach you to write your search queries so you don't need Advanced Search at all. Everything done in Advanced Search can also be performed on the regular Google search page; you just need to know the proper language to use.

There are information archivists, librarians, media specialists, researchers, academics, and museum personnel who function as skilled professionals in the field of information retrieval. We do not pretend to possess their level of expertise. Our goal in this chapter is to help people who know a little bit about searching to become better searchers. We're oriented toward the general education consumer. If you find yourself desiring more information about skilled searching, a good next step is to consult with your school library media specialist or a public librarian.

Accessing Advanced Search

Most people go to Advanced Search from the basic Google search page (www.google.com). Just click on Advanced Search, to the right of the search box. The direct URL for Advanced Search is www.google.com/advanced_search?hl=en/.

Working with Advanced Search

Figure 10.1 shows the Advanced Search page. If you have not used Advanced Search very much, a great place to start is the blue bar at the top right of the page, where it reads Advanced Search Tips. This links to Google's Help area, which provides clear assistance. Of course, some people would rather just get started and then read the directions later. That's fine, too.

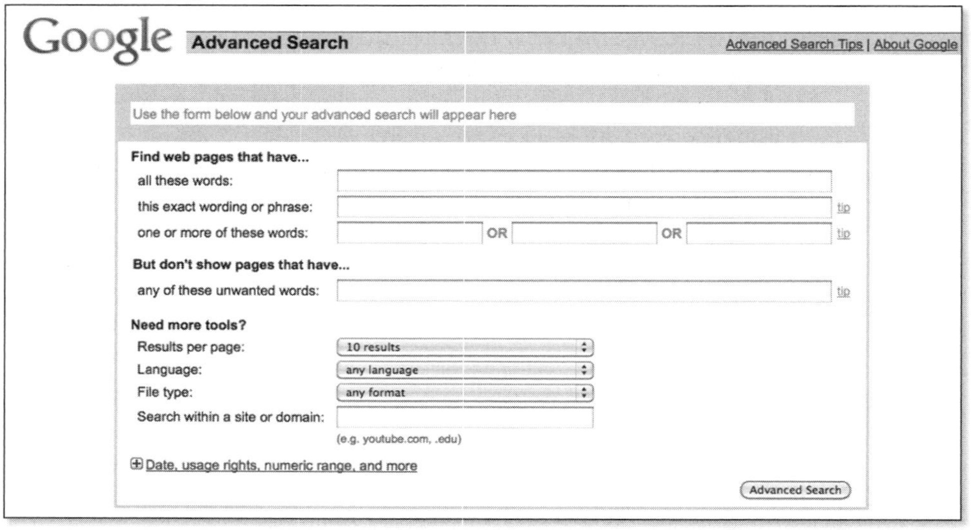

FIGURE 10.1. The Advanced Search page

Under that blue bar is a white box outlined in blue. The following phrase appears in the white box in gray letters: "Use the form below and your advanced search will appear here." As you enter information in the various boxes of the search form, you will see your search query being built, with all of Google's operators and syntax. As we said before, observing this is a good way to learn this language.

It is not necessary to use all the search boxes and tools in Advanced Search. You might use just one or two; that's fine. The idea is to use only the tools that will help shape your individual search.

Find the section headed "Find web pages that have … " followed by three lines of boxes. Let's explore them a bit.

All these words. The results of your search will contain all the words you type here. The words may be in the title or body of the resulting web pages, and they may not be all together in a phrase (ordered sequentially), but they will appear somewhere on the page of each returned result.

This exact wording or phrase. Words must appear exactly the way you have entered them—all together and in the same order. This is the same as putting a phrase in quotation marks in a regular Google search. Using this tool helps to focus, or narrow, your search; yielding results that are more likely to contain the information you seek.

One or more of these words. This tool can be useful when you have a general idea of what you're looking for, and are trying to get a clearer idea of the breadth and depth of the topic as a whole. After reading a few results, you should be able to go back and search again, this time with a more specific idea of what you'd like to zero in on.

For example, you might be interested in how the United States became involved in fighting in Afghanistan; so you might enter terms such as "Afghanistan," "United States," and "war" (without the quotation marks) in the All These Words box, since you know you definitely want information about that. In the One Or More Of These Words box you might enter "history," "21st century," and "bin Laden" (again, without the quotes). Try this example and then change some of the words to see how your results differ. As you go through the results, you may find you want to know more about Russia, the Taliban, Pakistan, and some other topics as well.

The next section of Advanced Search is titled "But don't show pages that have..." and consists of just one box: Any Of These Unwanted Words. Just as it reads, this is where to enter words you wish to exclude from the results. To continue with our example, suppose in our search about Afghanistan we decided to focus on only politics and were not particularly interested in economics. Words we might enter in this box might include "economics," "economy," "petroleum," "oil," and "opium" (again, no quotes).

The next section is titled "Need more tools?" and contains four lines of boxes that enable users to make a number of useful choices:

Results per page. This allows selection of anywhere from 10 to 100 results to be contained on each page of results. If you have to scan through hundreds or thousands of hits, it can be useful to make pages bigger.

Language. This allows specification of the language for results.

File type. This enables users to specify what type of file results should be. This can be quite helpful. For example, you may just be looking for PowerPoint files or Excel spreadsheets. When searching for articles, PDFs are likely to be better written than most websites. Shockwave Flash will yield videos.

Search within a site or domain. This enables users to indicate a single website to search within or a single domain, such as .edu, .org, .gov, or .com. You might be searching for images only from the Library of Congress or only want lesson plans from ThinkFinity (formerly MarcoPolo). Similarly, when searching a controversial topic such as birth control or global warming, you might only want results from .edu sites, to strive for objective presentations.

After filling in the desired search boxes for your particular query, click the Advanced Search button on the lower right, to obtain your results.

Note the topic-specific search engines located at the very bottom of the page; educators will likely be interested in several of them. Google Book Search, Google Scholar, and Google News Archive enable specialized full-text searches of a rapidly growing collection of hundreds of thousands of books (Book Search), scholarly publications (Scholar), and past news articles (News Archive). Book Search and Scholar have separate chapters devoted to them in this book. Educators may also be interested in the search engines for the U.S. Government and Universities.

More Advanced Search Parameters

Note the blue command with the plus sign (+) next to it near the bottom of the Advanced Search page. It reads: "Date, usage rights, numeric range, and more." Click on it to open more search options.

Date. Allows specification of results from within a few hours to a year.

Usage rights. Enables users to choose among levels of copyright protection. Using the Creative Commons categories, you may select results that are free to redistribute, redistribute and copy, redistribute and copy commercially, or subject to regular fair use controls. This is particularly useful for images and music.

Where your keywords show up. Where your key search terms are displayed on a website can be an indication of how important, or central, they are to the message of that particular site. This control enables users to select locations in the URL, title, and body of a page, as well as in links to a page.

Region. Allows users to specify the country of origin results. This can be particularly helpful when researching news reports, since national interests on particular topics can vary tremendously. For example, how do English-language newspapers in Egypt, India, Pakistan, China, Australia, and South Africa vary in their reportage of current events in Afghanistan and Iraq?

Numeric Range. Permits specification of a set of numbers between which results must fall. For example, users might search for camcorders costing between $200 and $500, cities in Russia located between 35 degrees and 42 degrees north latitude, or articles about pterodactyls appearing between 2002 and 2007.

SafeSearch. Turns Google's SafeSearch off and on. The default setting for Google Search is Moderate SafeSearch. The control located here enables users to go between Strict SafeSearch and Moderate SafeSearch. To turn SafeSearch off completely, one must go to the Google Global Preferences page (www.google.com/preferences/), or the Preferences command next to the search box on the regular Google search page, under the Advanced Search command.

According to Google, strict filtering is intended to address both explicit text and images, moderate filtering is intended to address explicit images, and no filtering doesn't screen anything. Bear in mind that Google's filtering is performed entirely digitally; human eyes do not scan the pages. As a result, *filtering does not capture all objectionable content.* When students encounter objectionable content, and they will, be prepared ahead of time for how you are going to deal with the situation. Your school's Acceptable Use Policy and Discipline Code should address these issues as well.

Under the heading "Page-specific tools," readers will find two additional search parameters. Both of them allow identification of additional websites that may contain information relevant to your particular search beyond the search specification entered in the search boxes. To obtain results using these tools, enter the URL of a specific website into the search box and click Search.

Find pages similar to the page. Provides links to pages that are comparable to the page entered in the search box. This can be particularly useful if your search does not yield a sufficient amount of information.

Find pages that link to the page. Provides a list of pages that are linked to the page entered in the search box. Either the site entered in the search box has decided a linked site is worthy of being connected to it, or the linked site has decided the site entered in the search box is one it wants to be connected to. This can be useful for the same reason previously mentioned, and also as a measure of reliability. Generally speaking, a site with a large number of links is more likely to be reliable than a site with only a few links. However, this should be used as only one factor among several in assessing a site's reliability.

Recent Additions to Search

Google constantly strives to improve its products and services by adding new features and refining old ones. Google Search, perhaps Google's premier service, receives a great deal of attention and may be updated or changed several times a year. While technically not part of Advanced Search, the following features are, nevertheless, important to note.

Personalizing the Search Homepage

Want something different from the plain, white, standard Google Search page? Now you can personalize the background with an image of your choice. Click on the words Change Background Image at the bottom left of the Search page to open the dialog box. You may select an image from your computer, a Picasa Web Album, a public gallery provided by Google, or one from a group of editor's picks.

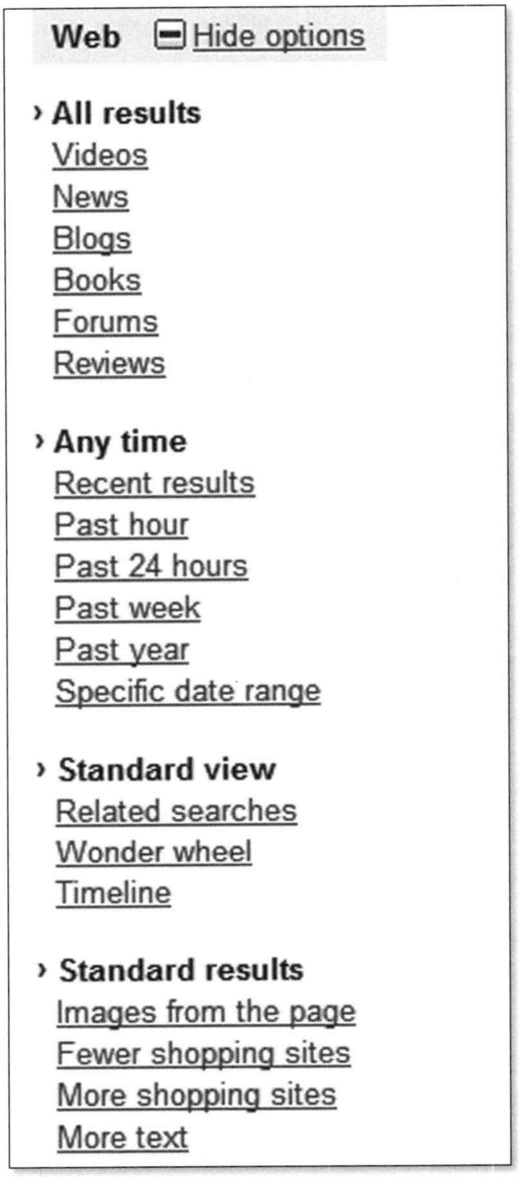

Web ⊟ Hide options

> **All results**
>   Videos
>   News
>   Blogs
>   Books
>   Forums
>   Reviews

> **Any time**
>   Recent results
>   Past hour
>   Past 24 hours
>   Past week
>   Past year
>   Specific date range

> **Standard view**
>   Related searches
>   Wonder wheel
>   Timeline

> **Standard results**
>   Images from the page
>   Fewer shopping sites
>   More shopping sites
>   More text

FIGURE 10.2. The list of Show Options commands

Stars in Search

Search makes it easy to note great sites you discover in the search results page. Just to the right of the title of every search result, or hit, there is a faint outline of a 5-pointed star. Click on the star and it turns yellow (i.e., the link has been "starred"). The next time you perform a search on the same, or closely related, topic, previously starred sites on that topic will be listed at the top of your results. Try it! It's very easy and very practical.

In addition, all of the starred results will show up on your Google Bookmarks page (www.google.com/bookmarks/). To use Bookmarks you need to have a Google account.

To remove a yellow star, just click on it. That site will no longer appear at the top of search results nor in your Google Bookmarks.

Search Options Panel

Whenever users conduct a search, the Show Options command displays at the top of the search results. Click the Show Options command and a panel opens on the left side of the screen (see Fig. 10.2).

These commands permit rapid filtering of search results and, in some cases, may be combined with each other. For example, suppose a student is researching volcanoes and wishes to see videos of volcanoes that have been posted within the past week. First, the student would enter "volcanoes" in the standard Google search box. When the 951,000 results come back in roughly one-tenth of a second, the student can click Videos to eliminate all results that are not videos. From the 32,800 videos returned, the student may select Past Week to narrow the list to a mere 837 videos. The student may then select the videos by length (short, medium, or long). In our search, there were 286 videos of volcanoes in the last week that were between 4 and 20 minutes long.

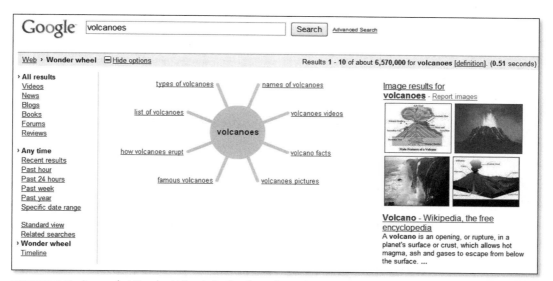

FIGURE 10.3. A sample Wonder Wheel display for *volcanoes*

Clicking on Forums returns results only from discussions of the search topic. These can be quite opinionated and also wildly inappropriate for a student population. Appropriate preparation is called for when using this option. Reviews returns only reviews on the topic under consideration. For example, suppose you were looking for a field trip destination, or a trade book for the class to read; Reviews could give you what you want very quickly. On a personal level, restaurant reviews, movie reviews, and product reviews are all at your fingertips. Once returned, you can filter them for the most recent, or simply sort them by the date posted. Google will surely add more ways to filter Search results in this manner in the future.

Wonder Wheel

Many young or inexperienced searchers often struggle to find the correct keywords to enter in a search in order to limit the number of results returned. The next four features (Wonder Wheel, Timeline, Related Searches, and Google Squared) are tailor-made to assist in this process. They will help not only the young or inexperienced but everyone to get better results faster.

As you can see in Figure 10.3, the Wonder Wheel takes the topic in the search box and places it at the center of a diagram that displays a number of associated search topics branching off from it. Many users of graphic organizers or writing webs will be familiar with this display scheme. Search results continue to be displayed on the right side of the page.

Each of the spokes of the Wonder Wheel may be clicked, and a new Wonder Wheel opens with the subtopic on display in the center and new sub-subtopics branching off from it. Users of Wonder Wheel may continue to branch off from a main topic until they arrive at the desired subtopic in a very short time. Try it; you'll love it!

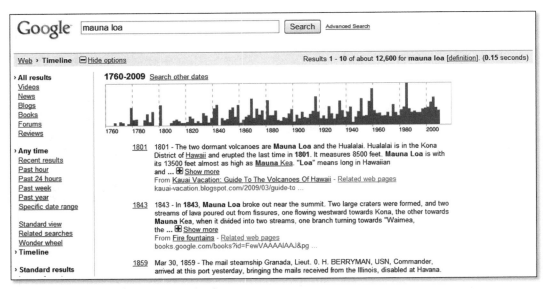

FIGURE 10.4. A sample Timeline display for *Mauna Loa*

Timeline

A second search simplifier in the Options list is Timeline. Often, searchers wish to find out about a topic as it develops over time, or what was happening with a particular topic at a certain time. For example, in a search about volcanoes, a searcher might become interested in a particular volcano; let's say Mauna Loa. Entering *Mauna Loa* in the standard search box and clicking on Timeline yields the page shown in Figure 10.4.

The searcher may then identify a particular period in time to examine more carefully. The period from 1940 to 1960 seems to have a fairly large number of spikes, perhaps indicating eruptions or other significant events related to the volcano. Click on the box for that time frame and obtain a similar timeline for only the period in question. The search results returned below the timeline will be for only the selected period. It is possible to get as detailed as one month within a particular year on the timeline; the results are listed chronologically by date within the month. Obviously, this enables rapid, precise searching by chronology.

Related Searches

The third search simplifier in the Options list is Related Searches. It functions similarly to Wonder Wheel, in that it provides a list of topics connected in some way to the original term entered in the search box. Some of the search terms returned by Related Searches will be the same as those returned by Wonder Wheel, but Related Searches will usually return more terms. Wonder Wheel may work more effectively if one has a reasonable idea of what one is looking for but doesn't quite know how to phrase the search. On the other hand, if searchers have a general idea of what they are looking for, Related Searches may provide a larger list from which to select and provide new ideas for investigation.

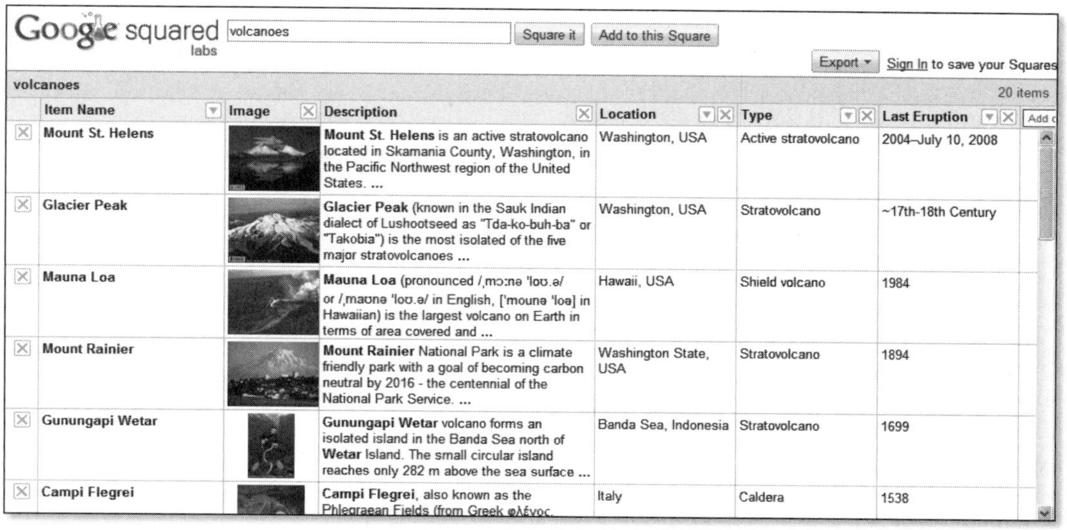

FIGURE 10.5. A sample Google Squared display for *volcanoes*

Google Squared

The fourth Search simplifier, Google Squared, is, as of the summer of 2009, still in an experimental phase at Google. It may not yet be fully functional or always yield the kinds of results you may be looking for, but when it works like it's supposed to, it's awesome.

Access Google Squared at www.google.com/squared/. There probably will be other ways to do this in the future. Google Squared takes the term for which you are searching and organizes facts related to the topic as a table. *Squared* comes from the idea that the cells of the table resemble squares. Let's search on "volcanoes" this time. Entering the word in Google Squared's search box returns the table shown in Figure 10.5.

If an item you don't want appears in the list, simply click on the faint Close icon at the beginning of the row and the item disappears from the list. Similarly, if you wish to remove a column of information, simply click on the Close icon at its top right heading.

Users may also add rows (items) and columns (information categories). To add an item, scroll to the bottom of the list and click in the Add Items box. A dialog box will open that allows you to type in your own item, import items from a table, or select items from a menu provided. Similarly, to add a column, look for the Add Columns box (to the top right of the last column). A dialog box will open affording a number of choices or the option to add your own information.

To save squares, you must sign in using your Google account. The Save command is located at the top right of the square. Squares are saved online. To access saved squares, click on the Saved Squares option on the top right of the screen. To save your square on your computer as a CSV file, which can be opened in Excel, use the Export command (next to the Save command).

Access to saved squares is available from the Google Squared home page or from any Squares results page. The Saved Squares command is located in the upper-right corner of the page in both instances.

To conduct another search and add its results to your existing square results, leave the square visible on your screen, enter a new search term in the Google Squared search box and click Add To This Square. The results will be added to your existing square using the same column information categories. To start a new search using an empty square, just click the Start With An Empty Square command at the bottom of the page.

Search Options for Images

Google has simplified the search process for images in much the same way as it has for general web search, by providing an Options panel. After conducting any Image Search, a Show Options command appears at the top left of the results. Clicking Show Options shows the Google Images Options menu (see Fig. 10.6).

Let's suppose you decide to search for images of birthday cakes. When we tried this, we received almost 12.5 million hits. Using the Image Options filters, we could add criteria to the search in numerous ways: by size, type, or color. By selecting medium-sized line drawings that are blue, we narrowed down the 12.5 million choices to six in less than five seconds.

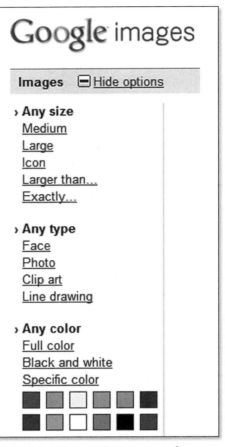

FIGURE 10.6. Images Options menu for Google Images

Creative Commons Image Search

As educators, we should teach our students proper respect for copyright when images are used in student work. Google has made it relatively easy to search only for images that carry an appropriate Creative Commons license for public use. To perform this type of search, it is necessary to use Advanced Image Search.

Access Advanced Imaged Search on the Image Search page, to the far right of the search box.

In the Usage Rights dialog box, users have the following choices:

- Not filtered by license

- Labeled for reuse

- Labeled for commercial reuse

- Labeled for reuse with modification

- Labeled for commercial reuse with modification

In most school situations, the first choice will be satisfactory. Select it and the only images returned in a search will be those that are OK to use without obtaining copyright permission from the owner (permission has already been given through Creative Commons).

TEACHER TIPS

- Help for Advanced Search is at Google's support page (www.google.com/support/?ctx=web).

- Information literacy has emerged as a top priority in today's schools—in our view, it is just as important as reading, writing, and mathematics. Searching exists as only one part of a well-articulated program of information literacy. Just as students are educated to engage in prewriting activities prior to commencement of a composition, so too, is it important for them to engage in a structured sequence of search strategy formulation prior to actually conducting a search. Then, when results are obtained, they must also learn to effectively evaluate the relevance and reliability of what they encounter. These are not simple skills, and they are especially crucial today. Unlike only 20 years ago, when simply finding information was a critical skill, today and in the future, knowing how to evaluate and apply information to solving problems have become the critical learning factors. Knowing how to effectively use Google's Advanced Search constitutes a key element in any adult or child's information literacy repertoire.

It is beyond the scope of this book to launch into an extended discussion of information literacy. However, we would like to suggest to readers a number of excellent resources on the web for further investigation:

Approaches to Information and Communication Literacy:
http://eduscapes.com/tap/topic72.htm
A brief overview of the field, with many useful links.

Big6: www.big6.com
A very popular information literacy model.

Evaluating Web Pages: www.sdst.org/shs/library//evaluating.html
Extensive quality links from Joyce Valenza, a great high school librarian in Pennsylvania.

IMSA 21st Century Information Fluency Project: http://21cif.imsa.edu
A complete online program with lesson plans, projects, and interactive student web tools.

Information Literacy: www.sunlink.ucf.edu/presentations/fetc2004/infolit.html
A very comprehensive and well-organized teacher portal providing access to an extensive collection of resources.

Google Guide: www.googleguide.com
> *An interactive tutorial and reference to Google search, with many tips and tricks. (Not affiliated with Google.)*

Lesson on Google Advanced Search: http://videos.webpronews.com/2008/04/09/lesson-on-google-advanced-search/
> *An informative 3-minute video on the basics of using Advanced Search, intended for adults.*

Search Education Lessons: www.google.com/educators/p_websearch.html
> *A collection of lessons developed by Google Certified Teachers for use in classrooms to teach effective searching skills.*

TRAILS: http://trails-9.org
> *Tools for real-time assessment of information literacy skills (TRAILS).*

Obe Hostetter, Rockingham County (VA) schools: www.rockingham.k12.va.us/resources/google.doc
> *A helpful tutorial handout for teaching advanced search skills.*

WebProNews: http://videos.webpronews.com/2008/04/09/lesson-on-google-advanced-search/
> *A great video tutorial (for teachers) on Google Advanced Search.*

Edublogs.tv: www.edublogs.tv/play.php?vid=2368
> *Another useful video on Google Search Tips.*

CHAPTER 11
CALENDAR

SNAPSHOT DESCRIPTION

When you start using Google Calendar, you'll be amazed at the many things you can do in addition to organizing your personal schedule. This application allows you to create, share, and collaborate on calendars with individuals or groups. You can easily create multiple, color-coded calendars as you work on various projects, and you can send invitations and receive automatic reminders on other devices, including your phone.

You may subscribe to public calendars that send automatic notices of events such as holidays, movie releases, cultural or sports events, and weather forecasts. One of the other great things about Google Calendar is how easy it is to embed a calendar in another Google App such as a Sites or Blogger page. You can also attach agendas or other types of Google Docs to any event in the calendar.

There's more! Calendar has a feature called Tasks, which enables you to create and maintain a very functional to-do list. You can check the availability of friends for meetings or events, and you can even use Calendar offline. That's right: by downloading Google Gears, you can use Calendar (and many other Google Apps, such as Docs) even when you are not connected to the Internet.

HOW IT WORKS

Getting Started

To get to Google Calendar go to http://calendar.google.com. A Google account is required for this application. Create or sign in to your Google account. This is how you will access features to create and share calendars.

The first time you sign in to Google Calendar, after you have logged in to your Google account, you will be required to provide information about yourself: your name, the country where you are located, and your time zone.

Get to Know Your Primary Calendar

Your primary Calendar is the first calendar you see when you sign in. The Google Calendar search box displays at the top left corner of the page. Use this to search your primary Calendar and any subcalendars you have created.

The current date range is always displayed in bold type and shows the current day, week, or month on view—depending on the view preference you have selected. To the left of the current date range are two arrow icons. Click on the left arrow to view past dates, and click on the right arrow to view future dates.

Today, the day on which you are currently viewing the Calendar, is always highlighted in yellow. The default view displays the current 24-hour day, presented hour-by-hour. No matter what your view preference is (Day, Week, Month, etc.), the current date will always be highlighted in yellow.

Spend a few moments choosing your view preference by clicking one of the tabs found on the upper right: Day, Week, Month, or 4 Days (this tab can be modified to show a custom range of 2 days to 4 weeks; select Settings > General > Custom view to modify). In Figure 11.1, Week has been chosen as the view preference.

Also note the Agenda option, to the right of the 4 Days tab. Click on Agenda to see a summary list of all events on the primary Calendar. The summary view may be expanded to show greater detail for each event by clicking on the Expand All command (upper-left corner) in the Agenda window. This is an alternative way to view your scheduled events without the display boxes of a typical calendar.

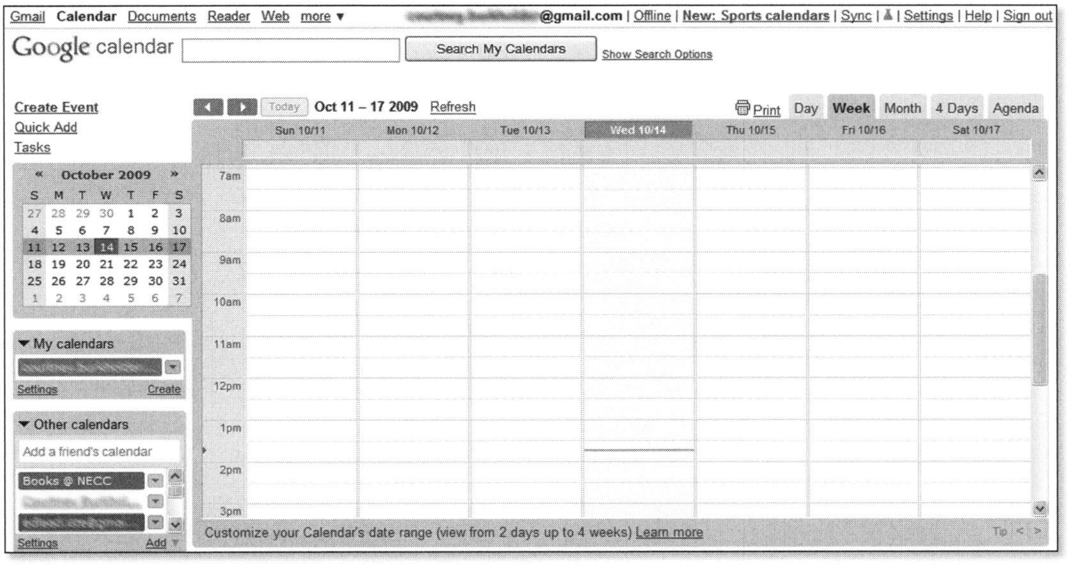

FIGURE 11.1. Week View of the primary Calendar page

Settings, or Calendar Settings (the terms are used interchangeably here), enables you to modify many preferences for your calendars.

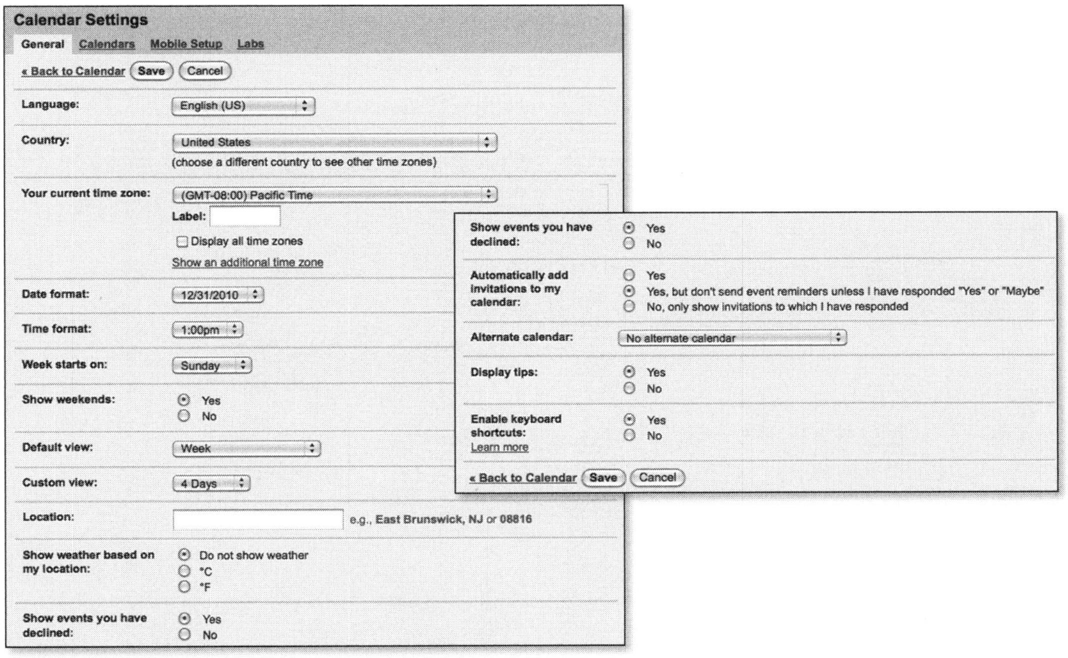

FIGURE 11.2. The Calendar Settings window

In Figure 11.2, the General menu is selected. This menu controls many of the display options for your calendars. Most of the choices are self-explanatory. Note the Custom View selection about halfway down Figure 11.2. This is where changes may be made to the 4 Days tab mentioned previously.

In addition to the General menu, there are three other menus: Calendars, Mobile Setup, and Labs. Click Calendars to view a list of all the calendars to which you have access. Mobile Setup enables a connection between your calendars and your cell phone. Calendars can display on an Internet-capable phone, and you may make entries to calendars using SMS text messaging. Labs lets you access experimental features that Google has released to the public. As of this writing, the list of features in Labs contains Background Image, Attach Google Docs (more on this later), World Clock, Jump to Date, Next Meeting, and Free or Busy (to check on which of your friends are free or busy right now). You may also access Labs directly from the primary Calendar page by clicking the small beaker icon.

Creating Events

There are five ways to enter events in your calendar: (1) Create Event, (2) Quick Add, (3) click and type, (4) add from My Calendars, and (5) SMS text messaging on your cell phone.

Create Event

The Create Event link, found on the upper left of the calendar page, opens a form allowing you to enter information about your event. As you complete this form, you can enable reminder features, invite guests via e-mail, and attach Google documents (if you have enabled this feature in Labs).

Click on Create Event, and the window shown in Figure 11.3 opens.

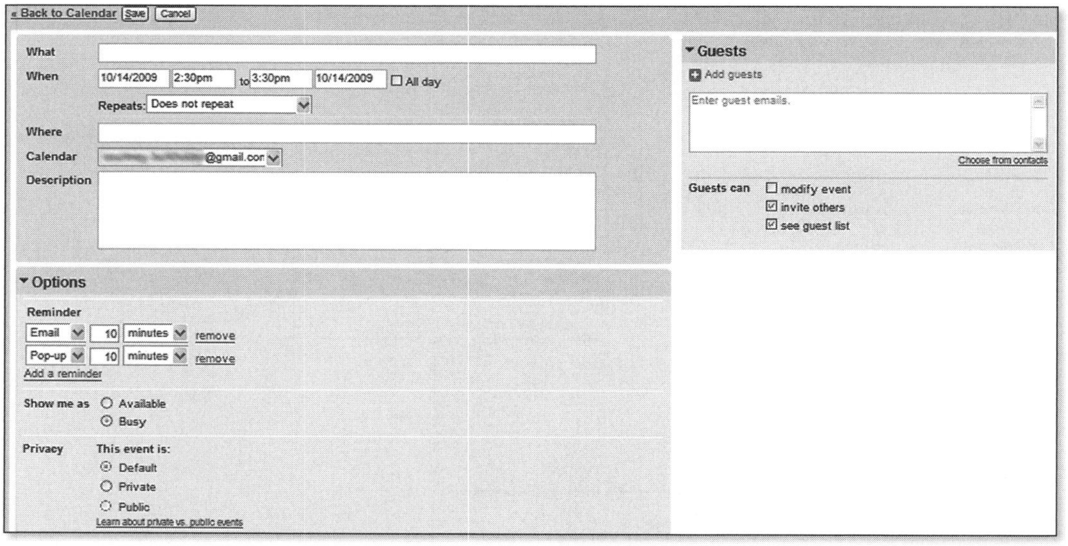

FIGURE 11.3. Create Event form

Let's look at some of the options in this window. The Repeats drop-down menu provides options for recurring events. Select the appropriate repeat cycle and the event will be entered into your calendar automatically, saving you from making repetitive entries. The Calendar drop-down menu specifies on which of your calendars the entry will display. Attachment enables attachment of a Google document. You must enable the Attachment option using the Labs menu described previously or the option will not be displayed.

The Reminder option allows you to enable an event reminder to be sent as either a pop-up message or an e-mail, according to the schedule you specify (from 5 minutes to 1 week before the event). For multiple reminders, click Add A Reminder. For no reminders, click Remove.

The Show Me As option displays your availability to others viewing your calendar. If you don't want your friends to disturb you during an event, check the Busy radio button. If you don't mind being contacted, check the Available radio button. The Privacy option sets the privacy status of an event. For more information about these choices, click on the link labeled Learn About Private Vs. Public Events.

Invite guests to this event by entering their e-mail addresses in the text box on the upper right (under the Guests menu). To add multiple guests, separate their e-mail addresses with a comma. Click the Choose From Contacts link if you have a Gmail account and would like to include individuals from your contact list. Finally, you can select permissions options for guests—Modify Event, Invite Others or See Guest List. (This is identical to permissions for collaborators in Google Docs.) Your invited guests need not have a Google Calendar account to view the calendars to which you have invited them.

Remember to click the Save button at the bottom of the form when you have finished.

Use Quick Add

With Quick Add, you just type the "what" and "when" of an event and Google Calendar can actually place the event on your calendar.

Click the Quick Add link on the upper left. In the text box that appears, type the "what and when" of your event. For example, type: "faculty meeting Sept 10 3 pm" and click the Add icon on the right. A highlighted message will be displayed across the top of your calendar, indicating that your event has been added. The message includes the title description of your event, along with the day, date, and time of your event. To edit or add additional details, click the title, which is your link to the event. There is also an Undo command in case you want to remove the event.

Click and Type to Add an Event

Another way of adding events to your calendar is to simply click the event date on the calendar. Click and drag your cursor from the desired beginning time to the ending time for the event. The space will be darkened and an abbreviated event form will pop up. Fill in the description of your event; the date and time will automatically be displayed. If you wish Calendar to provide viewers with a map of the event location, it is useful to give the address and city, or the name of a school or other well-known location and the city.

If you have more than one calendar, you will have to use the drop-down menu to specify a calendar for the event. Managing multiple calendars is discussed later in this chapter.

Click Create Event to save and place the event on your calendar, or click Edit Event Details to add more information.

Use My Calendars to Add an Event

Managing multiple calendars is discussed later in this chapter. When you have several calendars, it becomes useful to use the My Calendars menu to add events (see Fig. 11.1 to find the My Calendars option about halfway down on the left side). To add an event to any calendar on your list, click the drop-down menu next to its name and select Create Event On This Calendar. The Create Event form will open. When you save the information, it will be inserted into the correct calendar.

Use Your Phone to Add an Event

Simply send a text message to GVENT (48368). Provide the same information you would for a Quick Add. Google will enter the event into your primary calendar. This is a very convenient function when you're unable to access a computer. Text messaging charges may apply.

Creating Tasks

When you think about it, a task is a type of event—at least Google Calendar categorizes Tasks this way. Tasks functions as a very capable to-do list. It enters tasks into Calendars and enables users to print task lists, or view tasks by due date. Activate Tasks by clicking on the Tasks link just below the Quick Add link. A Tasks window will open to the right of the calendar view (see Fig. 11.4).

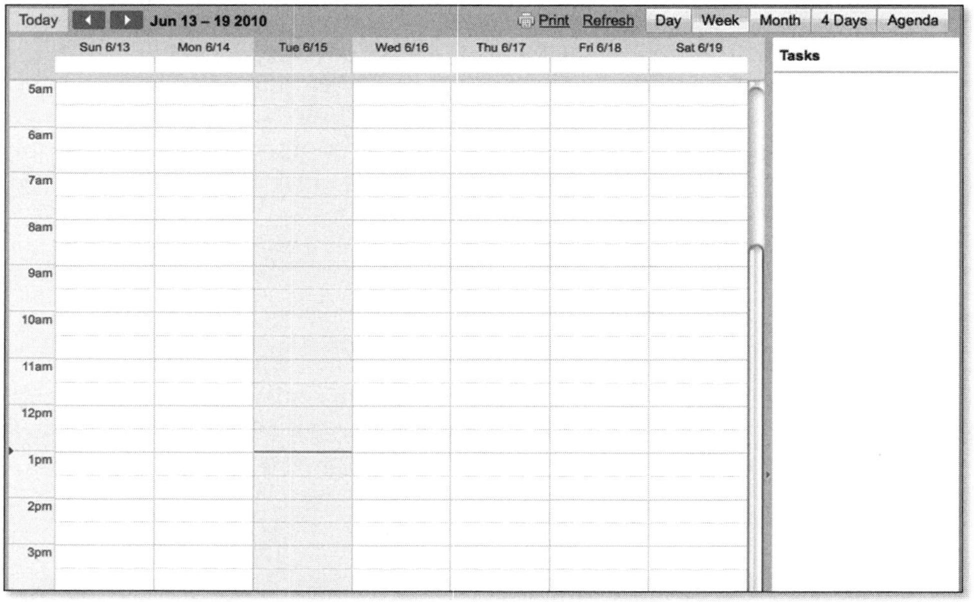

FIGURE 11.4. The Tasks window is shown to the right of a weekly calendar

Tasks works in Calendar and Gmail (more on this later). No doubt Google will add Tasks to more of its Apps in the future. The quickest way to add a task is to simply type in the first empty box that appears in the Task list. The Task box will expand as you type. It is good to get in the habit of starting each entry in the Task box with a due date so the task will be automatically entered into your calendar. If you forget to add the due date in the box, no problem, just click on the small > on the right end of the Task box and a new dialog box will open. You may add a due date, an explanatory note, or move the task to another Task list.

If the Task box already contains a task and another empty box is not visible, click on the Add icon (+) at the very bottom of the Task window. A new Task box will appear.

To change the order of your tasks, simply mouse over the Task box you wish to move. A dotted vertical bar will appear on the right end of the Task box. Mouse over the vertical bar and it will change into a hand. Click and drag the Task box using the hand, either up or down.

Another easy way to add a task is to click in the All Day area, which is the shaded row appearing directly below the calendar's dates (it does not have a time of day assigned to it). An all-day event is something that happens on a certain date but doesn't have a specific beginning or ending time, such as a holiday, birthday, anniversary, or due date for a task. In Figures 11.1 and 11.4, you can see the All Day area.

Click in the All Day area, and a dialog box will open. At the top, you have the choice to create an Event or a Task. The default setting is Event, and this dialog box may be used as an alternative way to enter an Event on the selected date. However, to enter a task, click the Task option, and the dialog box changes to allow entry of a task. Enter the description of the task in the Task box and any additional information in the Note box. Then click Create Task and the task will appear in the All Day area on your calendar and also in your Task list.

To mark a task as completed, click the small check box to the left of the Task box. A line will be drawn through the task title to indicate its completion.

To delete a task in the Calendar window, select the task in the All Day area and click Delete in the pop-up window. To delete the task in the Task window, select the task from the list and click the Delete icon (a trash can symbol) at the bottom of the Task window.

To manage lists within the Task window, click on the List icon (three bullet list lines) to the right of the trash can at the bottom of the Task window. This enables creation of new lists, renaming of existing lists, and deletions of lists. To take other actions in the Task window, click on the Actions menu at the bottom of the window. Actions include formatting the appearance of task descriptions, printing the task list, viewing completed tasks, sorting tasks by due date, and clearing the task list.

Mini Calendar

This at-a-glance, one-month view makes it easy to navigate to specific days, weeks, or months. It is located on the left side of the main calendar view, about one-third of the way down. Click on any date in the Mini Calendar to show the calendar for that date in the main work window. To display an entire week, click and drag across the week. To show the month view in the main area, click on the name of the month at the top. To display other months in the Mini Calendar, click on the left-pointing or right-pointing double arrows on either side of the month name.

Use My Calendars to Create and Manage Multiple Calendars

With the ability to create multiple calendars, you can manage different schedules for multiple projects, classes, and assignments. To add new calendars, go to My Calendars, which is found under the Mini Calendar on the left side of the page.

To create a new calendar, click on the Create command in the lower-right corner of My Calendars. Complete the form that opens and click Create Calendar when finished. The name of your new calendar will appear in My Calendars. To delete a calendar, click on the Settings command on the bottom left of My Calendars then select Delete for that calendar. Summary information for all of your calendars is shown here, and you may manage many of their properties. It is not possible to delete your primary calendar but if you select Delete, you can delete all the entries currently in the calendar.

To open a calendar in the main display area, click on its name in My Calendars. To manage a calendar in My Calendars, click on the drop-down menu on the right end of the calendar title. A window will open, enabling several options. The colored boxes allow you to choose the display color for the name of the selected calendar in My Calendars.

Other Calendars

Use Other Calendars (on the left, near the bottom) to add calendars from friends, subscribe to public calendars, add holiday or fun calendars, or view weather information.

To add holiday or fun calendars, click on Add > Browse Interesting Calendars at the bottom right of Other Calendars and select the calendars you wish. To add friends' calendars, go to Add > Add A Friend's Calendar. You will be prompted to add the e-mail address of your friend to view the calendar you seek. If your friend has not made a calendar public, you will see a message to send to your friend requesting that the calendar be shared.

To add a calendar by URL, click on Add > Add By URL. The calendar you are trying to add must be in iCal format. For further information about adding calendars by URL, follow the directions on the Google Calendar support site (www.google.com/support/calendar/bin/answer. py?answer=37104). For information on how to Import calendar events from other applications such as Microsoft Outlook, Apple iCal, and Yahoo! Calendar, go to www.google.com/support/calendar/bin/answer.py?answer=83126.

Embedding a Calendar in a Website, Blog, or Wiki

In addition to inviting friends to view your calendar, you can place your Calendar in a website, Google Site, blog, or wiki.

Please note that before you can embed a calendar, it must be in Public View. To make a calendar public, go to the My Calendars panel and find the name of the calendar you wish to make public. Click the drop-down menu to the right of the calendar title and select Share This Calendar then check the Make This Calendar Public box. If you prefer that viewers not be able to see the details of your events, also select Share Only My Free/Busy Information. If you want viewers to see your event details, leave this unselected. Then click Save. The calendar is now public.

To embed your calendar, go to the My Calendars panel and find the name of the calendar you wish to embed. Click on the drop-down menu and select Calendar Settings. A new window will open. Go to the Embed This Calendar area (see Fig. 11.5).

Copy all of the HTML code in the text box on the right and paste it into the code for the website, Google Site, blog, or wiki where you'd like it to appear.

FIGURE 11.5. The Embed This Calendar panel

To feed your calendar into an RSS reader, such as Google Reader or Bloglines, go to the box labeled Calendar Address (below Embed This Calendar). Click on the orange XML icon, copy the address that pops up, and paste it into the desired RSS reader. The pop-up address can also be pasted into applications such as Microsoft's. To feed your calendar into applications using iCal, click on the green iCAL icon and copy and paste the resulting address.

Tips

Calendar does so many things that it's pretty hard to remember them all. The Tip feature, displayed in the blue bar along the bottom of the calendar window, serves as a helpful suggestion and reminder tool. Scroll forward or backward through the list of tips by using the arrows in the lower right corner of the window. If the Tip feature bothers you, turn it off in the Settings window.

Using Calendar Offline

It's easy to access your calendar even when you are not connected to the Internet. You won't be able to make new calendar entries, or edit or delete existing entries, but you will be able to access and read your calendars.

To access this feature, you must enable it while you are connected to the Internet. To enable offline access, click the Offline link along the very top of the page (right corner). The program that enables this is called Google Gears. When you click Offline you will be prompted to download Gears. Click on Get Gears Now.

We strongly urge you not to make your calendars offline-accessible on a public computer; only use the offline feature on a computer that is fully under your personal control. It's too easy for your private information to fall into the wrong hands on a publicly accessible computer. When you download your calendar information for use on your computer offline, it is only available on that specific computer—not all computers to which you may have access.

Once you have downloaded Gears to enable offline access, log into Calendar by typing www.google.com/calendar/ into your browser address bar. At this time, this feature only works in the following browsers: Google Chrome, Internet Explorer 6 and 7, Firefox 2 and 3, and Safari 3. Google is working to add additional browsers.

You will be able to read all of the Calendar information you have selected to be available. Your primary calendar is available offline by default. Subcalendars must be selected for viewing offline *while you are still online*. To do so, go to Settings > Offline > Available Offline and check the boxes next to calendars you wish to see offline. Web content, such as weather, will not be visible while viewing offline.

TEACHER TIPS

- Color-coding is a great way to have separate subcalendars for the different categories in your life: family, school events, professional development, graduate school, clubs, or religious events, and perhaps one for each class or period of the day. It's simple to hide or show any of them, or show them all at the same time.

- Use Calendars to schedule resources too. Easily create calendars, visible to all users, for the library, computer lab, laptop cart, art room, gym, music room, science lab, assemblies, and so on. This makes sign-up easy for everyone and prevents double-booking and other types of conflicts. For more information on this, go to Google's Calendar support page (www.google.com/support/calendar/bin/answer. py?hl=en&answer=44105).

- Increase your productivity by organizing! Create class calendars for assignments, projects and activities. When setting up task-specific groups in class, invite student teams to meet in various locations for their work. Once they accept the invitation, the event will show up in their calendars, too.

- Reinforce connections with parents by publishing school happenings, sports events, parent conferences, evening meetings, and school board functions. It will decrease the distribution of paper, and parents will be more aware of what is going on. If you publish a class or school newsletter in the form of a Google Blog or Site, embed a calendar in the newsletter and have all the necessary information in one place.

- Communicate professional development activities, faculty meetings, or grade level curriculum planning sessions. Use the attachment feature to include notices, agendas, and minutes for colleagues. By attaching Google Docs of draft documents that are in progress, all people in a group can stay up-to-date and contribute their thoughts and ideas whenever it's convenient for them. And everyone involved knows where to locate needed items. Attach assignments, reading materials, and worksheets to calendar dates for student use.

- Here are some excellent blog posts and other resources on how people and schools have used Google Calendars with great results:

  Google Calendar Wins, Hands Down:
     http://mrmaher.wordpress.com/2008/09/22/google-calendar-wins-hands-down

  11 Reasons Schools Should Use Google Calendar Next Year:
     www.buzzmaven.com/2007/05/10-reasons-schools-should-use-google-calendar-next-year.html

Black Belt Scheduling with Google Calendar:
http://lifehacker.com/software/google-calendar/geek-to-live—
black-belt-scheduling-with-google-calendar-250939.php

Integrate Your Schedule with Google Calendar:
www.slideshare.net/dougdevitre/integrate-your-schedule-with-google-
calendar-presentation

Displaying Google Calendar Events on a Map:
http://ouseful.open.ac.uk/blogarchive/012594.html

CHAPTER 12
GROUPS

CHAPTER AT A GLANCE

- Snapshot Description
- How It Works
    - Logging In
    - Access Existing Groups
    - Creating a Group
    - Working within Groups as a Member
    - Creating a Page
    - Deleting or Removing Pages
    - Working within Groups as an Owner or Manager
- Teacher Tips

SNAPSHOT DESCRIPTION

Google Groups enables like-minded people to come together in their own space to share ideas, look for information, and carry on conversations. Users may search or browse for a group dealing with a topic of interest, start a new group, or join an existing group. They may join an existing discussion, start a new one, or just read others' comments. A group may customize the look of its space, make its own web pages within the space, and upload files for access by group members. Adding new people to the members list is simple.

HOW IT WORKS

Logging In

It is not necessary to have a Google account to simply read Groups; however, a great deal of functionality is lost without an account, so we recommend having one. People who do not have a Google account can be invited to be members of a Group by using their e-mail addresses.

Access the Google Groups home page (http://groups.google.com). If you are not already logged into your Google account, a page like the one in Figure 12.1 appears.

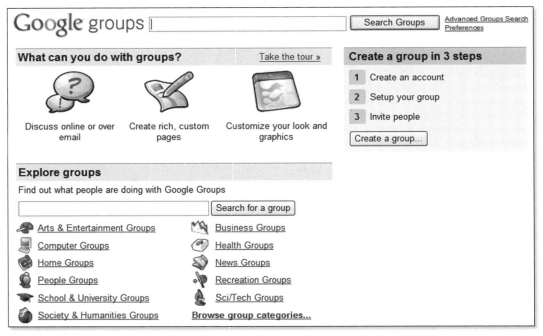

FIGURE 12.1. The Google Groups home page, before logging in

The top search box will search all groups on the Internet—those that are part of Google as well as all other services that provide groups. The lower search box (under Explore Groups) will search only for groups that are part of Google. Notice the option at the very bottom: Browse Group Categories. This allows viewers to look at all the group categories in Google.

Access Existing Groups

In Figure 12.2, a Groups home page is shown for a person who has already logged in to his Google account. It looks similar to the first example (the two search boxes function the same way), but there are some important differences.

FIGURE 12.2. The Google Groups home page after logging in

Notice the commands in the upper right toolbar:

My Groups. A drop-down menu that displays all the groups of which you are a member.

Favorites. In the Discussions area (see Fig. 12.3), there is a faint star to the left of each discussion topic. You may select any topic as a favorite by clicking on the star (it becomes bold). All posts in this topic will now appear in the Favorites area, if you click on the command. To delete a favorite, remove the star from the topic.

Profile. The custom description you have provided for yourself (including a picture if you wish).

Help. To access Google's Help for Groups.

My Account. Provides access to your Google account to modify settings.

Sign Out. Logs you out of your account.

The main heading, My Groups, displays the groups to which you belong. In this case, the person belongs to enewsletters and Happy Talk. The area under the heading My Profile & Stats shows thumbnail information about you and a summary of your activity in Groups over the previous week.

Creating a Group

Log in and click the Create A Group button. Follow the process to name your group and fill in the required information. After a couple of pages, you will come to the page where you can add members.

Enter the e-mail addresses of people you would like to invite to your group. Each one will receive an invitation and must respond to join the group. If you prefer a shortcut, click the Add Members Directly command. This option automatically adds members, whether or not they approve of being added. For classroom educators, it may be more efficient for you to add students as members by using the Add Members Directly option. (Of course, students may also create their own groups, but it would be wise to go over appropriate behavior expectations in student-created groups ahead of time.)

Write an invitation or welcome message, and select an e-mail subscription option for your members if you're directly adding them. Click the Invite Members or Add Members command. Google will send notifications or invitation to your group members.

It is Google's policy to review requests to add or invite a large number of new members. The company says that requests are usually reviewed within two business days and processed shortly thereafter.

Working within Groups as a Member

This is where the cool stuff happens. Once a Group is up and running, many ways exist to communicate, collaborate, and create.

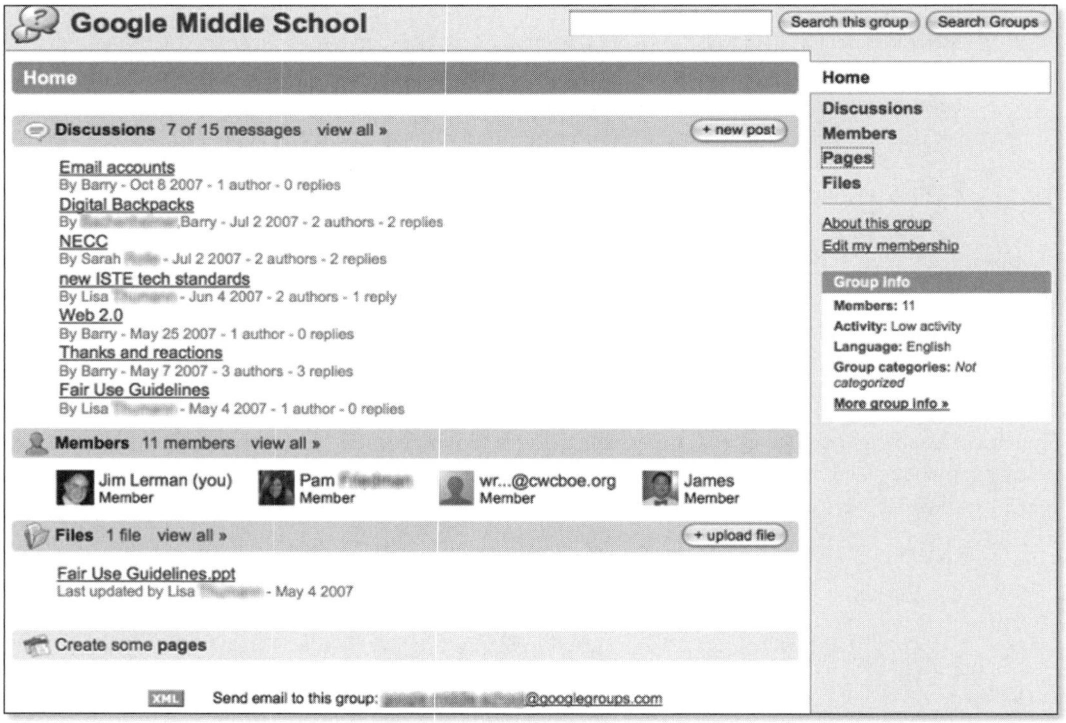

FIGURE 12.3. A sample home page for Group members

Figure 12.3 shows the home page for a group named Google Middle School. Note the search box that enables searching within this group or within all Google Groups.

The left three-quarters of the page consists of the main text area. For this particular group, there are abbreviated lists of Discussions, Members, and Files. No Pages have been created yet; near the bottom of the screen members are invited to do so.

On the right is the navigation bar, which appears on Groups pages. This makes it easy to navigate through all parts of the Group space. There are five main components of every group's space:

Home. Displays the home page, the one displayed in Figure 12.3. The command is in black, surrounded by white because this is the component that is currently selected.

Discussions. For most groups, this is the busiest area. Members post topics, respond to posts by other members, and comment.

Members. Takes you to group member profiles.

Pages. Members may create web pages here, without the need to use any code. Pictures may be uploaded, as well as links to other areas of the group or websites. HTML code may also be embedded, so that other Google Apps, such as Sites and Docs may be inserted into a page.

Files. Files and pictures may be uploaded to this area for storage; 100 MB is provided for each group. These files may be downloaded by group members.

Two useful commands are located at the bottom of the page. On the left, find the XML subscription button. This enables you to subscribe to group content. Whenever there is a new post, page, or file, it will appear in your news aggregator or reader.

To the right of the XML option, note the e-mail address for the group. Normally, e-mail sent to the group will be posted directly to it. Google notes that exceptions to this occur when: a group owner has decided that e-mails will be moderated or screened before posting; a group owner has decided that e-mails may be posted only by members; or announcement-only groups, which allow no incoming information at all.

Creating a Page

As group owner, you have the option to disable Pages or limit the editing rights to group moderators (see the upcoming section "Working within Groups as an Owner or Manager").

From the group's home page, click the Pages link in the navigation bar on the right side of the page. Click the Add A New Page button at the bottom of the page. A new page will open. Enter a name for your page in the New Page Name box at the top of the new page (see Fig. 12.4). Add content to your page by clicking into the empty box below the toolbar.

When finished, save your page by clicking the Save & Publish button. The page will be saved in Google Group and published to the group (in this case, Google Middle School). You can send a message or instructions to the members of your group announcing the creation of your page.

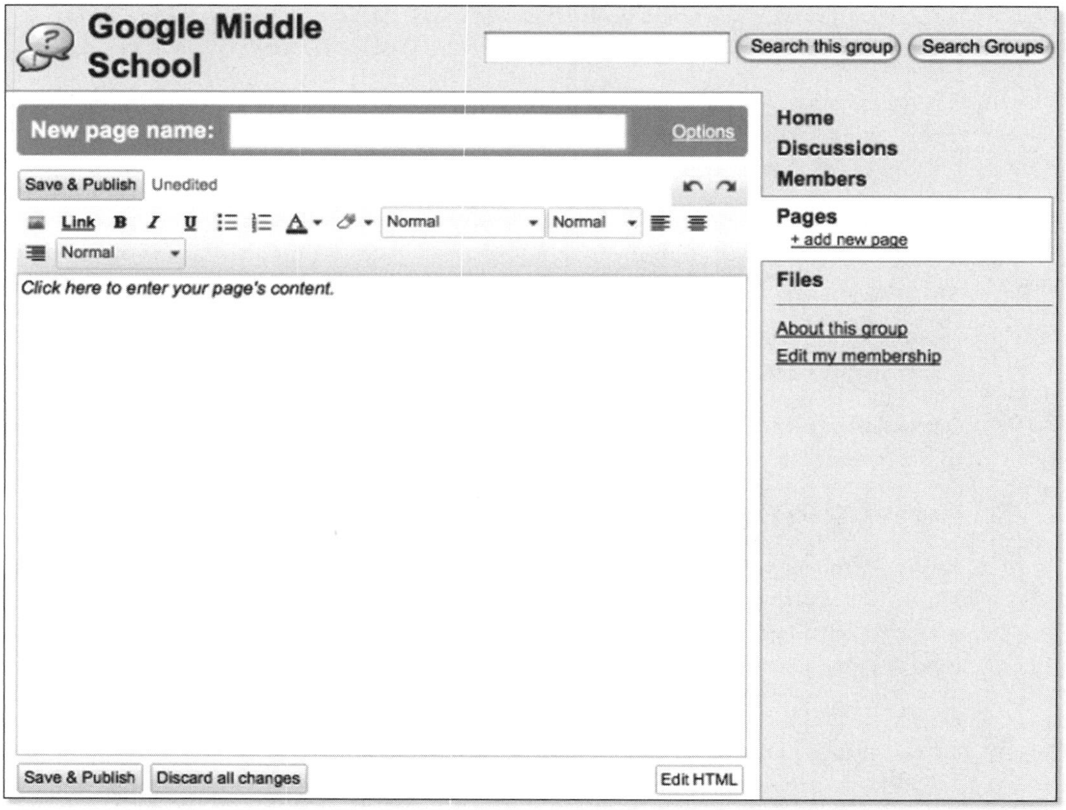

FIGURE 12.4. Creating a Page

If you are the owner of the group, you can rename the Pages link or remove the link from the group.

The Add Image icon (first icon, left of Link) is in the Formatting toolbar. Click it, and the window shown in Figure 12.5 will open.

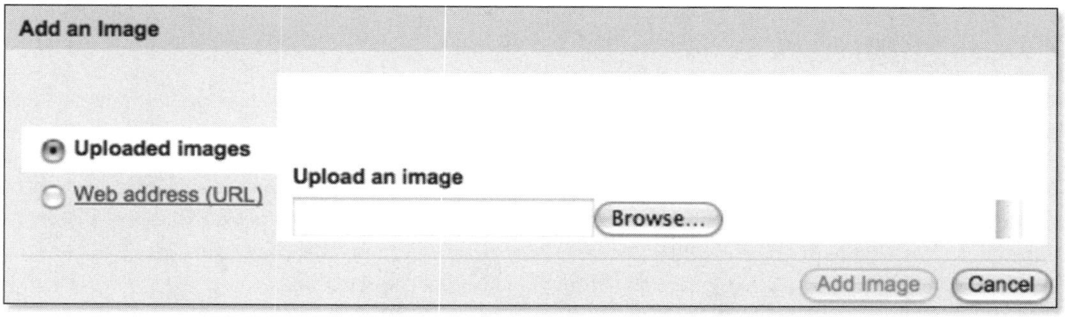

FIGURE 12.5. The Add An Image dialog box

If the image you wish to use is stored on your computer, use the Browse button to navigate to the image file. If you are using an image from the web, click Web Address (URL) to insert its correct location. Remember two things: (1) You must respect copyright; and (2) The image must exist all by itself on the URL you submit in order for it to upload correctly—no other text or images may be on the page. (In Firefox, right-click (Ctrl+click on a Mac) the image and select View Image. If you are unable to isolate the image so that it exists alone on a web page, then download it to your computer first and then use the Browse command to upload it to Groups.)

If you are uploading an image from the web, a thumbnail version of it will appear to indicate a successful upload. If the thumbnail does not appear, the image did not upload. Large pictures may take some time to upload.

After the image has been added, you can move it by dragging it to a different area on the page. Resize or remove the image by clicking on it and selecting one of the resizing option links or Remove Image.

To add a hyperlink, first highlight the text on the page that you wish to serve as the anchor. Then click on the Link option to the right of the Image icon. A window will open. The text you just highlighted will show in Text To Display. Then select whether you wish to link the selected text to one of your pages, one of your files, a web address, or an e-mail address.

Deleting or Removing Pages

You can delete any page you created as long as other members have not edited your page. Owners can also delete a page from a group. If you want to delete a page from a group follow these steps:

1. Click on the Pages link on your group's home page.

2. Find the page you want to delete and click on its title.

3. When the selected page opens, click the Edit command, located on the right end of the toolbar containing the name of the page.

4. Click Options > Delete This Page.

5. You will be prompted to confirm your decision. Click OK to delete the selected page.

Working within Groups as an Owner or Manager

Three levels of membership exist for groups: owner, manager (sometimes also called moderator), and member.

Google describes the difference between an owner and a manager: "The original owner is the person who created the group, invited the first members, and chose the group's posting and access settings. Once the owner selects a member to be a manager, both the owner and the manager can approve posts, invite new members, create managers, and change the group's management settings. Only the owner, however, can create a co-owner, transfer ownership to another user, or remove the group."

Owners and managers can change the rights enjoyed by members.

Let's assume you are either an owner or a manager and you want to perform some management tasks in your group's site. In the case we'll discuss, the group is called Google Book Project. As the owner or manager, when you go to the home page for the group, the top navigation bar looks a little different from that of a member. The right-side navigation bar now includes three additional commands: Group Settings, Management Tasks, and Invite Members.

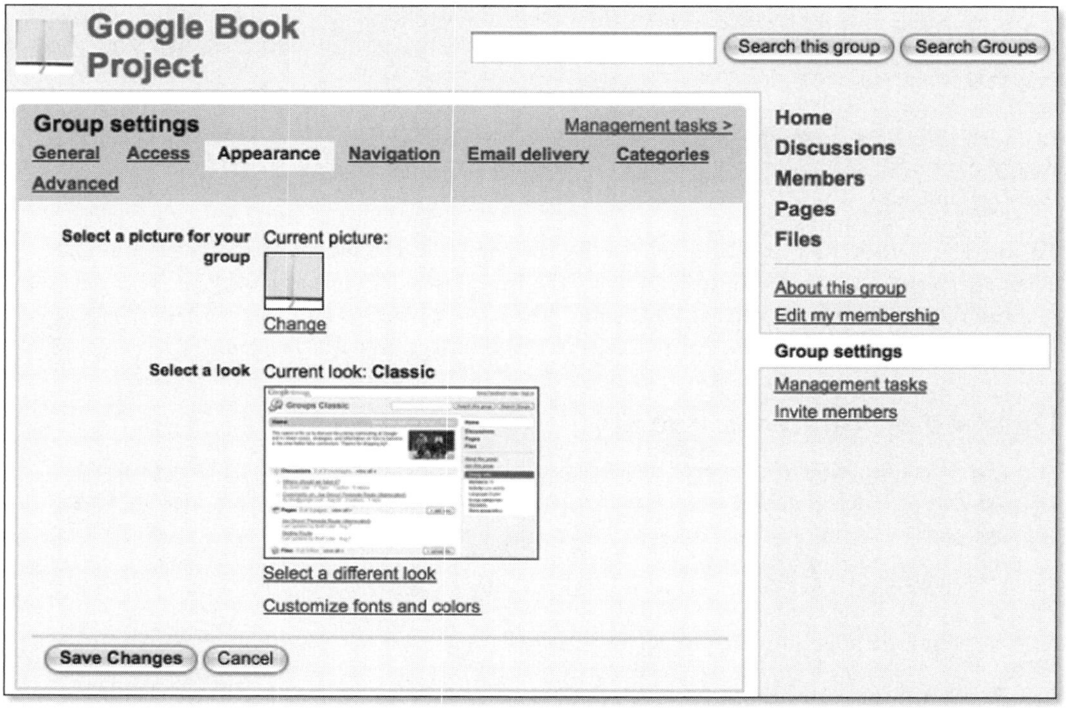

FIGURE 12.6. An owner's or manager's page. Group Settings is selected in the navigation bar, and the Appearance function is displayed.

Group Settings

This command is selected in Figure 12.6. Note that Group Settings contains seven separate functions: General, Access, Appearance, Navigation, Email Delivery, Categories, and Advanced. Appearance is the function depicted in Figure 12.6. It is highlighted in white in the menu. Owners and managers should familiarize themselves with the specific tasks that may be performed in each function:

> **General.** Controls the name, description, and addresses of the group; to modify these, click Edit.

> **Access.** Controls user permissions on the group site.

> **Appearance.** Controls the thumbnail displayed next to the group title and the style or look of the overall group site.

Navigation. Determines which commands appear in the navigation bar and their order of listing.

E-mail Delivery. Governs how e-mail messages from and to the group will be handled.

Categories. Permits choice of the categories, or tags, that will be applied to the group to make it easier for searchers to find.

Advanced. Contains a number of miscellaneous settings including, among others, deleting the group.

Management Tasks

Compared to Group Settings, these tasks are rather simple and consist of: Review Pending Messages, Review Pending Members, and Manage Members. Redundant commands to access Group Settings and Invite Members may also be found here.

Invite Members

This is a redundant command, found in several locations of Groups, to increase the number of members.

TEACHER TIPS

- According to Google, the following actions may be done in Groups without having a Google account:

    - Reading posts in public groups

    - Searching for groups, posts, or authors

    - Posting to unrestricted groups via e-mail or to groups of which a person is already a member

    - Joining a public group via e-mail

  The following actions require a Google account:

    - Creating and managing a group

    - Posting to groups using the web directly, instead of e-mail

    - Creating pages and uploading files

    - Joining a group using the web directly, instead of e-mail

    - Changing the way e-mail subscriptions are handled (no e-mail, abridged e-mail, digests, etc.)

  Thus, determining whether students will need Google accounts to use Groups appears to revolve mainly around the age of the students, what the teacher desires to accomplish with the group, and whether it is important that students are able to create pages and upload files.

For example, for students under the age of 13, it may not be worth the hassle of creating Google accounts because it requires parental permission. Also, if a group is going to be used only to conduct discussions, creating Google accounts will not be needed. On the other hand, if the group will be used as both a discussion and a workspace, the ability to create pages and upload files will be important to users; in this case, creating Google accounts for users is a good idea.

■ The most popular use of Groups is to conduct threaded discussions. Groups keeps discussion topics separate from one another and links all posts on a particular topic. This makes for easy continuation of conversations over extended periods of time. Because these conversations are archived and searchable, they can serve as a rich record of content over time. This provides excellent opportunities for directed or more freely flowing writing assignments in any subject area. In this way, a Group can function more like a forum than a simple listserv. To use this functionality, users should join the group but not have an e-mail subscription; otherwise the threaded conversations will clog up a user's inbox.

■ Groups offers a robust platform for collaborative projects within and across classes. Students may work together regardless if they live across the street or around the world from one another. Teachers will find Groups is a great way to share committee work or develop presentations collaboratively. Meetings, conferences, and social events of all kinds (e.g., class trips, special assemblies or observances, and reunions) also lend themselves to being organized with Groups.

■ One group of educators uses Groups for team agendas and meeting notes—keeping the archives for the life of the group easily accessible and searchable.

■ You can create a group for a particular subset of users, who should all become members. That way, an e-mail sent to one address is distributed automatically to everyone in the group. This is great for committees or group projects and is also an easy way to set up a communication network for a set of class parents.

■ Google's extensive Help for Groups may be found at http://groups.google.com/?hl=en.

CHAPTER 13
iGOOGLE

CHAPTER AT A GLANCE

- Snapshot Description
- How It Works
    - Accessing iGoogle
    - Starting to Work with iGoogle
    - Working with Gadgets (basic)
    - Working with Tabs
    - Themes
    - Working with Gadgets (advanced)
    - Making iGoogle Your Default Start Page
    - Help
- Teacher Tips

SNAPSHOT DESCRIPTION

The iGoogle App offers you the ability to design your own start page for the web. You can gather information from many different locations on the Internet and have it in one easy place; it's a way to create your own private portal to the web. Organize your iGoogle pages to suit your personal information needs and interests. iGoogle can work for you and your students as a kind of virtual information assistant, enabling you to manage the flow of information rather than be overwhelmed by it.

For example, on a single iGoogle page, you (or a student) can do all of the following:

- Keep a file of Internet bookmarks for ready access

- Check e-mail

- Keep a Google calendar

- Read all teachers' (or students') daily blog notices using RSS

- Chat with fellow teachers or students about group projects

- Access a dictionary or thesaurus

- Gather news stories from multiple sources

- Conduct a simple or advanced Google search

HOW IT WORKS

Accessing iGoogle

There are a few ways to get to iGoogle. Perhaps the easiest is to go to the regular Google search page (www.google.com). In the upper right of the page, you will see a link that reads iGoogle. Click on it. This will take you to iGoogle without signing in, which is fine if you are the only person who uses your computer. However, if the computer is shared, and most computers in schools (and many in homes) are shared, you are better off signing in to iGoogle. That way, you are password protected and only you (or someone with the password) can access your personal iGoogle space.

In other words, if you don't password protect your account, anyone who logs on to your computer can see your iGoogle page. If you choose to display anything private on your iGoogle page, such as your e-mail account or your financial information, you certainly don't want others to easily view it.

Sign in to iGoogle. Click on the Sign In option next to the iGoogle link on the upper right of the Google search page. You will be taken to another page that asks for your e-mail address and password. It is not necessary to have a Google account to use iGoogle, you need only an e-mail address. When you follow this procedure, you may access iGoogle from any web-connected computer (or cellphone, or PDA), and all your information will be private.

Another way to access iGoogle is via direct login at the iGoogle website (www.google.com/ig).

Starting to Work with iGoogle

The first thing you will want to do is personalize your iGoogle page. To do this, go to the box labeled "Create your own home page in under 30 seconds" (see Fig. 13.1), where you may select some of your interests and a theme for your page. All of these settings are very easy to change later, so don't spend any time worrying about your choices. In fact, it's easiest to just accept the default settings and move on because, if you're anything like us, you'll frequently change your mind about the appearance of your iGoogle page. It is important to enter your location so that the proper time zone will apply to your page.

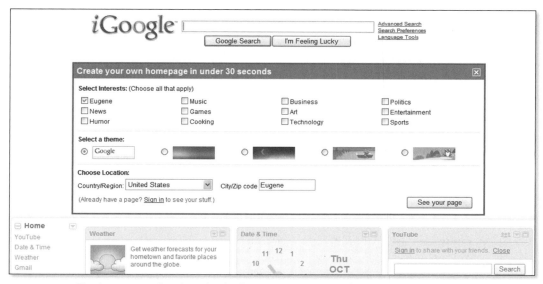

FIGURE 13.1. The home page for iGoogle, the first time it is accessed

Clicking on the See Your Page button will open a new page showing the options you selected (see Fig. 13.2).

FIGURE 13.2. iGoogle, showing the options you selected

Working with Gadgets (basic)

The iGoogle page is filled with little boxes, called gadgets, with blue bars across the top. Gadgets can contain all kinds of information and do many different things. The main way you personalize your page is by choosing which gadgets you want to display. The choices are amazing and rapidly expanding. You can add to or delete any of these gadgets and easily move them around the page. Popular gadgets include Google Calendar, To Do, Daily Horoscopes, and Joke of the Day. There are thousands of gadgets from which to choose.

To move a gadget on a page, place your cursor in the blue bar at the top of the gadget until the cursor changes into a hand; click and drag the gadget wherever you like on the page. To move a gadget from one tab (page) to another, click on the blue bar at the top of the gadget, and drag it to the name of the tab where you want it to appear. Tabs are listed on the left of your screen. (See the Section "Working with Tabs," in this chapter.)

The gadget control icons appear faintly in the upper-right corner of each gadget. Mouse over the blue bar and the icons will darken and turn into three (or more). The Crosshairs icon enables movement of the gadget around the page (click and drag). The drop-down menu displays specific commands related to the gadget. Included in the menu are commands to delete the gadget, minimize it (so that only the blue title bar shows) or share it, among others. The Maximize icon (small rectangle) opens the gadget in a larger window within iGoogle.

If you haven't already, you really should sign in. If you don't sign in, the iGoogle page you are working on will only be visible on the specific computer you are using. Once you sign in, the page will be stored on the Internet, and you will be able to access it from any computer with an Internet connection.

There are several ways to tell when you are logged in: your e-mail address will appear in the top right, the words *My Account* will appear in the same line, and the words *Sign out* will also appear in that line.

Working with Tabs

Eventually, your page will become cluttered with gadgets, or you may decide that you want separate pages with gadgets for home and school, or perhaps for different classes, subjects, or projects. Tabs can help. The term *tab* is used interchangeably with the term *page*. You go from one tab to another, or from one page to another.

Manage tabs in the navigation area on the left of the page. Figure 13.3 displays two tabs, or pages, on the left: Home and School. Note the Hide icon (little minus sign) next to Home and the Expand icon (little plus sign) next to School. A list of all gadgets that display on the Home page are listed in the Home panel because the Hide icon is showing. Notice that none of the gadgets' names are displayed in the School panel because the Expand icon is showing. If you want to see the gadgets for the School tab, click on the Expand icon, and they will appear.

To move a gadget from one page to another, click on the blue bar at the top of the gadget and drag it to the name of the page in the navigation area.

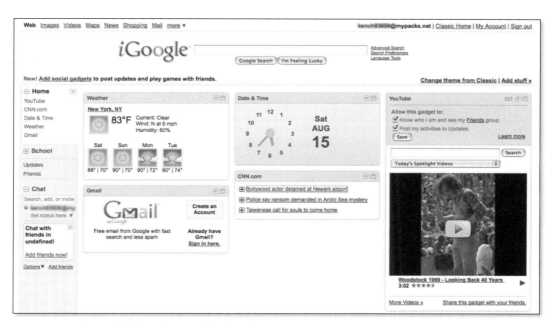

FIGURE 13.3. A sample iGoogle page after logging in

Themes

On the upper-right portion of the page, note the Change Theme command. Google offers hundreds of creative and artistic themes to customize the appearance of your iGoogle page. Many of the themes morph slightly over the course of the day, typically reflecting the change from day to night, while retaining their basic appearance. Some themes also change the color of the bars at the top of each gadget.

Working with Gadgets (advanced)

One of the most fun parts of iGoogle is choosing your gadgets. Right next to the Change Themes command is Add Stuff. Click this option and the page shown in Figure 13.4 opens.

There are hundreds and hundreds of gadgets, and their number increases constantly. Finding just the gadget you want can take some shopping ... be prepared to enjoy the experience. To assist you, Google has placed gadgets in groups, or categories, and listed them on the left side of the page. You'll find numerous gadgets in more than one category, so don't fret that you'll miss something important. You can sort gadgets by three criteria: Hottest (at the top of the current hit parade), Most Users (cumulative total over time), and Newest. You can also search for gadgets on the right side of the page.

The gadget menu occupies the center column of the page. (Please note at the top of this column that you may select a tab to display either the Gadgets or Themes menu.) Individual gadgets are listed in the column. There are many pages to the gadget menu. Each appears with a thumbnail picture, a name, and a brief description. If you click on either the thumbnail or the name, you'll be taken to a new page with more information about the gadget, including comments from users.

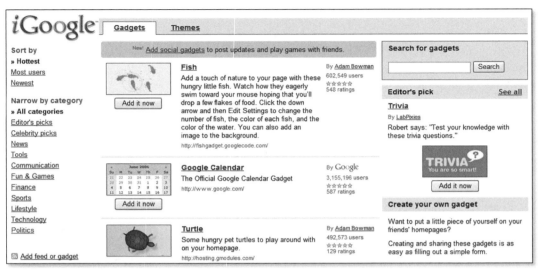

FIGURE 13.4. The Gadget menu page

Beneath the thumbnail is a command: Add It Now. Click on it to add the gadget to your iGoogle page. (Make sure that the last iGoogle page you were on before going to the gadget menu is the one you want the gadget to appear on. If the gadget appears on the wrong page, you can move it, as discussed earlier.)

To the right of each gadget title is a bit more information that identifies the author of the gadget, how many people use it, the number of times the gadget has been rated by users, and an average of user ratings—ranging from 1 to 5 stars. Clicking on the name of the author will take you to another page containing all the gadgets designed by that particular person or organization. If you like one gadget from an author, perhaps you will like others as well.

The right column on the page has a gadget search box, editor's pick, a link to information about how to create your own gadget, and links to learn more about iGoogle. The first three are aids to assist you in identifying gadgets that you will find useful. Please note that in addition to the one editor's pick featured on the page, the See All command takes viewers to a new page that lists all the editor's pick gadgets selected previously. Creating your own gadget is really quite simple (just fill out a form) and you can put it on your own iGoogle page as well as send it to friends and family. This is a very nice feature.

If you have your own website, blog, or wiki, be sure to visit "Learn more about iGoogle/iGoogle for feed owners" at the bottom of the column. It provides clear and concise directions for how to create an RSS feed from your site, blog, or wiki directly into a gadget in iGoogle. If all your students have iGoogle pages, this is a quick and easy way to communicate with them.

Imagine that Ms. Gonzalez has already set up her students with their own iGoogle pages. On these pages students are tracking newsfeeds for certain projects, accessing Google Calendars to manage their schedules, reading each other's blogs, and chatting. Now imagine that Ms. Gonzalez is planning a learning fair that requires frequent communication with students. She can place whatever information she wishes in her blog. She can have all the students subscribe to the RSS feed for her blog, and the messages will show up automatically on their iGoogle pages in the gadget created just for that purpose.

Near the top left of the page, please note the blue Back To iGoogle Home command. It takes you back to your iGoogle home page when you're finished with the gadgets menu.

Making iGoogle Your Default Start Page

If you would like to make iGoogle the first page that opens when you access the web, go to www.google.com/support/websearch/bin/answer.py?answer=25557&topic=13919 for easy instructions. This is one of iGoogle's greatest features—the ability to create your personal start page for the web. You can gather all the web features that are most important to you in one place. Instead of wandering all over the web to go to the sources you visit often, you can set them up in iGoogle so they're ready for you as soon as you go online.

Help

For some reason, the iGoogle Help command is located at the bottom of the page rather than the top right as in most Google applications. The direct URL for iGoogle Help is www.google.com/support/?ctx=web&hl=/.

TEACHER TIPS

■ The potential for users (teachers and students alike) to create their own Personal Learning Networks (PLNs) using iGoogle represents its greatest strength. Certainly other tools can be used for the same purpose, but two particular qualities that iGoogle offers (ease of integration with the other Google Apps, and that Google as an entity is likely to be around for a long time) lead us to recommend this tool most highly.

■ In their 2007 book, *In Command! Kids and Teens Build Their Own Information Spaces,* Robin T. Williams and David V. Loertscher provide a useful guidebook for teachers and library media specialists (www.lmcsource.com). Among the excellent recommendations the authors make, their template for organizing an iGoogle space stands out. They suggest that users set up three basic tabs to organize their iGoogle:

> **Personal Space.** Includes the content and tools that will be personally useful for school or work nearly every day.

> **Group Space.** Includes tools and projects that are used on a collaborative basis.

> **Outer Space.** Includes content and tools the user finds interesting or useful on a more general basis, or for infrequent use.

The authors don't mention it, but if any of these pages becomes too full of gadgets, it would be simple enough to create a Personal Space 2 page or Outer Space 3 page and so on. Williams and Loertscher advocate that every student and teacher have a PLN and that teachers use them to facilitate two-way communication with students and among each other, particularly through the use of blogs and RSS feeds.

■ iGoogle works with all of the following Internet browsers: Explorer, Firefox, Safari, Netscape, and Opera. It also works with web-enabled cell phones and PDAs.

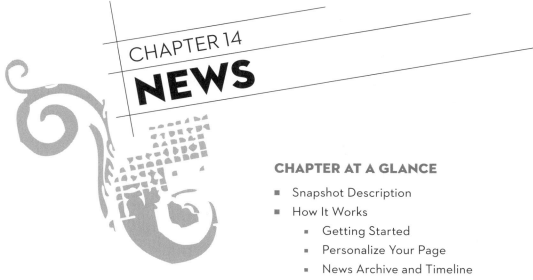

CHAPTER 14

NEWS

CHAPTER AT A GLANCE

- Snapshot Description
- How It Works
  - Getting Started
  - Personalize Your Page
  - News Archive and Timeline
  - Alerts
- Teacher Tips

SNAPSHOT DESCRIPTION

Using newspapers in the classroom is not a new idea, but Google News has advanced the way we get our news with the development of a website that pulls together news and stories from sources around the world. In the classroom, use Google News to bridge the gap to the outside world by gaining access to primary resource material for research and critical analysis. The archive search allows you to search for information dating back over 200 years. Available in over 40 regions and numerous languages, Google News keeps you informed with up-to-date information as the site is refreshed at regular intervals throughout the day.

HOW IT WORKS

Getting Started

When you first go Google News (http://news.google.com), the page defaults to showing Top Stories in the standard version. Notice the multicolored Section Menu to the far left, where Top Stories is highlighted. You may choose to view stories from any of the sections listed under Top Stories (World, U.S., Business, Sci/Tech, Entertainment, Sports, Health, Spotlight, and Most Popular). Click on the section, and you'll be taken to the area of the page where the stories in that section are displayed (or you may simply scroll down).

In Top Stories view, within different news sections, find a small Edit command and a small X icon in the upper right corner of each section. The Edit command allows selection of the country and language for display of stories within that section, as well as the number of stories to display at once. Click on the X icon to remove the section from the page.

Two sections appear below the Top Stories: Recommended For You and Local News. When you're signed in, Recommended For You will suggest stories based on your search history. Local News allows a custom section of the viewing page based on U.S. city, state, or zip code. This will show only stories based on the submitted geographic location.

Personalize Your Page

To get the most out of Google News, begin by personalizing your News home page (the topics below Top Stories). You can arrange the sections of news you need or those that most interest you.

Sign in to your Google account. While you do not need a Google account to use News, you will need a Google account to personalize your News home page. Near the top right of the default window, click the Edit This Page command. In the window that pops up, it is possible to rearrange the placement of story sections as well as complete other functions.

The sections displayed in the pop-up window are laid out as they appear on the News page. Click and drag the sections to rearrange them. Be sure to remember to click Save Layout after rearranging a page. If fewer than all sections are shown, click on Add A Section to display additional sections.

The Add A Custom Section command allows you to add a new section that includes news focused on keywords of your choosing. The Add A Local Section command does the same thing as Local News, described previously. The Add A Recommended Section command does the same thing as the Recommended For You section also described previously.

News Archive and Timeline

In addition to bringing the latest news and events to your classroom, Google News offers additional tools that provide access to a wealth of archived primary and secondary sources, as well as direct quotes from people as they lived through various events.

Let's say you have led your class into a discussion on the effects of nuclear war. The typical textbook might talk about the dropping of the atomic bomb in Japan during World War II.

As a method of bringing students a closer look at the event, use the News Archive Search link to begin your search by typing in the keywords "dropping of atomic bomb on Hiroshima."

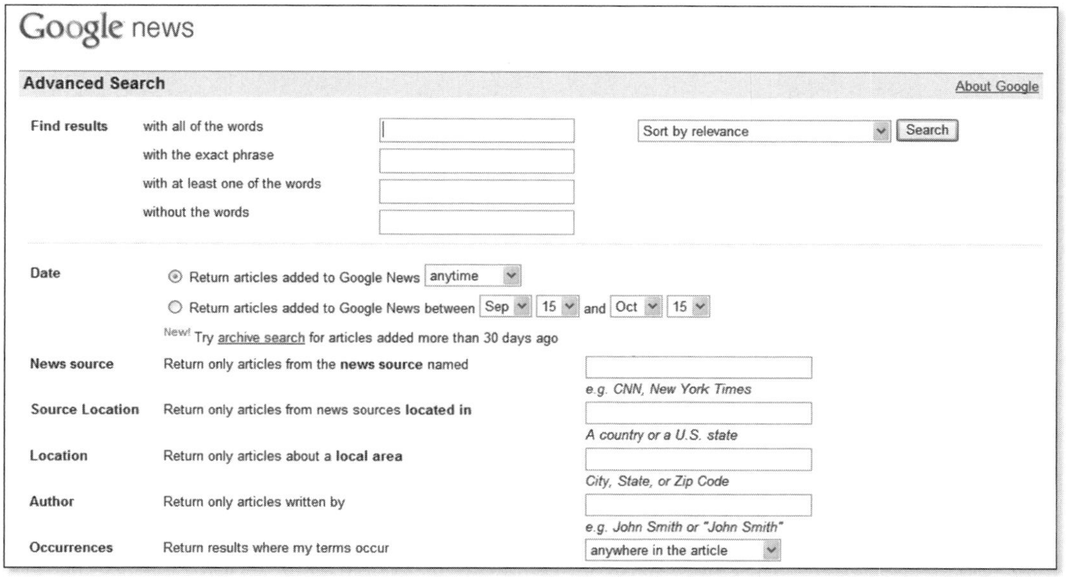

FIGURE 14.1. Access the News Archive Search from the Advanced Search page

Access the news archive search by clicking on Advanced News Search to the right of the search box at the top of the Google News page. Another way to get to the news archive search is to enter its direct URL (http://news.google.com/archivesearch?ned=us&hl=en&cf=all). The screen shown in Figure 14.1 will appear. Click on Archive Search.

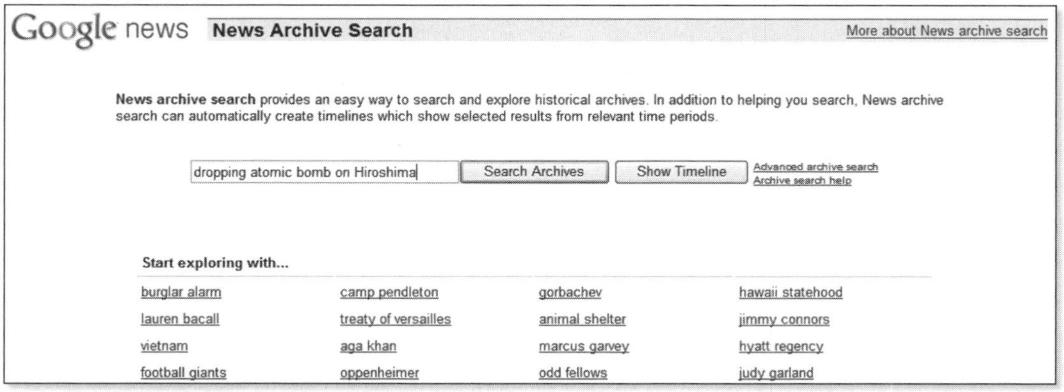

FIGURE 14.2. The News Archive Search window

In Figure 14.2, we have entered "dropping atomic bomb on Hiroshima" in the search box. We can display the search results in two ways. Search Archives returns articles in chronological order of their publication and also displays a timeline reflecting the publication date of the article. The Show Timeline command (upper-right side of page) returns articles in chronological order by the date referenced in the article, regardless of the article's publication date. For example, an article that mentions the dropping of the bomb on Hiroshima on August 6, 1941, will appear based on that date and will also be illustrated on the visual timeline according to that date, though the article itself may have been written in 1955, 1996, or 2010.

Many archived articles carry a cost of approximately $2–4 to be displayed or printed out. These funds are paid to the publications that own the rights to the stories, not to Google (although Google may realize some income for providing this service). Recent articles in Google News do not usually carry a fee. When there is a cost associated with an article, it is noted, either by the actual price or by generic dollar signs.

Alerts

Alerts are a great way to stay informed about a developing story or issue. Perhaps you and your class are following a natural disaster, a war, an election, or simply the rainfall in a particular location. It's a simple matter to set up an alert that feeds news to you via e-mail, your Google News page, your iGoogle page; or to embed the feed from the search in your blog or a Google Sites page. This way, Google will follow a developing story for you and send regular updates to you wherever you want them to arrive.

Whenever you conduct a search in Google News, a menu such as the one shown in Figure 14.3 appears at the bottom of the results. This particular menu comes from the search we conducted using the key words "dropping atomic bomb on Hirsoshima." The words in bold are the same as were entered for the original search.

> Stay up to date on these results:
> - Create an email alert for **dropping atomic bomb on Hiroshima**
> - Search blogs for **dropping atomic bomb on Hiroshima**
> - Add a custom section for **dropping atomic bomb on Hiroshima** to Google News
> - Add a news gadget for **dropping atomic bomb on Hiroshima** to your Google homepage

FIGURE 14.3. The Alerts option at the bottom of a News search results page

The first menu option sets up an e-mail alert for the search topic. Click on the link and a window opens, where one is able to set up both e-mail alerts and feeds to blogs and Google Sites. This window is pre-formatted to send results for the search terms we previously entered. Type allows a user to search not only for news stories—one can also search all the blogs on the web, regular websites, Google Video, or Google Groups. Or, if you select Comprehensive, you can search all of these possibilities. In How Often we can determine if information is sent to us daily, weekly, or as it happens. In Deliver To one can decide if the information is delivered via e-mail or feed. If the feed option is selected, Google will provide a URL that can be used to embed the results in a blog or Google Sites page, or to have the results appear in a Google Reader account.

Suppose, for example, you wish to follow an issue such as Israeli policy toward the Palestinians. By setting up separate alerts from news sources in the United States, Gaza (Palestine), Israel, Egypt, Saudi Arabia, and China, it is possible to see how very differently events and "facts" may be viewed from a variety of perspectives.

TEACHER TIPS

- Help for Google News is located at the bottom of each page.

- Because Google News gathers information from many sources, not all of it may be suitable for young children. It is wise to take reasonable precautions to prepare students, their families, and the school administration for this possibility. Controversial issues, and the variety of viewpoints concerning them in the media, may cause heightened excitement in the school community as well. All such moments can be teachable moments if thoughtful steps are taken ahead of time. We favor this approach. Wise educators are sensitive to the environment in which they work.

- Google News is available for many mobile phones that are web-enabled. For information about this service, go to www.google.com/mobile/products/more.html#news.

- Google News also has an interesting Quotes feature. Enter the name of a person who has been in the news lately into the search box. When the search results come back for that person, if they have been quoted in the news recently, one quote will be given at the top of the results list. To see more quotes from that person, click on the More By command below and to the right of the given quote. A new page will open containing many quotes from the individual (if they exist). These quotes are searchable and sortable.

- A creative way to emphasize the visual element of the news is to use the Image version of Google News. When an image is selected, mouse over it to see a summary of the story or click on it to see the full story. Students can write their own captions for the images after reading the story. Collect and display (either on a poster or on a Google Site) a number of student-captioned images to create themed summaries of the news. For example, one such summary could be News Around the World This Week, with images from different world news sources of key events in their countries during the week. Another could be a Kaleidoscope of Views on Global Warming or Images of the Global Economy or This Week in Iraq. Such summaries could be historical in focus too, such as Rocket Launches through the Decade or Top TV Show of the Year going back as far as the late 1940s.

- For students studying world languages, Google News is a great source of news stories from sources in languages other than English.

- Google has combined News with Google Earth. News exists as a separate layer in the Layers menu. When this feature is activated, zooming in on any location will yield Google News icons signaling that a story is available about that particular location. This is a great way to follow a continuing event that is particularly location-specific, such as a natural phenomenon, a violent flare-up, or a discovery. To activate the Google News layer, navigate to the Layers menu on the left-hand side of Google Earth. Expanding the Gallery node in the layers tree will expose the Google News layer. Check the box next to it (http://google-latlong.blogspot.com/2008/05/extra-extra-now-you-can-discover-worlds.html).

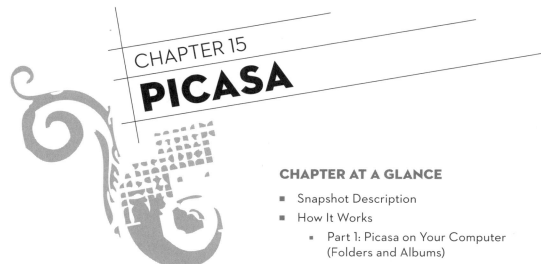

CHAPTER 15

PICASA

CHAPTER AT A GLANCE

- Snapshot Description
- How It Works
    - Part 1: Picasa on Your Computer (Folders and Albums)
    - Part 2: Picasa on the Internet (Web Albums)
- Teacher Tips

SNAPSHOT DESCRIPTION

As Google says, Picasa lets you "organize, edit, create, and share" your photos. It's an outstanding package that works quickly and continues to offer improvements on a regular basis. Full-featured versions of Picasa are available for users who work with Windows, Mac, and Linux operating systems—so nearly everyone is served.

With Picasa, you and your students can easily organize all your photos. Picasa locates all the photos on your computer and places them into folders according to your directions; it also enables users to create custom folders. Picasa makes it simple to import photos from many sources, including cameras, storage media, scanners, and screen shots.

Picasa comes with numerous controls to perform basic edits on photos. With one-click fixes, you can adjust color and lighting, add effects, and include captions. Changes made to photos in Picasa on your computer can be automatically synchronized with the versions of photos housed in your albums on the web. Picasa also offers quick back ups of photos to an external drive, CD, or DVD. Printing photos is easy, and photos may be easily previewed before printing as well.

Use Picasa creatively to mix your photos into new formats including collages and multimedia video presentations. Take screen shots of your computer's desktop, capture still-frame photos from videos (not for Macs yet, sorry), and add watermarks, too.

Share your photos online by inviting individuals to view your albums, or keep them private. You may choose to make your online albums public and searchable, or not. Picasa photos integrate with Blogger and can be e-mailed, uploaded elsewhere, and commercially printed. Picasa even comes with face recognition and tagging built in, to make organizing and searching easier and faster.

HOW IT WORKS

Picasa comes in two basic parts: software you download to your computer, and your albums that live on the web. The two parts communicate seamlessly. As you might expect, to use the Internet-based Web Albums function, you must have a Google account (not necessarily Gmail, just an account).

Like Picasa itself, this chapter also has two parts: Section 1 for Picasa on your computer, and Section 2 for Picasa on the Internet (Web Albums). Please note: all screen shots in this chapter will display the Windows version of Picasa. Nearly all of the uploading and downloading options, as well as display and sharing options, apply to videos as well as photos.

PART 1: PICASA ON YOUR COMPUTER (FOLDERS AND ALBUMS)

Starting Up

To download and install the free Picasa software, go to the Picasa website (http://picasa.google.com). Windows, Mac, and Linux versions are all accessible from this page. During the installation process, Picasa will look for photos on your computer. You will be given the choice to restrict its search to specific drives, or to allow a search of the entire hard drive. The choice is up to you. Depending on how many photos you have, it may take some time for this search to complete. Picasa works very quickly, but as you probably know, making copies of photos is not an instantaneous process.

Another screen prompt will appear during the installation process that will ask if you wish Picasa to become your default viewer for certain photo types (e.g., JPG, GIF, TIFF). Once you become comfortable with using the software, you may prefer to have Picasa serve this function.

Figure 15.1 shows what your screen will look like once your photos and videos have downloaded from your computer to Picasa. Google calls this Library View. Remember, we are working on your local computer.

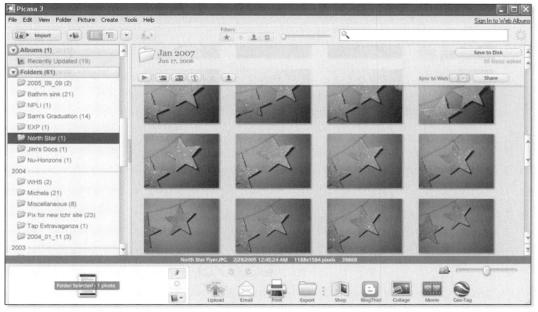

FIGURE 15.1. Sample Picasa page in Library View

Managing Photos

After Picasa has scanned your computer for photos, it displays them in the large central area. It uses the folder structure that you have already created. For example, if you have a folder containing 17 photos on your computer titled "Mom's birthday," they will display as a group in the large central area when the "Mom's birthday" folder is selected. You can see the available folders under the Folders drop-down menu, on the left side of the screen. Next to each folder is a little number indicating the number of photos the folder contains. In Figure 15.1, in the Folders drop-down menu you'll see that 61 folders with photos exist. Folders are listed by the date they were created on your computer, by default. You may alter the scheme by which they are displayed if you wish.

The Folders menu reflects your collections of photos as you have organized them on your computer. Changes made in folders within Picasa will be reflected in folders on your hard drive. For example, if you move a photo of Cousin Rita from "Mom's birthday" to "Our family album" in Picasa, the photo will also move from one folder to the other on your computer.

You may also create albums (see Fig. 15.1, above the Folders menu). Albums consist of new, custom collections of photos taken from anywhere on your computer. Making an album is sort of like making a scrapbook; the items come from all over. Creating an album is also like making a playlist in iTunes. (Come to think of it, the overall structure of Picasa resembles that of iTunes to a considerable degree, which makes it rather easy to understand if you're an iTunes user.) When you make an album, the photos do not change their locations within folders; they stay right where they always were. If you remove a photo from an album, or move it to another one, nothing happens to its location in its original folder on your hard drive. An album may be stored on your computer, or it may be created online. When it's online, such an album is called a web album.

There are several ways to organize your photos further. When taking any of these steps in relation to a particular photo, a small icon appears at the bottom of the photo to tell you what you did to it. The icons are explained below.

 Sync to Web. This means that edits (such as cropping, eliminating red eye, adjusting color, etc.) made to photos in an album or folder in Picasa on your computer will automatically show up in the corresponding web album (if you have created one).

 Favorites. Adding a star to a photo in Library View makes it one of your favorites. You may easily search for those photos that you've made favorites—a quick way to separate the best from the rest. To add a star, click on any photo in an album or folder in Library View. Then click the star button, located at the bottom center of the screen. A small star will then appear on the photo in your Library. To search for starred photos, click on the star button under Filters at the top center of the screen.

 Geotag a photo in Google Earth. If you have Google Earth installed on your computer, it is possible to embed location information in the file for your photo and have your photo display in a Google Earth satellite map. Directions for how to do this may be found at http://picasa.google.com/support/bin/answer.py?answer=43896. (At the time of this writing, this feature is not yet available for Macs.)

 Uploaded photos. This arrow appears on any photo that has been uploaded from your computer to Web Albums.

 Blocked photos. This arrow appears on any photo that you have chosen to block from being uploaded to Web Albums.

 Video files. This icon appears on all videos to distinguish them from photos.

The Photo Tray is located on the bottom left corner of the screen. It enables multiple photos to be worked on at the same time. See more about the Photo Tray in the upcoming Section, "Sharing Photos."

Folder Manager

This handy service in Picasa can automatically scan folders on your computer's hard drive to keep your Picasa Library up to date. You can select the hard drive folders you want Folder Manager to monitor. This way you never have to remember if you've added photos to Picasa that you've downloaded to your computer, because Picasa will do it for you.

To modify Folder Manager, click on the Tools menu at the top of the screen. Select Folder Manager from the drop-down menu and follow the prompts to select the folders you want to be scanned. The default setting is all folders, all the time. This service is particularly useful if you would like certain folders monitored and certain folders left alone.

Importing Your Photos

Photos can be imported from nearly any source. Picasa supports importing from:

- Digital still camera

- Camcorder

- Memory card

- CD or DVD

- Webcam (may not be available for Mac)

- Scanner

- Camera phone

- Screenshots from your computer

- Flash drive

- External hard drive

- Floppy disk

- Web pages

- E-mail

To import photos from a camera, click on the Import button in the upper left corner. The basic concept to keep in mind when importing photos is that you have to get the photos onto your hard drive and into a folder before Picasa can do anything with them. Every step in the import process proceeds from there. Specific steps to import from various sources may be accessed at http://picasa.google.com/support/bin/topic.py?topic=14159.

Editing Photos

Picasa offers a great many basic editing features for photos. More are almost certain to come in the future. For more advanced photo editing options, separate programs such as Photoshop or Gimp (free for PC, Mac, and Unix users) offer greater functionality. But for a free program that does so many other things so well, we think the editing capabilities Picasa offers are very good and will only get better.

To start editing, open Picasa and double click on any photo to open the Edit Photo window. Editing tools are clustered within tabs along the left side of the screen: Basic Fixes, Tuning, and Effects. To zoom in on a picture in the Edit Photo window, use the mouse to click and hold on the picture. Click and hold again to zoom back out. Note that Picasa never changes your original photo; it is always there for you. Changed photos are always saved as separate images.

The following editing functions are available:

Basic Fixes. At present, there are nine basic fixes; most are self-explanatory. Straighten allows approximately 15–20 degrees of rotation to straighten the vertical-horizontal axes of crooked shots. I'm Feeling Lucky is the one-click auto adjust feature for those who don't want to mess with the individual adjustment controls. Text enables typing of text right on the image (very customizable). Retouch is amazing. Use it to cover facial blemishes, scratches, or water marks, eliminate entire people or objects, or insert oddities such as third eyes. Fabulous!

Tuning. These fine adjustments help modify the lighting and color of the photo. Don't miss the Neutral Color Picker, which enables you to minimize the effect when a particular color washes over an entire photo too much.

Effects. These offer a dozen ways to further refine an individual photo. Depending on the photo, the results can be quite dramatic. Sharpen, Warmify, and Soft Focus are particularly effective in our view, but you should experiment.

Note the Caption Bar just below the main image. You may easily type in captions for photos. The captions display when photos are uploaded to Web Albums. In addition, captions are searchable in the search bar on the Library page, within Picasa. This is very helpful when searching for a particular photo.

The Sync to Web feature automatically makes changes to your web albums once you've edited photos in Picasa on your computer. Select the particular folder you wish to sync to the web. Click the Sync To Web button; the folder is uploaded to your web album, and any edits made to the pictures will automatically be saved in the web album from now on. To disable this feature, select the folder and click the Sync To Web button again. (Google advises Mac users that Sync To Web is not available for folders located in iPhoto Libraries.)

The Photo Tray

The Photo Tray shows photos that have been selected from within folders and albums. The Photo Tray may contain one or many photos. When multiple photos are displayed in the Photo Tray, any command applied to one will apply to all the photos currently in the tray.

To select a single photo, just click on it from its folder or album. A thumbnail image of the photo appears in the Photo Tray. To select multiple photos from the same folder or album, hold down the Ctrl key (PC) or Command key (Mac) while clicking. Thumbnails of all photos chosen this way will appear in the Photo Tray. To select all the photos in a folder or album, click Edit > Select All, or simply use the keyboard shortcut: Ctrl+A for a PC or Command+A for a Mac. An even faster way is to click on the name of the folder or album. A single thumbnail image then appears in the Tray that indicates how many photos are in the folder or album.

If you want to select multiple photos from different folders and albums, gather all the photos you want from a particular folder or album and then click the Hold icon (the pushpin). This keeps the selected photos safe in the Photo Tray. You may then proceed to repeat the process of adding more photos to the Tray from other folders or albums.

To remove photos from the Tray, click the Clear command, immediately under the Hold icon. All photos in the Tray will be removed (but *not* deleted). To remove a single photo from the tray, select it in the Tray and click Clear. Clicking on the Add To command will add all the photos in the Tray to a new or existing album.

Sharing Photos

To share an entire Picasa folder or album from your computer with one or many people, simply click the Share command. This will create a new web album online and open a window for you to send an e-mail to whomever you choose to invite to the new web album.

Most other sharing functions for Picasa on your computer are handled through use of the Photo Tray and its related commands (along the bottom of the screen). Use the nine larger icons located here to perform numerous sharing functions.

> **Upload.** Upload photos in the Tray to a new or existing web album. Users may also select the image size in pixels and degree of the web album's privacy.

> **E-mail.** Send the photos in the Tray by e-mail to whomever you choose.

> **Print.** Allows printing, with many selections for size, borders, captions, and layout.

> **Export.** Send the photos to folders on your hard drive, with choices regarding size and quality. Also add watermarks to images to preserve copyright.

> **Shop.** Purchase prints and custom merchandise from a list of vendors.

> **BlogThis!** Send images to Blogger for instant blogging.

> **Collage.** Create collages with the photos in the tray.

> **Movie.** Make a slide presentation or short movie, including photos, videos, and music.

> **Geo-Tag.** Place latitude and longitude of locations in your photos' files and have your photos placed on a map in Google Earth.

Collages

Collages present a great way to get creative with your photos. Picasa offers many options in terms of collage types, controlling the space between photos, how they are layered, their types of borders, and background choices. To make a collage, select the photos you want to use. There are two basic ways to do this: use the pictures located in a folder or album or use pictures you have placed in the Photo Tray.

Open the collage maker by clicking the appropriate command. If you are working from a folder or album, there is a Create Photo Collage command in the folder or album header. If you are working from the Photo Tray, the Collage command may be found on the right of 9 icons at the bottom of the window.

Whichever method you use to access the collage maker, the work space that opens is the same. Once you start making a collage, you don't have to finish it all in one sitting. To come back to your collage, click Close > Save Draft. To return to your collage later, go to the Collages folder.

Movies

With Picasa, users may combine photos, videos, and music into short movies to be saved as .wmv (PC) or .mov (Mac) files. Movies may be uploaded directly to YouTube.

Google intends movies to be brief, but does not specify a length. This is because Google is actually concerned with how much storage space the movie takes up, not necessarily how long it is. Storage space requirements are determined by the amount of audio and visual information in the presentation, as well as its length. A long presentation made of mostly slides, with just a few transition effects and no music takes up much less storage space than a 45-second movie that is almost all video, with complex transitions and a richly textured musical score. This is to say: it's pretty hard to know exactly how long a movie can be. It's probably wise to make your first few movies in the two- to three-minute range and then experiment with lengthening them bit by bit—taking into account the amount of video, audio, and complexity involved in each one.

As with Collages, users may navigate to the movie maker workspace either from a folder or album, or from the Photo Tray area. The command icons are in similar locations. Either command mentioned in "Collages" opens the same workspace window in Movie Maker. The movie maker workspace contains the controls for assembling and rendering your movie.

The left side of the movie maker window contains three tabs with most of the controls: Movies, Slides, and Clips. The right side holds a screen displaying the currently viewed slide or video. At the bottom, find thumbnail images of the slide and video clips that have been chosen for use in the movie.

The Movies tab options are as follows:

> **Audio Track.** Picasa permits uploading of a single audio track for the entire movie. If you want to include voiceover, fades, and mixing, it will need to be done outside of Picasa.

> **Transition Style.** Determine the visual effect used when transitioning from one frame to the next, such as Wipe or Fade.

> **Slide Duration.** The length of time each slide is displayed.

> **Overlap.** Modify how much slide transitions overlap one another.

> **Dimensions.** Control the resolution of your movie for viewing in different formats such as DVD or online.

> **Captions.** Determine if picture captions should be visible in a movie.

> **Full frame photo crop.** Edit movie images to fully fill the picture frame.

The Slide tab controls text on your movie's slides. You can write text onto any image or create slides that have only text to use for titles and dividers. Text font, size, style, color, and location may be modified along with the color of the background.

The Clips tab enables the addition or removal of photos from the movie and the placement of more photos from your Library into your movie.

When completing your movie, you have three options. You may click the Play Full Screen command on the lower right to view it. You may click the Create Movie command to simply activate the process of rendering, or making, your movie. You may click the YouTube command to both make the movie and upload it automatically to YouTube. Google advises that, based on the size of your audio file and how many images are in your movie, it may take a "significant amount of time" for the movie to be made once you activate one of these commands.

Finished movies and drafts of movies may be found in the Movies folder. For PCs, this folder is located in My Pictures > Picasa. For Macs, it's located in Pictures > Picasa. Drafts are movies that you're not finished with yet. To save a draft, click the Close command and you will be asked if you want to save the draft in the Movies folder. Drafts and finished movies may be edited at any time. Double click the movie you want to edit and then click the Edit Movie command.

The sequence of photos in the movie may be altered by dragging and dropping the photos in the filmstrip layout at the bottom of the window. To remove a slide from the filmstrip layout, click the Delete icon (X), located below Play in the bottom left area of the window. For more advanced information on making collages, movies, and slide shows in Picasa, go to http://picasa.google. com/support/bin/topic.py?topic=16057.

Backing Up Photos

It's definitely a good idea to back up your photos and videos. You never know when your hard drive will crash, when you might have trouble getting to your Picasa albums online, or when you want that one photo you didn't upload to the web. Backing up also makes it easy to transfer large amounts of photos to a new computer.

Photos may be backed up to any device or medium that has storage: an external hard drive, flash drive, iPod, CD, DVD, and numerous others. The most common ways are to an external hard drive or a CD or DVD. We'll explore both processes.

First, make sure the external hard drive is connected, or the CD/DVD is in the proper slot on your computer. In Picasa, click on Tools > Backup Pictures. Dialog boxes will appear at the bottom of a new window.

Follow the prompts in Box #1. Select New Set if this is the first time you are backing up your Picasa photos. Be sure to follow all the prompts carefully. If you wish to work with an already-created backup set, select it from the drop-down menu in the center of the box Backup Set. Click the Edit Set command to change the name of the set or the types of files to backup.

Follow the prompts in Box #2 to select the names of the folders and albums you wish to back up.

Please note: If you plan to copy your photos to a new computer, download them from the disc or external hard drive first, tell the computer if you want them installed in the same folders they came from or if you want them to go to new folders, and then download a fresh copy of Picasa from the web onto your new computer.

Picasa Photo Viewer

This tool offers a quick and easy way to view photos without having to open the entire Picasa program. It's especially useful if you just want to work with one or a few photos and you know exactly where they are. It works on your desktop or in Explorer.

To open a photo in Photo Viewer, just double click it.

The following operations may be performed in Photo Viewer:

- Add stars
- Zoom in and out with mouse scroll wheel
- Rotate photos
- Upload directly to Web Albums or Blogger
- E-mail directly
- Print directly
- Go to the full Picasa program

Screen Shots

Capturing and saving a screen shot on a PC is a quick and easy one-step process when Picasa is open. The program must be open first for this to work properly.

Bring up the screen you wish to capture. Push the PrntScrn key (or whatever variation on that spelling that shows up on your keyboard). This saves the entire screen currently displayed on your computer's screen to the Projects section of your Folder list. They're collected in a folder called Screen Captures. To capture a selected area of your screen, press Ctrl+PrntScrn at the same time.

Google advises that this automatic capturing of screen shots to Picasa is not available for Macs as of this writing (thus suggesting that it will be at some time in the future). The Grab feature on Macs will save a screen shot as a TIFF file to a folder on your Mac's hard drive. Once there, it may be moved to a Picasa folder or album as any other photo.

PART 2: PICASA ON THE INTERNET (WEB ALBUMS)

Starting Up

OK, so you're ready to put your photos online. Perhaps you wish to create an album for parents to view, or you want to create a collection from which students may draw when making presentations. Perhaps you just wish to free up some storage space on your computer. Using Picasa's online Web Albums gives you 1 GB of free online storage for putting your photos and videos on the Internet and managing who can see them.

There are two basic ways to get to Web Albums. From Picasa on your computer, select Web Albums from the very top toolbar, on the right. Web Albums takes you directly to your online albums. The other way is to use the URL http://picasaweb.google.com.

When first logging in to Web Albums, viewers encounter your Public Gallery (see Fig 15.2). These are the albums you have chosen to make visible to anyone.

FIGURE 15.2. The default page, My Public Gallery, in Web Albums

The default setting displays the My Photos tab in the large central area. The area on the right displays the owner of the gallery. You may upload a small photo of yourself there. In the same area, all galleries to which you have linked are listed with hotlinks.

Near the bottom of the screen, note the small RSS command. Click on this to subscribe to an RSS feed using your chosen RSS aggregator. This will send new photos from the albums you designate to your feed reader automatically. You probably won't be subscribing to your own album, but do know that this RSS capability exists on everyone else's Public Galleries. Subscribing in this manner can be more convenient than using the notifications function described below.

Click on the Explore tab to go to a display of Picasa's featured photos. Finding photos that appeal to you is a good way to begin to identify favorite photo sources. Select a photo you like from the Featured Photos page, and it opens in a new window.

The name of the web album appears in bold print above the image. In Figure 15.3, the album's name is Photowalking—USS Hornet. Below the title, you'll see four commands for viewing the album as a slide show, sending a copy of the photo to someone via e-mail, downloading the photo to your computer's hard drive, or ordering prints from a commercial service. Below the photo, other viewers may have entered comments about the photo, and you can as well.

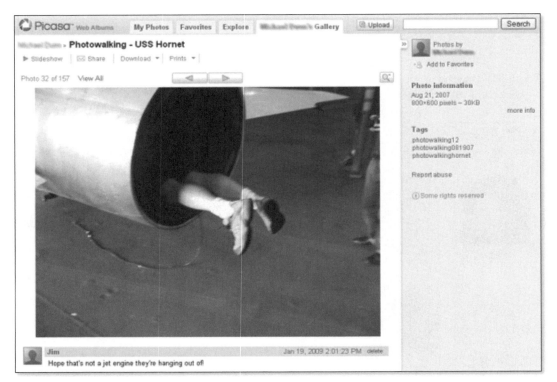

FIGURE 15.3. Display of an individual photo after selection in any web album

On the right side of the window, find information about the photo and the Add To Favorites icon. This icon adds the person who owns the album to your Favorites list. You may also choose to make a link between this person's Public Gallery and your own.

Clicking on the Favorites tab at the top of the screen opens a new screen that lists the owners of your favorite albums. From this list you may choose to receive update notifications whenever the owner makes changes to her or his Public Gallery, and also whether to list her or his Public Gallery as a link on your gallery. The update notifications, when received from your favorite gallery owners, are displayed in the area on the right, named Favorites Activity.

Uploading Photos

Users may upload photos and videos to Web Albums in three ways: directly from Picasa on your computer, using a web browser, or via e-mail. Let's look at each option in more detail.

From Picasa on Your Computer. As described previously in the Sharing Photos Section, use either the Share command in a folder or album tab or the Upload command in the area near the Photo Tray.

Using a Browser. First, sign in to Web Albums (http://picasaweb.google.com). Second, click the Upload command. Then, for Windows, use Basic Uploader in all browsers to upload as many as five photos at a time; use the Upload Control in Explorer to upload large numbers of photos simultaneously. For Macs, use the plug-in called Picasa Web

Albums iPhoto Exporter to upload from iPhoto to Web Albums or Picasa Web Albums Mac Uploader to upload from your hard drive to Web Albums.

Via E-mail. This is a great way to upload photos from your phone, or to have multiple people submit photos to the same album. It involves creation of a private e-mail address as a destination. Use the following steps to upload photos via e-mail:

1. Sign in to Web Albums, and click Settings on the top right.

2. On this page, select "Allow me to upload photos by e-mail."

3. You are prompted to enter a "secret word" of 6–15 letters or digits.

4. An e-mail address appears for you to use. Make a record of it.

5. Click Save Settings.

6. Attach photos to e-mails to send to the new address.

7. Enter the album name for the desired destination in the subject line of the e-mail.

8. Leaving the subject line blank, or entering a nonexistent album name, will result in the photos arriving in the Drop Box album.

9. Attachments may be up to 20 MB in size in JPG, GIF, and PNG formats.

Drop Box

The Drop Box Album (almost always referred to as just Drop Box) on Web Albums serves as a kind of miscellaneous file basket to hold uploaded photos until you decide what album to place them in. The Drop Box remains invisible in Web Albums until you upload a photo to it for the first time.

To delete photos in the Drop Box, first click on the album cover image to select the Drop Box. Then, click Edit > Organize and Reorder. Finally, select the photos you wish to delete and click the Delete command. To select multiple photos at once, hold down the Ctrl key while selecting files.

Sharing Photos and Albums

You may share entire albums or single photos in Web Albums. To share an entire album, click on the album cover image to select it. Then click the Share command in the row of commands just below the name of the album. A new window opens that requests e-mail addresses of the people you wish to invite, and provides space for a short invitation message. To share a single image, click on it and then follow the same procedure.

When you share an album with someone, that recipient's name appears in the Shared With list that appears below the album cover image in Web Albums. It contains the names of everyone the album has been shared with and is visible only to the album owner. Everyone on this list will always be able to view the album in the Web Albums gallery, no matter what privacy settings you put on the album.

Another way to share access is to e-mail the URL for your Web Album gallery. Anyone who arrives at your gallery using its URL can see all your public albums as well as any that you have shared with them through an invitation.

To add a caption to a photo in Web Albums, select the individual photo. Click the Add A Caption command. Write what you want to say and click Save Caption.

Captions added previously in Picasa on your computer will upload with the photo. However, be advised that captions have a 1024 character limit in Web Albums, so a caption longer than that from Picasa (which has no such limit) will be cut off in Web Albums.

Comments may be easily added to photos in Web Albums. Select the individual photo, write your comment in the text box under the photo, and click Post Comments. Comments are visible to anyone viewing the photo. Comments can't be edited, but the writer may delete his or her own comment. Album owners can also delete any comment.

Privacy for your photos can be a big concern. You may modify your privacy options at the time you upload photos to create a new album. After clicking the Upload command in Picasa on your computer, you are prompted to set your desired privacy level. If you wish to change the privacy level of an already existing web album, select that album, click Edit > Album Properties and then make your choice in the Visibility Of This Album area.

Managing Photos—Tagging, Name Tagging (Face Recognition), Mapping Photos, and Syncing

When you put a tag on a physical object, like an item in a garage sale, the tag provides information and may help people find things easier (with color coding of discounted items, for example). Tagging in Web Albums serves a similar purpose; it's a way to find things more easily and learn more about them.

We might place tags on all our pictures that have dogs in them, regardless of what album they are in. We can do the same thing with tags for houses, horses, hills, and handkerchiefs. Then we can search by one tag name, or many, to retrieve only those photos possessing the tags we desire. Makes searching for stuff pretty easy, right? The best time to add tags is when adding pictures to a collection. It can be tedious to go back and add tags to hundreds of photos after they've been uploaded.

To add a tag to a photo, sign into Web Albums and select the photo with which you want to work. On the right side of the screen, go to People & Tags and select the Add A Tag command (+Tag). Enter the tag word and click Add. If you wish to add multiple tag words, simply separate them by a space. To search for photos with particular tags, enter the tag words in the search box in the top right of the My Photos page.

Name Tagging (or Face Recognition) allows you to identify the names of people in your photos amazingly easily. The program uses face recognition technology to enable you to give a nickname (name tag) to a person in one photo; it then finds this person in all other photos in any of your albums and tags the photos with the same nickname. It's quite accurate for full face shots, except of course when poor lighting, profile views, big hats, and big sunglasses pose challenges. Using the tags, you can create new albums and slide shows containing only the people you want.

There are two ways to activate the name tagging feature. On the right side of the My Photos page, a command may appear titled Try It! (You may have turned this off inadvertently at some point ... we did. Never fear.). If the command is there, click Try It! > Start Processing Photos. The other method involves clicking on the Settings command on the top right of the page. A new page opens. Select Turn Name Tags ON.

Once started, the process of adding tags to photos can take a bit of time. When it is finished, a new command, Add Name Tags, will appear in the People tab. As new photos are added to your web albums, they will be automatically scanned for faces and be ready for name tagging. Name tags can be edited by selecting the People tab.

Once the people in your photos have been named, it's simple to make custom albums and slide shows. Under the People tab, first check the boxes for the people you wish to include in the album or slide show. Then, just click the View Photos or Slideshow commands to make an album or view a full screen slide show.

Privacy concerns are always important with photos, and so too with name tags. By default setting, tags are not shown in public web albums. You may choose, however, to display tags in albums you select, or to show or hide the name tags of specific people. Details for how to do this may be found at http://picasa.google.com/support/bin/answer.py?answer=97953&topic=14605. Google describes the particular steps it has taken to protect the identity of children at http://picasa.google.com/support/bin/answer.py?answer=106441&topic=14605.

In Web Albums, users may locate an album, a single photo, or multiple photos from a single album within a Google map for display. To map an album, open the My Photos page in Web Albums and click on the cover photo for the desired album. Click Edit > Album Properties. A new window opens. Add the requested information. After you enter the address, city name, or zip code in Place Taken, the map will move to that location and a red marker will appear. Move the red marker to exactly the spot you want. Complete the additional choices and click Save Changes. When you open your My Photos page, a map will show each of your mapped albums with a red marker.

To map a single photo, open the photo by itself from an album. Click the Add Location command on the right side of the page. A new window will open, prompting you to add location information and to place the red marker appropriately on the map. When finished, click Save Location. The map will display on the right side of the page for the individual photo, with the red marker indicating the location where the photo was taken.

To map multiple photos from the same album, open the My Photos page in Web Albums and click on the cover photo for the desired album. Click Edit > Album Map to see all the photos in the album and its map. Click Edit Map to alter previously made marker placements or to include more photos in the map. You may either drag and drop photos from the left of the page onto the map or select a photo on the left and then click where you want it to appear on the map. Small thumbnail images of the photos actually appear on the map on this work page. When finished, click Done. A small map displays on the right of the page when the album is selected, showing red markers for the photos. You may choose to view a larger version of the map in a new map view page, or open it in Google Earth, if Google Earth has been downloaded to your computer.

Creative Commons

Creative Commons was established by a group of people interested in creating an alternative to copyright restrictions. Creative Commons allows creators of intellectual property to control the extent to which others may reproduce, alter, or share their work.

Web Albums is set up to allow album owners to select the various Creative Commons permissions and apply them to individual photos. The default setting for Web Albums is to claim copyright on posted photos. The Creative Commons options must be selected by the album owner.

By applying Creative Commons licensing, you make it easier for others to legally share your photos. It is a very simple process to use. To make blanket, or general, use of Creative Commons for all your Web Albums, go to the Settings page and then to the Content Controls section to select the level you desire. For a single photo or video, the control is located on the page of the specific item.

People in education are often more interested in sharing their material and getting credit for it than in trying to make a profit. Creative Commons licensing was established precisely to facilitate this point of view. Marking one's work with a Creative Commons license will enable others to use it and require them to give credit where it is due. It is even possible to stipulate if works may be altered, shared, or used commercially.

For more about Creative Commons, visit their website (http://creativecommons.org). Simplified discussions of Creative Commons may be found at www.diaryofareluctantblogger.com/2009/05/creative-commons-explained.html and http://creativecommons.org/about/licenses. For more about copyright issues in Picasa, see the Terms of Service for the program at www.google.com/accounts/TOS.

More

There's more cool stuff to do with Picasa Web Albums:

Embedding an album, picture, or slide show in a blog or website. When viewing an embedded album, image, or slide show in a site, viewers are taken to the album in Web Albums once they click on the cover image. You accomplish this by copying a small piece of HTML code from the web album page to the website where you want to create the link.

For an album

- Click the desired album on the My Photos page.

- On the right side, click the Link To This Album command.

- There will be a small window titled "Paste HTML to embed in website." Copy all the code in this window.

- Paste the HTML code in the source code into the site where you want the embedded album cover to appear.

For a picture

- On the My Photos page, click the album and then the individual photo you wish to use.

- On the right side of the page, select the image size. Choose Hide Album Link if you don't want viewers to be able to go to the entire album that contains the single photo.

- Also on the right side of the page, find a small box titled Embed Image and copy all of this HTML code.

- Paste the HTML code in the source code into the site where you want the embedded image to appear.

For a slide show

- Click the desired album on the My Photos page.

- On the right side, click the Link To This Album command.

- Click Embed Slideshow.

- Select the options you wish to apply such as captions, image size, and autoplay.

- After choosing the options, copy all of the HTML code that is given.

- Paste the HTML code in the source code into the site where you want the embedded slide show to appear.

Accessing Web Albums from your phone. Using your web-enabled cell phone, you can get to and use your Web Albums features to browse and search your photos, share photos with others, comment on others' photos, create slide shows on your phone, and search all Web Albums photos. As Google says, "This service is free from Google; carrier charges may apply." For details, go to www.google.com/support/mobile/bin/topic.py?topic=13562.

Interoperability with Blogger. Any photos you upload using Blogger appear simultaneously in Web Albums. In this way, you can manage photos in both services from one location.

TEACHER TIPS

- Picasa Web Albums comes with 1 GB of free storage for photos and videos. More storage is available for a fee (http://picasa.google.com/support/bin/topic.py?topic=10765). Of course, photos and videos may be stored on CDs, DVDs, flash drives, iPods, and external hard drives as well.

- Google's excellent Help for Picasa may be found at www.google.com/support/picasa/bin/topic.py?topic=14609.

- Mark Wagner offers these creative ideas for how to use photos in school:

    - Create slide shows for Back to School Night or any Open House

    - Make slide shows of performances, assemblies, celebrations, or field trips

    - Photo yearbooks

    - Photojournalism, documentaries, or dramatizations

    - Time-lapse photography (especially in science)

    - Class books (even big books)

    - Story books (digital storytelling)

    - How-to guides (especially good for teaching sequential thinking)

    - Exercises in classifying, categorizing, or comparing and contrasting

    - Photos as anticipatory sets, writing prompts, or review

    - To document learning (great for parent conferences)

- Picasa Albums can function as a storehouse for a class full of pictures, where multiple collaborating parents can upload and download pictures.

- As a way of introducing or reviewing a unit, print out key images related to its big ideas or essential understandings. Seat two students back-to-back, one with the image, the other with a blank piece of paper. The first student must describe the image in sufficient detail for the second student to draw it. After a certain period of time, the students compare the drawing to the image and discuss them using Document Based Questions (e.g., www.edteck.com/dbq/basic/worksheet.htm) to elicit key understandings. All students in a class may engage in this activity, or it may be set up so that two additional students observe the pair while back-to-back and then in their discussion. Then all four students process what occurred.

- Do a five-minute community montage. Have students, armed with cameras, walk five minutes in any direction from their school, home, or other key location in the community and take a picture of what they see. They write a caption for the picture, perhaps describing the meaning or significance of the image. Collect the images and captions in a web album to create a portrait of the community.

- For deeper exploration of creative uses, here are some great websites for ideas about using digital photography in the classroom:

    100 Ways to Use Digital Cameras:
    http://content.scholastic.com/browse/article.jsp?id=3122

    Digital Photography in the K–5 Classroom:
    www.rockdale.k12.ga.us/personal/mholbrook/dig_photos/default.aspx

Adobe Digital School Collection: Teacher Resources:
www.adobe.com/education/instruction/adsc

Educational Uses of Digital Storytelling:
http://digitalstorytelling.coe.uh.edu

Kodak's Tips & Projects website:
www.kodak.com/eknec/PageQuerier.jhtml?pq-path=
11808&pq-locale=en_US&_requestid=7194

- If you use Picasa on your computer regularly, it's probably a good idea to store all your photos as subfolders within a single main folder. This way, when you set Folder Manager to keep your computer's Picasa Folders and Albums up to date (automatically bringing new photos into Picasa as you place them into folders on your hard drive) you only have to select one folder for the Manager to keep track of.

- A great collection of video tutorials on Picasa is located at the Learning Electric website (www.learningelectric.com/picasa2).

CHAPTER 16
SITES

SNAPSHOT DESCRIPTION

At its most basic level, Sites enables users to publish an attractive, collaborative website quickly and easily, with no knowledge of complicated code. Its strongest feature lies in its ability to share large amounts of information, either individually or among a team, and then communicate about it. Access to a created site may be tightly controlled or open to anyone. Websites built with Sites are very customizable in terms of their appearance and functionality, and allow easy insertion of rich media such as videos, spreadsheets, slide shows, dynamic questionnaires, and images. At its best, Sites offers users of all ages great facility in generating and sharing knowledge. Absolutely no software is required—only an Internet connection.

By employing Sites, users can:

- Collaborate with others

- Subscribe to receive notification of site changes

- Insert calendars, spreadsheets, videos, and more

- Upload documents as attachments

- Search the site for specific content

- Access the site from any Internet-connected computer

- Share the site with specific individuals, a group, or the world

- Automatically save all versions of pages and access them easily

There's a bit of a learning curve to Sites—we strongly encourage new users to persevere. This is a *vastly* easier way to create your own presence on the web than writing HTML code, and it can be about as collaborative as you want to make it, allowing visitors tremendous opportunities to interact with you. Once most people learn how to work with an application like Sites, they wonder how they ever lived without it. (Can you tell we think Sites is pretty awesome?)

The famous Wikipedia website was built with an application very much like Sites. You can do it too!

HOW IT WORKS

Getting Started

There is a slight learning curve to Sites. We suggest you first experiment by making a sample site before trying to create the site you are going to display publicly. Getting the hang of the basic tools takes most people about 30–60 minutes.

Access the Google Sites home page (http://sites.google.com). You must have a Google account in order to use Sites, but a Gmail account is not needed. Log in to your Google account. To begin creation of your site, click on Create New Site below the long, horizontal line. A new window will open, allowing you to choose a template, site name, and theme, as well as see more options (see Fig. 16.1).

The template controls the arrangement of the elements on the page. There are hundreds to choose from. For your first site, it might be best to use the blank template or one of the templates just to its right.

Your site name is important. Once you choose a name, you can't change it, so you should select a name carefully. Sites will tell you if the name you select has already been chosen by someone else. If that's the case, you won't be able to use it and will have to come up with another name. If the name is OK, Sites will accept it and include it in the box that indicates the URL for your site (found just below the name for your site).

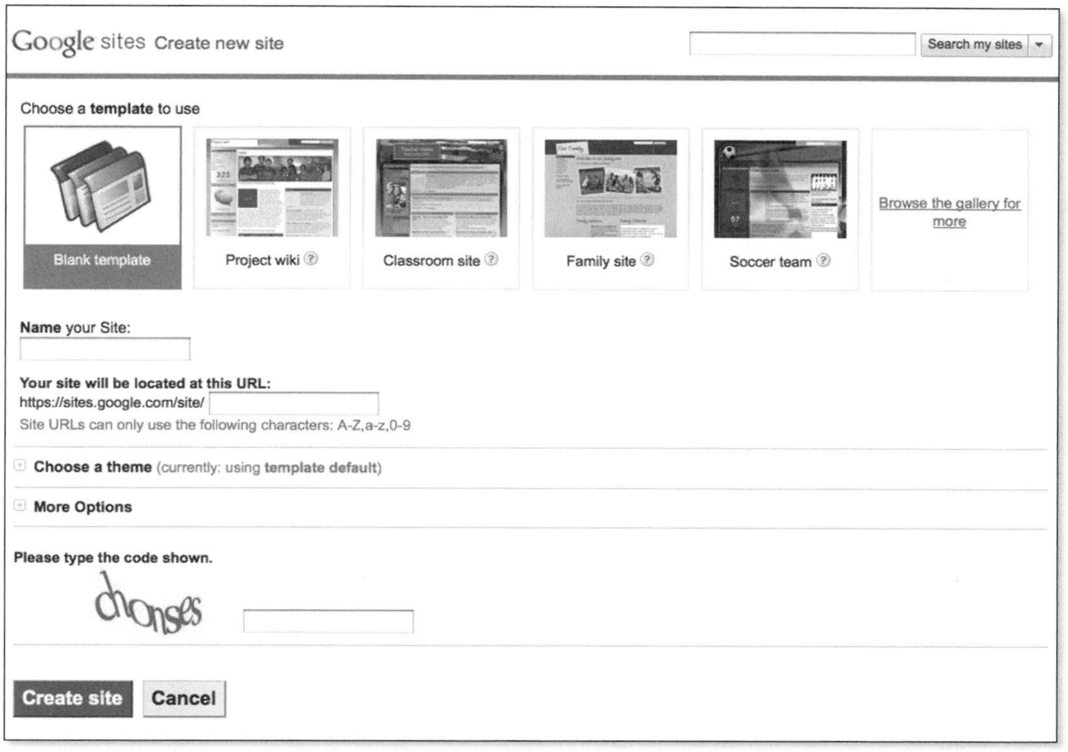

FIGURE 16.1. The Create New Site window

Themes control the appearance of your Site, including items such as color and illustrations. To see the theme choices available, click the small plus sign (+) just to the left of the word Choose. Again, for your first site, don't agonize over what you pick. It's easy to change the theme later. After making a choice, click on the minus sign (-) located where the plus sign used to be and the template selections will disappear.

Click the plus sign to the left of More Options to see further options for your site. The Site Description box offers a space for you to briefly describe your site. The Share With radio buttons control whether your site is public (viewable by anyone) or private (viewable only by those you specify). These choices can be changed at any time. We like to keep our sites private while we're setting them up, and when they are ready, change the setting make them public. The mature content check box is self-explanatory. Click the minus sign where the plus sign was to exit the More Options menu.

The Please Type The Code Shown request is a way to prevent machines from creating sites. You prove that you're a person by reading and typing the "captcha"—the partially garbled characters that appear. Sometimes the characters can be difficult to read. Don't worry if you get it wrong, Google will give you a new set of characters to work with.

Once you've filled out the form, click Create Site. A site has a storage capacity of 100 MB and may consist of an unlimited number of pages.

Working with a Page

As a regular user of the web, you probably know more about good web design than you realize. You can usually tell if a website is put together well by how easy it is to find commands that enable navigation, if the color scheme is harmonious, and whether the graphic arrangement of elements is aesthetically pleasing. As you put your pages together, you'll want to keep these criteria in mind.

The great thing about Sites is that you can change elements very easily. Every content change is saved, date- and time-stamped, and the identity of the person who made the change is recorded. This is very useful if you are working with one or more other people, and avoids a tremendous amount of confusion.

Figure 16.2 shows what a very basic first page might look like. There are lots of ways to get work done from this page. Let's take a look.

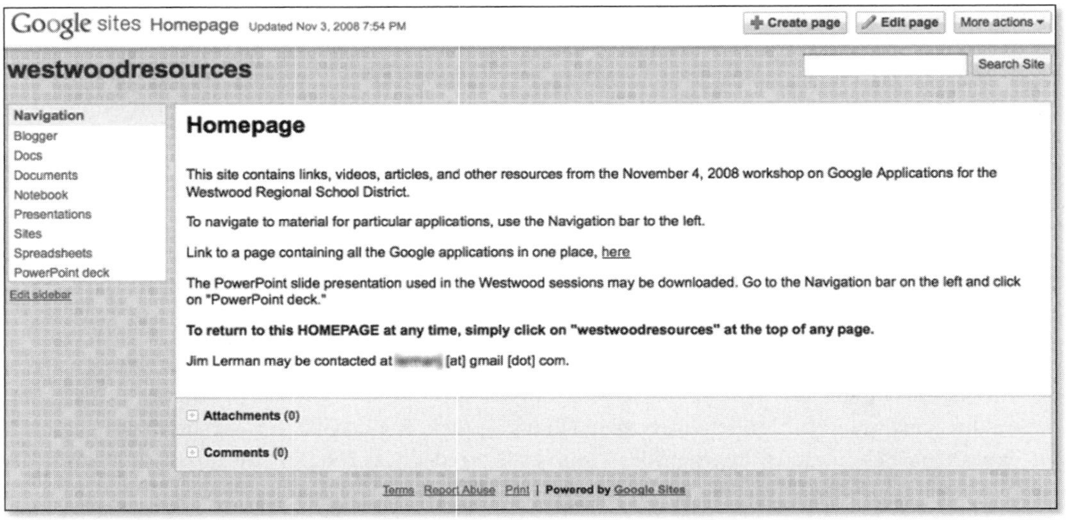

FIGURE 16.2. The first page of a new site, in view mode. Note that Attachments and Comments are enabled for this page.

Notice to the right of the Google Sites logo, that the date and time of the last site update is provided. This will change every time there is an update. You can change the logo if you like. Some people like the Google logo on their page; others want their own logo. To change the logo (which will appear on every page in your site), click on More Actions in the upper-right corner. Then select Manage Site > Site Layout (under Site Appearance). In the Header box, click Change Logo.

On your Sites page, there are three commands in the upper-right corner: Create Page, Edit Page, and More Actions.

> **Create Page.** Enables creation of a separate, new page. The current page will be saved, and a new one will open. There are five types of pages in Sites:
>
>> *Web page.* A basic page that allows you to write content and embed gadgets. This is your basic blank slate.

File cabinet. A page where you can upload and share files. You can create folders for different subjects.

List. This page can be used to create to-do or assignment lists. You can easily add or remove items.

Announcements. This is a perfect tool for adding recent announcements to your page. While much of your content remains static, this lets time-stamped information be placed anywhere on your site.

Dashboard. A two-column web page with four placeholder gadgets to make it easy to create an overview of information. You can create a Dashboard page by changing the layout of a web page to two columns and inserting gadgets in the page.

Edit Page. Allows editing of the current page. This command is covered in more detail in the Editing a Page section of this chapter.

More Actions. Opens a drop-down menu with the following options:

Revision history. Opens a list of all changes made to the page you are viewing, with the date and time along with the name of the person making the change. You may also change the version of the page that will be displayed here. This is a very important command because it allows users to see every version of the page, when it was edited, and by whom. Different versions may also be compared. Obviously, this detailed tracking of changes serves as both a wonderful memory aid and a great motivator of honesty. It also makes it easy to go back to earlier versions for information, or to even replace the current version with a previous one, if the group thinks the earlier one is better.

Subscribe to page changes. Click on this to receive an e-mail each time collaborators make changes to this page. Unsubscribe from this notification in the same manner. Subscribers receive notifications of page updates, comment insertions, and attachment of files. Some people love these notices, others find them annoying. Site owners usually fall into the first category, site viewers the second one.

Page settings. Controls a number of settings related to the current page. Users may show or hide the page title and turn the Attachments and Comments features on or off, among other functions. Adding attachments and comments can be quite a valuable feature and heighten the interactivity of your site. If you make an assignment on a page, for example, your students can upload their homework as attachments to the site. Using comments, students can peer review their classmates' writing assignments.

Print. Controls printing of the page currently being worked on. There is also a print command at the bottom of the window.

Move. Enables movement of the current page to another location within the website. All pages in the site are connected in a hierarchy, which may be viewed by clicking on Sitemap at the end of this list.

Delete. Deletes the current page. This removes all subpages and attachments as well as the current page. Read and understand "Deleting a page" in Google Help before performing this task (http://sites.google.com/support/bin/answer.py?answer=90551&topic=14064).

Preview page as viewer. Shows what the current page will look like to someone else viewing it on the web.

Subscribe to site changes. Click on this to receive an e-mail each time collaborators make changes to the site. Unsubscribe from e-mail notifications in the same manner. Note that this command applies to the entire site, not only a single page.

Manage site. Select this to open a menu of many controls regarding site content, site settings, and site appearance. To delete a site, click on Manage Site > General (under Site Settings) > Delete This Site.

Share this site. Opens the window for inviting people to your site as owners, collaborators, or viewers, along with choosing if the site will be viewable to anyone, or only those you invite.

Sitemap. Opens a diagram of the complete website you are working on, depicting the hierarchy of pages and how they are connected.

Use the Search box on the upper right of the Sites page to search through the entire site you are creating. This can be very helpful if users get lost while building the site or if they're uncertain of where to find information or functionality.

The Navigation Sidebar is located along the left side of the screen. To edit the sidebar, click on Edit Sidebar below the Navigation area. This permits additional elements to be shown in the sidebar.

Editing a Page

The remarkable versatility of Sites really shines in the page edit mode. Here, users may exercise a great deal of creativity in terms of the look of pages as well as the special features that may appear on a page. To begin the editing process, click on Edit Page. This opens a new version of your page, with two new toolbars near the top. You will notice that light dotted lines will appear around sections of text in the work area. This helps you to distinguish between edit mode and view mode.

In Figure 16.3, note that the toolbar just below the Google logo contains four commands:

Insert. Allows insertion of a great variety of navigation, formatting elements, and gadgets.

Format. Controls formatting of text.

Table. Controls insertion of a table into the workspace.

Layout. Enables choice of a one, two, or three-column format in the workspace and other modifications of a page's layout.

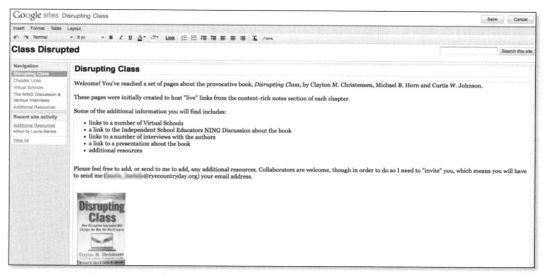

FIGURE 16.3. A Sites page in edit mode

The Insert menu is where Sites really sizzles. Click on Image to add a picture or graphic from your local computer or the web. To edit an image, you must be in the page edit mode, not page view. To activate image editing, click on the image and a set of controls will become visible at the bottom. The controls enable resizing of the image; aligning the image left, center, or right; and turning text wrapping around the image on or off. The maximum image size is 10 MB.

To create a link (to another page in your Site or the web), highlight the text you wish to serve as the anchor, and then click Link.

A table of contents enables easy navigation through a long or complex page. Text in the table of contents can be linked to different regions, or areas, of a page, so a simple click on text in the table jumps the viewer to the appropriate area. Click Insert > Table of Contents and follow the directions in the box that opens.

Clicking on Insert > Subpage creates a box that lists all the subpages associated with the current page. This is a great aid to navigation.

Insert > Horizontal Line inserts a horizontal line across the entire page to serve as a divider between sections.

The next selections come from Google Apps. It's likely that this list will grow. Each command enables placement of a Google App directly into your page. This means you can have an operational interactive calendar, a document (not an attachment, but a document itself), a map, a slide show from Picasa or Presentations, a spreadsheet, a spreadsheet form (see Chapter 6, Forms), or videos from YouTube or Google Video. Whenever you update one of these source applications back in its home space, it will be updated automatically in Sites. (Make sure to set the application to "automatically republish.") It is essential to use the Insert menu to add one of these applications; cutting and pasting will not work. These options add tremendous customizability to Sites pages.

The following commands round out the Insert menu. They're grouped into a category Google calls Gadgets.

Recent Posts. Takes the most recent posts from an Announcements page you have created and displays the first few lines in a textbox on your chosen page. You specify how many posts to display.

Recently Updated Files. Takes the most recent files you have uploaded as attachments to a File Cabinet page you have created and displays their names in a textbox on your chosen page. You specify how many file names to display.

Recent List Items. Takes the most recent list items you have placed on a Lists page you have created and displays them in a textbox on your chosen page. An obvious use for this function is to make to-do lists. You specify how many items to display.

Text Box. Creates a text box for you to type whatever you want into a text box that will appear on your chosen page.

More Gadgets. Opens a huge menu of Google Gadgets. These are the same gadgets that can be used in other Google Applications. There are scores of Gadgets to choose from, with many more on the way. These include all sorts of items such as clocks, calendars, to-do lists, RSS readers, online TV tuners, language translators, currency converters, weather stations, dictionaries, thesauri, image sources, games, stock charts, sports results, MP3 players, free software, and password storage. Installing these gadgets brings content to your page; users don't have to go out looking for it.

Google does not currently offer an application for users to make RSS feeds from their sites. With an RSS feed, viewers may subscribe to your site and receive updates to your site in their RSS reader (Google Reader or others). For instructions on how to set up an RSS feed from your site using a third-party application, go to http://siteshelp.kccloudsolutions.com/step-by-step-guides/googlesitesrssfeed/.

Also notice two additional commands near the top right corner of the window: Save and Cancel. Save saves the current page and all its contents. Cancel stops your work on the current page and returns you to that page in view mode. No work is saved.

Working with the Navigation Sidebar

As an experienced web navigator, you know that a good site needs to make it easy for visitors to go exactly where they want with a minimum of clicks. In Sites, that's the function of the Navigation Sidebar, which has its own set of controls.

The default location for the Navigation Sidebar is the left side of the page. It is possible to change the location of the sidebar to the right of the page, or to have two sidebars, by using the Layout menu. If you want to insert something in your site that will appear on every page, the place to do that is in the Navigation Sidebar.

The Navigation Sidebar's default setting displays Home, Sitemap, and Edit Sidebar as the only visible commands. Clicking Home takes you back to your site's home page from anywhere on

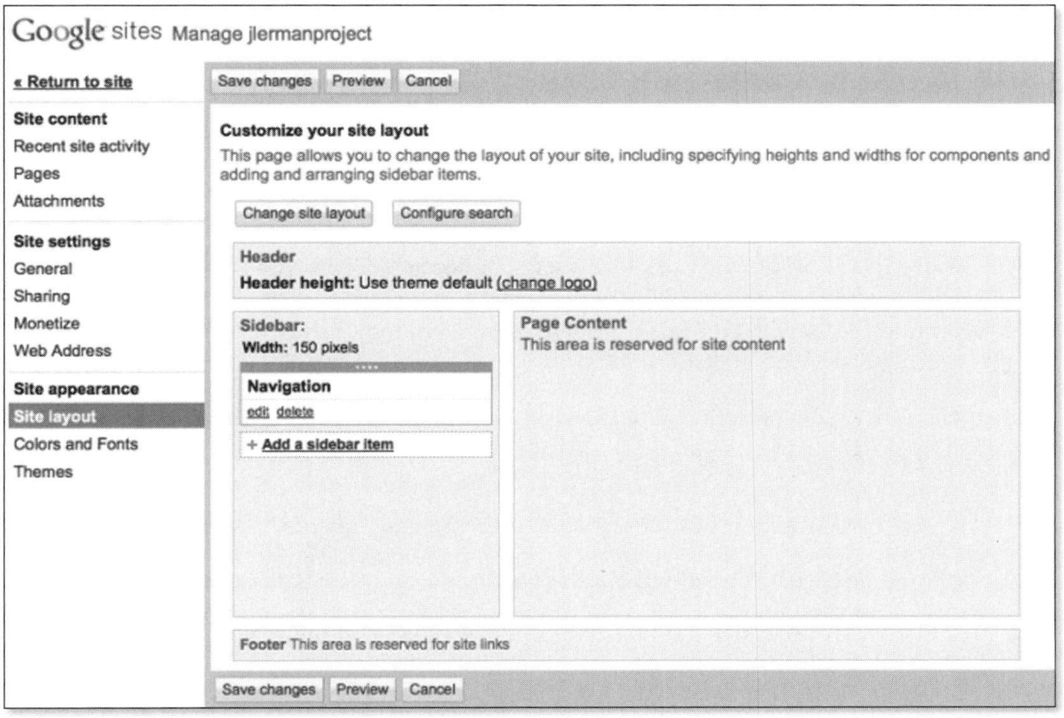

FIGURE 16.4. After clicking Edit Sidebar this screen appears

the site. The Sitemap automatically shows the connections among all site pages. A second link to the Sitemap may be found at the bottom of each page, in the center. Click Edit Sidebar to go to a new window that enables changes to the sidebar as well as your site as a whole (see Fig. 16.4).

Click on Add A Sidebar Item to choose from among many possible elements. Chosen elements will be shown in the Navigation Sidebar on every page on your site.

Collaboration

People you have invited as collaborators may all work on the site in real time. However, no two people may work on the same page simultaneously. If you try to work on a page someone is already editing, you will be told it is locked. It is possible to "break the lock" while someone is editing a page. This can be useful because sometimes people forget to log out and leave pages open after they have stopped working on them. However, if you "break the lock" and that person comes right back to edit the page you just worked on, the changes they make will over-write yours. So, if you do "break the lock," it's good to go back to the page to check it shortly after you log off.

TEACHER TIPS

- For examples of websites built with this App, visit Google's Help for Sites (http://sites.google.com/support).

- Savvy web users will recognize that Sites is actually a form of web tool known as a wiki. We don't understand why Google has chosen not to refer to Sites as a wiki, but the company must have its reasons. We mention this because there is a wonderful video that explains what wikis are, what they're good for, and basically how they work. It's short and very clear and will definitely help people who are trying to wrap their minds around this particular tool. It's produced by Common Craft (www.commoncraft.com/video-wikis-plain-english).

- Here are 27 ideas for ways educators might use Sites:

    - Create a showcase for student work

    - Make a drop-box for students to submit assignments

    - Have student work groups or faculty committees share work and ideas

    - Develop a space to house your personal files and thoughts—converse with yourself

    - Collaborate with a partner to share ideas and strategies

    - Develop a site as a parent/community newsletter

    - Have students publish an online class newspaper

    - Create a site for students to house portfolios of their work

    - Have students write content outlines and study guides collaboratively

    - Use a student portfolio for parent conferences to document progress over time and areas needing continued attention

    - Publish homework, announcements, and a class calendar for students

    - Have students publish lecture notes for those absent; rotate responsibility

    - Promote peer editing of student work and projects

    - Use Sites to collaborate on a project with another class across the hall or halfway around the world

    - Some people use Sites as a presentation tool as an alternative to PowerPoint or Keynote

    - Conduct a debate in Sites

    - Compile research data over time, documenting the processes by which it is gathered

- Create a branching story, starting with a single premise and moving in multiple directions simultaneously—with separate pages and subpages for new branches. Readers may follow their own path.

- Create multiple path scenarios in mathematics and science

- Students create lists of resources on a topic and evaluate their quality (websites, images, videos, audios, slide shows, past student papers, articles, etc.) Maintain these lists from year to year and have subsequent students critique and add to them.

- Have students write their own text material and evaluate one another's work

- Ask students to create collaborative memoirs for those who will come after them (next year's class)

- Have students create a homework help site. This will help both the creators and the visitors.

- Make a site as a time capsule, capturing a period in the past, present, or future

- Create a site around a particular issue, topic, problem, or conflict—with separate pages for different points of view

- Develop a hoax site and see if others will accept it as true

- Maintain a class diary, documenting what happens in each class every day, rotate student responsibility, make entries in real time

- It is possible to copy an entire Google Site and export it to another location on the web, while leaving the site that's being copied right where it is. The process is described step-by-step at the Unofficial Google Sites Help website (http://siteshelp.kccloudsolutions.com/step-by-step-guides/copysite).

- Molly Robbins, from the Cherry Creek Schools in Colorado, posted this description of using Sites on her website (https://sites.google.com/a/cherrycreekschools.org/google-literacy-presentation/if-you-were-one-of-our-students):

  I wanted to have my students keep track of their reading throughout the year through their own site. I started by having students break into their writing communities—which consist of no more than three students—to design and work on their sites. My hope was to have them present their thinking for each book so the students could see their growth in thinking and writing over time.

  My favorite post occurred when we read *How the Garcia Girls Lost Their Accents*. I got on to each group's site and posted a picture with directions for them to find a quote from the chapter read to match the picture.

  It was awesome to see my students flipping through their books and discussing in authentic ways the different thinking about which quotes would fit the picture. It became evident the discovery of many correct and fitting answers allowed the students to think and talk in authentic ways about their reading.

- Creation of a website can be a complex proposition, even after you have gathered all your resources. Try to allow yourself ample time in order to minimize frustration. Think about using a storyboard or other form of graphic organizer to plan out the organization and flow of your site. Leave time to master the technology. Start small, then work toward getting big. We learned the hard way and tried to make our first site in Sites in a big rush. To put it mildly, this was not a good idea.

- We have tried to make our instructions as easy to follow as possible, but there are many, many steps to this process; particularly the first time you try, it's likely to take longer than expected. Once you get the hang of it, it will start to seem pretty easy ... but getting the hang of it can take some effort. Don't give up. Sites is a wonderful tool.

- Helen Barrett has created a great Google Site titled "Creating an Interactive Portfolio with Google Sites." (That's right, this is a Site about Sites.) It is a detailed, step-by-step guide to creating an online portfolio in Sites for either personal or group purposes of learning, showcasing, or assessment (http://sites.helenbarrett.net/portfolio/how-to).

- If you make your website private, be aware that all users will need to have Google accounts to access it.

- Google has created a short, informative introductory tutorial about Sites. You can access it at http://services.google.com/apps/resources/overviews/welcome/topicSites/index.html.

- The folks at SmartTeaching.org have come up with a great list of ways to use a wiki (essentially the same thing as a Google Site) in school. Access "50 Ways to Use Wikis for a More Collaborative and Interactive Classroom" at www.smartteaching.org/blog/2008/08/50-ways-to-use-wikis-for-a-more-collaborative-and-interactive-classroom/.

SECTION IV

DO SCHOOL
DIFFERENTLY

CHAPTER 17

GOOGLE APPS
THE EDUCATION EDITION

Harold Olejarz

CHAPTER AT A GLANCE

- Description and Benefits
- Getting Started—Setting Up a Google Apps Account
- Administering Your Google Apps Account
  - Dashboard
  - Users and Groups
  - Adding Users
  - Domain Settings
  - Advanced Tools
  - Support
  - Service Settings
- Online Help
- Summary

DESCRIPTION AND BENEFITS

In previous chapters you learned about many individual Google applications (notice the small "a" in applications) such as Google Presentations and Google Spreadsheets. Many of these individual applications (small "a") are included in Google Apps. Google Apps (with a capital "A") refers to a collection or, as Google says, a group "of hosted communication and collaboration applications."

So now you might be wondering: what is Google Apps all about? How is it different from a single Google application or a single Google account? How can a teacher, class, or school use Google Apps to do things better, faster, or differently? How will using Google Apps improve teaching and learning, and engage students?

First, Google Apps comes in three different editions: Standard Edition, Premier Edition, and Education Edition. The Standard Edition is free but allows only as many as 50 users and does not include the Video application. The Premier Edition is designed for business use, and the cost is $50 per user account per year. The Education Edition is free and allows any number of users. All three editions of Google Apps provide the same set of Google applications, like Presentations, Docs, and Spreadsheets, and are administered in the same way. This chapter will focus on the Google Apps Education Edition, which most schools and teachers will want to use.

Once again, the Education Edition is a self-contained package of Google applications that any school or school district can easily manage for its own use. The applications contained in the Education Edition are Docs (Documents, Spreadsheets, Presentations, and Forms), Calendar, Contacts, Gmail, Chat, Sites, and Video. In order to avoid confusion, think of Google applications (with a small "a") as referring to specific applications like Google Calendar and Spreadsheets. Think of Google Apps (with a capital "A") as referring to the entire suite of Google applications named previously, all housed under one roof and administered by you.

As I said, the Education Edition provides your school with its own suite of Google applications that can be made as private or public as you wish, available to any or all of the students, staff, and families you choose ... all free and without advertising. You may choose to include as many or as few of the Google applications as you wish. This makes a very powerful collection of tools available to everyone in your community who has an Internet connection. There is no software to obtain, everything is compatible with everything else, and real-time collaboration is possible for everyone.

The Education Edition will help you administer Google applications and will put your entire school on the same page. It will make it easy for students, faculty, and administrators to share documents, websites, calendars, video, and more. These tools will enable students, teachers, and administrators to work on documents at home and at school without having to worry about software compatibility or the version of the document they are working on. All versions of documents are saved, time- and date-stamped, and identified by their author for easy retrieval and attribution. The Education Edition allows students and teachers to collaborate more effectively in a safe environment, free of ads and uninvited users.

Imagine several students working on the same document from different computers simultaneously. They will no longer need to worry about getting together face-to-face after school to work on a group project, because each can work from home, at the same time. With the Education Edition, collaborative projects will be more mutual and encourage all students to contribute.

The Education Edition also makes it possible for teachers to collect work online. No need to worry about large e-mail attachments, software incompatibility, or collecting students' work from 20 to 30 flash drives. Teachers can use the Education Edition to provide feedback directly on students' documents. If you can read the document online, you may no longer need a printed copy. In addition, students can use the Education Edition to share documents. This means that groups of students can review, revise, and comment on one another's work online. Just think of how many trees you will save.

With the Education Edition, your students and teachers will be able to use Google tools on a safe and secure network. Students will be able to use Google Docs without an e-mail login. Documents and websites can be set to be shared within your domain only. This means that no one without permission will be able to view or edit documents. The Education Edition also gives you the opportunity to create e-mail accounts for students that can only be used to contact teachers and other students within your private domain ... kind of like a walled garden for just those in your school.

On the other hand, if you want to share your websites with the world, you may allow students and teachers to publish their websites so that everyone on the Internet can see their pages. You will also be able to select the Google tools you want to make available to your students and staff. So, if you want your students to have access to Google Docs, and not to have access to Gmail or Chat, Google Apps Education Edition puts the power in your hands.

Another great reason to go with Google Apps Education Edition is that it runs on Google's servers. This will take the pressure off your IT department to run and maintain additional services. Since Google Apps Education Edition runs on Google's servers, reliability is not a problem. Google guarantees that Google Apps Education Edition will be available 99.9% of the time.

GETTING STARTED— SETTING UP A GOOGLE APPS ACCOUNT

The first thing you will need to do is create a Google Apps account (for the sake of brevity, we will just call it Google Apps from this point forward, but we really mean Google Apps Education Edition). To create the account, go to the Google Apps Application page (www.google.com/apps). This page is shown in Figure 17.1. Once you are on this page, click on the School IT manager's page, illustrated by the schoolhouse.

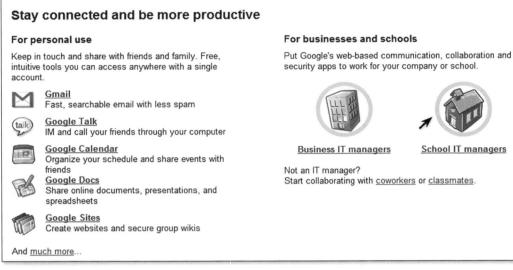

FIGURE 17.1. Google Apps page

The School IT manager's page, Figure 17.2, offers links to information about Google Apps Education Edition. There is also a video that describes the benefits of Google Apps and the problems Google Apps can solve for organizations. You may want to share this video with your administrators to help convince them of the value of Google Apps. Once you have explored some of the information on this page you will want to click on the Get Apps For Your School button just above the school building icon.

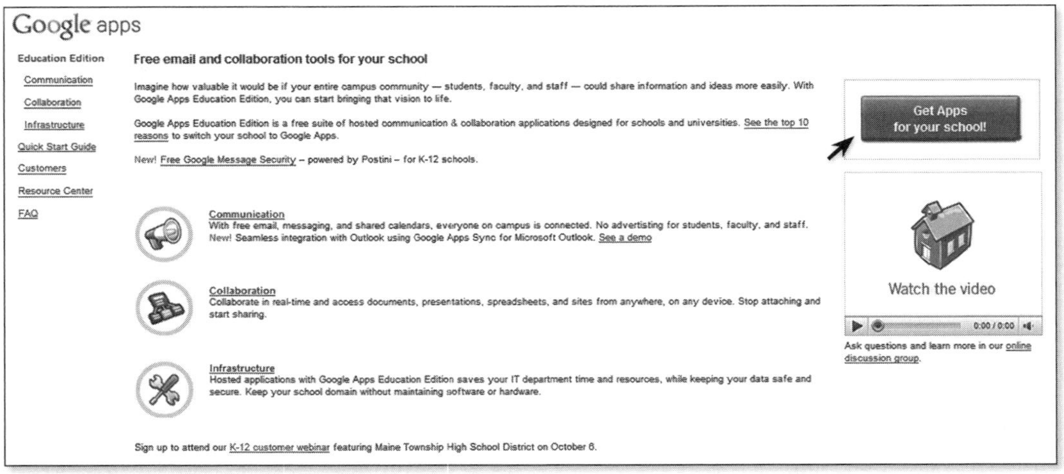

FIGURE 17.2. Google Apps Education Edition information

After you have clicked on the Get Apps For Your School button, you will go through a series of screens that will ask for information required to set up an existing domain for Google Apps. Even if your school already has a domain, you may choose to purchase a new domain name for Google Apps. If you are not sure what a domain name is, it is a website address like www.google.com. If your school has a website, it has a domain name. For example, in the web address www.shadyavenueschool.org, the domain name is "shadyavenueschool.org."

It's important to consider whether to use a domain name you already have or to create a new domain name for your Google Apps account. I strongly suggest that you create a new domain name for your Google Apps account. The cost is only $10 per year per domain name. Setting up a new domain will make it easier to manage your users and prevent any conflicts that may occur with your existing domain name, especially if you give teachers and students access to Google Sites and/or Gmail accounts. A new and separate domain name will enable teachers and students to use Google Sites to create websites that are viewable only by the users in your new domain. In effect, this gives you a private network where students and teachers can share and post files on a safe, secure, and private website. If you prefer to make Google Sites public and publish your pages to the public, you can do that too.

If you are a teacher who would like to set up a Google Apps account for your classes only, you will definitely want to set up your own domain name so that you can add or delete users and decide which tools to make available to your students. If you are in a large school district with several schools, you may want different schools to use different features of Google Apps. This can easily be done if each school has its own domain name for its Google Apps account.

TEACHER TIP

SELECT A DOMAIN NAME that is easy to remember, since this will be the URL (web address) people will use to access your Google Apps account. I teach at Eisenhower Middle School, so eisenhowerms.org was my choice. If your first choice is not available, try different names. Since this is an education site, you should choose the .org suffix from the drop-down menu.

TEACHER TIP

WHEN YOU SIGN UP for your Google Apps Education Edition account you can activate your account immediately by using one of three verification options—uploading an HTML file, Creating CNAME records, or configuring your MX records. In the Support Section you will find the Account Setup and Verification link. This will take you to a page that provides step-by-step instructions on how to verify your account. The Support Section is discussed later in this chapter.

If you already have a Google Apps account and want to upgrade it to the Education Edition, go to the request form (www.google.com/support/a/bin/request.py?contact_type=nonprofit) and enter the requested information in the required fields. In some cases, it may be easier to simply set up a Google Apps account and then upgrade it to the Education Edition. Unless you are a classroom teacher or small school that plans to have fewer than 50 users, you will have to upgrade to the Education Edition to have more than 50 users without having to pay any fees. Nonprofits are also eligible for Google Apps Education Edition.

ADMINISTERING YOUR GOOGLE APPS ACCOUNT

Once you have set up your account, you will have the ability to administer it. This means you will be able to add users, decide on which Google tools you want to make available to your users, and decide what level of sharing options you would like to give to your users. You can also share the administration of your account by giving other users administrator privileges. All of this is done using the account Dashboard.

Dashboard

When account administrators sign in, they are taken to the Dashboard screen (see Fig. 17.3). The Dashboard is the place to administer your Apps account. Notice the six sections on the bar just below the Google Search box. The six sections are Dashboard, Users and Groups, Domain Settings, Advanced Tools, Support, and Service Settings. Below the sections bar are links to manage account information and create new users. The Service Settings area is the place to administer the Google tools you will be giving your users.

On the Dashboard find the option Service Settings in large bold print. Below Service Settings are the Services enabled on this Apps account. As you can see, the services enabled are Chat, Docs, Mobile, Calendar, and Sites. If you want to add more services, click on the Add More Services link to the right of Service Settings. This will take you to a screen that will show you any available services that you have not yet enabled. If you want to manage or delete the services you have enabled, simply click on the service name—Docs, for example, and this will take

TEACHER TIP

EVERY GOOGLE APPS account has its own sign-in page. The model example of a sign-in page URL is https://www.google.com/a/yourdomainname. For example, I purchased the domain name ourschoolapps.com. To log in to this Apps account, I would go to https://www.google.com/a/ourschoolapps.com. This is why an easy-to-remember domain name is best. I will be using screen shots from ourschoolapps.com and eisenhowerms.org to illustrate the rest of this chapter.

The ourschoolapps.com account is a Standard Edition account and the eisenhowerms.org account is an Education Edition account. In most cases, there is little difference between the Dashboard screens in either account.

you to the Service Settings page. Service Settings enables you to manage the sharing options of a Google application. The settings are reviewed later in this chapter. You will also use Service Settings if you want to disable a Google service, such as Chat.

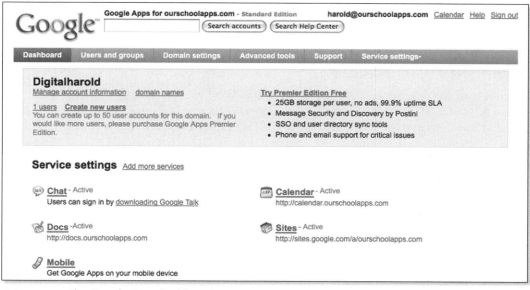

FIGURE 17.3. The Google Apps Dashboard

Users and Groups

Use this section to see a list of your users, enable contact sharing, create new users, and create groups of users. In Figure 17.4, only two users are listed, John Doe and me, Harold Olejarz. You can see that in the Status column, I am listed as the administrator, and I last logged in at 2:41 p.m. The Username column lists my username as harold. John Doe is a newly created user who has not logged in, and his username is 11JohnDoe. Once again, keep in mind that you can have more than one administrator for your Apps account.

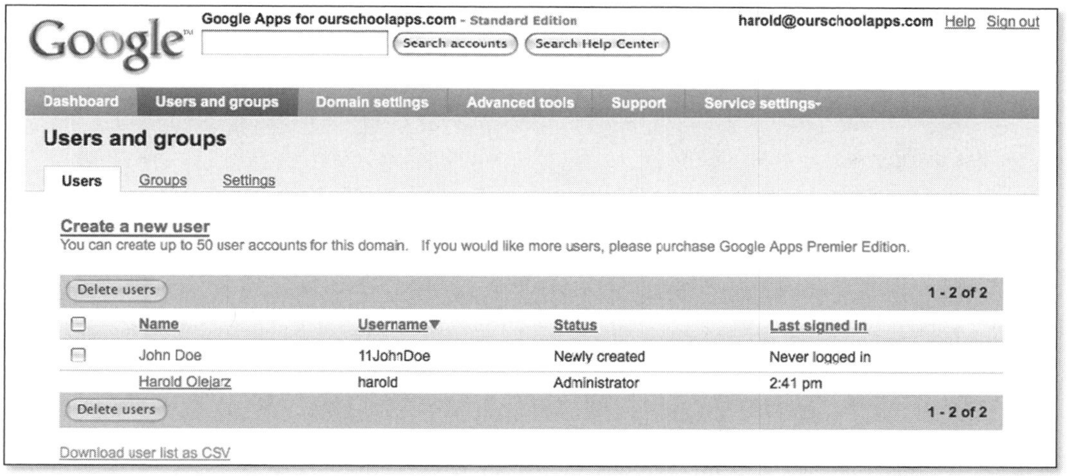

FIGURE 17.4. Google Apps Users and Groups

Adding Users

There are two ways to create new users. You can create individual users, one at a time, or upload a group of users from a CSV (comma separated value) file. If you have a Standard Edition, you may have up to 50 users. If you have the Education Edition, you may add more users without having to pay any fees. Before we get into adding users, consider the teacher tip that refers to adding teachers.

Creating New Users Individually

When you are in the Users and Groups section, you can create a new user by clicking on the Create A New User link. This will bring up a screen like the one in Figure 17.5. Enter your user's first and last name and username. Just below the Username box is your new user's temporary password. New users must use the temporary password to log in before setting a new personal password. Clicking on the Create A New User button will create your new user and take you to a screen with the login information for that user. You can simply copy this information and paste it into a new e-mail, or print the login information for your new user. If you would like to assign a password simply click on the Set Password link and follow the directions.

TEACHER TIP

IF YOU ARE ADDING TEACHERS you may want to add them individually. This way your teachers can create an individual password on their first sign-in. If you are adding large numbers of students or teachers, you will definitely want to do a bulk upload from a CSV file. In order to distinguish teachers from students, I suggest that teachers' usernames have a Mr., Ms., Miss, or Mrs. before their surname. For example, my username on my school Apps account is MrOlejarz. Notice there is no period between Mr and Olejarz. Google Apps does not accept a period in a username.

If you are adding large numbers of students from different grade levels, keep in mind that at some point you will want to remove students who are no longer in your school. I have found that since Google lists users by username it is useful to put the year of graduation in front of the student's username. In the example above, since John Doe will be graduating in 2011, his username is 11JohnDoe. This will organize your student users by graduation year and make it easier to delete them once they leave your school. Otherwise you will have to have a list of graduates and carefully go through all of your users, one by one, to find and delete graduates.

Identifying students by year of graduation will also make it easier for students and teachers to find the correct student if they are sharing a document. If, for example, there are five Johns in your school but only one is graduating in 2011, typing in 11John will immediately bring up the correct student.

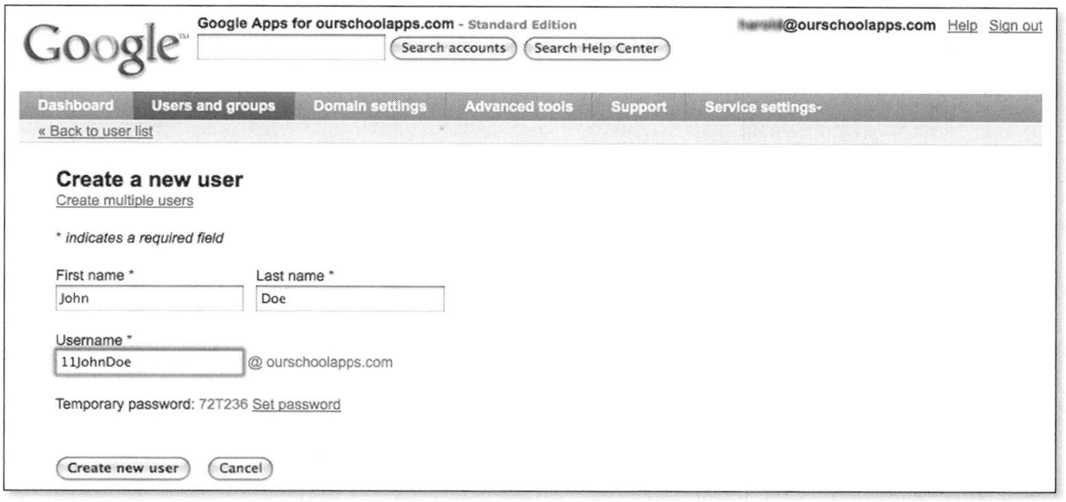

FIGURE 17.5. Create a New User

Creating Multiple New Users

To add multiple users click on the Create Multiple Users link. This will bring you to the screen shown in Figure 17.6. This screen enables you to add multiple users.

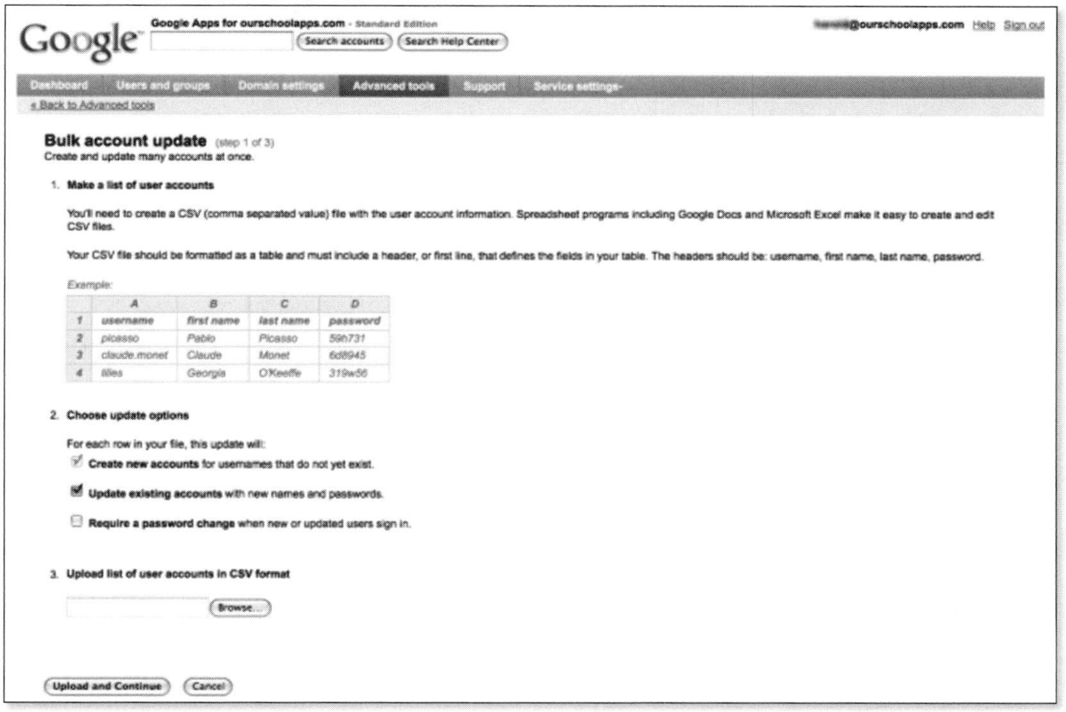

FIGURE 17.6. Create Multiple Users

Before you can add multiple users you will need to create a CSV file. The instructions as stated on the Google page are:

> You'll need to create a CSV (comma separated value) file with the user account information. Spreadsheet programs including Google Docs and Microsoft Excel make it easy to create and edit CSV files.
>
> Your CSV file should be formatted as a table and must include a header, or first line, that defines the fields in your table. The headers should be: user-name, first name, last name, password.

If you school or district uses a student information system, your IT department should be able to generate a CSV file of your students. If you have that information in an Excel spreadsheet, you can generate a CSV file by opening the file in Excel, going to the File menu, and selecting Save As. In the dialog box next to Format there is a drop-down menu from which you should select CSV (Comma Delimited). Save your file in this format. Then use the Browse button on the Bulk account update page to navigate to and upload your CSV file of users.

Domain Settings

The Domain Settings section, pictured in Figure 17.7, has four tabs: General, Account Information, Domain Names, and Appearance.

In the General tab, you will type your organization name. In the User support box, you can include a reminder to your users if they have a problem logging in. Select the language and time zone that is right for your school. In the New Services and Pre-release Features area, be sure that both checkboxes are *not* checked. You do not want Google to automatically enable new services and features until you and your administrators have had a chance to preview them. In the Education Edition, you are also given the option to hide all advertisements in any of the services provided in your domain.

You will want to check the Enable SSL box. This will make your users' connection to Google Apps more secure. I use the Current Version of the Control Panel just to be on

---

TEACHER TIP

IN ORDER TO successfully upload multiple users, you should make sure that all of the usernames contain no spaces, special characters, or periods. For example, if your student's user name is JohnDoe be sure that there are no spaces between the first and last name of the student's username. Also, if your teacher's user name is MrsSmith make certain that there is no period or space between *Mrs* and *Smith*. In order to successfully upload multiple users, you must make certain that all passwords are at least six characters long. In my district, students have six-character ID numbers so I use the students' ID numbers as their passwords. If you have the Education Edition of Google Apps and need more users, there is a link that allows you to request more users. This usually takes a day or two to process and is very easy.

the safe side. Be sure to click on the Save Changes button at the bottom of the page once you have made your changes.

In the Account Information tab you will set the primary administrator for the account and list a secondary e-mail address in case you need to reset a forgotten administrator's password. You will also be given the option to get e-mail notifications, provide feedback, and unsubscribe from Google marketing e-mails. Be sure to click on the Save Changes button at the bottom of the page once you have made your changes.

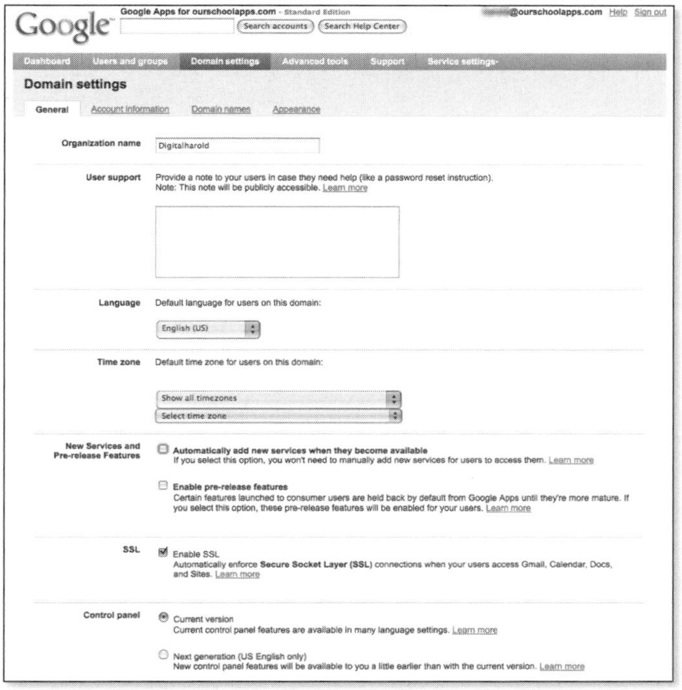

FIGURE 17.7. The Domain Settings section

In the Domain Names tab you will find information about your domain name and a link to access your Advanced DNS settings. These settings are used to update your domain information and change settings for e-mail and other services.

The Appearance tab gives you the opportunity to add a custom logo to your domain and select a color for the sign-in box. In order to upload your own logo, you will have to follow the requirements specified by Google. They are:

> Admins can upload images of varying sizes. If your image is smaller than the recommended size of 143 x 59 pixels, it should look fine. If your image is bigger, the image may overflow while portions are clipped. The file type can be JPEG, PNG, or GIF, and should be smaller than 20kb.

Once you have created the graphic in a program like Photoshop, simply use the Browse button to select and upload your file. Once again, be sure to click on the Save Changes button at the bottom of the page once you have made your changes.

Advanced Tools

The Advanced Tools section, pictured in Figure 17. 8, lives up to its name. The only tool that most users will use in this section is the User Accounts Bulk Update. This tool was discussed in the Users and Groups section earlier in this chapter. The "advanced" part of the Advanced Tools section allows you to manage authorization protocols, set up e-mail migration, and manage API references. Since most users will not use these tools without the assistance of an IT professional, they go beyond the scope of this chapter. After many of the tools listed in this section there is a Learn More link that you should use if you need to use one of these advanced tools.

FIGURE 17.8. The Advanced Tools section

Support

The Support section offers links to online and telephone support. The resources available from this page should provide the answer to nearly all of the questions you have. For additional online help see the "Online Help" section of this chapter.

Your Customer PIN and Support PIN numbers are located on this page. If you contact support, you will need this information.

Service Settings

The Service Settings section is the place to go to if you want to manage or disable any of the Google applications in your suite of Google Apps. For example, if you do not want your users to use Google Sites, simply click on the Service Settings tab and scroll down to Sites. Use the Disable Sites link near the bottom of the screen (shown in Fig. 17.9).

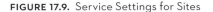

FIGURE 17.9. Service Settings for Sites

You can also set the Sharing options for Calendar, Docs, and Sites from the Service Settings section. Figure 17.9 shows the Service Settings for Google Sites, and the two main options are:

Users cannot share sites outside this domain. This means that only users with accounts in your Google Apps Education Edition domain will be able to view the sites posted. This option is a great way to keep teachers' and students' sites safe and private. It is also an excellent way to create a school network where teachers and students can publish and view documents and information such as student names and copyrighted material that you may not want to publish on your public website.

Users can share outside this domain, with or without a warning. This means that the sites created by students and teachers will be published to the Internet for anyone to view. If you choose this option, *make sure that your school has an effective Acceptable Use Policy that clearly communicates to students and teachers what is and is not appropriate for publication on the Internet.* You, or another responsible professional, should also monitor students' public sites to ensure that inappropriate or personal information is not published.

TEACHER TIP

IF YOU DO NOT ALLOW your users to share documents outside of your domain and still want to allow other people, who are not in your school, to share documents with your students and teachers, you can create new user accounts or set up guest accounts for people who are not part of your school. This is the best way to ensure that your students are working in a safe and secure environment.

ONLINE HELP

Google has launched a very comprehensive site to support teachers and schools in using Google Apps Education Edition (http://www.google.com/a/help/intl/en/edu/k12.html). A list of Google websites that I found especially helpful follows. Also included is a website I set up to help my school transition to Google Apps.

> The Google Apps Admin Help: www.google.com/support/a
> *This page provides deployment guides, admin basics, control panel tabs information, and information on managing and using services.*
>
> The Google Apps Admin Help—Training:
> www.google.com/support/a/bin/answer.py?answer=67784
> *This page has a great collection of short videos on Google Apps, Gmail, Sites, Calendar, and more. The videos are short and direct.*
>
> Google Apps Admin Help—E-mail:
> www.google.com/support/a/bin/topic.py?topic=9202
> *Setting up Gmail can be a complicated process. This page has links that deal with Mail Delivery, Gmail Training, Mail Migration, and Mail Setup. If you plan on enabling mail, be sure to review the links on this page.*
>
> The Google Apps Education Community: http://edu.googleapps.com/Home
> *This page has links to tutorials, tips, and blogs.*
>
> The Google Apps Education Community Help Forum:
> www.google.com/support/forum/p/apps-education?hl=en
>
> Google Apps Services Help: www.google.com/support/a/users/?hl=en
> *Links to Google's help forums for all of the Google services available in Google Apps.*
>
> Using Google Docs and Apps @ Eisenhower: http://eisenhowerms.pbworks.com
> *This is a page I set up for my school.*

SUMMARY

Google Apps Education Edition offers educational communities a variety of Google applications. These applications enable your students, teachers, and administrators to develop 21st-century skills using 21st-century tools. Google Apps gives you the power to administer all of these Google applications: Docs (Documents, Spreadsheets, and Presentations), Calendar, Contacts, Gmail, Chat, Sites, and Video. This power ensures that your school is using Google applications in a safe and secure environment. Google Apps will also lift a large burden from your IT department, since everything runs on Google servers. Best of all, it's free! Your district may actually save money by not having to purchase and install software and hardware upgrades.

Before implementing Google Apps Education Edition, your district's Acceptable Use Policy should be modified. Students need to be made aware of the fact that Google Apps is an educational tool that the district is providing for educational use only. Since Google Docs and Google Sites provide students with publishing opportunities, guidelines need to be provided so that students know what is permitted. If your district activates Gmail and Chat, you may be providing students with an opportunity to communicate with people inside and outside of your school. This needs to be carefully considered and spelled out in the AUP.

One of the most valuable applications in Google Apps is Google Docs. Google Docs, which includes word processing, spreadsheet, presentation, and form creation applications, makes it easy for everyone in your school community to collaborate and share documents in real time from any computer with an Internet connection. Once you have set up your Google Apps account, I suggest that you start by enabling Docs and Calendar and limit sharing to within your Google Apps domain. Give your students and staff a chance to get comfortable with Docs and Calendar before adding more services.

Google Video is another service in Google Apps Education Edition that you will want to activate as soon as you have set up your Apps account. Google Video provides up to 10 GB to store and share videos. The videos that you store using this App can be seen only by members of your Google domain. In effect, Google Video gives you the ability to set up a private video distribution network to host and share videos within your district or school.

Google Sites is the next application to explore and consider. Before activating Sites, your district should determine if the web pages created with Sites will be public or private. As with Google Docs, I suggest that you start out cautiously and limit the sharing options to within your Google Apps domain.

Activating Google Chat and Gmail should be carefully considered. Many school districts are reluctant to give students an open avenue to communicating with people outside of their school system. On the other hand, if our goal is to teach real-world skills, what better way to do this than to provide students with real-world tools? Limiting Gmail and Chat to users in your domain only is probably the best compromise when dealing with students in elementary schools.

When Google Chat is activated, users can automatically chat with other Google Apps and Gmail users. This means that your students will be able to chat with anyone in the world with a Gmail account. If you would like to limit students so that they can chat only with users in your school, you have two options.

A simple work-around solution is to use the Spreadsheet application in Google Docs, which has a chat function. A chat room can be set up by simply opening a Google Doc spreadsheet and sharing the spreadsheet with the people you would like to chat with. The spreadsheet has a chat window that will let you see who is viewing and/or editing the spreadsheet. This will enable you to chat with people who have access to and opened the spreadsheet. This ensures that your students will be able to chat with only the people who have accounts in your Google Apps domain.

Gmail is a great e-mail application that is part of Google Apps. If you enable Gmail, you will have to carefully go through the Gmail service settings to configure your account so that your users will be able to send and receive e-mail. If you decide to enable Gmail, make sure you work with your school IT department to ensure that it is set up properly. If you have set up your Apps account with a domain name you are already using for e-mail, keep in mind that you will have to transition from your old e-mail system to Gmail. This could be quite disruptive, so it is best to proceed with caution and be sure that your users have bought into the changeover. Google provides extensive help for setting up and managing e-mail. The Google Apps Admin

TEACHER TIP

I HAVE POSTED several handouts online that deal with Managing Google Apps Education Edition Gmail with Postini. They provide step-by-step instructions on how to limit Gmail to your domain, create filters that screen for inappropriate language and filters that allow only specific e-mail addresses and domains to e-mail users in your Apps domain. The directions may be found at www.olejarz.com/handouts/postinidomainonlye-mail.pdf.

Help page has an extensive section on e-mail (www.google.com/support/a/bin/topic.py?topic=9202). Setting up Gmail can be a complicated process. This page has links that deal with Mail Delivery, Gmail Training, Mail Migration, and Mail Setup. If you plan on enabling Gmail, be sure to review the material and links presented on this page.

If you choose to enable Gmail, all of the users in your Google Apps domain will have access to Gmail. Google does offer an e-mail security service that allows you to limit messaging to within your domain. This means that you can limit students' e-mail accounts so that they can only send and receive e-mail to and from school members. The service is called Postini. At this point, Google will offer this service free of charge for schools until July 2010.

Postini will enable you to give teachers and students separate e-mail systems, provide virus protection, filter e-mails with certain words, and generally manage your school's Gmail accounts. If you decide to give students Gmail accounts, Postini is a must.

Once again, you can avoid problems publishing Google Sites and setting up Gmail if you start by purchasing a new domain name for your Google Apps Education Edition account. Getting a new domain name for different schools, classes, and/or grade levels will give Apps administrators the ability to turn on or turn off the Google services that are appropriate for their users.

In my school, students are thrilled with Google Apps. It gives them the freedom to work at home and at school without having to worry about software incompatibility. The students no longer worry about having files stored on USB drives that are left at home or lost. Also, students can collaborate on projects without having to meet in the same place or even at the same time.

As a teacher, I find that my students are more productive. Google Apps gives me the ability to view student documents as they are worked on. I can easily see how much work each student did on a group project by checking the document's revision history. Students no longer have to print projects because I can read and grade their projects online. Also, I no longer have to worry about using a USB drive to collect student projects or worry about e-mail file attachments that are too large or don't open.

Google Apps Education Edition is a terrific suite of applications that enhances and improves teaching and learning. Once you and your students start using it, you will wonder how you got along without it.

LESSON PLANS

LESSON PLAN
INTRODUCTION

We have developed 43 original lesson plans using the six most popular Google Applications: Documents, Presentations, Spreadsheets, Blogger, Maps, and Earth. We hope these ideas will provoke your interest and your creativity.

The lessons are grouped into separate sections for elementary, middle, and high school levels. Each section includes a summary table that lists the lesson plan title, page number, grade level, age level, subject, and the Google Apps used. However, you may find something of interest in a level that is not the one you teach. If you can change something to better suit your situation, by all means do so.

We are very grateful to the wonderful educators who have contributed their ideas here. Sincere thanks to Jerome Burg, Cheryl Davis, Pamela Friedman, John Hrevnack, Carol LaRow, Sarah Rolle, Eleanor Funk Schuster, and Andrea Tejedor. They worked long and hard to share their enthusiasm for these great tools with you and your students.

The following standards were referenced in the lesson plans:

National Geography Standards

National Geography Standards, Geography Education Standards Project. 1994. Geography for Life: The National Geography Standard. Washington D.C.: National Geographic Society Committee on Research and Exploration. The full list of standards is available at www.nationalgeographic.com/xpeditions/standards/matrix.html.

National Science Education Standards

The full list of standards is available at www.nap.edu/openbook.php?record_id=4962/.

National Standards for Civics and Government

Reprinted with permission. National Standards for Civics and Govenment. ©1994, 2003. Center for Civic Education. Calabasas, California, USA. The full list of standards is available at www.civiced.org.

National Standards for History

The full list of standards is available at http://nchs.ucla.edu/standards/us-standards5-12.html.

NCSS Curriculum Standards for Social Studies

The full list of standards is available at www.socialstudies.org/standards/.

NCTE/IRA Standards for the English Language Arts

Standards for the English Language Arts, by the International Reading Association and the National Council of Teachers of English, ©1996 by the International Reading Association and the National Council of Teachers of English. Reprinted with permission. The full list of standards is available at www.ncte.org/standards/.

NCTM Principles and Standards for School Mathematics

Reprinted with permission from Principles and Standards for School Mathematics, ©2000 by the National Council of Teachers of Mathematics (NCTM) . All rights reserved. NCTM does not endorse the content or validity of the alignments in this book. The full list of standards is available at http://standards.nctm.org.

ELEMENTARY SCHOOL
LESSONS

LESSON PLANS

- After-School Activities
- Biomes of the Earth
- Calorie Counter
- The Camping Trip
- A Day at the Beach
- Discover Blogging
- Favorite Fruits
- The Gift Giver
- Google Earth Pen Pals
- Home Measurements
- How We Spend Our Time
- Mapping Our Community
- Sam the Trucker
- School News
- Travel of Our Ancestors
- U.S. Immigration
- The World in Our Classroom
- Writing Fables

LESSON TITLE	PAGE #	GRADE LEVEL (U.S.)	AGES	SUBJECT AREA(S)	GOOGLE APP(S) USED
After-School Activities	217	5	9–11	Math	Presentations, Image Search
Biomes of the Earth	220	2–4	6–10	Science	Earth
Calorie Counter	223	5	9–11	Math	Spreadsheets
The Camping Trip	227	3	7–9	Math	Blogger, Search
A Day at the Beach	230	3	7–9	Math	Documents
Discover Blogging	233	2–4	6–10	ELA	Blogger
Favorite Fruits	236	3	7–9	Math	Presentations, Image Search
The Gift Giver	239	5	9–11	Math	Spreadsheets
Google Earth Pen Pals	242	2–4	6–10	ELA	Earth
Home Measurements	244	4	8–10	Math	Blogger, Spreadsheets
How We Spend Our Time	248	4	8–10	Math	Spreadsheets
Mapping Our Community	251	1–2	5–8	ELA	Maps
Sam the Trucker	253	4	8–10	Math	Earth
School News	256	3–4	7–10	ELA	Documents
Travel of Our Ancestors	259	3	7–9	Math	Earth
U.S. Immigration	263	4	8–10	Social Studies/ History	Spreadsheets, Forms
The World in Our Classroom	266	K–4	4–10	ELA	Blogger
Writing Fables	268	2–4	6–10	ELA	Presentations

AFTER-SCHOOL ACTIVITIES

John Hrevnack

GRADE LEVEL: 5

SUBJECT: Mathematics

TIME REQUIRED: 2–3 class periods (45 minutes); 1 evening of homework

OBJECTIVES

Students will be able to:

- Add hours and minutes.

- Produce a presentation slide using Google Presentations.

- Collect information and use it to solve problems.

CORRELATIONS TO STANDARDS

NCTM Principles and Standards for School Mathematics

Problem Solving

- Solve problems that arise in mathematics and in other contexts

- Apply and adapt a variety of appropriate strategies to solve problems

Data Analysis and Probability

- Formulate questions that can be addressed with data and collect, organize, and display relevant data to answer them

Connections

- Recognize and apply mathematics in contexts outside of mathematics

ISTE National Educational Technology Standards for Students (NETS•S)

1. Creativity and Innovation

2. Communication and Collaboration

3. Research and Information Fluency

4. Critical Thinking, Problem Solving, and Decision Making

5. Digital Citizenship

6. Technology Operations and Concepts

MATERIALS AND RESOURCES REQUIRED

■ Internet access and necessary technology

■ Only one classroom computer is required

■ Google Presentations

■ Pencil and paper or Google Documents

LESSON DESCRIPTION

Check and/or teach the following prerequisite skills:

■ Students are able to use Google Presentations and Google Image Search, and import an image to a presentation.

■ Students are able to add time (including converting minutes into hours when necessary).

1. The teacher should commence the class with a discussion of activities that students engage in after school. (If the teacher wishes, he/she could also include the weekend in the activities.) The teacher should elicit from the students some of the things they do in their time after school (e.g., soccer, using the computer, etc.) Then, based on the responses, the teacher should create a master list of these activities. The teacher should have the students copy the final list. Next, the teacher should explain to the students that they are going to create a presentation showing how much time students spend on these activities. Students will be paired up, assigned an activity, and asked to create a slide that includes the name of the activity, the names of the students who developed the slide, and an imported picture illustrating the activity. The slide should also include the heading "Time spent per week," followed by a three-column table with the headers "Hours," "Minutes," and "Student." Students will enter information into this table later in the activity.

2. Next, the teacher should assign each pair of students an activity and specify the order in which the various pairs of students are to use the computer to develop the slide. One computer should be designated for this lesson and one pair of students at a time should be using the computer. The rest of the class should be engaged in seatwork or other activities.

3. The teacher should ask the students to record on their list of activities the time they spend on the various activities each week in hours and minutes. This can be assigned as homework.

4. The following day, the pairs of students should cycle back to the computer and enter their times and names for the various activities into the tables on the relevant presentation slides. Again, the rest of the class should be engaged in seatwork or other activities. When all students have input their individual times for the various activities, the teacher should inform them that each pair will now total the times for their assigned activity. At this point, the teacher should remind the students how to convert every 60 minutes into 1 hour. For example, 2 hours 136 minutes would be converted to 4 hours 16 minutes. The student pairs should cycle back to the computer to total the time spent on the activity.

5. The students should then take the total for the activity they were responsible for and input it on a "Time Spent on Activities" slide, which should be developed by the teacher after all the activities have been identified. A sample is shown immediately following. The teacher should check that the students have added the times correctly.

TIME SPENT ON ACTIVITIES		
ACTIVITY	TIME SPENT	
	Hours	Minutes
Baseball		
Dance		
Computer		
Soccer		
Total Time		

6. The teacher should conduct a summative activity and engage the class in a discussion of the importance of activities in becoming a well-rounded person. If one area is particularly under- or overrepresented with respect to time, the teacher may want to discuss that activity further with the class.

7. The teacher can view a sample presentation of this lesson at the following Google Docs address: http://docs.google.com/Presentation?docid=dc2nk7vh_286fpx94xf7&hl=en

ASSESSMENT

Students' grades can be based on the following sample assessment rubric:

CRITERIA	BELOW STANDARD	MEETS STANDARD	ABOVE STANDARD
Students were able to add hours and minutes			
Students were able to use Google Presentations			
Students were able to import images from Google			

BIOMES OF THE EARTH

Andrea Tejedor

GRADE LEVEL: 2–4

SUBJECT: Science

TIME REQUIRED: 4–8 class periods

OBJECTIVES

Students will be able to:

■ Collaborate in describing and/or summarizing one of the Earth's biomes.

■ Peer-evaluate and critique the work of fellow students in presenting their collaborative report.

■ Implement the use of Google Earth in a collaborative production of their report.

CORRELATIONS TO STANDARDS

National Science Education Standards

1. Unifying concepts and processes in science

2. Science as inquiry

4. Life science

6. Science in personal and social perspectives

ISTE National Educational Technology Standards for Students (NETS•S)

1. Creativity and Innovation

2. Communication and Collaboration

3. Research and Information Fluency

5. Digital Citizenship

6. Technology Operations and Concepts

MATERIALS AND RESOURCES REQUIRED

■ Internet access and necessary technology

■ Enchanted Learning (enchantedlearning.com/biomes) or other grade-appropriate website

■ Google Earth

FORMAT FOR GROUP PROJECT

- Each member of the group is to be responsible for writing the first draft of one section of the report. The report will have three sections: description of the biome, animals of the biome, and plants of the biome. Students will research one of the following biomes: desert, tundra, coniferous forest, temperate deciduous forest, grassland, tropical rainforest, temperate ponds, coral reef, or savannah.

- Each member of the group is responsible for checking all three sections of the collaborative report. Each person is responsible for confirming the accuracy of all three sections. Changes should be made directly in Google Earth. Content of the report is everyone's responsibility. All should agree on its accuracy and quality.

- Each member of the group must write a statement at the end of the report that they have read the report and approve of its contents. All members of each group will receive the same grade for content, but individual grades for teamwork.

LESSON DESCRIPTION

This lesson assumes students possess satisfactory understanding of the three components of the biome they are being asked to write about.

1. Pre-assess students to ensure necessary reading and writing competence.

2. Divide students into groups of three. Each student will use the Enchanted Learning website (enchantedlearning.com/biomes) or another grade-appropriate website to research one of the three components of the biome. The students will use a graphic organizer to record information on the component of the biome they are researching. Develop one rubric with the students for evaluating the final group project, including the following criteria:

    - Content

    - Presentation Clarity and Delivery

    - Preparedness

    - Comprehension

    - Use of Technology

    - Grammar and Syntax

    (80% of Group Grade). (1–2 class periods)

3. The teacher will create a model of a biome description in Google Earth. Teacher will show the students Google Earth. Teacher will show the students their school in Google Earth and "fly" to the placemark where the teacher created the description of the biome. The teacher will demonstrate how to find the different biomes using the students' research. The teacher will show the students how to create a placemark in Google Earth. (1 class period)

4. The teacher will model how to locate a biome using the Google Earth search function and create a placemark with the description of the biome. The students will follow as the teacher models the aforementioned process. (1–3 class periods)

5. The students will discuss how the project is working, what problems are occurring, and ways of addressing the problems. (ongoing)

6. The students will present the placemark they created as a group to the class and report on the biome they studied. Develop a second rubric for students to evaluate the quality and extent of their team members' participation.

   - Researches information

   - Identifies important information

   - Contributes to group

   - Manages time

   - Quality of work

   - Focuses on task

   - Comes prepared to work with group

   (50% of Individual Grade). (1–2 class periods)

7. The teacher will create a center in the classroom where the students will navigate Google Earth independently to locate the placemarks for the biomes created by their classmates. (ongoing)

ASSESSMENT—SUGGESTED METHODS AND CRITERIA

Students receive two grades: an individual grade for the quality and extent of their individual participation and a group grade for the quality of the report.

Individual Grade

25%	Teacher assessment of student participation in discussions
25%	Teacher assessment of student contributions to report as required (as documented in Google Earth)
50%	Student assessment of group participation using rubric

Group Grade

20%	Teacher assessment of quality of mechanics, grammar, and spelling
80%	Teacher assessment of quality of report using rubric

CALORIE COUNTER

John Hrevnack

GRADE LEVEL: 5

SUBJECT: Mathematics

TIME REQUIRED: 3 class periods; 1 evening of homework

OBJECTIVES

Students will be able to:

- Use Google Spreadsheets to compile data.

- Use the Sum spreadsheet function.

- Read tables to gather data.

- Measure people's height and weight.

CORRELATIONS TO STANDARDS

NCTM Principles and Standards for School Mathematics

Problem Solving

- Solve problems that arise in mathematics and in other contexts

- Apply and adapt a variety of appropriate strategies to solve problems

Connections

- Recognize and apply mathematics in contexts outside of mathematics

ISTE National Educational Technology Standards for Students (NETS•S)

1. Creativity and Innovation

3. Research and Information Fluency

4. Critical Thinking, Problem Solving, and Decision Making

6. Technology Operations and Concepts

MATERIALS AND RESOURCES REQUIRED

- Internet access and necessary technology
- Google Spreadsheets
- Pencils
- Food Intake Record Sheet (see sample at end of the lesson)
- Scale for weighing people
- Height measuring device

LESSON DESCRIPTION

Check or teach the following prerequisite skills:

- Students can use basic functions of Google Spreadsheets (including the Sum function).

1. The teacher should begin this lesson by introducing the concept of calories. As an anticipatory set the teacher should ask students their favorite foods. The teacher will write these foods on a board and provide the calorie count for these foods (from a calorie counter website). The teacher might also want to supply the calorie count for a sampling of healthy food choices. Then the teacher will supply each student with a Data Collection Sheet and explain that students are to write on the sheet everything they eat from the end of the class to the beginning of the same class tomorrow.

2. The next day the teacher will direct students to a website with information on counting calories. An example is www.caloriescount.com.

   Students will use this site to enter the number of calories for each item they ate the day before and fill in the data on the Food Intake Record Sheet. The students should find the sum of the calories they ate in the previous 24 hours.

3. With a partner, students should enter their weight and height information into a new spreadsheet. See example below.

MY PERSONAL DATA				
Name:				
My Age	Total Calories	My Height	My Weight	Recommended weight for my height & age

Sample student spreadsheet

4. Students should consult the age, weight, and height chart from Disabled World (www.disabled-world.com/artman/publish/height-weight-teens.shtml) and enter the

appropriate data for themselves into their spreadsheets. Each student should give a completed spreadsheet to the teacher, either in hard copy or digitally.

5. Prior to the next class, the teacher should compile a spreadsheet for the whole class with the data for each child entered anonymously, separated by boys and girls. Working as a whole group with the data, each student should determine:

   - The average calorie intake for the class the previous day for the appropriate gender group.

   - How much higher or lower this is than the recommended amount.

   - The total amount all the boys in the class should weigh.

   - The total amount all the girls in the class should weigh.

   - The total amount all the boys actually weigh.

   - The total amount all the girls actually weigh.

   - The average difference between what the boys and girls actually weigh and what they should weigh.

6. The class then discusses what they see as the possible relationship between their average calorie intake in the previous day and the average difference between their average actual weight and what they should weigh. They may also discuss steps to address discrepancies in the data, and the advantages of maintaining a healthy lifestyle.

Recommended caloric intake for students:

4–8 YEARS	9–13 YEARS
1400–1600 Calories	**Girls:** 1600–2000 Calories **Boys:** 1800–2200 Calories

Source: Baylor College of Medicine. www.bcm.edu/cnrc/consumer/archives/percentDV.htm

ASSESSMENT

Students' grades can be based on the following sample assessment rubric:

CRITERIA	DOES NOT MEET EXPECTATIONS	MEETS EXPECTATIONS	EXCEEDS EXPECTATIONS
Foods eaten were accurately transcribed			
Students performed research correctly			
Students entered data correctly			
Students were able to use Google Spreadsheet function			

WORKSHEET

Food Intake Record Sheet

My Name:	
WHAT I ATE AND DRANK TODAY	
NAME OF FOOD OR DRINK	NUMBER OF CALORIES
6:00 a.m. to 12:00 noon	
12:00 noon to 6:00 p.m.	
6:00 p.m. to 12:00 midnight	
Total Calories For 24 Hrs:	

THE CAMPING TRIP

John Hrevnack

GRADE LEVEL: 3

SUBJECT: Mathematics

TIME REQUIRED: 2 class periods

OBJECTIVES

Students will be able to:

- Add money to the thousands.

- Discuss the rationale for decisions made as to the importance of various items needed for survival.

- Critique the rationale of others.

- Enumerate items necessary for a camping trip.

CORRELATIONS TO STANDARDS

NCTM Principles and Standards for School Mathematics

Problem Solving

- Solve problems that arise in mathematics and in other contexts

- Apply and adapt a variety of appropriate strategies to solve problems

Data Analysis and Probability

- Formulate questions that can be addressed with data and collect, organize, and display relevant data to answer them

Connections

- Recognize and apply mathematics in contexts outside of mathematics

ISTE National Educational Technology Standards for Students (NETS•S)

1. Creativity and Innovation

2. Communication and Collaboration

3. Research and Information Fluency

4. Critical Thinking, Problem Solving, and Decision Making

5. Digital Citizenship

6. Technology Operations and Concepts

MATERIALS

- Internet access and necessary technology
- Blogger
- Pencils
- Guide sheet (see suggested sample guide sheet at the end of the lesson plan)
- Calculators (optional)

LESSON DESCRIPTION

1. Teach the students to use Blogger and Google Search.

2. Divide the students into groups of four at a computer with Internet access.

3. Begin by telling the students to imagine they are going on a camping trip. The trip will last for three days and will take place at a state park near a river. They will not have access to electricity on the trip. Their guide will provide them with food, water, and a tent, so they do not have to plan for these items. Tell the students that each student has $400 to spend on equipment for the trip. The students in the group act as a team and collaboratively plan for the trip. The teacher should lead a discussion on the items needed for the trip. Inform the students that the trip will be held in the summer so they should plan accordingly. The teacher should direct the students to appropriate websites that sell camping equipment. Students can be directed to fill out the guide sheet first, and then create their blog posts based on the guide sheet. Each student's blog entry should consist of a list of items, rationale for each item, item cost, and total cost.

4. Next the students should be directed to enumerate their choices and the rationale for these choices on Blogger. When all students have completed the assignment, the teacher should check each post and then allow the students to publish their posts.

5. The following day the students should be directed to log on to Blogger and comment on the posts of their classmates. Comments should address agreement or disagreement with items on the list (with an explanation), agreement or disagreement with the rationale (with an explanation), and agreement or disagreement with the total cost (with correct answer if there is a disagreement). Students should note especially which items can be shared. The teacher should monitor the activity and, in conclusion, reach consensus with the class on the items that should be bought. This should lead to the conclusion that a number of items could be shared by a group (e.g., a stove), and thus allow for greater efficiencies. The class can add up the total cost for each student, as a group activity, to get a total cost for the class.

ASSESSMENT

Students' grades can be based on the following sample assessment rubric:

CRITERIA	BELOW STANDARD	MEETS STANDARD	ABOVE STANDARD
Relevant items for a camping trip were identified			
Items were correctly added			
Blog post and rationale			
Response to blog posts			

WORKSHEET

Sample Guide Sheet

ITEM	INDIVIDUAL USE OR SHARED?	WHY THIS ITEM IS NEEDED	COST
		Total:	

A DAY AT THE BEACH

John Hrevnack

GRADE LEVEL: 3

SUBJECT: Mathematics

TIME REQUIRED: 2 class periods

OBJECTIVES

Students will be able to:

■ Develop word problems involving addition and subtraction.

■ Solve word problems involving addition and subtraction.

■ Use Google Documents.

CORRELATIONS TO STANDARDS

NCTM Principles and Standards for School Mathematics

Problem Solving

■ Solve problems that arise in mathematics and in other contexts

Data Analysis and Probability

■ Formulate questions that can be addressed with data and collect, organize, and display relevant data to answer them

Connections

■ Recognize and apply mathematics in contexts outside of mathematics

ISTE National Educational Technology Standards for Students (NETS•S)

1. Creativity and Innovation

2. Communication and Collaboration

3. Research and Information Fluency

4. Critical Thinking, Problem Solving, and Decision Making

6. Technology Operations and Concepts

MATERIALS AND RESOURCES

- Internet access and necessary technology
- Google Documents
- Writing implement
- Paper

LESSON DESCRIPTION

Check and/or teach the following prerequisite skills:

- Students are able to use Google Documents.
- Students are able to add and subtract dollars and cents.
- Students can navigate to a preselected site. For example: Toy Splash (www.toysplash.com/Category/Beach).

1. The teacher should begin the lesson with a discussion about why it is so much fun to go to the beach. Then the class should discuss what things students want to take to the beach that adds to their fun. The students should be led to include beach balls, games, floats, goggles, masks, etc. The teacher should then tell the students that they will go to a website that has all kinds of things that can be used at the beach, and then make up a word problem that can be solved using addition or subtraction.

2. The teacher should (prior to the lesson) identify a site appropriate for the lesson. **Note:** In this lesson the teacher could use other activities instead of the beach. Camping, sports, arts, cooking, or another activity may serve as the basis of the lesson. For this example, Toy Splash was used (www.toysplash.com/Category/Beach).

3. The teacher should ask the class, what items might we want to buy for a trip to the beach? After students have selected an item, the teacher should write the item on the board or a projected, shared Google Document. When three items have been selected the teacher should go to the website. For example, the students may identify an inflatable boat. The teacher would go to the site and look under "inflatable boats." When the page with the inflatable boats is displayed, the students can discuss the merits of the various boats and decide on one. For this example, the students could decide on the Junior Pro Inflatable Kayak for $49.99. The same procedure should be followed for the next items. For the purpose of this example, the students selected a "sand and beach playset" for $9.99 and a "pool baseball game" for $14.99. The teacher should also note that certain items, although listed in the catalog, are out of stock and thus not available. The teacher should ask the students to help think of a problem. For example, the students may come up with the following problems:

   - If Johnny bought an inflatable boat for $49.99, a sand and beach playset for $9.99, and a pool baseball game for $14.99, how much did he spend?

   - If Yvonne had $80.00, could she buy an inflatable boat for $49.99, a sand and beach playset for $9.99, and a pool baseball game for $14.99?

> ■ How much change would Carlos receive if he bought an inflatable boat for $49.99, a sand and beach playset for $9.99, and a pool baseball game for $14.99, and gave the clerk $80.00? If there is change left over, what else could Carlos buy?

4. The teacher then solves the problems cooperatively with the students.

5. The teacher should tell the class that they are going to have the opportunity to go to a website, pick out items, and then write a problem using the information from the site. The problem could be an addition or subtraction problem. Next the teacher should have each child go to the computer and develop a problem based on the theme presented. **Note:** The students could go back to a computer to input their problem at one of the learning centers in the room or the whole class as a group could input the problems into a group Google Doc in a computer lab (if available).

6. The following day (when all the students have posted the problems) the teacher should have each child solve the problems either online or on a printed hard copy. The teacher could have the students solve all the problems, have half the class solve the odd problems and the other half the even, or any other variation that meets the individual needs of the students. It is suggested that the teacher review selected problems with the class and stress the proper labeling of the problems.

7. At the conclusion of the problem solving, have the class discuss what they liked and disliked about writing their own problems and solving problems created by their classmates (rather than out of a book). Did this experience help them understand word problems any better?

ASSESSMENT

The assignment can be graded in two ways:

1. Scoring the number of problems right and wrong, or

2. Using the following sample assessment rubric:

CRITERIA	BELOW STANDARD	MEETS STANDARD	ABOVE STANDARD
Students were able to navigate the selected website			
Students were able to use Google Documents			
Students were able to create problems			

DISCOVER BLOGGING

Andrea Tejedor

GRADE LEVEL: 2–4

SUBJECT: English Language Arts

TIME REQUIRED: 4–6 class periods

OBJECTIVES

Students will be able to:

- Make predictions about a book by looking at the front and back cover of the book and by looking at the pictures.

- Confirm or disconfirm their predictions when the teacher reads the book aloud.

- Evaluate and respond to the comments of fellow students.

CORRELATIONS TO STANDARDS

NCTE/IRA Standards for the English Language Arts

4. Communications Skills

ISTE National Educational Technology Standards for Students (NETS·S)

2. Communication and Collaboration

5. Digital Citizenship

6. Technology Operations and Concepts

MATERIALS AND RESOURCES REQUIRED

- Internet access and necessary technology

- Picture book

- Blogger

LESSON DESCRIPTION

1. The teacher will create a classroom blog using Blogger.

2. The teacher will read a picture book aloud.

3. Each member of the class will respond to the teacher's questions, read the comments left by their classmates, and respond to at least two classmates' comments. Each student will receive a grade for answering the teacher's question and responding to at least two classmates' comments.

LESSON

This lesson assumes students possess satisfactory reading and writing skills appropriate for the grade level.

1. Pre-assess students to ensure necessary reading and writing competence.

2. The teacher will ask the students if they know what a blog is. The teacher will tell the students that she has created a class blog, and the teacher will show the students what the class blog looks like. The teacher will tell the students that a blog is like a personal diary. The teacher will demonstrate how to enter a comment in the blog. The teacher will tell the students that they will use the class blog to discuss the literature that they will be reading together. (1 class period)

3. The teacher will read a picture book to the students. In this example, the students respond to the picture book *When the Relatives Came* by Cynthia Rylant. Prior to reading the book, the teacher shows the students the front and back covers of the book. The teacher facilitates a discussion and helps the students make predictions about the story. For example, the teacher might ask:

   ■ What does the front cover tell us about the story?

   ■ How do you think the characters are feeling?

   ■ Who do you think the main character is?

   ■ What does the title of the story tell us about what may happen?

4. The teacher will tell the students that after reading the book aloud, the teacher will ask the students different questions, but instead of discussing the book as a class, they will be using a class blog to write their answers. (1 class period)

5. The teacher will read the book aloud. Then the teacher will tell the students that the following questions have been posted in the class blog: How did the story differ from your prediction? Do the relatives in the story remind you of your own relatives? Explain. The teacher will demonstrate how to access the class blog and post a response. Then the students will go to the class blog, read the questions, and post answers to the questions. Develop a rubric to evaluate the quality and extent of the students' responses, including the following criteria:

   ■ Uses evidence from the story to support position

   ■ Identifies important information and details

   ■ Makes a logical connection between story and self

   (1–2 class periods)

6. The students will read the answers their classmates have posted to the blog. After reading the answers, each student will post a comment to at least two of the responses, using the following questions as a guide:

- Do you agree or disagree with the prediction? Explain.

- Did you have a similar experience with your relatives?

- Would you like to know more about the situation your classmate describes?

The teacher will model how to leave a comment and discuss proper netiquette (Internet etiquette) for leaving a comment. Develop a rubric to evaluate the quality and extent of the students' response, including the following criteria:

- Uses evidence from the story to ask questions and respond

- Identifies important information and details

- Uses proper netiquette

(1–2 class periods)

ASSESSMENT—SUGGESTED METHODS AND CRITERIA

Students receive two grades: a grade for the quality of their response to the teacher's questions, and a grade for the quality and extent of their response to their classmates' responses.

FAVORITE FRUITS

John Hrevnack

GRADE LEVEL: 3

SUBJECT: Mathematics

TIME REQUIRED: 2 class periods

OBJECTIVES

Students will be able to:

- Add numbers to the tens place.
- Produce a presentation slide demonstrating preferences.
- Take information and use it to solve problems.

CORRELATIONS TO STANDARDS

NCTM Principles and Standards for School Mathematics

Problem Solving

- Solve problems that arise in mathematics and in other contexts
- Apply and adapt a variety of appropriate strategies to solve problems

Data Analysis and Probability

- Formulate questions that can be addressed with data and collect, organize, and display relevant data to answer them

Connections

- Recognize and apply mathematics in contexts outside of mathematics

ISTE National Educational Technology Standards for Students (NETS•S)

1. Creativity and Innovation
2. Communication and Collaboration
3. Research and Information Fluency
4. Critical Thinking, Problem Solving, and Decision Making
5. Digital Citizenship
6. Technology Operations and Concepts

MATERIALS AND RESOURCES REQUIRED

- Internet access and necessary technology
- Google Presentations
- Google Image Search
- Only a single classroom computer is required

LESSON DESCRIPTION

Check and/or teach the following prerequisite skills:

- Students are able to use Google Presentations and Google Image Search.
- Students are able to import an image to a presentation.

1. The teacher should introduce the lesson by discussing with the class that fruits are a healthy food. Then the teacher should engage the class in a discussion of different types of fruits and ask the students to identify some of their favorite fruits. The teacher should tell the students that they are going to create a slide that shows how many students like the various fruits and explain that each group will be asked to fill in the name of the fruit that they are assigned at the top of the slide, their names at top, the phrase, "Those who like [name of fruit]," and a picture of the fruit.

2. Next the teacher should assign each pair of students a fruit and an order in which the various pairs of students are to use the computer. While the rest of the class is engaged in seatwork or other activities, two students at a time will be using the computer. The students will create a slide with their names at the top, the phrase "Those who like [name of fruit]," and a picture of the fruit. Students can use Google Image Search to locate appropriate images, or the teacher may download images to choose from ahead of time.

3. When all the students are finished providing the required information, the teacher should direct the first pair of students to go back to the computer and view all the slides (their own, and those created by all other student pairs). Students who like the fruit should add their names under the section: "Those who like ..." Students who do not like the fruit noted should not add their names to the section. **Note:** students may place their names next to as many fruits as they like.

4. When all the students have noted their favorite fruits, each pair of students (that developed the slide) should add the number of students who like the various fruits and give the teacher the information for the slide "Class Totals." This slide should be prepared by the teacher.

5. The teacher should then discuss the results of the class totals with the students stressing the importance of making wise decisions in the choices they make of foods. The teacher should engage in a concluding discussion that could focus on the reasons why one fruit was the "favorite" and why one was "least favorite." If the class is advanced, the teacher may compute the percentages for the various fruits and discuss these percentages with the students as a concluding activity.

6. The teacher can view a sample presentation of this lesson at the Google Docs website (http://docs.google.com/Presentation?docid=dc2nk7vh_3gbzq4fgd&hl=en).

ASSESSMENT

Students' grades can be based on the following sample assessment rubric:

CRITERIA	BELOW STANDARD	MEETS STANDARD	ABOVE STANDARD
Items were correctly added			
Students were able to use Google Presentations			
Students were able to import images from Google			

THE GIFT GIVER

John Hrevnack

GRADE LEVEL: 5

SUBJECT: Mathematics

TIME REQUIRED: 2 class periods

OBJECTIVES

Students will be able to:

- Use Google Spreadsheets.

- Estimate and add items so that they do not exceed a given amount.

- Total items to identify the rank order of spending by the class in various categories.

CORRELATIONS TO STANDARDS

NCTM Principles and Standards for School Mathematics

Problem Solving

- Solve problems that arise in mathematics and in other contexts

Data Analysis and Probability

- Formulate questions that can be addressed with data and collect, organize, and display relevant data to answer them

Connections

- Recognize and apply mathematics in contexts outside of mathematics

ISTE National Educational Technology Standards for Students (NETS•S)

1. Creativity and Innovation

3. Research and Information Fluency

4. Critical Thinking, Problem Solving, and Decision Making

5. Digital Citizenship

6. Technology Operations and Concepts

MATERIALS

- Internet access and necessary technology
- Google Spreadsheets
- Writing implement
- Paper

LESSON DESCRIPTION

Check and/or teach the following prerequisite skills:

- Students are able to use Google Spreadsheets.
- Students are able to add and subtract dollars and cents.
- Students can navigate to preselected site.

1. The teacher should begin the lesson by initiating a discussion about why we give gifts and how people feel when they give and receive gifts. Then the teacher should discuss with the students what gifts they liked most and why. The teacher should then tell the students that they will be given an imaginary bank account with $100.00. (Depending on the number of members in the family, the teacher may want to make the limit $200.00 or $25.00 per family member.) With the money in the account, students are to buy gifts for members of their family. This would include their brothers, sisters, mother, father, stepfather, stepmother, grandmother, and grandfather. The teacher could lead the discussion of which relatives should be included. (Friends of the students should NOT be included, because if one "friend" were to be omitted from a present list the feelings of that child could be hurt.) The teacher should inform the class that they will use several websites to search for presents.

2. Prior to the lesson, the teacher should identify websites appropriate for the lesson. For this example the following websites were used:
   - Sears (www.sears.com)
   - J.C. Penney (www.jcpenney.com)

3. The teacher should model the activity for the class by asking the class what presents to buy for the teacher's mother, father, sister, and brother. After the students have selected an item the teacher should write the name of the item on the board. For this example the students could decide that the teacher should buy the father an electric screwdriver, mother a vase, brother a baseball bat, and sister a stereo radio/CD player. When all the items have been selected the teacher should go to one of the websites.

4. The teacher should then list the items and their prices. **Note:** The teacher should show the class that there may be many examples of an item at varying prices, and the students would need to choose one; or, if it's too expensive, students may need to choose a different gift. For example: there are several types of electric screwdrivers, and one needs to be chosen at a price that will allow for the purchase of other gifts.
   - Father—Black & Decker 3.6 Volt Rechargeable 3-Position Screwdriver: $27.99
   - Mother—Whole Home Green Reactive Glaze Vases: $19.99

- Brother—Rawlings 242J Big Stick Youth Wood Baseball Bat: $14.99

- Sister—Emerson AM/FM Stereo Clock Radio with CD Player: $29.99

5. The teacher could then solve the problem cooperatively with the students (i.e., add the amounts together to see if their total is less than $100.00). In this example the total cost of the items is $92.96.

6. The teacher should tell the class that they are going to have the opportunity to go to a website, select gifts, and then, using Google Spreadsheets, log in the information from the website. Next the teacher should have each child go to the computer and do the activity. The following is an example of a student spreadsheet:

Name: *Sammy*

RELATIVE	ITEM	COST
Father	electric screwdriver	$27.99
Mother	vase	$19.99
Brother	baseball bat	$14.99
Sister	clock radio/CD player	$29.99
	Total:	$92.96

7. The following day the teacher should list each of the relatives for whom gifts were bought on the board or on a projected Google Spreadsheet. Then the teacher should have students predict which one of the relatives would have the greatest number of gifts, and which relative would have the most money spent on gifts. When the raw data is assembled the students could be directed to add the totals for each relative and then rank relatives by the number of gifts and by the amount spent. When the students finish the assignment the teacher should review the results with the class.

ASSESSMENT

The assignment can be graded in two ways:

1. Student was able to add amount of the gifts correctly and not overspend the $100.00

2. Using the following sample assessment rubric:

CRITERIA	BELOW STANDARD	MEETS STANDARD	ABOVE STANDARD
Student was able to navigate the selected website(s)			
Student was able to use Google Spreadsheets			
Student was able to rank the data by the number of gifts			
Student was able to rank the data by the amount of money spent on gifts			

GOOGLE EARTH PEN PALS

Andrea Tejedor

GRADE LEVEL: 2–4

SUBJECT: English Language Arts

TIME REQUIRED: 2–3 class periods, then ongoing throughout the school year

OBJECTIVES

Students will be able to:

- Use Google Earth to compare and contrast landscapes.
- Employ a wide range of strategies to communicate.

CORRELATIONS TO STANDARDS

NCTE/IRA Standards for the English Language Arts

4. Communication Skills
5. Communication Strategies
12. Applying Language Skills

ISTE National Educational Technology Standards for Students (NETS•S)

1. Creativity and Innovation
2. Communication and Collaboration
3. Research and Information Fluency
6. Technology Operations and Concepts

MATERIALS AND RESOURCES REQUIRED

- Internet access and necessary technology
- e-Pals (www.epals.com)
- Google Earth
- Venn diagram

LESSON DESCRIPTION

1. The teacher will use e-Pals to identify a classroom in another country that the students can communicate with throughout the school year. The teacher will tell students that they will be communicating with students who live in a different part of the world.

2. The teacher will facilitate a class discussion about what is unique about where they live.

3. The teacher will show the students the location of their town using Google Earth. The teacher will ask the students to identify the mountains, rivers, and lakes, and other identifying characteristics around the town.

4. The teacher will show the students the location of the partner school that they will be communicating with. Using a Venn diagram, the teacher will ask the students to compare their town to the location of the partner school.

5. Students receive a safe and protected e-mail account to use to communicate with an e-Pal from the partner school.

LESSON

1. As a whole class, open up Google Earth on one computer.

2. Teach the students the different tools and how to navigate in Google Earth (e.g., zoom, tilt, turn).

3. Show students their school building in Google Earth.

4. Students go to their computers and launch Google Earth.

5. Students navigate through Google Earth to find their houses.

6. Students use keywords or latitude and longitude to locate the partner school.

7. Students take notes about the similarities and differences of the landscape of their own town and the partner school's town.

8. Students fill out their Venn diagram from the notes that they have taken.

9. Students will write an e-mail to their e-Pal about the similarities and differences between their locations. Students will ask their e-Pals questions about life in their town and whether they have visited the landmarks students identify using Google Earth.

ASSESSMENT

Students are assessed based on the e-mail they compose to their e-Pal and their Venn diagram, using the following criteria:

E-mail

- Does the e-mail have a recipient and a subject?

- Is proper grammar and spelling used to write the e-mail?

- Does the student ask relevant questions based on the comparison conducted using Google Earth?

Venn diagram

- Did the students use Google Earth to compare the landmarks in both locations?

- Are similarities and differences clearly identified?

This lesson was designed in cooperation with Tina Villardi-Kakascik, Deborah Gilson, and Laurie Santos.

HOME MEASUREMENTS

John Hrevnack

GRADE LEVEL: 4

SUBJECT: Mathematics

TIME REQUIRED: 5–10 minutes of 1 class period and 2–3 additional class periods; 1 evening of homework

OBJECTIVES

Students will be able to:

- Measure feet and inches.

- Analyze information and use it to solve problems.

- Organize objects based on their size.

- Identify why certain items in the home are a standard size.

CORRELATIONS TO STANDARDS

NCTM Principles and Standards for School Mathematics

Problem Solving

- Solve problems that arise in mathematics and in other contexts

- Apply and adapt a variety of appropriate strategies to solve problems

Data Analysis and Probability

- Formulate questions that can be addressed with data and collect, organize, and display relevant data to answer them

Connections

- Recognize and apply mathematics in contexts outside of mathematics

ISTE National Educational Technology Standards for Students (NETS•S)

1. Creativity and Innovation

2. Communication and Collaboration

3. Research and Information Fluency

4. Critical Thinking, Problem Solving, and Decision Making

6. Technology Operations and Concepts

MATERIALS AND RESOURCES REQUIRED

- Internet access and necessary technology
- Blogger
- A ruler of at least 12 inches
- Writing implement
- Paper or Google Spreadsheets

LESSON DESCRIPTION

Check and/or teach the following prerequisite skills:

- Students are able to use Blogger and Google Spreadsheets.
- Students are able to add feet and inches (with regrouping, as needed, of inches into feet).
- Students are able to measure in feet and inches.

1. The teacher should begin the lesson with a discussion of why certain household items/objects are built to specific sizes: for example, why a doorway needs to be a certain height and width. What would happen if doorways were only 5 feet tall? What if dining room chairs had legs that were higher than the table? Next the teacher should ask the students to identify objects and items they have in their houses and could measure. The students could identify, for example, the width of the front door, the height of the backs of a kitchen chair, the height of the kitchen table, the height of the seat of a kitchen chair, the width of the refrigerator, the width of the television, and so on. Then, based on the responses, the teacher should then develop a master list of these objects.

    Sample Data Sheet (with a possible list of items):

Name:	
ITEM	MEASUREMENT
Width of front door	
Height of the top of the back of a kitchen chair (from floor)	
Height of the seat of a kitchen chair	
Width of kitchen table	
Length of kitchen table	
Height of the kitchen table (from floor)	
Width of the refrigerator	
Width of my bed	
Height of window sill (from floor)	
Width of bathroom door	

The teacher should have the students copy the final list on a sheet of paper or on a shared Google Doc that the students save. In conclusion, the teacher should direct the students to measure the various objects identified for homework.

2. Students should enter the answers to the following questions in their blog the next day:

    ■ The widest object I measured was …

    ■ The narrowest object I measured was …

    ■ The difference between the widest and narrowest objects was …

    ■ The highest object I measured was …

    ■ The lowest object I measured was …

    ■ The difference between the highest and lowest objects was …

    ■ One thing I liked about this assignment was …

    ■ One thing I didn't like about this assignment, or I found difficult was …

    ■ One thing I learned that I didn't know before was …

    ■ Something I have a question about is …

3. Assign students to partners and have partners check the accuracy of the responses to the first six questions, based on their partner's Data Sheet.

4. Ask students to make a comment in the blog on their partner's answers to the last four questions about one thing they didn't know before or one question they would like to ask their partner.

5. Have students read several blog postings and comments.

6. Have students enter the data from the Data Sheets into a Google Spreadsheet (objects down the side, dimensions across the top). All students should use the same format.

7. Display a correct spreadsheet for all to see and have partners correct each other's spreadsheets.

8. Conduct a discussion on patterns students are able to discern from the data (width of front door vs. width of bathroom door, seat heights all approximately the same from floor, tallest, lowest, widest, and narrowest objects, etc.)

9. Students make one more blog entry addressing:

    ■ One thing they have learned about measurement

    ■ One thing they learned about the size of objects

    ■ Anything else they wish to add

ASSESSMENT

Students' grades can be based on the following sample assessment rubric:

CRITERIA	BELOW STANDARD	MEETS STANDARD	ABOVE STANDARD
Items were correctly measured			
Completion of blogging activities			
Worked with partner in collaborative manner			
Demonstrated critical thinking skills			

HOW WE SPEND OUR TIME

John Hrevnack

GRADE LEVEL: 4

SUBJECT: Mathematics

TIME REQUIRED: 3 class periods; 2 evenings of homework

OBJECTIVES

Students will be able to:

- Use Google Spreadsheets to compile data.
- Use the Sum function in Google Spreadsheets.

CORRELATIONS TO STANDARDS

NCTM Principles and Standards for School Mathematics

Problem Solving

- Solve problems that arise in mathematics and in other contexts
- Apply and adapt a variety of appropriate strategies to solve problems

Connections

- Recognize and apply mathematics in contexts outside of mathematics

ISTE National Educational Technology Standards for Students (NETS·S)

1. Creativity and Innovation
2. Communication and Collaboration
3. Research and Information Fluency
4. Critical Thinking, Problem Solving, and Decision Making
6. Technology Operations and Concepts

MATERIALS AND RESOURCES REQUIRED

- Internet access and necessary technology
- Google Spreadsheets
- Data collection sheet (see sample at end of the lesson)
- Pencil

LESSON DESCRIPTION

Check and/or teach the following prerequisite skills:

- Students can use the basic functions of Google Spreadsheet (including the Sum function).

- Students understand how to compute averages.

1. The teacher should introduce the lesson by asking the students to name things they do during the course of a day. As the students provide responses the teacher should list them on the board. After several are provided the teacher should say, "We're going to see how much time we spend on different activities and then we will find the average for our class for the various activities." The teacher should also discuss the meaning of the term *average*. At that point the teacher should distribute data collection sheets to the students and direct them to keep track of the amount of time they spend on each activity (everything they do) for the next two days and then bring the information back to school. The students should be told to keep track of the activities in minutes.

2. When the students have compiled two days of data they should be instructed to open Google Spreadsheets and complete the chart. **Note:** the teacher may want to have the students treat the Spreadsheet as a collaborative document rather than having each student complete an individual spreadsheet.

   To see a sample, go to the Google Spreadsheets website (http://spreadsheets.google.com/pub?key=pJFPjEcnR9a28EaOOshDbRw).

   The teacher should circulate among the students, praising the students for their work or, when necessary, prompting students who are having difficulties. When the data has been recorded the students should use the Sum function to add the minutes for each day, find a grand sum for both days, and then save their data. The students should be told that each day's total should add up to 1440 minutes (60 minutes/hour x 24 hours = 1440 minutes/day). Next the students should total the time for each individual activity.

3. The teacher should direct the students to their computers and on a master (or collaborative) spreadsheet compile a grand time total for the various activities. This could be done by the teacher or individual students, or groups could be assigned the task. When the totals have been compiled the teacher should compute the class averages for the activities and discuss the comparisons of the individual students to the class average. The teacher may want to compile a chart of the data (e.g., a pie graph) to display in the class.

ASSESSMENT

Students' grades can be based on the following sample assessment rubric:

CRITERIA	DOES NOT MEET EXPECTATIONS	MEETS EXPECTATIONS	EXCEEDS EXPECTATIONS
Activity times were accurately transcribed			
Students were able to use Google Spreadsheet function			

WORKSHEET SAMPLE

Data Collection Sheet

TIMES FOR DAY 1		TIMES FOR DAY 2	
Activity	Time Spent	Activity	Time Spent
Studying		Studying	
Playing		Playing	
In Class Time		In Class Time	
Eating		Eating	
Chores		Chores	
Homework		Homework	
Sleeping		Sleeping	
Other Activities		Other Activities	
TOTAL	1440 minutes	TOTAL	1440 minutes

MAPPING OUR COMMUNITY

Sarah Rolle

GRADE LEVEL: 1–2

SUBJECT: English Language Arts

TIME REQUIRED: 3–5 hours

OBJECTIVES

Students will be able to:

- Mark on a digital map where they live and go to school.

- Describe the relationship between where they live and their school using the words *closer* and *farther.*

- Write three observations about using their new vocabulary.

CORRELATIONS TO STANDARDS

NCTE/IRA Standards for the English Language Arts

4. Communication Skills

ISTE National Educational Technology Standards for Students (NETS•S)

2. Communication and Collaboration

MATERIALS AND RESOURCES REQUIRED

- Internet access and necessary technology

- Google Maps

- Paper and pencil or word processor

- Color printer for printing maps to be posted with written descriptions

LESSON DESCRIPTION

(**Note:** this lesson is part of a larger unit on community.)

Pre-Activities

1. Students need to have home and school addresses written down before this activity starts.

2. Introduce students to communities and locations on Google Maps.

3. Introduce students to the words *closer* and *farther*. Demonstrate these words by having students stand in your room *closer* to, and *farther* from, an object or area in the room. Have other students describe the relationship of the students to one another and the object. For example: Jon is closer to the blackboard than Sue.

Activity

1. Go to Google Maps and use the Get Directions tab.

2. Students will work in pairs, plotting each child's home address on the map. One student types his or her address in Start Address box, and the other student types his or her address in End Address box.

3. Students can add more locations. The address of the school is necessary for the activity, but you may want to provide another address (e.g., the fire house, post office, or another important community location) so that each student gets to add a second address. Once the first two locations have been plotted, click on Add Destination below the directions in order to add additional locations to the map.

   Note: If time allows, explore the Terrain and Satellite buttons on the maps with the students so that they can see different types of maps with the same locations marked.

   To print the maps: Go to File > Print. Do not use Google's Print link because it will not display a large map.

   Note: Any type of map (terrain, satellite or regular) can be printed this way. As an extension of this assignment, students might print more than one type of map and compare them.

4. Students will cut out the map(s) to be posted.

5. Each student will write three or more sentences, including the following:

   ■ My house is closer to (or farther from) school than [fill in partner's name]'s.

   ■ [Fill in partner's name]'s house is farther from (or closer to) school than mine.

   ■ Teachers may have students write a sentence that starts: The school is closer to or farther from …

6. Have the students write one more sentence of their choice. It could involve writing their address or something related to the fourth address marked on the map. If they printed more than one map, they could write something about the difference between the maps.

7. Post the maps and paragraphs so that all the students can see them and learn more about their community.

8. Discuss with the students what they learned from making the maps and looking at one another's maps.

ASSESSMENT

Did students do each of the following?

■ Place one or two addresses on Google Maps

■ Write three sentences about their map using the words *closer* and *farther*

SAM THE TRUCKER

John Hrevnack

GRADE LEVEL: 4

SUBJECT: Mathematics

TIME REQUIRED: 2 class periods

OBJECTIVES

Students will be able to:

- Add distances.
- Add minutes and hours.
- Use Google Earth to find the directions between two cities.
- Work cooperatively in a group.

CORRELATIONS TO STANDARDS

NCTM Principles and Standards for School Mathematics

Problem Solving

- Solve problems that arise in mathematics and in other contexts
- Apply and adapt a variety of appropriate strategies to solve problems

Measurement

- Understand measurable attributes of objects and the units, systems, and processes of measurement

Communication

- Analyze and evaluate the mathematical thinking and strategies of others

Connections

- Recognize and apply mathematics in contexts outside of mathematics

ISTE National Educational Technology Standards for Students (NETS·S)

1. Creativity and Innovation
2. Communication and Collaboration
3. Research and Information Fluency
4. Critical Thinking, Problem Solving, and Decision Making
6. Technology Operations and Concepts

MATERIALS AND RESOURCES REQUIRED

- Internet access and necessary technology
- Google Earth
- Pencils
- Paper
- Calculators (optional)

LESSON DESCRIPTION

Check and/or teach the following prerequisite skills:

- Students can use the basic functions of Google Earth (including locating a given section of the United States, being able to use the Direction and the Compass features).

1. Divide the students into groups of four at a computer. Assign roles as specified:

   - Leader—responsible for keeping the group on task and making sure that everyone participates
   - Recorder—records the work of the group
   - Inputter—responsible for inputting data on the computer
   - Reporter—gives oral responses to the teacher and class about the activities of the group

2. Model the activity. The teacher should activate the Google Earth website and make sure the Borders and Labels, International Borders, Country Names, 1st Level Admin Borders, and Populated Places features are activated. The teacher tells the class that Sam the Trucker is going to start out in Philadelphia, Pennsylvania, and end at Chicago, Illinois. He also needs to make stops in Pittsburgh, Pennsylvania, and Columbus, Ohio. Using the Directions feature, the teacher demonstrates how to plot the route from one city to the next. The distance and time are recorded for each leg of the trip; total distance and total time are computed.

3. The teacher then provides the class (or each group) with a beginning city, a final destination, and several cities where Sam the Trucker needs to stop along the way. The groups then plot a route and add the distance and the total time to make the trip.

4. As a summative activity the teacher should have the students come to the board to add the distances and time involved in the activity. The teacher could finally engage the class in a discussion of how various goods are transported to the stores in their neighborhood and the time necessary to ship them.

Sample Log Form

	FROM	TO	DISTANCE	TIME (Hours)	TIME (Minutes)
1.					
2.					
3.					
4.					
5.					
6.					
		Total Distance:		Total Time:	

ASSESSMENT

Students' grades can be based on the following sample assessment rubric:

CRITERIA	DOES NOT MEET EXPECTATIONS	MEETS EXPECTATIONS	EXCEEDS EXPECTATIONS
Distances were accurately added			
Times were accurately added			
Group worked cooperatively			
Group was able to use Google Earth			

SCHOOL NEWS

Sarah Rolle and Eleanor Funk Schuster

GRADE LEVEL: 3–4

SUBJECT: English Language Arts

TIME REQUIRED: 5 class periods

OBJECTIVES

Students will be able to:

- Construct basic interview questions.

- Conduct an interview.

- Use Google Documents for collaborative work on an interview, including inserting a picture.

CORRELATIONS TO STANDARDS

NCTE/IRA Standards for the English Language Arts

4. Communication Skills

6. Applying Knowledge

ISTE National Educational Technology Standards for Students (NETS•S)

2. Communication and Collaboration

6. Technology Operations and Concepts

MATERIALS AND RESOURCES REQUIRED

- Internet access and necessary technology

- Google Documents

- Digital camera

LESSON DESCRIPTION

Students will collaborate to gather school news through interviews.

Preparation

The teacher collects two or three sample news broadcast interviews for students to view. At this point, the teacher will need to coordinate schedules with potential interview subjects to ensure availability during Activity #2 of the lesson.

Pre-Activity

1. Familiarize students with Google Documents.

2. Students view sample broadcast interviews then participate in a teacher-led discussion related to interview questions.

3. Discussion questions:

    - What questions did the interviewer ask that would be essential for any interview?

    - What questions were specific for this interview?

    - What else would you like to know?

4. The teacher should introduce the following elements of a good interview if not thought of by students:

    - Every interviewer should begin by asking name and position of interview subject.

    - Every interviewer should state the purpose of the interview: to gather news about the school.

    - Open-ended questions are important to ask at the end of an interview. For example: "Is there something more you would like to add? What have you learned from this? What would you like others to know? What was this experience like for you?"

Activity 1

1. In groups, students pick whom they are going to interview.

2. Students generate interview questions in a Google document.

3. Teacher should remind students of the 5 Ws (Who, What, Where, When, Why) as prompts for interview questions.

4. Once questions are generated, another group should review them and indicate if they feel there are any missing questions.

5. Students revise questions based on feedback.

    (1 class period)

Activity 2

1. Students interview subjects and take notes in their Google document. **Suggestion:** use different colors for question and answers.

2. Students take digital photograph of subject. **Note:** teacher uploads photographs for students to access and insert later.

    (1 class period)

Activity 3

1. Each student takes responsibility for editing a different question. Students can work independently on the same document simultaneously. Students will:

    - Put notes into full sentences

    - Check spelling and grammar

    (1 class period)

Activity 4

1. Peer review: students share interviews with the class in oral presentations.

2. Class provides feedback based on the following questions:

    - Is the information clear?

    - Were each of the relevant five Ws addressed?

    - Is there anything else you would like or need to know?

    (1 class period)

Activity 5

1. Students meet in groups to insert photo and to create additional questions based on class feedback.

2. Group shares document with interviewee who answers questions and checks facts for accuracy.

3. Group conducts final edit based on feedback.

    (1 class period)

EXTENSION

Consider adding the interviews to the school website.

ASSESSMENT

Students' grades can be based on the following sample assessment rubric:

CATEGORY	EXCELLENT	GOOD	NEEDS IMPROVEMENT
Creative Contribution	Contributed constructive, creative ideas with enthusiasm	Contributed constructive ideas	Did not contribute ideas
Working with Others	Considerate and kind Listened to others' ideas with an open mind	Able to accept others' ideas	Difficulty with accepting others' ideas
Work Input	Extra effort and time given to helping group achieve goal Remained engaged in group work throughout project	Contributed meaningfully to project Remained engaged in group work throughout project	Little or no contribution
Spelling	Great care given to spelling	Sufficient care given to spelling	No revisions or effort evident in spelling
Sentence Structure	Words are capitalized at beginning of sentences Periods are used at end of sentences Sentences include a noun and verb	Words are capitalized at beginning of sentences Periods are used at end of sentences	No effort given to sentence structure
Inserting an Image	Image is clear Image is relevant to topic	Image is relevant to topic	No image
INTERVIEW QUESTIONS			
Name and Position of Interview Subject	Both name and position of interviewee are listed, capitalized and spelled correctly	Both name and position of interviewee are listed	Name and/or position of interviewee not listed in document
Quantity	More than one relevant question per student, not including name, position, and concluding remarks	One question per student, not including name, position, and concluding remarks	Less than one question per student
Quality	Questions were very thorough in covering topic	Questions adequately cover topic	Not enough questions were generated to cover topic
Open-ended Closing Question	Multiple open-ended questions included	One open-ended question included	No open-ended questions were included
Use of Google Docs	Students independently edit document Students organize ideas using formatting options in Google Docs	Students independently edit document	Students need help with editing document

TRAVEL OF OUR ANCESTORS

John Hrevnack

GRADE LEVEL: 3

SUBJECT: Mathematics

TIME REQUIRED: 2 class periods; 1 evening of homework

OBJECTIVES

Students will be able to:

- Add numbers to the ten-thousands place.

- Identify the countries from which their ancestors migrated.

- Measure the distance between two points using appropriate strategies.

CORRELATIONS TO STANDARDS

NCTM Principles and Standards for School Mathematics

Problem Solving

- Solve problems that arise in mathematics and in other contexts

- Apply and adapt a variety of appropriate strategies to solve problems

Measurement

- Understand measurable attributes of objects and the units, systems, and processes of measurement

Communication

- Analyze and evaluate the mathematical thinking and strategies of others

Connections

- Recognize and apply mathematics in contexts outside of mathematics

ISTE National Educational Technology Standards for Students (NETS•S)

2. Communication and Collaboration

3. Research and Information Fluency

4. Critical Thinking, Problem Solving, and Decision Making

5. Digital Citizenship

6. Technology Operations and Concepts

MATERIALS AND RESOURCES REQUIRED

- Internet access and necessary technology
- Google Earth
- Pencils
- Paper
- Guide Sheet (see sample at the end of the lesson)

LESSON DESCRIPTION

Check and/or teach the following prerequisite skills:

- Students can use the basic functions of Google Earth (including locating a given country, being able to use the Pin, Rule, and Compass features).

1. Divide the students into groups of four at a computer.

2. Begin by discussing with the students that our ancestors may have come from different countries. The teacher may share personal ancestry or the ancestry of a famous person. The teacher should then model the activity for the students. First, the teacher should type in the Fly To area the name of the state and city in which the students go to school, and then fly to that area. A placemark should be placed on the city. Next the teacher should input the area the teacher's (or famous person's) ancestors came from in the Fly To area. Then the teacher should activate the Ruler feature and move the marker to the the placemark. Finally, the teacher should activate the Fly To feature, which will provide the distance between the two locations. The teacher should then use the Pan Out tool of Google Earth to show how far the ancestors had to travel, and the teacher should read the number provided in the Ruler results. The teacher may, at this point, have the students try several examples in their groups.

3. At the end of the period the teacher should ask the students to go home and discuss their ancestry with their parent or guardian. Each student should write on a sheet of paper their ancestor's place of origin. If a student has more than one location of ancestry, they should, for this exercise, select the location that comes last in the alphabet. (Students who are adopted may research the ancestry of their adoptive parents.)

   It is important to be sensitive to the fact that not all families may be willing to share their immigration information for a variety of reasons, and you should plan alternative ways for students from these families to be included in the lesson.

4. The next day the teacher again has the students go to their assigned groups. Recreating the activity from the day before, they find out the distance between their ancestor's place of origin and the city where the student lives.

5. The teacher should circulate among the groups, providing assistance as needed. The students should, when they complete the individual computations, add the total miles traveled for all the ancestors of those in the group.

6. The teacher should add the mileage totals from all the groups to obtain a grand total of miles (this could be done by the teacher or students). The teacher should engage the class in a mathematical discussion about place value and the process of addition. Did the students see any patterns emerge in the data (about the places of origin or the numbers)? It is suggested the teacher conclude the lesson with a discussion of how far students' ancestors traveled, why their ancestors might have left their homelands, what sacrifices they might have made, and so on.

ASSESSMENT

- Students will be judged as a group on their ability to fill out the guide sheets appropriately.

- Students will be graded on their ability to work cooperatively.

WORKSHEET SAMPLE

Guide Sheet

STUDENT	USA-TOWN/CITY	ANCESTOR- TOWN/CITY	TOTAL MILES
		Total miles:	

U.S. IMMIGRATION

Sarah Rolle

GRADE LEVEL: 4

SUBJECT: Social Studies or History

TIME REQUIRED: approximately 5 class periods, plus time for the homework assignment

OBJECTIVES

Students will be able to:

- Make a personal connection between own family history and the immigrant experience.

- Summarize collected data and draw conclusions about their family and about the class data as a whole.

CORRELATIONS TO STANDARDS

National Standards for History

Standards in History for Grades K–4

TOPIC 3   The History of the United States: Democratic Principles and Values and the Peoples from Many Cultures Who Contributed to Its Cultural, Economic, and Political Heritage

ISTE National Educational Technology Standards for Students (NETS·S)

6.   Technology Operations and Concepts

MATERIALS AND RESOURCES REQUIRED

- Internet access and necessary technology

- Download this chart with immigration data for reference during the lesson: http://teacher.scholastic.com/activities/immigration/pdfs/multiline2.pdf

- You may want to refer to some of these websites for more historical immigration data:

  Migration Policy Institute—MPI Data Hub: Migration Facts, Stats, and Maps:
     www.migrationinformation.org/DataHub/charts/final.immig.shtml
     www.migrationinformation.org/DataHub/historicaltrends.cfm

  Reach Every Child—Research immigration and family histories:
     www.reacheverychild.com/feature/immigrate.html

LESSON DESCRIPTION

This lesson is part of a larger Social Studies unit on immigration. The focus of this lesson is to help students gain a personal connection to American immigration.

1. Introduce spreadsheets. Explain that spreadsheets were designed as a grid of cells with rows and columns that can contain alphanumeric, text, or numeric data. The cells can also contain formulas. They are often used for mathematical purposes. If the number in one cell is changed, the other cells that refer to that cell will change automatically. Sometimes charts or graphs are created to visualize the data that is in a spreadsheet. Sometimes spreadsheets are used as a grid to organize data. Show the class a blank spreadsheet and input information or have various samples so that they will understand how spreadsheets can be used.

2. Explain that, for this lesson, the class will be asking their families for help filling out a form (questionnaire) so that the class can learn about everyone's family immigration history. Explain that Google Spreadsheets allows a form to be created that will put all the information into a spreadsheet automatically. Create a sample form for students to answer two or three personal questions so that they understand how this will work. Your form could include name, number of siblings, and favorite color. Students fill out the form individually and then see the collective data. Mention that conclusions can be drawn from that data, for example, how many people like a certain color, and so on.

3. Brainstorm with the students what questions they think would be important to ask about their families. Talk about the kinds of questions that will help students relate to historical data you intend to use in the class. Explain that there are five types of questions that can be used in creating the form: Text, Paragraph Text, Multiple Choice, Checkboxes, and Choose From A List. Though you can include any questions you want, for this lesson the form will need to gather the following information: relationship, where the family member was born (country and continent), and, if they were born abroad, the year of immigration.

   It is important to be sensitive to the fact that not all families may be willing to share their immigration information for a variety of reasons, and you should plan alternative ways for students from these families to be included in the lesson.

4. Create the form on a new spreadsheet using whichever questions you decide upon. Once the form has been created, give the students the web address (URL) to fill out the form for homework.

5. Look at the data spreadsheet that has come together once everyone has filled out the form. Sort the spreadsheet to consider the answers to different questions. Ask the students to summarize the information about their class. How many countries are represented? How many continents?

6. Look at historical data and discuss how it compares to the class data.

7. Have the students draw conclusions based on the data collected.

8. In order to have students understand more about their particular heritage, have them go to The Migration Policy Institute website (www.migrationinformation.org/DataHub/whoswhere.cfm), where they can select their heritage and the state in which they live, and the combination will produce information to read about that particular group in that state.

9. Have students write a few sentences about what they have learned in this lesson. Suggest that they share some of the conclusions they reached about their family's heritage and how the class as a whole compared to the historical data presented.

ASSESSMENT

Create a rubric to assess the following:

15%   Participation

15%   Homework completion

70%   Written work

THE WORLD IN OUR CLASSROOM

Sarah Rolle

GRADE LEVEL: K–4

SUBJECT: English Language Arts

TIME REQUIRED: 4 class periods

OBJECTIVES

Students will be able to:

- Take a digital photograph.

- Post an entry on a blog.

- Comment on someone else's blog entry.

- Describe part of their classroom.

CORRELATIONS TO STANDARDS

NCTE/IRA Standards for the English Language Arts

4. Communication Skills

5. Communication Strategies

ISTE National Educational Technology Standards for Students (NETS•S)

2. Communication and Collaboration

6. Technology Operations and Concepts

MATERIALS AND RESOURCES REQUIRED

- Internet access and necessary technology

- Blogger

- Digital camera

LESSON DESCRIPTION

1. Talk about the idea of the students sharing their "world" with others (e.g., older students at school). Ask them for ideas as to how they might accomplish this. Explain that they will take a picture of part of the classroom and describe it in order to give others a glimpse into their classroom. Show some examples of other blogs, or create a post or two on the class blog as examples for the students.

2. Students take a photograph of any area in the classroom. Once everyone has taken a photograph, upload the pictures to the computer. Keep track of the order in which the students took their pictures so that they will be able to find their picture without having to search all images.

   Note: if your students each take photos of different parts of the room, you will later be able to discuss how well they think they have represented the room to others.

3. Show the class how to create posts or help each student create a post on the classroom blog. Students will upload their photos and then write a few sentences about them. You may decide to have your students save their posts in draft form and finish at another time, or write their sentences before creating the blog post.

4. Have older students comment on the blog so that your students get feedback and have an audience for which to write.

5. Share those comments with each student individually.

EXTENSIONS

Your students could reply on the blog to the older student who left a comment. You may also write comments as you would give feedback on any other writing done by your students.

ASSESSMENT

Teacher will read all blog entries and comments. Did students, at their ability level, do each of the following?

- Post a picture and description on the class blog

- Successfully share a part of their classroom with others

- Write appropriate to their ability and your requirements

- Give feedback to others through the comments feature
  (If you chose to have them comment a second time on the blog.)

WRITING FABLES

Eleanor Funk Schuster

GRADE LEVEL: 2–4

SUBJECT: English Language Arts

TIME REQUIRED: 7 class periods

OBJECTIVES

Students will be able to:

- Recognize and describe the elements of Aesop's fables.

- Write an original fable and accompanying moral.

- Collaborate with other students using Google Presentations to create a project.

- Publish and present to an audience.

CORRELATIONS TO STANDARDS

NCTE/IRA Standards for the English Language Arts

2. Understanding the Human Experience

4. Communication Skills

6. Applying Knowledge

12. Applying Language Skills

ISTE National Educational Technology Standards for Students (NETS•S)

1. Creativity and Innovation

2. Communication and Collaboration

MATERIALS AND RESOURCES REQUIRED

- Internet access and necessary technology

- Google Presentations

- Aesop's Fables books and/or Internet sites

- Aesop's Fables can be found at the University of Virginia Library, Electronic Text Center website (http://etext.virginia.edu/toc/modeng/public/AesFabl.html) or at the University of Massachusetts, Amherst, website (www.umass.edu/aesop).

PREPARATION

- Teacher selects images that represent the fables (animals, objects, settings). These will be used as prompts for the students when creating their fables. Save images in a place students can easily access. Teacher should test the Image Save process in order to refine and model the process for students.

- Teacher selects fables to read aloud to students.

- Teacher selects pairs or groups of students to collaborate on project. Consider creating groups of students with diverse abilities such as storytellers and those comfortable with technology.

PRE-ACTIVITIES

- Read a variety of Aesop's Fables to class.

- Explain that fables are moral tales that use animal personification.

- Present simple story elements: character, setting, plot and structure, main character, motivation, problem, and resolution to provide basis for fable writing activity.

- Model use of the Google Presentations tool.

- Evaluate and reinforce basic skills as necessary.

- Discuss the Presentations format as a tool for sharing.

DESCRIPTION

Students will learn the basic elements and structure of Aesop's Fables through listening to fables read aloud, independent reading, teacher-led instruction, and class discussion. Students will then write (in groups or independently) original fables and morals. Students will create a Google presentation that tells their original fable and will share the fable with an audience. The presentation will consist of at least three slides: title slide, story slide (more than one story slide is OK), and image/moral slide.

1. Teacher models the following Presentation tools to create three slides (title slide, story slide, image slide):

   - Open Google Docs page

   - Click File > New Presentation

   - Create title slide: insert fable name, student name, teacher's name, and date in subtitle. Expand subtitle box by dragging corners so that text fits inside box.

   - Choose theme

   - Create new slide

   - Select Text layout

   - Write fable title as heading

   - Write fable story in body of slide

- Format text (font, size, color, alignment)
- Create new slide
- Select Caption layout
- Insert image in main body
- Write fable moral in caption box

Teacher guides class in practicing skills and reinforces skills as necessary.

(1 class period)

2. Students write their own fables and morals in groups or pairs. (Modification: students choose an existing Aesop Fable to use in presentation.)

    (2 class periods)

3. Students select an image and save it for easy access.

    (1 class period)

4. Students create their presentations.

    (2 class periods)

5. Teacher publishes project and links to school website.
    Whole Class Activity: students share fables with own class and other classes.

    Alternative/Extension: Teacher creates a Presentation slide entitled "Fable Morals." Students do not write moral under image in their own project; morals will instead be listed on "Fable Morals" slide. Audience will try to match correct morals to fables.

    (1 class period)

ASSESSMENT

Grade based on individual or group performance at teacher's discretion for a total of 100 points.

20 points   Student or group produces original fable and accompanying moral or finds an Aesop Fable to share.

35 points   Fable incorporates animal personification along with a plot that illustrates moral.

25 points   Final presentation includes:

- Creating new slide (5 points)
- Theme selection (5 points)
- Layout selection (5 points)
- Text formatting (5 points)
- Image (5 points)

20 points   Student or group shares project with an audience.

MIDDLE SCHOOL
LESSONS

LESSON PLANS

- African American History Heroes
- Book Review Blog
- Candidate Watch
- Creating a Study Guide
- Current Events Blog
- Group Memoirs
- Literature Genre Study
- Middle School Favorites
- National Parks
- Our Community Speaks
- Story Starters
- Vocabulary Spreadsheet

LESSON TITLE	PAGE #	GRADE LEVEL (U.S.)	AGES	SUBJECT AREA(S)	GOOGLE APP(S) USED
African American History Heroes	273	5–8	9–14	Social Studies/ History	Presentations
Book Review Blog	276	6–8	10–14	ELA	Blogger
Candidate Watch	279	7–12	11–18	Social Studies/ History	Earth, Maps, Search, Documents
Creating a Study Guide	282	5–8	9–14	Social Studies/ History	Spreadsheets
Current Events Blog	285	5–8	9–14	Social Studies/ History	Blogger
Group Memoirs	288	5–8	9–14	ELA	Documents
Literature Genre Study	291	5–8	9–14	ELA	Blogger
Middle School Favorites	295	5–8	9–14	Math	Spreadsheets, Forms
National Parks	298	5–6	9–12	Social Studies/ History	Earth
Our Community Speaks	302	5–8	9–14	ELA/ Social Studies/ History/Math	Spreadsheets, Forms
Story Starters	305	5–8	9–14	ELA	Presentations
Vocabulary Spreadsheet	308	5	9–11	ELA/Any	Spreadsheets

AFRICAN AMERICAN HISTORY HEROES

Pamela Friedman

GRADE LEVEL: 5–8

SUBJECT: Social Studies

TIME REQUIRED: 5–6 class periods

OBJECTIVES

Students will be able to:

- Research famous African Americans.

- Evaluate the contributions of famous African Americans.

- Analyze the character traits of the African American chosen.

CORRELATIONS TO STANDARDS

National Standards for Civics and Government

I.   Civic Life, Politics, and Government

V.   Roles of the Citizen

National Standards for History (U.S. History for Grades 5–12)

Era 4. Expansion and Reform (1801–1861)

Era 5. Civil War and Reconstruction (1850–1877)

Era 6. The Development of the Industrial United States (1870–1900)

Era 7. The Emergence of Modern America (1890–1930)

Era 8. The Great Depression and World War II (1929-1945)

Era 9. Postwar United States (1945 to early 1970s)

Era 10. Contemporary United States (1968 to the present)

NCTE/IRA Standards for the English Language Arts

2.   Understanding the Human Experience

3.   Evaluation Strategies

4.   Communication Skills

5.   Communication Strategies

6.   Applying Knowledge

7.   Evaluating Data

11. Participating in Society

12. Applying Language Skills

ISTE National Educational Technology Standards for Students (NETS·S)

1. Creativity and Innovation

2. Communication and Collaboration

3. Research and Information Fluency

4. Critical Thinking, Problem Solving, and Decision Making

5. Digital Citizenship

6. Technology Operations and Concepts

MATERIALS AND RESOURCES REQUIRED

■ Internet access and necessary technology

■ Google Presentations

■ Books, periodicals, and magazines for research purposes

LESSON DESCRIPTION

Black History Month is celebrated in classrooms across the U.S. during the month of February. Researching important African Americans, the history of their arrival and progress, and the impact blacks have had on the U.S. could be considered during any month of the school year. Pre-assess students to ensure necessary competence in Google Presentations. Teach where necessary.

1. The teacher should separate students into small groups, or pairs, depending on the size of the class. Each group will select an African American as its focus for this project.

2. After discussing the importance of African Americans' influence in the U.S., the teacher should allow students time to gather information on their chosen person.

3. Each group is responsible for evaluating websites and choosing appropriate sources. The Biography website has reliable information (www.biography.com/blackhistory/index2.js).

   Students will be expected to include the following in their reports:

   ■ Biography—this includes early life, schooling, career, and family life

   ■ Contributions—how this person contributed to change in the U.S.

   ■ Characteristics—identify one characteristic they admire most and why they chose it

   ■ Graphics—images from the Internet of their person

   ■ Resources—cite all sources used for this project

4. Once a group has completed its research, the group will log onto the Google presentation set up by the teacher. A sample presentation can be viewed at http://docs.google.com/Presentation?id=dcphsvkf_49cfq6xfcp.

5. Each group will begin by posting an image of its chosen person on the title slide.

6. Each group will create three slides and add them to the Google Presentation document. One slide will contain biographical information, one slide will contain information about the contributions of this person, and one slide will contain character traits of the person.

7. Each group will be responsible for adding its sources to the final slide.

8. The teacher will remind students to keep their backgrounds simple and appealing, allowing the viewer to easily read the text.

9. When each group has completed their contribution to the slide presentation, the teacher will publish the slide show and share it with the class, the school, and the community.

ASSESSMENT

Students' grades will be based on the following assessment rubric:

CRITERIA	DOES NOT MEET EXPECTATIONS	MEETS EXPECTATIONS	EXCEEDS EXPECTATIONS
Biography			
Contributions			
Identification of character traits			
Proficiency in using technology			

BOOK REVIEW BLOG

Pamela Friedman

GRADE LEVEL: 6–8

SUBJECT: English Language Arts

TIME REQUIRED: 5–6 class periods

OBJECTIVES

Students will be able to:

- Critique a biography from the perspective of understanding the human experience.

- Peer evaluate and critique the book reviews written by fellow students according to established criteria.

- Compare and contrast characteristics of the subjects of several different biographies.

CORRELATIONS TO STANDARDS

NCTE/IRA Standards for the English Language Arts

1. Reading for Perspective

2. Understanding the Human Experience

3. Evaluation Strategies

4. Communication Skills

5. Communication Strategies

6. Applying Knowledge

7. Evaluating Data

11. Participating in Society

12. Applying Language Skills

ISTE National Educational Technology Standards for Students (NETS·S)

1. Creativity and Innovation

2. Communication and Collaboration

4. Critical Thinking, Problem Solving, and Decision Making

5. Digital Citizenship

6. Technology Operations and Concepts

MATERIALS AND RESOURCES REQUIRED

- Internet access and necessary technology
- All students must have read a biography
- Google Blogger

FORMAT FOR BOOK REVIEW BLOG

Each student will write a book review using the following format:

1. The title of the biography should be the subject of the blog post. Discuss the following:

   - What was the subject best known for?

   - Critique the book using the following criteria:

     - In your opinion, did the author provide a balanced view of the subject's life? Explain.

     - What were the strengths/weaknesses of the book? Explain.

     - What value is to be gained by the reader from reading the book? Why or why not is this book important?

     - What is your response to the book? Was it interesting, moving, or dull? Why? What did you like or dislike? Why? Did anything surprise you? How or why?

     - Would you recommend the book to everyone, just some people, or no one? Why?

   - Write a very brief summary of the subject's life, including something important that might not be widely known.

   - Describe the subject's character strengths and weaknesses.

   - Has society been affected by this person? If so, how?

   - List several of the subject's major accomplishments.

2. Once all students have posted a book review on the blog page, students will be assigned to peer review a post, and students will revise their blog posts. After the revisions are posted, each student will comment on at least two of their peers' posts. The following questions should be addressed when commenting:

   - Compare and contrast the personality traits of the subject in your biography to the subject in your peer's biography.

   - Compare and contrast any hardships you had to overcome versus those of your character. What was similar and what was different?

   - What have you learned about this person that you didn't know before, based on your peer's book review?

   - What are one or two questions you would like to ask the reviewer about the book or their review of it?

LESSON DESCRIPTION

Pre-assess students to ensure necessary competence in use of Blogger. Teach where necessary.

1. Prior to students' beginning to write, share examples of excellent and poor book reviews. Work with students to generate a rubric to evaluate their book reviews.

2. Have students choose a biography they will be using for the book review. The teacher must approve the book.

3. Students read biographies and write their reviews in something other than Blogger.

4. After students have completed writing their book review, the teacher will approve (but not edit) the review before having it uploaded to Blogger.

5. Students will upload an image of the subject of their book next to their blog post.

6. Once students have completed entering their book reviews, assign each student to peer critique a post written by someone else, using the class-developed rubric. Peer critiques should be posted as signed comments. Students should then post the revised book review as a new, separate post (both revised and original posts should remain visible). Review the process of giving constructive feedback and receiving feedback constructively before the peer critiques take place.

7. Students comment on at least two of their classmates' revised book reviews using the questions given above.

ASSESSMENT

Students' grades are based on three criteria:

50%	Quality of review
30%	Quality of peer critique
20%	Quality of two comments

CANDIDATE WATCH

Cheryl Davis

GRADE LEVEL:	7–12
SUBJECT:	United States History
TIME REQUIRED:	3 class periods to set up, continues over an election cycle

OBJECTIVES

Students will be able to:

- Identify and analyze the issues and candidates in an election.
- Connect geography to the election process by creating a collaborative Google Map and Google Earth file.
- Collect and plot data and statistical information about an election.

CORRELATIONS TO STANDARDS

NCSS Curriculum Standards for Social Studies

- X. Civic Ideals and Practices

ISTE National Educational Technology Standards for Students (NETS·S)

1. Creativity and Innovation
2. Communication and Collaboration
3. Research and Information Fluency

MATERIALS AND RESOURCES REQUIRED

- Internet access and necessary technology
- Google Earth
- Google Maps
- Google News Search Archive
- Google Documents

LESSON DESCRIPTION

Locally or nationally, the election process provides an opportunity for teachers to engage students in participatory civic literacy. In this lesson, students will integrate geography with the election process to identify presidential candidates and understand the primary process and the electoral college. Students will work in teams to collaborate on a Google map identifying and outlining a candidate's position on issues and analyzing the location of campaign events. For a national presidential election, placing candidates on Google Earth and identifying the electoral college numbers for each state gives students a geographic understanding of the process. Students will also write a collaborative "white paper" in Google Docs on the issues in the election. During the campaign and election season, students will track statistics and polling information using Google Spreadsheets. See Step 3 in the following list for thoughts on congressional and state election campaigns.

1. Group students in teams and assign them a candidate or election issue to follow.

2. Each student team sets up one collaborative Google map. Instruct students on how to access and add placemarks to the map. Also show students how to export the Google map to Google Earth. Google Maps give students the ability to collaborate on one map that they can update and then export to Google Earth as a KMZ file for a final presentation.

3. Introduce students to Google Earth. Instruct students on how to upload exported KMZ Google Map files. Show students how to view the layers in Google Earth, and have students check the U.S. Government layer which is located within the More layer. This will outline the congressional districts in the United States. If you are studying the national presidential election, have students placemark each state in Google Earth and include the number of electoral votes that the state is assigned. You can assign specific states to each of your teams. Dates and outcomes of the state primaries can also be included in the placemark of each state. For congressional or state elections, students may follow the candidates from location to location within the candidates' districts, reading local newspaper accounts or monitoring local media broadcasts to see the ebb and flow of issues over time and locality.

4. Each student team locates and creates placemarks for their candidates on a Google map. In the placemark descriptions, teams include pertinent information on the candidate or election. That information might include:

   ■ Date of candidate's announcement

   ■ Links to the candidate or campaign website

   ■ Links to videos of candidate or campaign speeches

   ■ The state electoral number

   ■ Candidate party affiliation

   Reliable primary resource video footage and information on the candidates for national office can be found at C-SPAN Classroom (www.c-spanclassroom.org).

5. As the campaigns progress, teams update their candidate's placemark with additional videos and links (including campaign ads).

6. Each student team sets up a collaborative Google document and spreadsheet. In the document, each team contributes to a "white paper" on the candidate or issue, outlining and analyzing the candidate's position on the issues. Direct students to the Google News Search archives, where they'll be able to access past newspaper articles on their candidates. In the spreadsheet, team members post and update statistics and polling information on the candidate. Spreadsheets can include updated information on primary wins or the electoral college numbers.

7. Throughout the election cycle, student teams continue to share, update, and revise their documents.

8. Student teams prepare for a presentation on their candidates or issues. Student teams export their final Google map to a Google Earth KMZ file. Finalized Google Earth files are collected by the teacher and opened in one Google Earth file. The combined election issues and/or candidate profiles are shown in a presentation to the class in a combined Google Earth tour. Each team takes a turn at showing their placemarks and summarizing for the class the information in their Google Docs white paper and Google spreadsheets. The tour can be displayed using an LCD projector. The class discusses and evaluates the election issues and research.

ASSESSMENT

Create a rubric to assess the following:

10%	Student participation in class discussion/presentation on issues and candidate.
30%	Quality and accuracy of candidate information on Google Earth tour. Tour placemarks link to meaningful primary source information on the candidate or issue.
40%	Quality and extent of analysis in student team "white paper."
20%	Accuracy of data information in spreadsheet.

CREATING A STUDY GUIDE

Sarah Rolle

GRADE LEVEL: 5–8

SUBJECT: Social Studies

TIME REQUIRED: 1 or 2 class periods

OBJECTIVES

Students will be able to:

- Format a spreadsheet to contain information in an organized fashion.

- Summarize and record information to be used as a study guide.

- Synthesize information in order to determine the significance of the battles of the American Revolution.

CORRELATIONS TO STANDARDS

National Standards for History

United States History Standards for Grades 5–12

Era 3 Revolution and the New Nation (1754–1820s)

ISTE National Educational Technology Standards for Students (NETS·S)

6. Technology Operations and Concepts

MATERIALS AND RESOURCES REQUIRED

- Internet access and necessary technology

- Google Spreadsheets

- Students will need any and all resources and/or notes already taken regarding the battles of the American Revolution

LESSON DESCRIPTION

This lesson is part of a larger social studies unit on the American Revolution. Although this lesson plan focuses on the American Revolution, any subject matter could be used with this format for organizing information into a study guide.

Pre-Activity

Students will have already studied the battles of the American Revolution and have reference material to use while working on their study guides.

1. Introduce spreadsheets. Explain that spreadsheets were designed as a grid of cells with rows and columns that can contain alphanumeric, text, or numeric data. The cells may also contain formulas. They are often used for mathematical purposes. If the number in one cell is changed then the other cells that refer to that cell will change automatically.

2. Explain that you will be using the spreadsheet because it is an adjustable grid—each column will hold specific information related to the battles, and each row will contain information about a single battle. Create and share an example containing one battle so students will see what is required of them.

3. As a group, have students format their spreadsheet as follows:

    -   Highlight seven rows and five columns below the sortbar.

    -   Under the Format menu, select Normal.

    -   Place the mouse pointer between columns A and B, at the top, and drag to double the width of the columns. The same needs to be done for the rows, but they need to be 3 or 4 times as high as they were by default. This will give students space to type in the details. Mention to students that once they start typing the cells will get "longer" if the text does not fit. They will not need to resize the cells manually. *Note:* You may decide that certain columns should be wider or narrower based on the amount of information that will be entered. Also, keep in mind that you will want all of your information to fit on one page, if possible. Students should print in landscape mode, giving you approximately 10" of width.

4. Students fill in the heading for each column in row 1 as follows: Name of Battle, Year Fought, Location, Causes of the Battle (if known), Winner, Significance of the Battle, Other Details. *(Extension: you may want students to list causes of the revolution in addition to battles.)*

5. Discuss with the students that they will need to input the details, summarize what they know, and draw some conclusions about the significance of each battle. Go through an example, showing how you would expect them to think through the rest of the battles.

6. Have students type in the names of the battles you want them to cover. At this point, they can work independently to fill in the spreadsheet. You may want them to work with a partner, discussing the significance of the battles before typing them in.

7. Check students' work before continuing with the lesson. A partial grade can be given at this point.

8. When students' spreadsheets are returned, have a discussion about the significance of the various battles. Give them time to make corrections and additions if others share ideas they have not thought of.

9. Let them know how you expect them to use this study guide. Will there be a test? Do they have to write a paper using this information?

10. After students have used the study guide, ask them if it was helpful. How was it helpful? As a class, generate a list of ways they found this to be a good study guide. You may want to explain that rewriting and rewording information along with drawing conclusions from the information given often helps people remember things better.

11. Discuss with students how they could apply this type of study guide to other subjects.

ASSESSMENT

Create a rubric to assess the following:

20%   Formatting spreadsheet

50%   Summarizing and recording information

30%   Synthesizing for the significance of the battles of the American Revolution

Teacher may choose to adjust grade after students make corrections and additions after Step 8 in the Lesson Description.

This lesson was adapted from one originally created by Susan Smolin.

CURRENT EVENTS BLOG

Pamela Friedman

GRADE LEVEL: 5–8

SUBJECT: Social Studies

TIME REQUIRED: 5–6 class periods or ongoing throughout the year

OBJECTIVES

Students will be able to:

- Examine a current events issue.

- Use higher-level thinking skills to analyze current events.

- Compare and contrast their point of view with other students' points of view.

CORRELATIONS TO STANDARDS

NCTE/IRA Standards for the English Language Arts

1. Reading for Perspective

2. Understanding the Human Experience

3. Evaluation Strategies

4. Communication Skills

5. Communication Strategies

6. Applying Knowledge

7. Evaluating Data

11. Participating in Society

12. Applying Language Skills

National Standards for Civics and Government

5–8 Content Standards

I. Civic Life, Politics, and Government

II. Foundations of the American Political System

III. Principles of American Democracy

IV. Other Nations and World Affairs

V. Roles of the Citizen in American Democracy

ISTE National Educational Technology Standards for Students (NETS·S)

1. Creativity and Innovation

2. Communication and Collaboration

3. Research and Information Fluency

4. Critical Thinking, Problem Solving, and Decision Making

5. Digital Citizenship

6. Technology Operations and Concepts

MATERIALS AND RESOURCES REQUIRED

■ Internet access and necessary technology

■ Google Blogger

FORMAT FOR CURRENT EVENTS BLOG

1. Periodically, the teacher will create a post on the Current Events Blog. It will vary depending upon local, national, and world events. The post will require students to comment on a specific news article or video news clip. Some suggested ideas for current events are:

    ■ The teacher will provide students with a copy of a specific article on a given topic and have students read the article and then comment.

    ■ The teacher will have students watch a video clip and comment on the blog.

    ■ Teachers will provide students with a website with a news article, have students read the article online, and then post an opinion on the blog.

    ■ Students may visit Google News and compare and contrast stories from media from different parts of the world on the same topic in order to see variations in perspectives.

2. Each student is responsible for responding to the current events article or news clip using the following criteria:

    ■ What is the main idea of the article or news story?

    ■ What is your reaction to this current event? What do you like or dislike about what happened? Why? Did anything surprise you? Why? Do you think it is important or not important? Why?

    ■ Answer the questions of who, what, when, where, and why regarding the news piece.

    ■ What are one or two questions you would like to ask the person or people the article is about, or the reporter/author?

    ■ Why do you think the news media thought this story was important enough to write about or broadcast?

3. Each student will make at least two comments on the current events blog. The comments must include the following:

    ▪ What do you find interesting about what your classmate had to say?

    ▪ What are one or two questions you would like to ask your classmate based on what they wrote?

    ▪ Do you agree or disagree with something your classmate wrote? Explain why.

LESSON DESCRIPTION

Pre-assess students to ensure necessary competence in use of Google Blogger. Teach where necessary.

1. At the beginning of each week, the teacher will share with the students a current event. This can take the form of a newspaper article, an online editorial, or a news story from television. The teacher can record news stories at home, and then show them to the students in school, if the necessary technology is available.

2. Before students use the current events blog, the teacher should explain how to evaluate a news article or story:

    ▪ Who is providing the report?

    ▪ What techniques are used to convey the facts?

    ▪ How might others interpret what they are seeing, hearing, or reading differently from me?

    ▪ In addition to the basic facts of the story, what values are being expressed, if any?

    ▪ Why do you think this media outlet chose to report this particular story? Who is their intended audience?

    ▪ What has this report omitted that you would like to know about?

    These questions are modified from Alliance for a Media Literate America (http://amlainfo.org/classroom-resources/hurricane-katrina-lesson-one-basic).

ASSESSMENT

Create a rubric to assess the following:

50%   Quality of student's original blog entry

50%   Quality of each of two comments

GROUP MEMOIRS

Eleanor Funk Schuster

GRADE LEVEL: 5–8

SUBJECT: English Language Arts

TIME REQUIRED: 3 class periods

OBJECTIVES

Students will be able to:

■ Use Google Documents in a collaborative production of a brief nonfiction narrative.

■ Understand the concept of memoirs.

■ Implement a strategy for writing memoirs.

CORRELATIONS TO STANDARDS

NCTE/IRA Standards for the English Language Arts

4. Communication Skills

6. Applying Knowledge

9. Multicultural Understanding

12. Applying Language Skills

ISTE National Educational Technology Standards for Students (NETS·S)

1. Creativity and Innovation

2. Communication and Collaboration

MATERIALS AND RESOURCES REQUIRED

■ Internet access and necessary technology

■ Google Documents

LESSON DESCRIPTION

The purpose of this lesson is to introduce the art of writing memoirs. Students may find it easier to share a common memory with peers than to jump immediately into writing about themselves. This exercise can help to prepare them for writing their own memoirs.

Students will work together in small groups to write a short piece on "The school lunchroom/lunchtime." The final projects may be shared with another class in school or with a school in another geographic location as part of a larger collaborative project.

The group will choose an event, a moment, an accomplishment, a new, exciting food selection, a situation, or a memory about lunchtime.

- The project must be nonfiction and approximately one to two paragraphs in length.

- Students will use figurative language including at least three of the following: simile, metaphor, alliteration, personification, and imagery.

- Students will insert at least one picture that represents the topic. The more specific students are, the better it will be.

- The following suggestions may help students in writing their narratives.

  - Use the five senses in descriptions, so the readers will feel like they can see, hear, smell, taste, and touch the scene. You remember what it was like; your challenge is to recreate that scene in your reader's mind.

  - Use dialogue and describe characters' personalities, appearances, and actions. Remember that you, too, are a character; be sure to give a sense of your own physical presence.

  - Imagine a reader who knows nothing about you, your family, or your geographic area. Pretend that you are explaining your story to that person so that you add essential background.

Preparation

- Teacher collects images that may be used by students during the project.

- Teacher plans grouping of students. Each group should be between 2–4 students.

  Note: Consideration should be given as to what kind of common memories each group may share. A class discussion may be helpful to encourage creative thinking in this aspect.

Pre-Activity (optional)

- Students take photographs of the lunchroom.

- Students or teacher uploads photos into project folder.

- Model use of Google Documents. Run practice session using toolbar features. Evaluate and reinforce basic skills as necessary.

Lesson

1. Working in assigned groups, students decide which memory they would like to write about.

2. Each group creates and names a Google Document project. (Example: Grade 8 Lunch: The First Day, by Ann, Tom, and Greg.)

3. Students search the Internet for images that represent their topic. Images may be of food, people eating, school lunchrooms, or other representative pictures.

4. Photographs are uploaded and placed with other images for easy access.

   (1 classroom period)

5. Students work in assigned groups of 2–4 students to write a short memoir on the "school lunchroom/lunchtime" to be read at the end of class or during the next class period. Groups may choose an event, a moment, an accomplishment, a new exciting food selection, a situation, or a memory about "lunchtime." It must be nonfiction; the more specific, the better it will be.

6. Students insert at least one image they saved earlier.

   (1 classroom period)

7. Students share project with class.

   Extension: students share projects with another class or school.

   (1 classroom period)

ASSESSMENT

Students' grades will be based on the following assessment rubric:

CATEGORY	POINTS/100	FANTASTIC	GOOD JOB	NEEDS IMPROVEMENT
Working Together as a Group	20	Listened to others' ideas with an open mind	Able to accept others' ideas	Difficulty with accepting others' ideas
Figurative Speech	20	Used figurative language skillfully including at least three of the following: simile, metaphor, alliteration, personification, or imagery	Used three examples of figurative language	Used less than three examples of figurative language, or not used correctly
Image	20	Image was inserted correctly and is an accurate representation of the written memoir	Image inserted correctly and represents broad topic	No image inserted or does not relate to topic
Spelling and Grammar	20	Great care given to check spelling and grammar	Sufficient care given to check spelling and grammar	No care given at all to spelling and grammar
Length and Content	20	Project was meaningfully written in one to two paragraphs	Project was one paragraph with some care given to content	Memoir was not of sufficient length and little care given to content

With thanks to Kristi Ann McGrath, English teacher at Suffern Middle School in New York.

LITERATURE GENRE STUDY

Eleanor Funk Schuster

GRADE LEVEL: 5–8

SUBJECT: English Language Arts

TIME REQUIRED: 4–7 weeks per genre

OBJECTIVES

Students will be able to:

- Implement the use of Blogger for posting and commenting.

- Identify the elements of the assigned literary genre.

- Understand importance and elements of evaluating Internet resources.

- Create hyperlinks within text and as lists to credible resources on the Internet.

- Analyze reading, in a simple fashion, to make connections with the human experience.

CORRELATIONS TO STANDARDS

NCTE/IRA Standards for the English Language Arts

1. Reading for Perspective
2. Understanding the Human Experience
3. Evaluation Strategies
4. Communication Skills
5. Communication Strategies
11. Participating in Society
12. Applying Language Skills

ISTE National Educational Technology Standards for Students (NETS•S)

1. Creativity and Innovation
2. Communication and Collaboration

MATERIALS AND RESOURCES REQUIRED

- Internet access and necessary technology

- Blogger

- The following resources are not required, but highly recommended:

  Richardson, W. (2006). *Blogs, wikis, podcasts, and other powerful web tools for classrooms.* Thousand, CA: Corwin Press.

  Genre Study: A Collaborative Approach:
  www.readwritethink.org/lessons/lesson_view.asp?id=270
      Helpful resource on the elements of literary genres, book review templates and discussion topics.

  Evaluating Web Pages: Techniques to Apply & Questions to Ask:
  www.lib.berkeley.edu/TeachingLib/Guides/Internet/Evaluate.html
      This resource from the University of California–Berkeley Library is valuable for evaluating websites.

  Kathy Schrock's Guide For Educators: Teacher Helpers: Critical Evaluation Information:
  http://school.discoveryeducation.com/schrockguide/eval.html

  American Library Association Award Lists:
  www.ala.org/ala/alsc/awardsscholarships/literaryawds/literaryrelated.cfm
      This is a good reading list for genre book choices.

  Young Adult Library Services Association: http://blogs.ala.org/yalsa

LESSON DESCRIPTION

Preparation

- Teacher chooses genre and 4–6 book choices.

- Teacher assigns reading groups.

- Teacher sets up main teacher blog and one blog for each reading group.

- Teacher determines audience, considering whether the discussion is to remain within the class or if parents and the larger community will be invited to participate.

- Write a "Blogging Letter" (see Richardson, p. 13) to families explaining the project and inviting participation.

- Consider inviting an author or expert to participate as well.

Pre-Activity

- Model use of Blogger.

- Run practice posting and commenting session.

- Evaluate and reinforce basic skills as necessary.

Overview

- The questions to be addressed in this unit progress from identifying the concrete traits of a specific genre to essential questions that encourage deep reflection and responsive journaling.

- Teacher posts assignment and questions on main blog. Students take turns posting teacher's current question (not the entire assignment) on their group blog and beginning the discussion thread. Each student is responsible for one comment in response to the teacher's question and two comments in response to other students' comments.

- The teacher's page will function as an instructional center with the teacher posting assignments, relevant news, instructions, and the teacher's own reflections on the students' work and discussions.

- The student blogs function as separate groups. Students comment within the community of their own group. Visiting authors and experts can pose questions on the main teacher blog, which can be discussed on the main blog or in separate student groups at the teacher's discretion.

The Basic Elements of Fiction and Genre

1. Students begin reading and blogging at same time for purpose of immersion and immediate relevancy.

2. Students should finish reading their books by the end of step one.

3. The number of questions posted by the teacher is determined by class needs and time constraints. The teacher should post to the teacher blog in the following format:

   - The teacher describes the traits of a specific genre and the elements of fiction. External links that address the traits of a specific genre will further support instruction.

   - Teacher poses questions that ask students to find examples in what they are reading that support the genre format.

   Example: Some elements of fantasy are the presence of talking animals, magical powers, and parallel worlds. Give two examples from this book that would characterize it as a fantasy.

   (2–4 weeks)

Reflective Journaling on Essential Questions

4. This stage encourages students to seek connections between their reading and life. These open-ended questions posted by the teacher provide a platform for discussion and journaling on a higher level of reflection with the foundation of Steps 1–4. Sample essential questions:

   - How do a person's point of view, culture, and experiences affect how they perceive themselves and the world?

   - To what extent does an experience define who we are?

   - To what extent does how we react to an experience define who we are?

- To what extent are you responsible for your environment?

- What can you learn about yourself by studying the lives of others?

- How do the desires of individuals drive their choices and shape their goals?

- How is a protagonist changed by the events of a story?

- To what extent does the setting affect conflict?

Time Required: 1–2 weeks

Source: Suffern Middle School, Suffern, NY. Grade 8 English Department Curriculum Map (http://ramapocentral.org).

Student-Generated List of Recommended Further Reading on Genre Topic

5. Each blog group creates a recommended list of at least five books within the genre. The list may be published as a blog entry in Google Documents as a link. The reading list format should be as follows: Author (last name, first name). Title. Two-to-three sentence summary. The blog group also creates a list of three or more hyperlinks to Internet resources on the genre topic. The students must evaluate the validity and quality of sites.

    Time required: 1 week

ASSESSMENT

Students will be assessed on the following individual and group criteria:

Individual

20%	Writing: punctuation, grammar, and organization of thoughts.
35%	Expressive language. Students respond thoughtfully in their comments by addressing the subject matter, formulating clear discussion points, and displaying original thinking. Students describe connections among the literature, genre styles, and the human experience.
10%	Students must respond at least once to main post. They may add additional responses to clarify or continue their points of discussion.
10%	Students must respond at least twice to comments of other students on each posting assignment.

Blogging group

10%	Reading list: proper format; five or more books listed.
10%	Internet resources: websites are valid sources of information and fulfill at least four of the following requirements: title, author, organization, date, working links, and useful information.
5%	Activity level, mechanics (e.g., working links), and appearance of blog.

MIDDLE SCHOOL FAVORITES

Pamela Friedman

GRADE LEVEL: 5–8

SUBJECT: Mathematics

TIME REQUIRED: 3–5 class periods

OBJECTIVES

Students will be able to:

- Use ratios and proportions to represent quantitative relationships.

- Understand the meaning of integers, and represent and compare quantities with them.

- Understand the meaning and effects of arithmetic operations with fractions, decimals, and integers.

- Develop, analyze, and explain methods for solving problems involving proportions.

CORRELATIONS TO STANDARDS

NCTM Principles and Standards for School Mathematics

Number and Operations

- Understand numbers, ways of representing numbers, relationships among numbers, and number systems

- Understand meanings of operations and how they relate to one another

- Compute fluently and make reasonable estimates

ISTE National Educational Technology Standards for Students (NETS·S)

1. Creativity and Innovation

2. Communication and Collaboration

3. Research and Information Fluency

4. Critical Thinking, Problem Solving, and Decision Making

5. Digital Citizenship

6. Technology Operations and Concepts

MATERIALS AND RESOURCES REQUIRED

- Internet access and necessary technology
- Google Spreadsheets and Spreadsheet Forms
- Survey sheets
- Student e-mail accounts

LESSON DESCRIPTION

The teacher will begin this lesson by discussing the use of surveys to gather information and make determinations based on survey results. The teacher will discuss different types of survey questions with students: multiple choice, rank order questions, matrix questions, and free-form text questions. For this assignment, students will be using rank order questions. Pre-assess students to ensure necessary competence in use of Google Spreadsheets. Teach where necessary.

1. The teacher will conduct a simple survey with the class as a model. For example, "What is your favorite subject?" Teacher will provide several choices for students. Results of the survey can be displayed on the board or projected.

   Students will be given the opportunity to create their own survey questions, which will be used for this assignment. The teacher will have final approval. As an example: "For the following question, rank the choices on a scale of 1–5. Use the formula of 5 = always and 1 = seldom/never. Question: How often do you use each of the following as your daily news source: television, radio, newspaper, Internet, magazines?"

   Other question formats and topics may be used.

2. Each student will be responsible for surveying 10 people. The students will need the e-mail address for each of the people they survey.

   - Students should log onto the Google Spreadsheet document.
   - Students should choose the Form option on the Spreadsheet.
   - Each student will type at least 5 questions on their form and invite at least 10 different people to answer their survey, 5 adults and 5 students.
   - Once the students have completed their forms, and invited up to 10 people, they will need to wait until everyone has responded. It is wise to let the people know ahead of time that the survey is coming.

3. The teacher will show the class how to create graphs from each survey category. Have students make bar graphs, with each graph representing a different question and the chart title reflecting the question asked. Once all of the graphs have been created, students will calculate percentages for each category of each graph. Then have students use the same data to create pie graphs. Have students compare and contrast the outcomes of the two graphing methods.

4. Students should write a brief paper describing how they used the tools in Google Spreadsheets, made their graphs, and what they learned about the differences between bar graphs and pie graphs.

ASSESSMENT

Students' grades can be based on the following sample assessment rubric:

CRITERIA	BELOW STANDARD	MEETS STANDARD	ABOVE STANDARD
Students were able to use the Spreadsheet function			
Students were able to generate appropriate survey questions			
Students were able to produce charts using the Chart function			
Students were able to create a form using the Forms function			
Students were able to explain how they did their work and the differences between bar and pie graphs			

NATIONAL PARKS

Sarah Rolle

GRADE LEVEL: 5–6

SUBJECT: Social Studies

TIME REQUIRED: 8–10 class periods

OBJECTIVES

Students will be able to:

■ Give a presentation about a National Park using Google Earth.

■ Add and remove layers to display various pieces of information in Google Earth (i.e., show borders of states and parks).

■ Plot placemarks in Google Earth.

■ Create a tour in Google Earth.

CORRELATIONS TO STANDARDS

National Geography Standards

1. The World in Spatial Terms

5. Environment and Society

ISTE National Educational Technology Standards for Students (NETS•S)

1. Creativity and Innovation

2. Communication and Collaboration

3. Research and Information Fluency

6. Technology Operations and Concepts

MATERIALS AND RESOURCES REQUIRED

■ Internet access and necessary technology

■ Google Earth

■ Research previously done on a national park

LESSON DESCRIPTION

This lesson is part of a larger research and geography unit on national parks. Each student will have researched a national park. This lesson will give them the opportunity to create a presentation that they will share with the class using Google Earth. Students will need to organize their ideas and thoughts into a format for speaking before they create their presentations.

Pre-Activity

Students will need to organize their research based on a list of required elements for their presentation or a rubric you provide. Some areas to highlight might be:

- Location
- Founding of the park
- Geographical features
- Activities for visitors
- Wildlife

Lesson

1. Introduce students to Google Earth. Create a presentation in advance and show it to your students. Create a presentation that has placemarks that are familiar and will engage the students—perhaps a tour of the school grounds or the town where you are located. Use this as a jumping-off point for a discussion about why they like Google Earth and how they could share information about their national park with others. From this discussion move on to discuss what makes a good presentation. In addition to creating the visual tour in Google Earth, students will need to be prepared to speak about their national park.

2. Show students how to use Google Earth:

    - Students map their own addresses. Show them how to turn on and off the layers in Google Earth. Ask students to share what they saw change as they explored the various layers. Did they turn on all the layers? If so, did that pose a problem in finding helpful information? Discuss which layers might be helpful in their presentation.

    - Talk about how a presentation is a visual aid to what you are saying, and that they need to pick the most important things to share (e.g., having 50 Panoramio balls that show pictures when clicked upon is not good because you can't display all those pictures while presenting). Students have to understand that it's better to find pictures that are specific to their presentation.

    - Set placemarks. Show students how to string together a few locations to create a tour. Show them how to place a picture and a link into the placemark. Make sure they understand that everything has to be in the same folder to be saved as a single tour.

3. Students begin planning their presentations in a storyboard format. Give students a piece of paper with six boxes on it (they may need more than one piece), or have them do their storyboarding in Google Documents. In each box, they should indicate what they will be discussing and the address of the placemark for their tour. They will also need to indicate any special items being included in that placemark, for example, a picture. As students plan, they will need a checklist of required elements. For example:

   ■ Show the state, including borders, in which the park is located.

   ■ Zoom into the boundaries of the park.

   ■ Show a particularly famous item or part of the park, or possibly more than one—for example, a mountain or waterfall.

   ■ Show a few different locations to give the audience a sense of the terrain from different angles.

   ■ Display some pictures of flora/fauna in the different parts of the park where they might be found.

   ■ Specify how many placemarks students should include in their presentation so that it will be manageable. If time allows, students can add an additional element of their own choosing.

4. Students search for, and save, online images. Images must have a proper citation. Provide a format model. A suggested online bibliography tool is Citation Machine (http://citationmachine.net).

5. Give students a set amount of time to create their tour. Students should share ideas with the class when they learn something new or if they figure something out that might help others with their presentations.

6. Lead a class discussion. What have students learned about Google Earth? How are the presentations different from a slide program like Google Presentations? How else do they see themselves using Google Earth? Would they share the program and/or their presentation with their families or friends?

7. Students update their tours based on what they learn during the class discussion.

8. Students give their presentations.

ASSESSMENT

Create a rubric to assess the following:

10%   Preparation

30%   Use of Google Earth including:

   ■ Student navigated well around Google Earth.

   ■ Student added placemarks to create a tour to compliment their presentation.

   ■ Student used layers to aid presentation.

- Student put pictures in placemarks that exemplified the student's remarks.

60%   Overall presentation, including speaking about and showing the following:

- Show the state, including borders, in which the park is located.

- Zoom into the boundaries of the park.

- Show a particularly famous item or part of the park, or possibly more than one—for example, a mountain or waterfall.

- Show a few different locations to give the audience a sense of the terrain from different angles.

- Display pictures of animals in the different parts of the park where they might be found.

This lesson was adapted from a lesson originally created with Yonne Prata.

OUR COMMUNITY SPEAKS

Eleanor Funk Schuster and Sarah Rolle

GRADE LEVEL: 5–8

SUBJECT: English Language Arts (or Social Studies, or Mathematics)

TIME REQUIRED: 4–6 class periods

OBJECTIVES

Students will be able to:

- Develop a questionnaire/survey.
- Draw conclusions from data collected.
- Use Google Spreadsheets to create a form and sort the data collected.
- Communicate the results to the community.

CORRELATIONS TO STANDARDS

NCTE/IRA Standards for the English Language Arts

7. Evaluating Data

12. Applying Language Skills

ISTE National Educational Technology Standards for Students (NETS·S)

2. Communication and Collaboration

3. Research and Information Fluency

6. Technology Operations and Concepts

MATERIALS AND RESOURCES REQUIRED

- Internet access and necessary technology
- Google Spreadsheets

LESSON DESCRIPTION

Using Google Spreadsheet Forms, students will collaborate in groups to conduct research on a chosen topic. Data will be collected using the survey tool in Google Spreadsheets. Students will sort and analyze the data in spreadsheet format to draw conclusions and communicate the results on their individual projects to the school community.

Project Requirements

- Create a spreadsheet.

- Create a survey form with five or more questions relating to topic.

- Share results with class.

- Summarize findings in paragraph format; share with the community.

Teacher Preparation

- Gather sample surveys to share with class.

- Gather sample topic questions that may include open-ended, Likert-scale, multiple choice, or ordinal questions that rank the answers.

- Create sample spreadsheet to show students how data is automatically transferred from a survey into a spreadsheet.

- Plan student groups and assign topics (or allow groups to select topics). Ideas for topics include:

    - Dress codes

    - School clubs

    - Activity nights

    - Friends

    - Lunchroom

    - Homework

    - Music

    - Sports

Lesson

1. Introduce spreadsheets. Explain that spreadsheets were designed as a grid of cells with rows and columns that can contain alphanumeric, text, or numeric data. The cells can also contain formulas. They are often used for mathematical purposes. If the number in one cell is changed then the other cells that refer to that cell will change automatically. Sometimes charts or graphs are created to visualize the data that is in a spreadsheet. Sometimes spreadsheets are used as a grid to organize data. Show the class a blank spreadsheet and input information, or have various samples so that they will understand how spreadsheets can be used.

2. Explain that for this lesson, the class will be asking members of their school community to fill out a form (questionnaire) on a given topic. Explain that Google Spreadsheets allows an online form to be created that will put all the submitted information into the spreadsheet automatically.

3. Brainstorm with the students what questions regarding their topic would be important to ask. Talk about the kinds of questions that will help them in gathering information. Explain that there are six types of questions that can be used in creating the form: Text, Paragraph Text, Multiple Choice, Checkboxes, Choose From A List, and Scale (1–n). For data collection, multiple choice is ideal, but students may want to explore other options.

4. Give examples of open-ended and close-ended questions. An open-ended question opens up possibilities, whereas a close-ended question is good when there are limited responses and quantitative results are desired. Discuss the variety of options with the class.

   (1 to 2 class periods)

5. Students work in groups to decide survey questions and then practice creating spreadsheets and surveys. Students submit questions to the teacher for feedback. Questions may also be shared with the class for feedback, if time permits.

   (1 class period)

6. Student groups create their forms and questions in a new blank spreadsheet. Once the forms have been created, the data will automatically be collected in the spreadsheet in which the form was created. Each survey submitted will have data in its own row of the spreadsheet. Ask the school community to fill out the forms. You can invite people by e-mail or you can give them the web address directly.

   (1 class period)

7. Once enough surveys have been filled out, students will look at their spreadsheet to see all of the data that has been collected. We suggest that at least 20 responses should be received, since this is a good minimum number to be able to discern trends. Fewer responses tend to make the survey more anecdotal than quantitative. They should sort the spreadsheet and consider the answers to different questions. Ask the students to summarize the information and draw conclusions about their topics.

8. Students share their conclusions with school community through the following activities:

   - Write summary about findings.
   - Publish spreadsheets on school web page.

   (1 to 2 class periods)

ASSESSMENT

Create a rubric to assess the following:

20%	Contribution to group.
20%	Created spreadsheet.
20%	Created form consisting of five or more survey questions relating to topic.
20%	Shared results with class.
20%	Communicated results to school community through article of summarized findings and recommendations.

STORY STARTERS

Pamela Friedman

GRADE LEVEL: 5–8

SUBJECT: English Language Arts

TIME REQUIRED: 5–6 class periods

OBJECTIVES

Students will be able to:

- Develop a story using five story elements.

- Write constructively using a variety of sentence types.

- Critique and respond to other students' writing.

CORRELATIONS TO STANDARDS

NCTE/IRA Standards for the English Language Arts

1. Reading for Perspective

2. Understanding the Human Experience

4. Communication Skills

5. Communication Strategies

6. Applying Knowledge

11. Participating in Society

12. Applying Language Skills

ISTE National Educational Technology Standards for Students (NETS•S)

1. Creativity and Innovation

2. Communication and Collaboration

3. Research and Information Fluency

4. Critical Thinking, Problem Solving, and Decision Making

5. Digital Citizenship

6. Technology Operations and Concepts

MATERIALS AND RESOURCES REQUIRED

- Internet access and necessary technology

- Google Presentations

LESSON DESCRIPTION

1. The teacher will begin the lesson by supplying the students with a sample story starter. For example, "I'll never forget the worst day of my life ..." Have students write one or two sentences as a response to the story starter.

2. Once all students have written a response, they will read their ideas to the rest of the class. The teacher should emphasize the different ways students react to suggestions and the creative writing process.

3. Pre-assess students to ensure necessary competence in Google Presentations. Teach where necessary.

4. The teacher will explain that students will be creating stories using several different story starters. Each day, students will log onto the Google Presentation set up for the purpose of creating the stories.

5. The teacher should discuss the five elements of a good story: characters, setting, problem, events, and solution.

6. The lesson will begin with each student or student group being assigned a story starter.

7. Students will be responsible for writing one full paragraph (equal to one full Google Presentations slide) for each portion of their story.

8. On the first day, students will log onto the Google presentation and add their paragraphs to a blank slide. Students should be reminded to Insert A New Slide after the Main Slide of the story starter they received. They should also put their names in the bottom left corner of every slide they create. A sample presentation can be seen at http://docs.google.com/Presentation?id=dcphsvkf_57hmfgk9f5/.

9. At this point, the teacher should assign a random number to each story. Each day, students will be given a number randomly. This way, they will be adding to different stories almost every time.

10. The teacher will also decide how many slides each story will have. To fully develop a plot, there should be a minimum of five slides per story.

11. Each day, when students receive their story number, they should review and peer-edit all the slides created previously for that story.

12. In order to fully develop every story, the teacher should assign a different story element each day. For example, Day One: student entries must contain the setting and the development of at least one character. Day Two: student entries must contain some type of rising action and/or problem encountered. Day Three: student entries must contain a new character and the start of problem solving. In this way, the stories will follow a general pattern of similarity and will contain all the necessary elements.

13. Each student or group will be responsible for adding at least one image to their slide that is relevant and meaningful to the portion of the story they added. Add additional slides as necessary to avoid cluttered pages.

14. The teacher will remind students to keep their backgrounds simple and appealing, allowing the viewer to easily read the text. Also, the teacher should remind students to put their names in the bottom left corner of each slide they work on.

15. As a culminating activity, each student will be assigned a story. After reading the entire story, that student will be responsible for establishing a meaningful title.

16. When each story is completed, the teacher will publish the slide show and share it with the class.

ASSESSMENT

Students' grades will be based on the following assessment rubric:

CRITERIA	DOES NOT MEET EXPECTATIONS	MEETS EXPECTATIONS	EXCEEDS EXPECTATIONS
Uses effective language and appropriate word choices			
Sentences appropriately varied in length and structure			
Follows the rules of grammar, spelling, and punctuation			
Shows creativity and originality in the writing process			

VOCABULARY SPREADSHEET

Pamela Friedman

GRADE LEVEL: 5

SUBJECT: English Language Arts (or any subject with vocabulary lists)

TIME REQUIRED: 1–2 class periods

OBJECTIVES

Students will be able to:

- Use various sources to identify synonyms and antonyms.
- Distinguish between synonyms and antonyms.
- Identify words with several meanings.
- Use vocabulary words in a sentence to show understanding of the definitions.

CORRELATIONS TO STANDARDS

NCTE/IRA Standards for the English Language Arts

1. Reading for Perspective
2. Understanding the Human Experience
4. Communication Skills
5. Communication Strategies
6. Applying Knowledge
11. Participating in Society
12. Applying Language Skills

ISTE National Educational Technology Standards for Students (NETS•S)

1. Creativity and Innovation
2. Communication and Collaboration
3. Research and Information Fluency
4. Critical Thinking, Problem Solving, and Decision Making
5. Digital Citizenship
6. Technology Operations and Concepts

MATERIALS AND RESOURCES REQUIRED

- Internet access and necessary technology
- Google Spreadsheets

LESSON DESCRIPTION

This lesson can be used as an extension of an assigned book or project, or as a stand-alone vocabulary lesson. Pre-assess students to ensure necessary competence in Spreadsheets. Teach where necessary. Create a Google spreadsheet containing the base words students will use.

1. The teacher should discuss the difference between a synonym and an antonym. At this point, you may want to put some sample words on the board and ask for students to volunteer synonyms and antonyms for those words.

2. Each student will log onto the Google Spreadsheets document created by the teacher. The spreadsheet should have all base words already entered by the teacher.

3. Students will be responsible for entering at least five synonyms and five antonyms on the document. (This amount may vary depending on the number of vocabulary words and number of students in the class). After each entry, the students should enter their names. Additionally, each student should pick one of the words and provide a meaningful sentence using the word.

4. By the end of this lesson, the teacher will have an excellent source for students to use when studying for vocabulary tests. It can also be used as a pre-assessment activity before reading a new novel. A sample presentation can be seen at http://spreadsheets.google.com/pub?key=pbf1d_mrOLTw6JHcEbay-TQ/.

5. At this point, the teacher may decide to continue creating vocabulary documents that can be used throughout the year. Students will have access to each spreadsheet as the teacher publishes it on the web. This will be an excellent tool for students to use.

6. When each vocabulary spreadsheet is completed, publish it and share it with other classes, if desired.

ASSESSMENT

Students' grades will be based on the following assessment rubric:

CRITERIA	DOES NOT MEET EXPECTATIONS	MEETS EXPECTATIONS	EXCEEDS EXPECTATIONS
The student provided five synonyms and five antonyms			
Synonyms and antonyms provided were unique			
The student showed understanding of the original meaning of the word by providing an appropriate sentence			

HIGH SCHOOL
LESSONS

LESSON PLANS

- A Brush with History
- Candidate Watch
- Election Central
- Google Lit Trips
- *The Great Gatsby* Great Debate
- Imperialism's Impact
- Issues of Our Times
- Mapping Foreign Policy Doctrines
- A Place in Time
- Political Cartoon Analysis
- Postcards from the Past
- Road Trip
- The Statistical World

LESSON TITLE	PAGE #	GRADE LEVEL (U.S.)	AGES	SUBJECT AREA(S)	GOOGLE APP(S) USED
A Brush with History	313	10–11	14–17	Social Studies/History	Groups
Candidate Watch	316	7–12	11–18	Social Studies/History	Earth, Maps, Search, Documents
Election Central	319	9–12	13–18	Social Studies/History	iGoogle, Documents
Google Lit Trips	322	9–12	13–18	ELA	Earth
The Great Gatsby Great Debate	326	9–12	13–18	ELA	Spreadsheets
Imperialism's Impact	329	11	15–17	Social Studies/History	Presentations
Issues of Our Times	332	9–12	13–18	Social Studies/History	Blogger
Mapping Foreign Policy Doctrines	335	9–12	13–18	Social Studies/History	Earth, Groups
A Place in Time	338	9–12	13–18	Social Studies/History	Earth, News Search
Political Cartoon Analysis	341	9–12	13–18	ELA/Social Studies/History	Spreadsheets
Postcards from the Past	345	11	15–17	Social Studies/History	Maps
Road Trip	348	9–12	13–18	Social Studies/History	Maps, Documents
The Statistical World	351	9–10	13–18	Social Studies/History/Math	Spreadsheets

A BRUSH WITH HISTORY

Cheryl Davis

GRADE LEVEL: 10–11

SUBJECT: History

TIME REQUIRED: 1–3 class periods; homework; 30-minute interview

OBJECTIVES

Students will be able to:

- Research primary source descriptions of historic events.

- Conduct primary source interviews and create written accounts of those interviews.

- Compare and contrast primary source accounts of history with secondary source accounts.

CORRELATIONS TO STANDARDS

NCSS Curriculum Standards for Social Studies

I.   Culture

II.   Time, Continuity, and Change

III.   People, Places, and Environments

ISTE National Educational Technology Standards for Students (NETS•S)

1.   Creativity and Innovation

2.   Communication and Collaboration

3.   Research and Information Fluency

MATERIALS AND RESOURCES REQUIRED

- Internet access and necessary technology

- Student or class Google account

- Google Groups

LESSON DESCRIPTION

In December 1989, *American Heritage* magazine began a unique series of articles called "My Brush with History" (www.americanheritage.com/articles/magazine/ah/1989/8/). The magazine asked its readers to recall a moment in their lives when they were touched by events or forces that became a part of the historic record. The powerful and sometimes humorous accounts have added personal insight to the events of our times. After introducing the concept of oral histories to students, challenge them to contribute to the historical record by "collecting" a brush with history from a friend, relative, or acquaintance, or by analyzing and describing their own encounter with a historic event. Once students interview and write about a source's personal encounter with an historical event, they post it for comments in a Google Group. This gives students a clearer understanding of the historical record as described in the words of those who were touched by its events.

1. Introduce students to the idea of the lesson by accessing several copies of *American Heritage* (starting with December 1989). Read (or have students read) "My Brush with History" accounts. These are all first-person accounts. Inform students that they will be collecting similar accounts, and they should use the same descriptive writing style as in the magazine stories.

    American Heritage has a few of its "My Brush with History" stories online. Visit the American Heritage website (www.americanheritage.com) and search for "My Brush with History."

2. Instruct students to find a person (primary source) who was a witness to, or participated in, an event described in history sources (text or history books). That person could have encountered a famous person or have been caught up in the events of a time. They should recall what they experienced when something important happened, such as what it was like for them when President Kennedy was shot, or when men walked on the moon, when the Berlin Wall came down, or when 9/11 happened. This must be a firsthand experience. Students should make an appointment for a formal interview with the source.

3. Go over the definition and process of collecting oral histories with students. A good resource site for students is the Library of Congress, American Memory, Learning Page—Using Oral History (http://memory.loc.gov/learn/lessons/oralhist/ohhome.html).

4. Students research the historical event or person their source will describe. For example, if a source was fighting in the European Theater during World War II or was deployed during Desert Storm, students should research and read about those events prior to the interview. If the source participated in the voter registration drives in the South during the Civil Rights movement, students should research the efforts involved in that cause.

5. Students write several interview questions that they will ask their source based on their reading and research. The teacher should give students feedback on these questions.

6. Students schedule an interview with their source. This can be a face-to-face, e-mail, or phone interview.

7. Students compose an accurate, well-written, and powerful (or entertaining) account of the events they glean from their source's brush with history.

8. Teacher creates a class Google group for the Brush with History project. Students access the Google group and post their written accounts to the discussion board. They include web links to their research sources.

9. Once the Brush with History accounts are posted, students read other accounts and post comments as replies.

ASSESSMENT

Create a rubric to assess the following:

30%   Quality and accuracy of research information: Interview questions show evidence of content research and subject matter knowledge. Sources are cited correctly.

50%   Student written accounts are accurate, powerful, and/or entertaining. They have a clear and meaningful description of the primary source account and show an understanding of the events of the time.

20%   Quality and amount of participation in discussion board posts to the Google group: in their posts students are able to compare and contrast the interviews with secondary source or textbook accounts.

CANDIDATE WATCH
FOLLOWING AND UNDERSTANDING THE ELECTION PROCESS

Cheryl Davis

GRADE LEVEL: 7–12

SUBJECT: United States History

TIME REQUIRED: 3 class periods to set up; continue over an election cycle

OBJECTIVES

Students will be able to:

- Identify and analyze the issues and candidates in an election.

- Connect geography to the election process by creating a collaborative Google Map and Google Earth file.

- Collect and plot data and statistical information about an election.

CORRELATIONS TO STANDARDS

NCSS Curriculum Standards for Social Studies

X.   Civic Ideals and Practices

ISTE National Educational Technology Standards for Students (NETS•S)

1.   Creativity and Innovation

2.   Communication and Collaboration

3.   Research and Information Fluency

MATERIALS AND RESOURCES REQUIRED

- Internet access and necessary technology

- Google Earth

- Google Maps

- Google News Search archive

- Google Documents

LESSON DESCRIPTION

Locally or nationally, the election process provides an opportunity for teachers to engage students in participatory civic literacy. In this lesson, students will integrate geography with the election process to identify presidential candidates and understand the primary process and the electoral college. Students will work in teams to collaborate on a Google map identifying and outlining a candidate's position on issues and analyzing the location of campaign events. For a national presidential election, placing candidates on Google Earth and identifying the Electoral College numbers for each state gives students a geographic understanding of the process. Students will also write a collaborative "white paper" in Google Docs on the election issues. During the campaign and election season, students will track statistics and polling information using Google Spreadsheets. See Step 3 for thoughts on congressional and state election campaigns.

1. Group students in teams and assign them a candidate or election issue to follow.

2. Each student team sets up one collaborative Google map. Instruct students on how to access and add placemarks to the map. Also show students how to export the Google map to Google Earth. Google Maps give students the ability to collaborate on one map that they can update and then export to Google Earth as a KMZ file for a final presentation.

3. Introduce students to Google Earth. Instruct students on how to upload exported KMZ Google Map files. Show students how to view the layers in Google Earth, and have students check the U.S. Government layer which is located within the More layer. This will outline the congressional districts in the United States. If you are studying the national presidential election, have students placemark each state in Google Earth and include the number of electoral votes that the state is assigned. You can assign specific states to each of your teams. Dates and outcomes of the state primaries can also be included in the placemark for each state. For congressional or state elections, students may follow the candidates from location to location within the candidates' districts, reading local newspaper accounts or monitoring local media broadcasts to see the ebb and flow of issues over time and locality.

4. Each student team locates and creates placemarks for their candidates on a Google map. In Placemark Descriptions, teams include pertinent information on the candidate or election. That information might include:

   - Date of candidate's announcement
   - Links to the candidate or campaign website
   - Links to videos of candidate or campaign speeches
   - The state electoral number
   - Candidate party affiliation

   Reliable primary resource video footage and information on the candidates for national office can be found at the C-SPAN Classroom website (www.c-spanclassroom.org).

5. As the campaigns progress, teams update their candidate's placemark with additional videos and links (including campaign ads).

6. Each student team sets up a collaborative Google document and spreadsheet. In the document, each team contributes to a "white paper" on the candidate or issue, outlining and analyzing the candidate's position on the issues. Direct students to the Google News Search archives, where they'll be able to access past newspaper articles on their candidate. In the spreadsheet, team members post and update statistics and polling information on the candidate. Spreadsheets can include updated information on primary wins or the Electoral College numbers.

7. Throughout the election cycle, student teams continue to share, update, and revise their documents.

8. Student teams prepare for a presentation on their candidate or issue. Student teams export their final Google map to a Google Earth KMZ file. Finalized Google Earth files are collected by the teacher and opened in one Google Earth file. The combined election issues and/or candidate profiles are shown in a presentation to the class in a combined Google Earth tour. Each team takes a turn showing their placemarks and summarizing for the class the information in their Google Docs white paper and Google spreadsheets. The tour can be displayed using an LCD projector. The class discusses and evaluates the election issues and research.

ASSESSMENT

Create a rubric to assess the following:

10%   Student participation in class discussion/presentation on issues and candidate.

30%   Quality and accuracy of candidate information on Google Earth tour. Tour placemarks link to meaningful primary source information on the candidate or issue.

40%   Quality and extent of analysis in student team "white paper."

20%   Accuracy of data information in spreadsheet.

ELECTION CENTRAL

Cheryl Davis

GRADE LEVEL: High School

SUBJECT: United States History or Government

TIME REQUIRED: 1 class period to set up; continue over an election cycle

OBJECTIVES

Students will be able to:

- Search and collect Internet news sources on issues in an election.
- Identify the validity of, and possible bias in, election news coverage.
- Compare and contrast election coverage by a variety of Internet news sources.

CORRELATIONS TO STANDARDS

NCSS Curriculum Standards for Social Studies

X.   Civic Ideals and Practices

ISTE National Educational Technology Standards for Students (NETS·S)

1.   Creativity and Innovation

3.   Research and Information Fluency

MATERIALS AND RESOURCES REQUIRED

- Internet access and necessary technology
- Google account
- iGoogle Site
- Google Documents

LESSON DESCRIPTION

Watching and analyzing media coverage during an election can be an important part of teaching students about civic literacy. It also provides students with practice in comparing media coverage and improving their media literacy skills. In this lesson, students will individually create their own "Election Central" by setting up a Google account and adding a tab on their iGoogle page dedicated to election coverage. On the iGoogle tab, students will add gadgets that bring in election information from news sources and video sites that update current information.

Once the tab is set up, students will share the gadgets they have collected with a class Election Central tab that will be used as a basis for class discussion of media coverage on election issues. Students will evaluate each of the gadgets and sources of information they collect via a Google document that is shared with the teacher. The students will also share their evaluations in a class discussion, analyzing how different Internet news and polling organizations are covering the events and issues in the election.

1. Explain to students that they each will be setting up an Election Central tab in iGoogle as a way to watch how the media and Internet sites are covering an election. Show students how to set up a Google account and add an iGoogle interface to that account.

2. On their iGoogle interface, students click Add A Tab, name that tab "Election Central," and add their initials. Adding their initials to the name will help to distinguish the Election Central tabs if they are shared with the teacher or with other students.

3. The teacher also sets up a class iGoogle account by creating a new Google account and setting up one iGoogle tab per class. This will be a place where students can share the election gadgets they collect on their personal iGoogle accounts with the class account.

4. Once students have their iGoogle Election Central tab set up, they search and add gadgets to the tab that track media stories and information about the election. To find gadgets, students click on the Add Stuff link to the right of the iGoogle tabs on their screen. Next, they type in an appropriate search term to locate a gadget. Students can select from a variety of gadgets such as election maps, polls, news results, quotes of the day, and surveys. Also, gadgets for iGoogle can be found on some Internet news sites, on Google Maps, and are also searchable from sites such as Netvibes Open Widget Platform (http://eco.netvibes.com). Gadgets available for the 2008 Presidential election included:

    ■ techPresident

    ■ msnbc.com: Candidate + Issue Matrix

    ■ Election Results from Google

    ■ *Times*—Quote of the Day

    ■ Election Collection by *The Washington Post*

    ■ U.S. Primary Results by Google

    ■ Election 2008 (date of election)

    ■ Election News

    ■ Election Map from Google

    ■ My Favorite Presidential Candidate

    ■ DaylifeIssueDex

    ■ Jodange's "Political Pundit"

    ■ Survey Google Gadget

    ■ Poll Tracker CQ Politics

    ■ Gadgets from state news organizations

5. Instruct students to evaluate each of the gadgets they add to their iGoogle site in a Google document. Share with the students some site evaluation resources and discuss what they might look for to determine the validity or bias of a source. For example:

   ■ Kathy Schrock's Guide for Educators—Critical Evaluation Surveys and Resources: http://school.discoveryeducation.com/schrockguide/eval.html

   ■ Schrock's Guide also has a downloadable evaluation document students can fill out titled "Critical Evaluation of a Website, secondary school level": http://school.discoveryeducation.com/schrockguide/evalhigh.htm

   ■ FAIR—"Fairness and Accuracy in Reporting—How To Detect Bias In News Media": www.fair.org/index.php?page=121

   On the Google document, students include the URL for each gadget they add, and outline the features that make it a valid source of information. They should also indicate any bias they can document.

6. Students can create their own gadgets in iGoogle by clicking on Add Stuff > Make Your Own Gadget > Try Now. They can add a candidate's YouTube videos to the YouTube Channel gadget and an election countdown via the Countdown gadget. For YouTube videos added to iGoogle, students will also include the URL on their Google Doc Election Central and evaluate the validity of the sources. If students take pictures of local election events or campaign signs in their neighborhoods, they can add those with the Framed Photo gadget.

7. As the election progresses, students update their iGoogle Election Central tab with additional gadgets. Students share gadgets they collect by sending them from their iGoogle tab via the Share This Gadget drop-down menu on the menu bar of each gadget. From this menu bar students can e-mail the gadget to the teacher-created class iGoogle account. The teacher will receive the links to these gadgets in the class account e-mail and add them to the iGoogle class Election Central tab. The teacher displays the gadgets to the class via an LCD projector. Students discuss the gadgets they added and explain why they found the sources to be valid.

8. Students share their Election Central Google Doc analysis of sources with the teacher.

9. Teacher and students follow and analyze the election via class discussions sparked by the stories, polls, and analysis accessed via the class iGoogle Election Central tab.

ASSESSMENT

Create a rubric to assess the following:

20% Student collects and shares at least three election gadgets with the class iGoogle Election Central tab.

60% Quality and extent of analysis on the validity of each shared gadget as a news source. Student explains why each source meets validity criteria based on what was discussed in Schrock's "Critical Evaluation of a Website."

20% Quality and extent of student participation in class discussion comparing and contrasting election coverage of sites displayed on the iGoogle Election Central tab.

GOOGLE LIT TRIPS

Jerome Burg

GRADE LEVEL: 9–12

SUBJECT: English Language Arts

TIME REQUIRED: 15–20 minutes per day in class for as many days as it takes to read the literature piece; 10–20 minutes per evening after reading assigned homework pages

OBJECTIVES

Students will be able to:

■ Track the geographical locations along the route taken by characters in a work of travel literature such as *Catcher in the Rye*, *The Grapes of Wrath*, or *The Motorcycle Diaries*.

■ Identify elements of a developing theme while reading a story.

■ Articulate examples of the universal themes of literature dealing with the human experience.

■ Articulate the significance of real-world references and allusions within a piece of literature.

CORRELATIONS TO STANDARDS

NCTE/IRA Standards for the English Language Arts

1. Reading for Perspective

2. Understanding the Human Experience

3. Evaluation Strategies

4. Communication Skills

5. Communication Strategies

6. Applying Knowledge

7. Evaluating Data

8. Developing Research Skills

11. Participating in Society

ISTE National Educational Technology Standards for Students (NETS•S)

1. Creativity and Innovation

2. Communication and Collaboration

3. Research and Information Fluency

4. Critical Thinking, Problem Solving, and Decision Making

5. Digital Citizenship

MATERIALS AND RESOURCES REQUIRED

- Internet access and necessary technology

- Students will have a copy of a piece of travel literature where characters travel through actual, real-world locations (as opposed to fictional, virtual, or simulated ones). Examples include *The Grapes of Wrath* by John Steinbeck, *Night* by Elie Wiesel, and *Into the Wild* by Jon Krakauer.

- Google Earth

LESSON DESCRIPTION

This lesson is based upon the Google Lit Trips project (www.GoogleLitTrips.com). As students read through the literature, they will collect the following information:

- Specific geographical locations used as settings for the story

- Any website URLs containing relevant supplemental information regarding historical, geographical, biographical, social, and political references made in the story

Students will also develop questions designed to stimulate higher-level synthesis of the story's themes and the relationship between those themes and the real historical and social settings within which the story is set.

As students read through the story, they will build a Google Lit Trip that tracks the travels of the story characters and includes pop-up windows at each point along the route, containing:

- URL links to websites providing supplementary information about real-world references made in the story

- Thought-provoking questions about the thematic content of the story and the thematic impact of setting a work of fiction within real locations

Procedure

1. The teacher should be familiar with the resources available on the GoogleLitTrips.com website found in the Downloads Etc. area under the Lit Trip Tips submenu. Among the resources are several downloadable guides that can be reproduced to help support students in the creation of their projects.

2. The teacher demonstrates how to use the Google Earth interface, including the basics of how to:

   - Create placemarks

   - Add content to placemarks

   - Draw path lines between pushpin markers indicating the route traveled by the characters

3. As students read through the literature as homework, they will:

   ■ Make notes on any indicators within the reading assignment that help identify specific locations.

   ■ Make notes on any real-world references such as names of people, references to historical events, and so on.

   ■ Find 1–2 websites that provide accessible supplementary information about the real-world references made in the assigned reading.

   ■ Write down 1–2 discussion starters that pose thought-provoking thematic questions worthy of class discussion for the next day. Unless the class is primarily one of struggling readers, these should not be low-level plot questions, but higher-level questions designed to stimulate a class discussion. Questions might be of the following types: compare and contrast; what's the relationship or connection between; why or why not something happened; what would be the difference if; imagine that; what would make it better (or worse), and why; analyze the reasons for; how do you justify; what might someone do in a different situation; can you see a connection between this work and … ; if a different character were in a situation what might they do.

4. Depending upon the academic level of the students, the collection of this data can be divided so that students are not responsible for collecting all of the information for all reading assignments. A suggestion for rotating which part of the information harvesting students are to collect each night can be found in the Lit Trip Tricks subsection of the Downloads Etc. area of GoogleLitTrips.com.

5. Class discussions on the day following the reading should begin with collection of the specific geographic locations from the previous night's reading and the placement of placemarks in Google Earth.

6. The teacher facilitates a discussion of the themes and real-world connections brought in by the students, and the class selects the most appropriate supplemental website URLs to be included in the placemark pop-up descriptions.

7. The class can also discuss the various discussion starters brought in by the students. Then, the class should decide which 3–5 discussion starters are the most significant and include them in the pop-up descriptions.

8. Adding the actual pop-up description content and the path lines between locations can be done live while students are discussing the reading, or can be done later by volunteer students who have learned some basic HTML code for dressing up the pop-up description formatting. A guide with some basic HTML tips is also available in the Lit Trip Tips section of the Downloads Etc. section of the Google Lit Trips website.

9. This process can be repeated as the class continues to read the literature. Optional: when the project is completed, it may be submitted to the Google Lit Trips website for possible publication by e-mailing submissions@GoogleLitTrips.com.

   Option for all students: Rather than providing supplementary links and discussion starters for the placemark pop-up windows, students might instead be asked to use the pop-up windows for fictitious diary entries or reflective journal entries written from characters' points of view, thus tracking not only the path of the characters' journeys, but also the development of their awareness and understanding of the thematic issues of the story.

Option for struggling students: Struggling students might focus their efforts on articulating significant plot summaries as the story develops along the journey, or constructing dialogue to act out.

ASSESSMENT

The assessment of the project will rest upon three evaluations:

1. Student participation in the data collection process. Teachers and students should be aware that this portion of the project is essentially a modernized brainstorming process. Therefore, evaluation should be based more upon willingness to collect data, locations, and supplementary information URLs rather than on the level of sophistication of their preliminary understanding of the developing thematic threads.

2. Student participation in the class discussion of the data entered from the previous evenings' readings. Students are evaluated on:

    ▪ The quality of the data collected for the Google Lit Trip pop-up descriptions and placemarks

    ▪ The quality of student contribution to the class discussion based upon their collection of information for the Google Lit Trip pop-up descriptions

    ▪ Student syntheses of the commentaries generated during the class discussion into more refined articulations of the thematic concepts being developed by the author as the story proceeds

3. Students will write a major paper in an appropriate writing genre in which they articulate their individual levels of thematic understanding and their understanding of writing structure. The exact writing assignment can be adjusted to meet the course expectations for various types of writing. Some suggestions include:

    ▪ An analysis of the relationship between the fictitious nature of the story and the real-world setting and references within the story.

    ▪ A persuasive essay arguing the relevance of the story's thematic messages to the real world in which the students live. (What's that old story got to do with my story?)

    ▪ An analysis of one character's development as the story progresses. (How and what has this character come to know about life as a result of his or her experiences? How might I benefit from it in my own life?)

    ▪ A comparison paper between the student's experiences with life's journey and one of the character's experiences on his or her fictitious life's journey.

THE GREAT GATSBY GREAT DEBATE

Jerome Burg

GRADE LEVEL:	9–12
SUBJECT:	English Language Arts
TIME REQUIRED:	25–35 minutes of homework over 9–10 days of reading *The Great Gatsby*.

OBJECTIVES

Students will be able to:

■ Track indicators of character development while reading the novel.

■ Use specific references from a novel to justify opinions about a character.

■ Weigh evidence supporting opposing opinions about a character.

■ Write a persuasive essay supporting their final opinion about the character that includes an intelligent concession to the opposing point of view regarding the character.

CORRELATIONS TO STANDARDS

NCTE/IRA Standards for the English Language Arts

1. Reading for Perspective

2. Understanding the Human Experience

3. Evaluation Strategies

4. Communication Skills

5. Communication Strategies

6. Applying Knowledge

7. Evaluating Data

11. Participating in Society

12. Applying Language Skills

ISTE National Educational Technology Standards for Students (NETS•S)

1. Creativity and Innovation

2. Communication and Collaboration

3. Research and Information Fluency

4. Critical Thinking, Problem Solving, and Decision Making

6. Technology Operations and Concepts

MATERIALS AND RESOURCES REQUIRED

- Internet access and necessary technology

- Google Documents and Spreadsheets

- *The Great Gatsby*, by F. Scott Fitzgerald

- Students will have collaborator privileges to modify a copy of "*The Great Gatsby* Great Debate" Google Spreadsheet available at on the Google Docs website (http://docs.google.com/Doc?id=djhtswt_34ck6536gf).

LESSON DESCRIPTION

As students read through the novel, they will use "*The Great Gatsby* Great Debate" Google Spreadsheet template to collect references and to record evaluative comments regarding the development of their opinions of whether the character Gatsby is great. Students will use class discussions to weigh validity of the various references and comments posted the previous evening.

At the end of the reading, students will write a persuasive argument paper defending their final evaluation of Gatsby's "greatness." The essay will include one concession paragraph indicating students' realization that there are valid arguments to be made for the opposing opinion.

1. The teacher provides students with directions for accessing the shared "*The Great Gatsby* Great Debate" Google spreadsheet.

2. The teacher demonstrates the process for adding references and commentary, reviewing the protocols for identifying the page numbers, chronological numbering, and student self-identification in the comments process.

3. As students read through the novel for homework, they will make contributions to the chart indicating specific references from the story and their interpretation of how these specific references affect their developing opinion of Gatsby's character.

4. Class discussions on the day following the reading and posting of references and comments will include a group evaluation of the references and the interpretations offered in the comments. Teachers may want to allow students to refine comments on the chart live (in real time) as the class discussion focuses students' understanding of the character development in the story. It is important to have students maintain an open-minded "data collection" mode during this processing rather than to make each day a "debate" where students lock into a position on Gatsby's character and become less receptive to considering the opposing views as they read through the novel.

5. After students have finished reading the entire novel, they will write a persuasive argument paper which defends their final opinion on Gatsby's character and includes a concession to an opposing view. It is important for students to know that a good paper can be written in support of either position and that a great paper is not determined by the student's position but rather by the quality of the argument and the concession presented in the paper.

ASSESSMENT

The assessment of the project will rest upon three evaluations:

1. Student participation in the data collection process (contributing to the *"The Great Gatsby* Great Debate" Google spreadsheet). Teachers and students should be aware that this portion of the project is essentially a modernized brainstorming process. Therefore, evaluation should be based more upon willingness to contribute rather than on the level of sophistication or accuracy of the comments. It should also be kept in mind that there are only so many references to make within a chapter and many students may not be able to make as many contributions to the chart as others who might get to the chart first because they do their homework earlier, or do not have sports or a job after school.

2. Student participation in the class discussion of the data entered from the previous evenings readings. Students can be evaluated on:

   ■ The quality of their contribution to the class discussion

   ■ Their ability to maintain an open mind during the class discussion.

   ■ Their synthesis of the commentary into more refined articulations of the value of a particular reference in defending a positive or negative opinion of Gatsby's character

   This is also an opportunity for students who have contributed less frequently to the chart development to express the reasoning for their developing opinions about Gatsby.

3. Students will write a persuasive argument paper with a concession paragraph defending their final opinion about Gatsby's character. This paper should be evaluated using a rubric that focuses on the following:

   ■ Understanding of the structure of a persuasive argument (introduction, concession, defense, and conclusion)

   ■ Quality of content of the arguments presented (articulation of thesis, sophistication of concession, significance of defense references and commentary, quality of final evaluation presented in conclusion)

   ■ Mastery of traditional elements of formal writing skills including mechanics, usage, and grammar

IMPERIALISM'S IMPACT

Cheryl Davis

GRADE LEVEL: 11

SUBJECT: United States History

TIME REQUIRED: 4–5 class periods

OBJECTIVES

Students will be able to:

- Research the influence of the United States on a specific country or region between 1865–1918.

- Collaboratively prepare a presentation that tells the story of the impact of American imperialism on one country or region.

- Analyze the impact of American imperialism between 1865–1918 on the nations or regions affected.

CORRELATIONS TO STANDARDS

NCSS Curriculum Standards for Social Studies

I.   Culture

III. People, Places, and Environments

IV. Power, Authority, and Governance

ISTE National Educational Technology Standards for Students (NETS·S)

3. Research and Information Fluency

4. Critical Thinking, Problem Solving, and Decision Making

6. Technology Operations and Concepts

MATERIALS AND RESOURCES REQUIRED

- Internet access and necessary technology

- Student Google accounts

- Google Presentations

LESSON DESCRIPTION

In this lesson, student teams research and create a Google slide show presentation on a specific world nation or region that came under the influence of the American government between 1865 and 1918. Student teams will be assigned a country or region to research. They will combine their research notes into a slide show and oral presentation that will inform the class about the impact of American imperialism on their assigned country or region. Their slide presentation, created collaboratively in Google Presentations, will augment, with images and bullet points, the oral presentation they give on the country or region. The research and presentation will include resource citations. When all teams have completed their oral presentation, the class will synthesize the information in a discussion on the impact of American imperialism between 1865–1918.

1. Assign student background and overview reading covering the age of American imperialism from 1865–1918.

2. Divide students into three-member teams and explain that they will research and prepare a slide and oral presentation teaching the class specifics on America's quest for empire between 1865–1918. They will be researching the impact of American imperialism on one country or region.

3. Assign each team one of the following countries or regions:

   ■ Alaska

   ■ China

   ■ Cuba

   ■ Hawaii

   ■ Nicaragua

   ■ Panama

   ■ Philippines

   ■ Puerto Rico

4. Allow library or lab time for student teams to research their assigned region or country. Instruct students to cite sources in MLA format or another format used by the school. Team research should include at least one primary source and should reflect a variety of valid sources.

5. Demonstrate how to use Google Presentations to collaboratively create slides. Explain that each slide should include a visual aid and important bullet information relevant to the presentation. All members of the group should participate in the creation of the slide show, so students should divide the work accordingly. Students should assign slide numbers to each team member, working individually at first and then working together to edit the overall presentation. This will ensure that students don't write over one another's work. Students should be prepared to cover the following areas during the research and presentation:

   ■ What is the relevant historical background? Detail the U.S. involvement in the assigned country/region.

   ■ Define any terms that are important to the presentation.

- Describe U.S. involvement with and/or acquisition of the territory.

- What were the motives of the United States? Was there a hidden agenda behind U.S. actions in that area?

- What are some perspectives on the particular situation other than those of the United States?

- What were the effects of U.S. government involvement on the United States, on the people in the region/country, on other regions or countries?

6. Develop criteria for effective oral presentations with the students. The oral presentation should be enhanced by the slide show and include enough background information and detail to give the audience a basic understanding of the topic. The person(s) making the presentation are what is most important, not the images on the screen. Oral presentation skills should apply. Note cards may be used, but enthusiasm and demonstrating knowledge of the topic is the key. The slides should not be heavily text-based but display graphics or include bullet points that outline the presentation.

7. During the presentations, the presenting team shows their Google presentation via an LCD projector. The student audience takes notes focusing on the impact of American imperialism on each region. When all the presentations are complete, facilitate a class discussion on the impact of American involvement. Encourage students to synthesize the information from the presentations, seeking to identify trends or patterns.

ASSESSMENT

Create a rubric to assess the following:

30%   Quality and accuracy of research information—shows evidence of content research and subject matter knowledge. Sources are cited correctly.

60%   Student oral presentation and slide show are accurate and interesting. All team members are able to explain the history of American imperialism in the region they researched and show how American actions influenced the history of the region.

10%   Quality and type of participation in class discussion. Students are able to analyze and synthesize the information given during the class presentations.

Thanks to James Lathrop, a teacher at Miramonte High School, for this lesson idea.

ISSUES OF OUR TIMES

Cheryl Davis

GRADE LEVEL: 9–12

SUBJECT: History or Government

TIME REQUIRED: semester or quarter

OBJECTIVES

Students will be able to:

- Create and update a blog that informs the public and analyzes a contemporary issue.

- Research a contemporary issue using primary sources and interviews.

- Advocate in a Google presentation for beginning solutions to the issues they have researched.

CORRELATIONS TO STANDARDS

NCSS Curriculum Standards for Social Studies

    IX.   Global Connections

    X.   Civic Ideals and Practices

ISTE National Educational Technology Standards for Students (NETS·S)

    2.   Communication and Collaboration

    3.   Research and Information Fluency

    4.   Critical Thinking, Problem Solving, and Decision Making

    5.   Digital Citizenship

MATERIALS AND RESOURCES REQUIRED

- Internet access and necessary technology

- Student Blogger accounts

LESSON DESCRIPTION

This project-based lesson encourages students to learn about and become advocates for an issue. Students will choose a contemporary issue, or trend, to follow and educate others about. They will research the issue and journal in a blog, sharing the information they learn. In the research process, students will interview people involved with or affected by the issue, or attend an organizational meeting or lecture on the issue. Students will also volunteer at a local organization that is related to their issue. The project culminates with a class presentation where students discuss what they learned and reflect on their experiences.

1. Explain the project to the students and brainstorm with the class the types of trends or contemporary issues they might choose for the project. Each student will be assigned an issue to follow, or may negotiate choice of issue with the teacher.

    Possibilities

    -   Residential development
    -   Commercial development
    -   Safety/Security
    -   Health
    -   Recreation
    -   Gangs
    -   Environment
    -   Natural resources
    -   Peace
    -   Justice
    -   Ethics
    -   Technology
    -   Media
    -   Gender
    -   Family relations
    -   Transportation

2. Introduce the concept of blogging to the students and show them several professional blogs that follow issues or cover news themes. Explain the public nature of a blog. Discuss the importance of accuracy of information and citing sources. Formulate with the class blog etiquette rules that the class will be expected to follow. A reference resource is David Warlick's Class Blogmeister Bloggers Contract from The LandMark Project (http://classblogmeister.com/bloggers_contract.doc).

3. Each student signs up for a Google account and creates a blog using Blogger. The purpose of the blog is for students to journal their research on their selected issue and educate readers about the issue. Student blog requirements can include the following elements:

    -   Links to a total of 10 current event sources. Sources should include news articles from reputable resources, video, websites, RSS feeds, and podcasts— at least one of each source.

    -   Images with sources cited.

- An opinion piece or commentary by the student on each linked source.

- Opposing viewpoints.

- Comments enabled, with moderation by the student, so the public can respond to the student research. Students can be encouraged to comment on one another's blogs.

4. Instruct students on research techniques. As they investigate their issues, tell them they need to go beyond print and Internet research to include the following elements in their investigation:

   - Interview a person involved with or affected by the issue or attend an organizational meeting, or lecture, related to the issue. Type a summary of and reflection on the interview or event. Include a photo of the interview subject or the lecturer.

   - Volunteer two hours of time at a local organization related to the issue or trend. Include pictures from the volunteer experience and a written reflection on the experience.

   - Write a letter to an editor of a local paper or edit a Wikipedia entry on the issue.

5. Students present their final projects to the class. Their presentation includes an analysis of the issue, and they engage the class in a reflective discussion of their experience. Student presentations include the discussion of the blogging experience and an overview of the research, videos, and comments posted to the blog.

ASSESSMENT

Create a rubric to assess the following:

50%   Quality, accuracy, and extent of research and information posted on the blog. Sources are cited correctly. The blog is organized and balanced. Student makes specified minimum number of blog entries.

20%   Student participation in, and account of, interviews and volunteer experience.

30%   Student presentation and reflection on their experience. Students demonstrate a strong understanding of the complexity of the issue they followed and propose workable steps toward solutions.

Thanks to Kim Everist, a teacher at Miramonte High School, for this lesson idea.

MAPPING FOREIGN POLICY DOCTRINES

Cheryl Davis

GRADE LEVEL: 9–12

SUBJECT: United States History

TIME REQUIRED: 1–2 class periods integrated with the study of each foreign policy doctrine

OBJECTIVES

Students will be able to:

- Identify and geographically map countries or locations affected by U.S. foreign policy doctrines.

- Research, analyze, and post Internet sites that accurately describe U.S. foreign policy doctrines.

- Analyze the nature and impact over time of U.S. foreign policy doctrines.

CORRELATIONS TO STANDARDS

NCSS Curriculum Standards for Social Studies

II.   Time, Continuity, and Change

IX.   Global Connections

ISTE National Educational Technology Standards for Students (NETS·S)

3.   Research and Information Fluency

4.   Critical Thinking, Problem Solving, and Decision Making

MATERIALS AND RESOURCES REQUIRED

- Internet access and necessary technology

- Google Earth

- Google Groups

LESSON DESCRIPTION

In this lesson students will, throughout the school year, create and build a Google Earth KMZ file that geographically depicts world areas affected by foreign policy doctrines. As each foreign policy doctrine or initiative is studied in class, students research and collect URLs that accurately describe the policy and its results. In a class Google group, created by the teacher, the students will post the collected URLs in the discussion area.

As each foreign policy doctrine is studied in class, the teacher facilitates a class discussion of the foreign policy initiative and brings up Google Earth on an LCD projector so it is displayed during the discussion. A student "driver" will be assigned and, using class prompts, the "driver" outlines the area of the world that was affected by the doctrine using the polygon tool in Earth. The student will also add placemark descriptions to indicate the areas affected by the doctrine. The URLs from the Google group will be added to the placemark.

At the conclusion of the discussion, the KMZ file will be saved and posted to the Google group. The process will repeat each time foreign policy doctrines are covered in the course of the U.S. History class. The KMZ file will be downloaded from the group and the next doctrine will be added. At the end of the school year students will have created a comprehensive Google Earth KMZ file outlining all the geographic areas impacted by foreign policy doctrines and linking to researched information on the policies. Then the Earth file will be used to compare and contrast the impact of the doctrines on the relationships of the United States with countries of the world.

1. Create a Google group dedicated to foreign policy doctrines and invite the class to the group via student e-mails. Show the students how to post URLs in the threads that they will add to the group discussion area. Show students how to post links to the group via e-mail.

2. Explain that, during the school year, students will be studying and geographically outlining foreign policy doctrines pronounced by presidents and their advisers. The doctrines studied might include:

    ■   Monroe Doctrine

    ■   Freeport Doctrine

    ■   Polk Doctrine

    ■   Roosevelt Corollary to the Monroe Doctrine

    ■   Truman Doctrine

    ■   Eisenhower Doctrine

    ■   Kennedy Doctrine

    ■   Nixon Doctrine

    ■   Reagan Doctrine

    ■   Bush Doctrine

    ■   Powell Doctrine

3. As the class studies the first doctrine, give students research time to find history websites with valid and reliable information on the doctrine under study. Research questions for focus:

    ■   What is the historic background on the pronouncement of the doctrine?

    ■   How is this doctrine similar to other presidential doctrines?

    ■   According to historians, how effective was the doctrine?

    ■   How might this doctrine have changed the course of history?

- How is this doctrine different from previous approaches to foreign policy?

- What geographical area or areas did the doctrine refer to?

To help them with research, share with the students some website evaluation resources and discuss how to determine the validity or bias of a source. One site to use is Kathy Schrock's Guide for Educators—Critical Evaluation Surveys and Resources—(http://school.discoveryeducation.com/schrockguide/eval.html). Schrock's Guide also has a downloadable evaluation document students can fill out titled "Critical Evaluation of a Website secondary school level" (http://school.discoveryeducation.com/schrockguide/evalhigh.html).

4. As students find sites that answer these questions, they post the answers in well-thought-out and complete posts to the Google group. Students also post the URL where they located the answers.

5. When research on the doctrine is complete, start a class lesson on how to outline shapes and post placemarks in Google Earth. With an LCD projector connected to the computer, demonstrate how to use the polygon tool to draw, show color, and set opacity in Google Earth.

6. Start a class discussion on the foreign policy doctrine with Google Earth displayed on the LCD projector from a computer. Select one student to outline, with prompts from the class, the geographic area in the Google Earth file that the doctrine covered. Next, select another student to add a placemark in Google Earth on the area that was affected by the foreign policy doctrine. With class participation, the student writes a brief description of the doctrine in the placemark and adds links that students posted to the Google group. The class discusses the foreign policy doctrine. When the discussion has concluded, the student saves the class Google Earth file to the Google group.

7. As each foreign policy doctrine is covered in the history class repeat Step 6 so that the Google Earth KMZ file continues to gain placemarks and polygon outlines of U.S. foreign policy doctrines.

8. At the end of the school year, revisit the Google Earth KMZ foreign policy "tour" that has been created and in a written paper or small group discussion with a share-out, have students analyze the nature of foreign policy doctrines over time and compare and contrast their impact.

ASSESSMENT

Create a rubric to assess the following:

20%	Participation in class discussion that accurately outlines and placemarks the foreign policy doctrine(s) in a Google Earth file
30%	Accuracy and quality of links posted to the Google Groups discussion area on the foreign policy doctrines
50%	Depth of analysis and ability to compare and contrast foreign policy doctrines in United States history via an individually written paper or a small group discussion that is shared with the class

A PLACE IN TIME

Cheryl Davis

GRADE LEVEL: 9–12

SUBJECT: World History or United States History

TIME REQUIRED: 2 class periods; continued over the school year
                 to identify and add photos/video to the project

OBJECTIVES

Students will be able to:

- Identify photographs or video footage that has had an impact on events.

- Locate and place historic photographs or video footage on a map.

- Analyze the significance of the role of media and images on our history and the impact of place on the images and media.

CORRELATIONS TO STANDARDS

NCSS Curriculum Standards for Social Studies

II.   Time, Continuity, and Change

III. People, Places, and Environments

ISTE National Educational Technology Standards for Students (NETS•S)

1.   Creativity and Innovation

3.   Research and Information Fluency

6.   Technology Operations and Concepts

MATERIALS AND RESOURCES REQUIRED

- Internet access and necessary technology

- Google Earth

- Google News Search archive

LESSON DESCRIPTION

Media, in the form of photographs, and more recently video, can affect history and influence events. In the 20th century, television coverage of the Vietnam War and photographs of the aftermath of Hiroshima and Nagasaki stirred public opinion and contributed to changes in policy. In this lesson, students will identify photographs and video footage that have influenced events and anchor this media to the places of origin using Google Earth. Throughout the course of a history class, or in each unit of study that applies, students will identify and select photographs and video that have had impact, and create a Google Earth tour of that media. By anchoring the photographs or video on Earth and reflecting on the impact in a Google Earth placemark, students will be incorporating geographic literacy into their learning and be challenged to focus on the significance of the place, captured in time, that influenced events.

1. Build a Google Earth tour for your students by selecting several photographs that have influenced either U.S. or world opinion. Good examples can be found at Digital Journalist, "100 Photos that Changed the World—*Life Magazine*" (www.digitaljournalist. org/issue0309/lm_index.html), and at the teachers' pages of the American Memory Collection from the U.S. Library of Congress (http://memory.loc.gov/learn/index.html). Places to start looking for videos of historical events: The History Channel (www.history. com/media.do) and EASE History from Michigan State University (www.easehistory.org/ index2.html).

2. Start your example tour by creating a new Folder in the Google Earth My Places sidebar. Click on Add Folder. Name the folder "A Place in Time." Select the placemark tool in Google Earth and anchor the location of each of the example photos you have in your Earth file.

3. In the Description box that pops up with each new placemark, name the placemark with the date of the photograph. Include the photograph in the placemark Description box by typing in the simple HTML image code <img src ="URL of your photograph">. Use the address or URL of the image as you View Image in your browser (right-click or Ctrl+click on image to View Image). Add several more placemarks and then highlight the "A Place in Time" folder by clicking once. In the top Earth menu, choose File > Save > Save Place As and save as a KMZ file to share with students.

4. Present to the class your Google Earth tour using an LCD projector. Students study the images and describe the details in each photograph. As the students take your "A Place in Time" tour, ask the following questions:

    ▪ What is the significance of the photograph?

    ▪ What is the significance of the place where the photograph was taken? How did the place influence the importance of the event(s) depicted in the photo?

    ▪ Discuss how this photograph could have influenced an event in history or public opinion. What did the photographer seem to be saying with the image?

    ▪ What does research say about this photograph? Cite that research.

    ▪ What effects might photography or other media have on history?

5.   Students record the date and discuss the significance of the photograph in the context of the event under study. They formulate conclusions about how the object or subject of the photograph might have been affected by or contributed to the sequence of events under study.

6.   Instruct students that they will be building a tour over the course of a unit, or over the course of the class, that will include photographs or video that they believe have changed the course of events. Demonstrate how to build a Google Earth tour and link photos and video.

7.   Direct students to the Google News Search archives, where the will be able to access newspaper articles and create timelines covering the events depicted in the photos or video.

8.   Over the course of a unit of study, have students create placemarks for their historic photographs or video in Google Earth. Each placemark includes the date and biographical information about the media, the significance of the media to events in history, and an analysis of the impact made by the photograph or video footage.

9.   At an appropriate time, or the end of the unit or course of study, the completed Google Earth tours are shared in class presentations. Each student explains the impact on history of the photographs or video that they selected.

ASSESSMENT

Create a rubric to assess the following:

10%   Student participation in class discussions.

40%   Quality and accuracy of information on Google Earth tour using the following criteria:

   ■   Location of events and photographs or video marked correctly on Google Earth

   ■   Date and biographical information of photographs and video included on Google Earth placemarks

   ■   Significance of photograph or video on events in history outlined in the Google Earth placemark

   ■   Relevance or impact of the location of the photo or video on the events depicted

50%   Quality and extent of analysis using the following criteria:

   ■   The student presentation shows evidence of historical knowledge of events and the significance of the geographic location of the media. Students draw insightful conclusions about the effect of media and images on history.

POLITICAL CARTOON ANALYSIS

Jerome Burg

GRADE LEVEL: 9–12

SUBJECT: English Language Arts or Social Studies

TIME REQUIRED: 30–40 minutes on first day; 10–15 minutes a day for two weeks

OBJECTIVES

Students will be able to:

- Determine if the critical commentary made by political cartoonists generally favors a liberal, neutral, or conservative point of view.

- Determine if a specific political cartoonist leans toward a liberal, neutral, or conservative point of view.

- Determine if a specific news source leans toward a liberal, neutral, or conservative point of view.

- Create charts representing their findings and embed them into their individual final report.

CORRELATIONS TO STANDARDS

NCTE/IRA Standards for the English Language Arts

1. Reading for Perspective

2. Understanding the Human Experience

6. Applying Knowledge

7. Evaluating Data

11. Participating in Society

ISTE National Educational Technology Standards for Students (NETS·S)

2. Communication and Collaboration

3. Research and Information Fluency

4. Critical Thinking, Problem Solving, and Decision Making

6. Technology Operations and Concepts

MATERIALS AND RESOURCES REQUIRED

- Internet access and necessary technology

- Google Documents

- Editorial section of a local newspaper, nearby metropolitan newspapers, and/or national newspapers

- A copy of the Political Cartoon Analysis Excel Spreadsheet (http://web.mac.com/jburg/PCA/Political_Cartoons.html)

LESSON DESCRIPTION

Students will use the "Satire: Political Cartoon" Spreadsheet template to record data regarding the political positions found in political cartoons from a single source over the course of a two-week sampling. The teacher will determine what sources are appropriate for the class. Suggestions for sources might include the following:

- A local newspaper

- A nearest major metropolitan newspaper

- A national newspaper such as *USA Today*

Prior to commencing the lesson, the teacher will:

- Download the Political Cartoon Analysis Excel Spreadsheet available at http://web.mac.com/jburg/PCA/Political_Cartoons.html

- Import the Political Cartoon Analysis Excel Spreadsheet into a Google Docs Spreadsheet for collaborative student access

- Determine appropriate "collaborative teams" for the project and establish collaborative access privileges for all students

- Each team will collect data from a single source. The collaborative teams can be created in any of the following ways:

- Within a single classroom, students can be divided into groups of 3–5 students, each group being assigned or allowed to select its political cartoon source based upon availability. (Some students' families may already subscribe to a local, metropolitan, or national newspaper.)

- Teachers who teach multiple periods of the same course might choose to create groups that are "blends" of students from different classes. This offers an opportunity for students to collaborate with students they may not know.

- Teachers may want to recruit colleagues teaching in other parts of the country to join the project. This offers students an opportunity to evaluate whether there are geographical influences upon the bias found in newspapers from different parts of the country.

PROCEDURE

1. Teachers should be familiar with the basic structure of the "Satire: Political Cartoon" Spreadsheet template. The template already has the appropriate formulas built in to generate percentages, frequency of publication totals, and three different evaluation charts.

2. On the first day of the project, teachers should lead a brainstorming session on the following general topics:

    -   Lists of what students understand or think they understand about the definitions of the terms *liberal, moderate,* and *conservative*

    -   Lists of what students know or think they know about the terms *left, far left, right,* and *far right*

    -   Lists of what students know or think they know about the political, social, and economic issues that are current concerns and might be satirized by political cartoonists

    -   Lists of what students know or think they know about the positions generally taken by liberals and conservatives on the political, social, and economic issues from the previous list

3. Each day students will read the political cartoons published in their source publication. Students will collaborate either face-to-face or by using the Discuss feature in the Google spreadsheet template, and come to a consensus as to whether they believe the cartoon leans in favor of a liberal, neutral, or conservative position. Although the group must cast only one vote on the spreadsheet in this regard, students will be invited to note dissenting views in their individual final assessment paper. The intention of the requirement for groups to come to a consensus is to encourage students constantly to be evaluating exactly what the determining factors are for assigning the "liberal" or "conservative" label to a position presented within a cartoon.

4. Students will then enter the name of the cartoonist onto the spreadsheet if that cartoonist has not already been added on a previous day, and type a "1" into the appropriate cell indicating a liberal, neutral, or conservative lean.

5. Each collaborative team member should keep a copy of all evaluated cartoons to be included in a final report and to be used by teachers for final evaluations.

6. The teacher should spend a few minutes daily using a projection system to lead a brief discussion on a current political cartoon, focusing on students analyzing a political cartoon for its political position. Teachers can use these discussions to help guide students towards contextual indicators within a cartoon that can be used to determine the cartoonist's position. Teachers can easily find current political cartoons at: www.cagle.com or http://blog.cagle.com. Teachers might also incorporate some of the ideas available in the teacher's guide (http://cagle.msnbc.com/teacher/teachertour.asp).

7.   At the end of the two-week sampling period, the spreadsheet will have calculated:

   ■   Individual cartoonist's percentage of liberal, neutral, or conservative cartoons

   ■   Individual cartoonist's frequency of publication

   ■   Overall percentages of liberal, neutral, or conservative cartoons published in specific publication

ASSESSMENT

At the end of the two-week sampling, students will create individual projects presenting their findings. Suggested topics for inclusion in the report might include the following sections:

■   Brief explanation of the reasoning behind the labeling of 3–6 sampled cartoons as having been liberal, neutral, or conservative

■   Brief review of the issues most addressed by cartoonists during the sampling

■   Identification of the general positions taken on these issues by the liberal cartoonists and by the conservative cartoonists (pro/anti gun control, pro/anti abortion, pro/anti taxes, pro/anti government control, etc.)

■   Evaluation of the source publication's political leanings: liberal, neutral (balanced), conservative

■   Brief summary of the political lean and area of focus of the 2–3 most frequently published cartoonists in the sampling

■   Brief section explaining if they themselves are more attracted to the positions put forth by the liberal-leaning or the conservative-leaning cartoonists

   Optional: As a variation of the traditional "concession" included in higher-level writing, students can be challenged to end their project with a section where they list the positions taken by those with political leanings opposite themselves that they are willing to admit are worthy or even attractive to them in spite of their overall tendency to lean the "other way."

POSTCARDS FROM THE PAST

Cheryl Davis

GRADE LEVEL: 11

SUBJECT: United States History

TIME REQUIRED: 1–3 class periods; 1–2 evenings of homework; optional field study

OBJECTIVES

Students will be able to:

- Research primary source photos from records of the past.

- Compare, contrast, and combine primary source images with current photography, showing changes over time.

- Analyze and document the impact of these changes.

CORRELATIONS TO STANDARDS

NCSS Curriculum Standards for Social Studies

II. Time, Continuity, and Change

III. People, Places, and Environments

ISTE National Educational Technology Standards for Students (NETS·S)

2. Communication and Collaboration

3. Research and Information Fluency

4. Critical Thinking, Problem Solving, and Decision Making

MATERIALS AND RESOURCES REQUIRED

- Internet access and necessary technology

- Student or class Google account

- Digital cameras, or phone cameras and online storage

- Google Maps

LESSON DESCRIPTION

Postcards from the Past is a primary resource history activity integrating the geographic location of an event with a "now" and "then" visual view of a place or subject. This lesson works well in the study of local history, where students can visit the actual event location. However, the lesson can also be used in the context of visualizing national events and having students analyze change or continuity in a location through time. In pairs or small groups, students research a variety of historic photos of an event or place under study. These photographs include the buildings or landscape where the event occurred. Students then research current photographs taken at the same location, or they visit the location and use a digital camera to capture the changes. Adding a geographic perspective, students place both the "now" and "then" photographs on a collabora-tive map and engage in a class discussion of their findings and an evaluation of the changes that have taken place.

1. In the context of a history unit of study, have students in pairs or small groups research and select historic photographs from digital resources, books, local history societies, or museums.

2. Students study the images and describe the details in the photograph. They record the date of the photograph and discuss the significance of the photograph in the context of the event under study. They formulate conclusions about how that same location might look today (what changes will have occurred) and how the object or subject of the photograph might have been affected by, or have contributed to, the sequence of events under study.

    If time permits, teachers may wish to engage students in a more in-depth analysis of how to analyze photographs. See the following resources:

    ■ Document Analysis Worksheets (www.archives.gov/education/lessons/worksheets)

    ■ Photo Analysis Guide (www.bright.net/~dlackey/pguide.html)

    ■ Photojournalism Tiered Lesson Plan (www.bsu.edu/web/latracey/PortfolioPages/phototiered.htm)

    ■ Process Guide—Viewing Photographs (http://projects.edtech.sandi.net/staffdev/tpss99/processguides/photographs.html)

3. If the photographs are of local sites or events, students conduct a field study and visit the location where the event occurred. They retake a photo with a digital camera from the same perspective as the original photo (or as close as possible). If students are unable to do a field study, they research current photographs of the place or event through Internet searches.

4. With both the current photograph and the historic photograph in hand, students test their conclusions about the changes to the place or subject. They compare the past photograph with the present and research the connections between the photograph and the larger historical developments of the time.

5. The class sets up a collaborative Google map and receives instruction on how to access and add photographs to the map.

6. The students create placemarks for their historic and current photographs on the Google class map. Each placemark includes the date and biographical information about the people in the photographs, the significance of the photograph in relation to events in history, and an analysis of the change that has occurred.

7. The completed Google class map is shared during a class discussion with each student pair explaining the historic change between then and now and discussing the impact of that change.

ASSESSMENT

Create a rubric to assess the following:

Teacher Assessment Only

20% Student participation in class discussions

50% Quality and extent of analysis using rubric that includes the following criteria:

- The student discussions and placemarks should show evidence of historical analysis that is clear and meaningful.

- Students should produce documented research on the subject or location they photographed and placed on the map.

- Students draw conclusions about the location they photographed and evaluate the consequences of the change they documented.

Student and Teacher Assessment

30% Quality and accuracy of information on class map using a rubric that includes the following criteria:

- Location of events and photograph marked correctly on Google map

- Photographs of "now" and "then" taken from similar perspectives

- Date and biographical information of photographs included in placemarks

- Significance of photograph in relation to events in history outlined in the placemarks

- Analysis of change between then and now outlined in the placemarks

ROAD TRIP

Cheryl Davis

GRADE LEVEL: 9–12

SUBJECT: United States History

TIME REQUIRED: 4 class periods and collaborative homework

OBJECTIVES

Students will be able to:

- Identify and map American historical destinations.

- Create a collaborative, themed history trip.

- Present a multimedia tour to American historical or cultural destinations of significance.

CORRELATIONS TO STANDARDS

NCSS Curriculum Standards for Social Studies

II. Time, Continuity, and Change

III. People, Places, and Environments

ISTE National Educational Technology Standards for Students (NETS·S)

1. Creativity and Innovation

2. Communication and Collaboration

3. Research and Information Fluency

MATERIALS AND RESOURCES REQUIRED

- Internet access and necessary technology

- Google Maps

- Google Documents

LESSON DESCRIPTION

Road Trip is an activity where students plan a summer trip around a history theme. Student "cartographers" create and present a virtual field trip to American historic or cultural destinations and research the significance of these destinations. Working in pairs, students access a collaborative Google map to plot their two-week, eight-destination journey. They produce a timeline for the trip, research each destination, and write a guidebook in a Google document that includes historical background for each destination. Then, in a class presentation, they take the class on a virtual trip with visual and/or auditory links in the Google map placemarks to help the class experience each destination.

1. Introduce students to the lesson by telling them they will plan a road trip to see American historic destinations. In pairs, they are to create and map a two-week trip with at least eight destinations that have American historical and/or cultural significance. Their trip should have a theme, and they will write a trip guide or journal.

2. Divide students into pairs and have each choose a trip theme. The class can brainstorm for trip or tour ideas. Some suggested themes are:

    - Presidential tour: Mt. Vernon and Hermitage, and so on

    - New Deal tour: Wall Street, Hoover Dam, and so on

    - Teddy Roosevelt National Park tour

    - Music tour: Graceland, Motown, New Orleans, and so on

    - Amish tour: Pennsylvania, Idaho, California, and so on

    - John Muir tour: follow his trail

    - Civil Rights tour: Birmingham, Montgomery, and so on

    - Gold tour: South Dakota, Colorado, California, Alaska, and so on

    - Baseball tour: Fenway Park, Yankee Stadium, Dodger Stadium, and so on

    - Civil War tour

    - Sam Houston tour

    - Jack Kerouac tour

    - Colonial America tour

    - Native American tour

    - Olympics tour

    - American art tour

    - Summer of Love tour

    - American immigrants tour

3. Students research and plan their tours. They use Google Maps to plot their locations. They also create a timeline for their trip, determining which day of the trip will be in which location. The timeline can be planned in a shared Google Docs document.

4. Students create a Google account and access Google Maps. They click on My Maps and sign in to their Google account. Have students explore some of the featured Google My Maps content so they can visualize the possibilities. Next, have one student in the pair click the Create A New Map link and give the map a title and description. That student shares their new Google map by clicking the Collaborate link in the Google map's left menu and adding the e-mail addresses of partners.

5. Instruct students on how to create placemarks for their destinations in a Google map. They will need to add a placemark for each destination. Show students how to use the Rich Text formatting in the placemark Description box to add images, format text, and link web addresses to the destinations. Adding creative information to placemarks will make the presentations more dynamic. Show students how to create the travel route using the line tool. Also show them how to edit destinations by clicking on the placemarks they create.

6. While students are creating the map they should also create and share a Google document that will be the trip's journal or guidebook. The Google document should include historical information on the selected destinations. Students will explain the significance of their destinations and how the locations relate to their theme. Research sources should be cited. The document can include a link to the Google map or the map can be embedded in the document using the HTML edit mode in Google Docs.

7. When the road trips are complete, schedule students for class presentations. Using an LCD projector, student pairs will access their Google map and Google document. Each presentation should include visual and/or auditory multimedia linked to the Google map placemark to help the class experience each destination. Presentations should last no longer than 15 minutes. It is recommended not to have more than two or three presentations in any one class period to alleviate the boredom factor. The teacher may wish to divide the class into a number of groups to have several audiences for presentations.

ASSESSMENT

Create a rubric to assess the following:

33.3% Quality and accuracy of Google map and placemark information.

33.3% Variety and creativity of trip journal or guide in Google Docs. Each location visited includes accurate historical information and proper citation.

33.3% Presentation information is interesting and informative. It includes links from the placemarks to multimedia (sound, video, or images) of the sites visited.

Thanks to James Lathrop, a teacher at Miramonte High School, for this lesson idea.

THE STATISTICAL WORLD

Cheryl Davis

GRADE LEVEL: 9–10

SUBJECT: World History

TIME REQUIRED: 2–3 class periods

OBJECTIVES

Students will be able to:

- Create, collaborate, and analyze a spreadsheet and its data.

- Chart statistical information on a selected group of the world's countries.

- Compare and contrast the quality of life in the world's countries and share in a class discussion or reflective essay.

CORRELATIONS TO STANDARDS

NCSS Curriculum Standards for Social Studies

VII. Production, Distribution, and Consumption

VIII. Science, Technology, and Society

IX. Global Connections

ISTE National Educational Technology Standards for Students (NETS•S)

1.   Creativity and Innovation

2.   Communication and Collaboration

3.   Research and Information Fluency

4.   Critical Thinking, Problem Solving, and Decision Making

MATERIALS AND RESOURCES REQUIRED

- Internet access and necessary technology

- Student or class Google account

- Google Spreadsheets

LESSON DESCRIPTION

Students look at statistical data to make comparisons on the quality of life in countries throughout the world. Using the interactivity and collaboration tools in Google Spreadsheets, students will collaborate in teams or pairs to select indicators and to research and gather data on selected countries. Student pairs or teams will input data into the group spreadsheet. Students will then chart their information using the charting feature of Google Spreadsheets, and graphically display the results they have obtained. Student analysis of the charts will be shared in a classwide discussion, or reflective essay, where they will present their statistical charts and hypothesize on contributing factors to the information they have gathered about quality of life in various locations.

1. Introduce students to the lesson by showing the Internet-based movie *Miniature Earth* (www.miniature-earth.com). The movie looks at the world's population and correlates those population statistics so they reflect a world village of 100 people. The text of the movie can be accessed at http://blog.miniature-earth.com/?p=30. Discuss the use of statistics in the movie to compare and contrast the quality of life.

2. In small groups, students brainstorm and form a list of the indicators they feel are important for quality of life. Have the groups share the information and create a class list of those qualities. Discuss why each quality might be important to the quality of life. The qualities might include:

    - Population

    - Capital (economic)

    - Government

    - Infant Mortality

    - Average Life Span

    - Unemployment Rate

    - Literacy Rate

    - GDP/per capita

    - Health

3. In a computer lab, with laptops, or on a teacher station with a classroom LCD display, explore visual statistics using Gapminder (http://tools.google.com/gapminder/). Select several countries by using the check boxes to the right of the Gapminder chart, and then click the Play button in the bottom left. Discuss what the visual representations show as the chart animates through the timeline. For further exploration of statistics using Gapminder, refer students to Gapcast movies (www.gapminder.org/video/gapcast). The Gapminder software is now incorporated in Google Spreadsheets and is available for free use. For more information, see Google's information on motion charts (http://tinyurl.com/4r6a7e/).

4. Next have students sign up for a Google account and access Google Spreadsheets. Review how to use a spreadsheet. Divide students into teams or pairs and have one member of the team start the group's "Statistical World" spreadsheet and share it with the teacher and other member(s) of the group.

5. Assign, or have each team select, blocks of world countries to chart and analyze. Teachers can determine how many countries each group will research depending on the time frame or parts of the world under study. Determine with the class which indicators will be researched. Have students start their spreadsheet by typing in the column headings with "Country" in column A and the indicators listed across the subsequent columns. They should then type the list of countries assigned in the A column under the "Country" heading. Student teams should then assign group members an equal number of countries to research. They can simultaneously work on the same spreadsheet.

6. Students use the Internet to research their data. They can use resources such as the World Fact Book (https://www.cia.gov/cia/publications/factbook/) to build the spreadsheet. In addition, Google Spreadsheets has a built-in search feature. By using Lookup on the Formula tab, and choosing Google Lookup, students can research the information they need and obtain a cited source. Students can also type information into a cell and right-click (Ctrl+click on a Mac) on the cell to search the Internet for information.

7. Once the research and spreadsheet data entry are complete, students select the cells they want charted and click the Chart icon to bring up the Charting Box. Students select the type of chart and labels to create a graphical display of their data. These charts can be saved as images by clicking on the chart menu and choosing Save Image.

8. In a class discussion or writing assignment have students reflect on what they have learned from the statistical comparisons of the countries. Each team can show their chart via a video projector or share their chart with the class by clicking the Share or Publish tab of their spreadsheet. Depending on the indicators they chose, some reflective questions might include:

    - What three factors do you consider to be the most important when determining quality of life? Explain.

    - What relationships do you find between the various indicators? When looking at your data which two columns have the most similar tendencies? Why might this be true?

    - Where did your data come from, and how can you be sure it is reliable?

ASSESSMENT

Create a rubric to assess the following:

20% Quality and accuracy of research information as displayed on the spreadsheet; sources are cited correctly.

30% Student charts are accurate, creative, and display collected data.

50% Student presentation of chart and in-class discussion or reflective essay demonstrates the ability to use data to compare and contrast the quality of life in the world's countries and an understanding of how selected statistical indicators affect the quality of life.

Thanks to James Lathrop and Kevin Honey, teachers at Miramonte High School, for this lesson idea.

REGARDING STUDENTS
UNDER 13 YEARS OF AGE

Until it was struck down by the U.S. Supreme Court in 2008, the Children's Online Privacy Protection Act (COPPA) regulated the collection of personal information from children under the age of 13. The other principal federal law regulating use of the Internet by children is the Children's Internet Protection Act (CIPA). In this chapter we are primarily concerned with how COPPA affected the legality of students under 13 obtaining Google accounts and Gmail addresses.

In a nutshell, COPPA required specific parental consent for students under 13 to subscribe to a Google account or to obtain a Gmail address. Since the law was overturned by the Supreme Court, most companies and schools have continued to follow its requirements regarding obtaining personal information from children younger than 13. We thought it would be useful to provide readers with some sample documents developed for these purposes by two school districts and one independent school.

BACKGROUND

The two quotations that follow are from official websites of the Federal Trade Commission (FTC) and the Federal Communications Commission (FCC), the bodies charged with implementation of COPPA and CIPA, respectively.

> The Children's Online Privacy Protection Act, effective April 21, 2000, applies to the online collection of personal information from children under 13. The new rules spell out what a Website operator must include in a privacy policy, when and how to seek verifiable consent from a parent and what responsibilities an operator has to protect children's privacy and safety online. (www.coppa.org/comply.htm)

> The Children's Internet Protection Act (CIPA) is a federal law enacted by Congress to address concerns about access to offensive content over the Internet on school and library computers. CIPA imposes certain types of requirements on any school or library that receives funding for Internet access or internal connections from the E-rate program—a program that makes certain communications technology more affordable for eligible schools and libraries. In early 2001, the FCC issued rules implementing CIPA. More recently, Congress enacted additional protections for children using the Internet. (www.fcc.gov/cgb/consumerfacts/cipa.html)

Basically, COPPA requires parental consent for online student accounts for organizations such as Google, and CIPA has resulted in the filtering and site blocking often used in schools and libraries.

DISCLAIMER

We are not attorneys, nor did we consult attorneys in preparing this material. We have gathered these examples from people whom we consider reputable, and they have provided this information to us and given their permission to include it in this book. We strongly urge readers to consult their school or school district attorney before requesting parental permission to use Google accounts or Gmail. At the same time, we expect most readers will find this information helpful in developing documents that can be crafted to suit your local situation.

We commend the Lawson Middle School, Sparta Public Schools, and Milpitas Christian School for taking the pioneering steps to assemble these materials and extend our deep gratitude for their willingness to share their work with the educational community. Special thanks go to Steve Burrell, Erica Hartmann, Patrick Higgins, and Diane Main for their assistance.

SAMPLE DOCUMENTS

The sample parent permission form on the following page comes from Lawson Middle School, Cupertino, California.

GOOGLE ACCOUNT PERMISSION REQUEST

As part of an Enhancing Education Through Technology (EETT) grant, our class has access to laptop computers on a daily basis. A major part of our language arts class involves the integration of technology into our writing and free reading program. Students will be using a web-based word processing application for all of their writing at school. They will also be keeping a reading journal. In the past, I used to give each student a "Mead Composition Notebook" in which to record his or her entries. This year I would like to try something new for their reading journals: a **blog**.

My reasoning behind the shift to online resources is threefold. To begin with, last year I became a Google Certified Teacher and learned about the benefits of these online tools. Second, students will be using a technology that they are already comfortable with, and there are built-in features that will allow for quicker responses to their writing and reading journals (entries are e-mailed to me and I can respond quicker). Finally, by going paperless, there will be fewer notebooks to weigh down your child's already heavy backpack.

We will be creating Google accounts for students to use Google Docs for writing and Blogger, a subsidiary of Google (http://www.blogger.com), for their reading journal. The Google account and both programs are free to set up and use. Students will set up accounts in class with my guidance, and we will be using a naming convention so that students' full names are not available online. For example, Jane Smith's account name would be Jansm34. Also, students will not fill in the optional profile and only invited users may post to their blog; therefore students are writing and posting journal entries in a safe Internet environment.

More information will be available about the program at back-to-school night. If you do not feel comfortable with this style of writing program, your child may use paper and pencil for all of his or her work.

Regards,

[Your child's teacher]

Lawson Middle School

[Contact information]

This form is to grant permission for:

Student's Name _____

Valid e-mail _____
(This e-mail will be used as the log-in for the Google account)

☐ Yes, my child may participate in the online writing program with a **Google account**.

☐ No, I would prefer my child to use paper and pencil for the writing program.

Please return by *(date)* _____

Parent Signature _____ Date _____

The following parent permission letter comes from the Sparta (New Jersey) Public Schools:

Dear Parents/Guardians,

Students in Mrs. Hartman's Connections class will be piloting a special Web 2.0 tool this year. This free tool is Google Apps for Education. Google Apps for Education streamlines and organizes student work. Flash drives are no longer needed. All student documents and presentations will be stored online and will be accessible from home, school, and anywhere there is an Internet connection. This means students can also work on assignments at the library and while traveling, if they choose. Students can access Mrs. Hartman's Google Apps for Education site at: **http://welcome.hartmanstudents.com**

At the site, they will have access to the class calendar, collaborative tools, all of their Google documents and presentations, as well as current events pertinent to our Connections classes. They will be assigned a Gmail account and password to log in to the site. I encourage you to record this information in a safe place. The e-mail and password are on page 4 of this document. Students will also have extensive training on how to use Google Apps for Education. We hope they will share what they learn with you.

Google Apps for Education is just one of the Web 2.0 tools we will be using this year in Mrs. Hartman's Connections classes. In an effort to increase our students' ability to work collaboratively on writing and research projects, we will be using a variety of free Web 2.0 applications. Here is a quick glossary for those who may not be familiar with all of the terms used throughout this document.

The term **Web 2.0** refers to the trend in World Wide Web technology and web design that aims to enhance creativity, information sharing, and most notably, collaboration among users. *(Wikipedia)*

A **wiki** is a website that may be edited collaboratively, anytime, anywhere. Wikipedia is an example of an encyclopedia built through a wiki. A wiki provides students and educators the opportunity to collaborate and share information on certain subjects. Students will use a wiki provider named Wikispaces to work collaboratively on a group project. Wikispaces is a safe, teacher-controlled environment, where only invited participants can edit the information, and no personal information is shared with readers of the page.

A **blog** is a shortened form of the words "web log" where people can publish their own content in written, audio (podcasts), video, or other multimedia formats. Blogs can be publicly accessible, accessible to only certain groups of people, or completely private. Most blogs operate as personal journals, on which readers may add comments.

Google is a search engine and much more; it offers a multitude of services such as Documents, Spreadsheets, and Presentations, which enable students to edit and collaborate on documents, spreadsheets, and PowerPoint-like presentations online. Additional Google services include Google Earth, Sketchup, and Blogger.

(continued)

Multimedia creation sites allow users to upload video, audio, images, or text in order to remix it into a new creation. Some examples of these sites are Voicethread, Scrapblog, Animoto, Jumpcut, YouTube, and CCMixter.

Moodle is a course management system that enables students to access course content and discussion forums at any time that is convenient for them. Some of our teachers will be using Moodle this year to run their classes. Moodle is hosted by us and does not need an e-mail account for the student to be registered.

The main reason we are writing this letter is to ask permission to create an online account for your child, which consists of an e-mail address and a password. The account will be used to access the services described in this letter. Federal law requires that students under the age of 13 have parental permission to submit any information of this type to a website.

We encourage you to participate with your child in his/her online activities. Our students create amazing work when they collaborate with one another. However, as with any other online pursuit, your involvement in their work is beneficial to their development as an informed user of the Internet. In an effort to be as clear as possible, we have outlined our policies below for using online applications, such as wikis, blogs, and other online applications with students. Once they are members of the sites they can create and participate in online classroom activities. Please note, in the case of Wikispaces, they will be able to participate in any public Wikispace; their access will not be limited to their teacher's pages.

Agreement and Purposes

We will be using Web 2.0 applications for the purposes of:

- Responding to and commenting on curriculum topics as we study them
- Creating written projects and commenting on each others' work
- Encouraging process writing
- Practicing persuasive writing
- Writing creatively
- Practicing taking varied points of view on a topic
- Sharing classroom events with families
- Sharing special projects with local, national, and global audiences
- Discussing current events
- Making classroom suggestions
- Creating dynamic and vibrant research
- Working with multimedia in a collaborative environment

(continued)

Terms and Conditions

All students and participants in these projects must agree to the terms and conditions of this agreement.

The teachers will make every reasonable effort to monitor student conduct related to class content in order to maintain a positive learning community. All participants will respect the teachers' time and professionalism by supporting the same positive approach.

No student, or other participant, may include any information or images on the site that could compromise the safety of him/herself or other class members. Participants should avoid specific comments about our location or schedules, if they would be visible to outsiders.

All participants will be respectful in their postings and comments. No trash-talk, inappropriate language, personal insults, profanity, spam, racist, sexist or discriminatory remarks, or threatening comments will be tolerated.

No student or other participant may post, comment, or change settings on the sites in violation of these terms and conditions.

Usernames may not contain any identifying information, including first or last names, but instead may be created at random by the teacher.

All participants must protect their login and password information, as well as class passwords (if any. If participants suspect that a password has been compromised, they must notify the teacher immediately.

No participant may share his/her login information or protected information about the site with anyone who is not a participant. This includes adding trackbacks or other means by which outsiders can access the site without permission.

Any participant who is aware of violations of this agreement by others must report these violations to the teacher immediately both verbally and in writing (e-mail or note).

All use of these services must be in accordance with the Sparta Board of Education's Acceptable Use Policy, including entries made from computers outside of school.

Uncited use of copyrighted material in any student work will be deemed as plagiarism and disciplined accordingly.

No posting or comment may facilitate or promote illegal activity, either overtly or by implication.

Consequences

Any violation of the above terms and conditions shall make the violator subject to both immediate termination from one or all of these services and/or additional disciplinary action. At the teacher's discretion, a warning may be given in the case of minor infractions.

(continued)

Signatures

I agree to the terms and conditions in this document, and permit my child to participate in these services.

Student Signature _____ Date _____

Parent/Guardian Signature _____ Date _____

Parent/Guardian e-mail *(please print)* _____

Please keep the information below for your records and return the signature page.

Student First and Last Name _____

Gmail address _____

Password _____

website address: http://welcome.hartmanstudents.com

Our class blog *(updated weekly by students)*: http://hartmanhoopla.blogspot.com

We welcome your comments and questions on our class blog!

Please contact me at erica.hartman@sparta.org with any questions.

The following Acceptable Use Policy (AUP) comes from Milpitas Christian School, San Jose, California.

Milpitas Christian School Acceptable Use Policy for students using computers

Access to the Internet is a privilege, not a right, and inappropriate use will result in the consequences show below.

The Following Are Not Allowed

- Using profanity, obscenity, or other offensive language
- Sending or receiving inappropriate files
- Harassing another person
- Revealing personal information on the Internet such as home address and phone number
- Posting personal information about another student
- Using material without proper citation of source
- Damaging computers, computer systems, or computer networks
- Logging onto a computer using another student's user name and password.

Consequences

- First offense: Warning and detention with parent notification.
- Second offense: In-school suspension with possible academic consequences.
    - Computer/Internet privileges may be suspended as a result of any second offense, and may affect grades in technology or other subjects.
- Third offense: At-home or in-school suspension with academic consequences as above.
- Severe: First offenses deemed severe can be elevated to third offence consequences.
- Any assignment that involves any breach of this policy will result in the assignment being given zero credit.

Student Agreement

I have read this policy and agree to follow the rules. I understand that violation of these rules will lead to the above listed consequences.

Student Name _____

Student Signature _____

Date _____

(continued)

Parent Agreement

I have read this policy. I release Milpitas Christian School and its personnel from any and all claims and damages of any nature arising from my child's use of the computer system.

Parent Name _____

Parent Signature _____

Date _____

This document expires on September 30, 2010

APPENDIX B

TECHNOLOGY STANDARDS

NATIONAL EDUCATIONAL TECHNOLOGY STANDARDS FOR STUDENTS (NETS·S)

All K–12 students should be prepared to meet the following standards and performance indicators.

1. **Creativity and Innovation**

   Students demonstrate creative thinking, construct knowledge, and develop innovative products and processes using technology. Students:

   a. apply existing knowledge to generate new ideas, products, or processes

   b. create original works as a means of personal or group expression

   c. use models and simulations to explore complex systems and issues

   d. identify trends and forecast possibilities

2. **Communication and Collaboration**

   Students use digital media and environments to communicate and work collaboratively, including at a distance, to support individual learning and contribute to the learning of others. Students:

   a. interact, collaborate, and publish with peers, experts, or others employing a variety of digital environments and media

   b. communicate information and ideas effectively to multiple audiences using a variety of media and formats

   c. develop cultural understanding and global awareness by engaging with learners of other cultures

   d. contribute to project teams to produce original works or solve problems

3. **Research and Information Fluency**

   Students apply digital tools to gather, evaluate, and use information. Students:

   a. plan strategies to guide inquiry

   b. locate, organize, analyze, evaluate, synthesize, and ethically use information from a variety of sources and media

    c. evaluate and select information sources and digital tools based on the appropriateness to specific tasks

    d. process data and report results

4. Critical Thinking, Problem Solving, and Decision Making

Students use critical-thinking skills to plan and conduct research, manage projects, solve problems, and make informed decisions using appropriate digital tools and resources. Students:

    a. identify and define authentic problems and significant questions for investigation

    b. plan and manage activities to develop a solution or complete a project

    c. collect and analyze data to identify solutions and make informed decisions

    d. use multiple processes and diverse perspectives to explore alternative solutions

5. Digital Citizenship

Students understand human, cultural, and societal issues related to technology and practice legal and ethical behavior. Students:

    a. advocate and practice the safe, legal, and responsible use of information and technology

    b. exhibit a positive attitude toward using technology that supports collaboration, learning, and productivity

    c. demonstrate personal responsibility for lifelong learning

    d. exhibit leadership for digital citizenship

6. Technology Operations and Concepts

Students demonstrate a sound understanding of technology concepts, systems, and operations. Students:

    a. understand and use technology systems

    b. select and use applications effectively and productively

    c. troubleshoot systems and applications

    d. transfer current knowledge to the learning of new technologies

NATIONAL EDUCATIONAL TECHNOLOGY STANDARDS FOR TEACHERS (NETS·T)

All classroom teachers should be prepared to meet the following standards and performance indicators.

1. **Facilitate and Inspire Student Learning and Creativity**

   Teachers use their knowledge of subject matter, teaching and learning, and technology to facilitate experiences that advance student learning, creativity, and innovation in both face-to-face and virtual environments. Teachers:

   a. promote, support, and model creative and innovative thinking and inventiveness

   b. engage students in exploring real-world issues and solving authentic problems using digital tools and resources

   c. promote student reflection using collaborative tools to reveal and clarify students' conceptual understanding and thinking, planning, and creative processes

   d. model collaborative knowledge construction by engaging in learning with students, colleagues, and others in face-to-face and virtual environments

2. **Design and Develop Digital-Age Learning Experiences and Assessments**

   Teachers design, develop, and evaluate authentic learning experiences and assessments incorporating contemporary tools and resources to maximize content learning in context and to develop the knowledge, skills, and attitudes identified in the NETS·S. Teachers:

   a. design or adapt relevant learning experiences that incorporate digital tools and resources to promote student learning and creativity

   b. develop technology-enriched learning environments that enable all students to pursue their individual curiosities and become active participants in setting their own educational goals, managing their own learning, and assessing their own progress

   c. customize and personalize learning activities to address students' diverse learning styles, working strategies, and abilities using digital tools and resources

   d. provide students with multiple and varied formative and summative assessments aligned with content and technology standards and use resulting data to inform learning and teaching

3. **Model Digital-Age Work and Learning**

   Teachers exhibit knowledge, skills, and work processes representative of an innovative professional in a global and digital society. Teachers:

   a. demonstrate fluency in technology systems and the transfer of current knowledge to new technologies and situations

b. collaborate with students, peers, parents, and community members using digital tools and resources to support student success and innovation

c. communicate relevant information and ideas effectively to students, parents, and peers using a variety of digital-age media and formats

d. model and facilitate effective use of current and emerging digital tools to locate, analyze, evaluate, and use information resources to support research and learning

4. Promote and Model Digital Citizenship and Responsibility

Teachers understand local and global societal issues and responsibilities in an evolving digital culture and exhibit legal and ethical behavior in their professional practices. Teachers:

a. advocate, model, and teach safe, legal, and ethical use of digital information and technology, including respect for copyright, intellectual property, and the appropriate documentation of sources

b. address the diverse needs of all learners by using learner-centered strategies and providing equitable access to appropriate digital tools and resources

c. promote and model digital etiquette and responsible social interactions related to the use of technology and information

d. develop and model cultural understanding and global awareness by engaging with colleagues and students of other cultures using digital-age communication and collaboration tools

5. Engage in Professional Growth and Leadership

Teachers continuously improve their professional practice, model lifelong learning, and exhibit leadership in their school and professional community by promoting and demonstrating the effective use of digital tools and resources. Teachers:

a. participate in local and global learning communities to explore creative applications of technology to improve student learning

b. exhibit leadership by demonstrating a vision of technology infusion, participating in shared decision making and community building, and developing the leadership and technology skills of others

c. evaluate and reflect on current research and professional practice on a regular basis to make effective use of existing and emerging digital tools and resources in support of student learning

d. contribute to the effectiveness, vitality, and self-renewal of the teaching profession and of their school and community

NATIONAL EDUCATIONAL TECHNOLOGY STANDARDS FOR ADMINISTRATORS (NETS·A)

All school administrators should be prepared to meet the following standards and performance indicators.

1. **Visionary Leadership**

   Educational Administrators inspire and lead development and implementation of a shared vision for comprehensive integration of technology to promote excellence and support transformation throughout the organization. Educational Administrators:

   a. inspire and facilitate among all stakeholders a shared vision of purposeful change that maximizes use of digital-age resources to meet and exceed learning goals, support effective instructional practice, and maximize performance of district and school leaders

   b. engage in an ongoing process to develop, implement, and communicate technology-infused strategic plans aligned with a shared vision

   c. advocate on local, state, and national levels for policies, programs, and funding to support implementation of a technology-infused vision and strategic plan

2. **Digital-Age Learning Culture**

   Educational Administrators create, promote, and sustain a dynamic, digital-age learning culture that provides a rigorous, relevant, and engaging education for all students. Educational Administrators:

   a. ensure instructional innovation focused on continuous improvement of digital-age learning

   b. model and promote the frequent and effective use of technology for learning

   c. provide learner-centered environments equipped with technology and learning resources to meet the individual, diverse needs of all learners

   d. ensure effective practice in the study of technology and its infusion across the curriculum

   e. promote and participate in local, national, and global learning communities that stimulate innovation, creativity, and digital-age collaboration

3. **Excellence in Professional Practice**

   Educational Administrators promote an environment of professional learning and innovation that empowers educators to enhance student learning through the infusion of contemporary technologies and digital resources. Educational Administrators:

   a. allocate time, resources, and access to ensure ongoing professional growth in technology fluency and integration

b. facilitate and participate in learning communities that stimulate, nurture, and support administrators, faculty, and staff in the study and use of technology

c. promote and model effective communication and collaboration among stakeholders using digital-age tools

d. stay abreast of educational research and emerging trends regarding effective use of technology and encourage evaluation of new technologies for their potential to improve student learning

4. Systemic Improvement

Educational Administrators provide digital-age leadership and management to continuously improve the organization through the effective use of information and technology resources. Educational Administrators:

a. lead purposeful change to maximize the achievement of learning goals through the appropriate use of technology and media-rich resources

b. collaborate to establish metrics, collect and analyze data, interpret results, and share findings to improve staff performance and student learning

c. recruit and retain highly competent personnel who use technology creatively and proficiently to advance academic and operational goals

d. establish and leverage strategic partnerships to support systemic improvement

e. establish and maintain a robust infrastructure for technology including integrated, interoperable technology systems to support management, operations, teaching, and learning

5. Digital Citizenship

Educational Administrators model and facilitate understanding of social, ethical, and legal issues and responsibilities related to an evolving digital culture. Educational Administrators:

a. ensure equitable access to appropriate digital tools and resources to meet the needs of all learners

b. promote, model, and establish policies for safe, legal, and ethical use of digital information and technology

c. promote and model responsible social interactions related to the use of technology and information

d. model and facilitate the development of a shared cultural understanding and involvement in global issues through the use of contemporary communication and collaboration tools